بسم الله الرحمن الرحيم

THE BOOK *of* WISDOMS

KITĀB AL-ḤIKAM

A Collection of Sufi Aphorisms

In the name of Allāh, Most Gracious, Most Merciful.
All praise be to Allāh, Lord of the Worlds, and peace and blessings be upon His Messenger Muḥammad, Mercy to the Worlds.

THE BOOK *of* WISDOMS

KITĀB AL-ḤIKAM

A Collection of Sufi Aphorisms

Shaykh Ibn ʿAṭāʾillāh al-Iskandarī

Translated by Victor Danner

With commentary Ikmāl al-Shiyam by

SHAYKH ʿABDULLĀH GANGŌHĪ

Introduction by

SHAYKH ZAKARIYYĀ KĀNDHLAWĪ

Edited by

ANDREW BOOSO &

ABDUR-RAHMAN IBN YUSUF

White Thread

PRESS

First Edition May 2014

ISBN 978-1-933764-05-4

Published by
White Thread Press
White Thread Limited, London, UK
www.whitethreadpress.com
info@whitethreadpress.com

Distributed in the UK by Azhar Academy Ltd. London
sales@azharacademy.com Tel: +44 (208) 911 9797

Library of Congress Cataloging-in-Publication Data

Ibn ʿAtaʾ Allah, Ahmad ibn Muhammad, -1309.
[*Hikam al-ʿAtaʾiyah*. English]
The book of wisdoms: *Kitab al-hikam*, a collection of Sufi aphorisms / Shaykh Ibn ʿAta'illah al-Iskandari; translated by Victor Danner. With commentary *Ikmal al-Shiyam* / by Shaykh ʿAbdullah Gangohi; introduction by Shaykh al-Hadith Maulana Zakariya Kandhlawi; edited by Andrew Booso and Abdur-Rahman ibn Yusuf Mangera. — First edition.
pages cm
Includes bibliographical references and index.
ISBN 978-1-933764-05-4 (hardcover: alk. paper)
1. Sufism. 2. Mysticism—Islam. 3. Spirituality—Islam. 4. Aphorisms and apothegms. I. Danner, Victor, 1926-1980. II. Booso, Andrew. III. Ibn Yusuf, Abdur-Rahman, 1974- IV. Gangohi, Muhammad ʿAbdullah, 1898-1921. *Ikmal al-shiyam*. V. Title.
BP189.62.I2613 2013
297'.4—dc23

2013037717

British Library Cataloguing in Publication Data. A catalogue record for this book is also available from the British Library.

♾ Printed and bound in the United States of America on premium acid-free paper. The paper used in this book meets the minimum requirement of ANSI/NISO Z39.48-1992 (R 1997) (Permanence of Paper). The binding material has been chosen for strength and durability.

Book design and typography by ARM,
Cover design by Abdallateef Whiteman and ARM

Cover image: ﴿إِنَّ الْمُتَّقِينَ فِي جَنَّاتٍ وَنَهَرٍ، فِي مَقْعَدِ صِدْقٍ عِندَ مَلِيكٍ مُّقْتَدِرٍ﴾ The righteous will live securely among gardens and rivers, secure in the presence of an All-powerful Sovereign (Qur'an 54:55).

ٱللَّهُ يَجْتَبِيٓ إِلَيْهِ مَن يَشَآءُ

وَيَهْدِيٓ إِلَيْهِ مَن يُنِيبُ

Allāh chooses whoever He pleases

for Himself and guides towards

Himself those who turn to Him.

The Glorious Qur'ān 42:13

TRANSLITERATION KEY

ء (أ إ)	’ (A slight catch in the breath. It is also used to indicate where the *hamza* has been dropped from the beginning of a word.)
ا	a, ā
ب	b
ت	t
ث	th (Should be pronounced as the *th* in *thin* or *thirst.*)
ج	j
ح	ḥ (Tensely breathed *h* sound.)
خ	kh (Pronounced like the *ch* in Scottish *loch* with the mouth hollowed to produce a full sound.)
د	d
ذ	dh (Should be pronounced as the *th* in *this* or *that.*)
ر	r
ز	z
س	s
ش	sh
ص	ṣ (A heavy *s* pronounced far back in the mouth with the mouth hollowed to produce a full sound.)
ض	ḍ (A heavy *d/dh* pronounced far back in the mouth with the mouth hollowed to produce a full sound.)
ط	ṭ (A heavy *t* pronounced far back in the mouth with the mouth hollowed to produce a full sound.)
ظ	ẓ (A heavy *dh* pronounced far back in the mouth with the mouth hollowed to produce a full sound.)
ع	‘, ‘a, ‘i, ‘u (Pronounced from the throat.)
غ	gh (Pronounced like a throaty French *r* with the mouth hollowed to produce a full sound.)
ف	f
ق	q (A guttural *q* sound with the mouth hollowed to produce a full sound.)
ك	k
ل	l
م	m
ن	n
و	w, ū, u.
ه	h
ي	y, ī, i

ﷺ	*Ṣalla ’Llāhu ‘alayhi wa sallam*—used following the mention of the Messenger Muḥammad, translated as, “May Allāh bless him and give him peace.”
	‘Alayhi ’l-salām—used following the mention of a prophet or messenger of Allāh, translated as, “May the peace of Allāh be upon him.”
	Raḍiya ’Llāhu ‘anhu—used following the mention of a Companion of the Messenger ﷺ, translated as, “May Allāh be pleased with him.”
	Raḍiya ’Llāhu ‘anhā—used following the mention of a female Companion of the Messenger ﷺ, translated as, “May Allāh be pleased with her.”
	Raḥimahu ’Llāh—used following the mention of a scholar or pious individual, translated as, “May Allāh have mercy on him.”
	Raḥimahumu ’Llāh—used following the mention of more than one scholar or pious individual, translated as, “May Allāh have mercy on them.”

Publisher's Note

In the name of Allāh Most Gracious Most Merciful. All praise is to Allāh Most High for allowing this work to come to print. White Thread Press undertook the project to edit and publish this valuable work several years ago. This is a work recommended by many of our sages as essential study for any seeker wanting to traverse the higher stations of the Path. It combines the profundity of Shaykh Ibn ʿAṭā'illāh al-Iskandarī's upliftingly beautiful aphorisms and Shaykh ʿAbdullāh Gangōhī's lucid unwrapping and exposition of them in his *Ikmāl al-Shiyam*, meaning "to perfect the innate character or natural disposition."

We are immensely thankful to Andrew Booso for editing the entire commentary and remarkably heightening its lucidity to match the eloquence of Victor Danner's translation of the aphorisms. His preface provides details on the background of the Islamic spiritual path and how the *Ikmāl* fits into the corpus of spiritual writing of the Indian subcontinent. Shaykh al-Ḥadīth Mawlānā Zakariyyā Kāndhlawī wrote a detailed introduction to the original Urdu commentary. He discusses, in his unique and inspiring style, the life and spirituality of the commentator, Shaykh ʿAbdullāh Gangōhī and provides a longer biography of Mawlānā Khalīl Aḥmad Sahāranpūrī. Mawlānā Khalīl Aḥmad was both his and Shaykh ʿAbdullāh's spiritual guide in the Path and had translated the aphorisms of Shaykh Ibn ʿĀṭā'illāh into Urdu. He was also responsible for inspiring his student Shaykh ʿAbdullāh to pen this commentary on his translation. Shaykh Zakariyyā's lengthy introduction therefore adorns this English edition, as it provides much-needed insight into the scholarship behind the commentary.

We are indebted to Mawlānā Ismail Nakhuda for revising the translation of the introduction. The only addition we have made to it is to include the Gregorian dates with the Ḥijrī dates to better assist the Western reader in placing the events discussed. The original South African translator's notes end with (trans.) while those by Shaykh Zakariyyā end with (sz). The remaining notes are by Mawlānā Ismail Nakhuda and remain unmarked.

The commentary *Ikmāl al-Shiyam* begins on page 89. The aphorisms are presented both in their original Arabic and English translation according to the subject-wise arrangement of Shaykh ʿAlī Muttaqī. The commentary is interspersed after each. Ibn ʿĀṭā'illāh no doubt had his reasons for arranging the aphorisms in the way he did. To facilitate their reading according to his original arrangement, the relevant numbering is provided in brackets with each aphorism according to the order they are found in Danner's work. The Arabic text of the aphorisms has been compared with Paul Nwyia's critical edition, although other editions were consulted when discrepancies were found in it. It has also been carefully vocalized and punctuated. Since the Arabic text is present, the interlinear transliterations of Arabic terms found in Danner's translation have been removed. All references to Qur'ānic verses both in Danner's translation (in brackets) and the commentary (in parentheses) have been added by us.

In closing, we would like to thank all those who have assisted in bringing this work to completion. In particular, I would like to thank our shaykh Mawlānā Yusuf ibn Sulayman Motala, who is one of the foremost inheritors of the *Ikmāl's* legacy today, and through whom I was first introduced to it. His valuable guidance was indispensible. May Allāh reward them all and the authors abundantly in this world and the next for providing this inspiration and may He make it a source of benefit for one and all.

Abdur-Rahman ibn Yusuf Mangera
London, 25 Shaʿbān 1434 | 4 June 2013

Contents

Part Two
THE TREATISES   311

Part Three
THE INTIMATE DISCOURSES   329

Editor's Preface

DEFINING SUFISM WITHIN ISLAMIC SPIRITUALITY

IBN ʿĀSHŪR (d. 1393/1973) has expounded at length the goals of Islamic law, and stated in the process that it "aims at the acquisition of what is good and beneficial (*jalb al-maṣāliḥ*) and the rejection of what is evil and harmful (*dar' al-mafāsid*)"—which, for him, is the "fundamental universal rule" of the Sacred Law. He elaborates that the attainment of this goal is dependent "on the righteousness and virtue of the human being," who "is the predominant creature (*muhaymin*) in this world." Therefore we see, in Ibn ʿĀshūr's formulation, that Islam

> started its call by reforming matters pertaining to faith and belief, for it is right belief that constitutes the foundation of sound and correct human thinking that leads the mind to proper reflection on the affairs of the world. Then, Islam addressed itself to purifying the human psyche and uplifting the human soul, since it is the inner person that actually motivates one to righteous deeds, as indicated in the Prophet's saying ﷺ: "Beware! There is in the body a piece of flesh (*mudgha*), if it becomes good (reformed), the whole body becomes good, but if it is spoilt, the whole body is spoilt, and that is the heart" (*Bukhārī*). . .Human beings have a natural propensity for perfection. However, their actual achievement of perfection develops only gradually in tandem with their spiritual purification and moral uplifting.[1]

The discipline of Islamic spirituality has—as pointed out by Muftī Taqi Usmani (b. 1362/1943)—a variety of titles in Arabic, such as *iḥsān* (perform-

---

1 Muḥammad al-Ṭāhir Ibn ʿĀshūr, *Treatise on Maqāṣid al-Sharīʿah*, trans. Mohamed El-Tahir El-Mesawi (London: IIIT, 2006), 94–5.

ing good deeds), *ṭarīqa* (the Path), *sulūk* (good manners) and *taṣawwuf* (often translated as *sufism*).[2] The most popular English title for Islamic spirituality is *sufism*, with the practitioner of sufism being called a *sufi*—the latter corresponding to its Arabic equivalent. It is prudent to distinguish between general Islamic spirituality and *taṣawwuf*. The distinction is necessary because *taṣawwuf* has now developed numerous forms and nomenclature that are not shared by many who are concerned with Islamic spirituality in general.[3] *Taṣawwuf*, strictly speaking, is now the method of the Orders (*ṭuruq*, sing. *ṭarīqa*) and their Masters (simply called *shuyūkh*, sing. *shaykh*).[4] Although *taṣawwuf* is, in addition, used more generally by some non-Order scholars to simply denote the spiritual teaching of the Qur'ān and Sunna, or "way," of the Prophet Muḥammad ﷺ.[5]

There is much discussion regarding the etymology of the term *ṣūfī*. Abū 'l-Qāsim al-Qushayrī (d. 465/1072) discusses the various linguistic models, and then concludes: "However, this group is certainly too famous to have to be defined by a linguistic model or vindicated by means of derivation."[6] Ibn Khaldūn (d. 808/1406) has indicated that the terms *ṣūfiyya* (sufis) and *ahl al-taṣawwuf* (people of *taṣawwuf*) became popular around the "second generation," as a means of describing those who were "dedicated solely to worship"—at a time "when people started to rush headlong into the world and mix with it." Ibn Khaldūn linked *taṣawwuf* to the Companions of the Prophet ﷺ, and he provided a very basic definition of *taṣawwuf*:

> The basis of the spiritual path is dedication to worship, devotion to Allāh Most High, turning away from the adornment and ornamentations of this

---

2 Taqi Usmani, *Spiritual Discourses* (Karachi: Darul-Ishaat, 2001), 1:27.

3 Ibn al-Jawzī, Ibn Taymiya, Ibn al-Qayyim and Ibn Rajab (all Ḥanbalīs, incidentally) are examples of scholars profoundly concerned with Islamic spirituality who are not considered to have a strict allegiance to one of the normative Orders nor close adherence to normative nomenclature, expositions and methods of the Orders. Moreover, Ibn al-Jawzī and Ibn Taymiya are known for even criticising the spiritual theory of such sufic luminaries as Abū Ḥāmid al-Ghazālī and Muḥāsibī.

A comprehensive study of general Islamic spirituality in English—with a negative reading of sufism, it must be said—can be found in Jamaal al-Din M. Zarabozo, *Purification of the Soul: Concept, Process and Means* (Denver, USA: Al-Basheer, 2002).

4 Some of the most famous Orders are the Naqhsbandī, Chishtī, Qādirī, and Shādhilī.

5 Yusuf Qaradawi has discussed this in his *Priorities of the Islamic Movement in the Coming Phase* (Swansea, UK: Awakening, 2002), whereby he has defended "true *tasawwuf*" (op. cit. 83), and called it a "necessity" (op. cit. 61); and he has defended Ibn Taymiya against the charge of being opposed to "all of *tasawwuf*" (op. cit. 61).

6 Qushayrī, *The Risalah: The Principles of Sufism*, trans. Rabia Harris (Great Books of the Islamic World, 2002), 337.

worldly life, renunciation of what most people crave of pleasure, wealth and prestige, limiting one's interaction with the creation and being free for worship.[7]

Many Masters of the Orders have explicit statements on the necessity of the Sufic Path and submitting to one of the Masters. Due to the fact that we are here handling a commentary by an Indian sufi, I will suffice with a quotation on the issue of taking a Master from someone connected to the same spiritual lineage as our commentator Shaykh ʿAbdullāh Gangōhī:

> Improving character traits is not possible except though spiritual struggle at the hands of an accomplished spiritual guide (*shaykh*) who has struggled with his own self, opposed his caprice, abandoned base character traits, and adorned himself with praiseworthy ones. Whoever thinks they can achieve this through mere knowledge and the study of books has erred and gone far astray. Just as [outward] knowledge is only acquired through study with scholars, good character is acquired by struggling to attain it at the hands of the knowers of Allāh.[8]

---

7 Ibn Khaldūn, *Al-Muqaddima*, as cited by ʿAbd al-Qādir ʿĪsā, *Realities of Sufism* (Netherlands: Sunni Publications, 2009), 367.

Numerous famous scholars of early Islam such as Mālik, Shāfiʿī and Aḥmad ibn Ḥanbal have been quoted by later great scholars as having spoken of "sufis" and "*tasawwuf*"—see Gibril Fouad Haddad, *The Four Imāms and their Schools: Abū Ḥanīfa, Mālik, Al-Shāfiʿī, Aḥmad* (Muslim Academic Trust), in regards to these scholars and the sufis. As Haddad's examples show, there are both positive narrations as well as negative. An example of the latter is attributed to Shafiʿī: "A rational man does not become a sufi except he reaches noon a dolt" (see op. cit. 230). Haddad mentions that many scholars quoted Imām Mālik saying, "He who practises *taṣawwuf* without learning Sacred Law corrupts his faith (*tazandaqa*), while he who learns Sacred Law without practising taṣawwuf corrupts himself (*tafassaqa*)"—but Haddad states that this quote has been "cited without chain of transmission." See op. cit. 179–180.

Ibn al-Qayyim wrote in *Al-Dā' wa 'l-Dawā'*: "Shāfiʿī ﷺ said: 'I accompanied the sufis and I did not benefit from them other than for two words. One was their saying: Time is like a sword, if you do not cut it, it will cut you.' He mentioned the other saying [as being]: 'Your soul, if it is not kept busy with the Truth, it will busy you with falsehood'"—cited in the translator's notes in ʿAbd al-Raḥmān al-Saʿdī, *The Exquisite Pearl: The Journey to Allāh & The Home of the Hereafter*, trans. Abu Aaliyah Surkheel Sharif (London: Jawziyyah Press, 2002), p. 31, n. 23.

8 Ẓafar ʿUthmānī, *Sufism & Good Character*, trans. Faraz F. Rabbani (Santa Barbara, USA: White Thread, 2004), 25.

ʿAbdullāh Gangōhī apparently reiterates the same view as ʿUthmānī later in this work, in chapter twenty-six: "If one desires to perceive His beauty and grandeur, then one should lift this veil of egotistic cravings by means of struggle [against the ego], righteous actions, invocation and obedience to a genuine shaykh (*shaykh kāmil*)."

For a standard description of the Master of an Order and the manners due to him—again taken from a Master connected to Gangōhī's spiritual lineage (see Masīḥullāh Khān, *The Path*

Nevertheless, Mawlānā Ẓafar ʿUthmānī (d. 1394/1974) does take a slightly revised view on this matter later in the same work:

> As for spiritual struggles, performing good works, and acquiring good character, these may be possible without the company of a spiritual guide. However, acquiring these in their company with a keen spiritual will (*himma*) is realized with relative ease, and, outside their company, with much difficulty and hardship.[9]

A rejection of the absolute necessity of submitting to a Master of an Order is the position of Shaykh ʿAbd al-Fattāḥ Abū Ghudda (d. 1418/1997), in his notes to Muḥāsibī's *Risālat al-Mustarshidīn*:

> These words of Imām al-Muḥāsibī 🙐 show that the matter concerning guidance is in the hands of Allāh the Exalted, and that the righteousness of the soul and its purification is not dependent on confining oneself to a shaykh and to *bayʿa* (allegiance). Rather, it is dependent on confining oneself to knowledge and practising on what Allah the Exalted ordered. This entails the Qurʾān, the Sunna and the way of the pious imāms.[10]

Nonetheless, Abū Ghudda's stance is not an absolute rejection of allegiance to a Master. This is proven in the same section of the aforementioned work, as he recounts a written encounter between Shāṭibī (d. 790/1388), the great jurist, and Ibn ʿAbbād (d. 792/1390), a famous sufi and commentator of Ibn ʿAṭaʾillāh's *Ḥikam*. Ibn ʿAbbād distinguishes between the *shaykh al-tarbiya* (the teacher of spiritual training) and the *shaykh al-taʿlīm* (the teacher of knowledge). For Ibn ʿAbbād, the latter is necessary for "every *sālik* (traveller to God)," but the former is only necessary for a person who is "mentally foolish and has a refractory soul." Ibn ʿAbbād writes that the "sufficiently intelligent" person who has no need for a spiritual Master "will reach his goal by the will of Allāh the Exalted." Furthermore, Ibn ʿAbbād writes: "Relying on a *shaykh al-tarbiyah* is the way of the latter day sufi imāms (leaders) while relying on a *shaykh al-taʿlīm* is the way of the early sufi imāms." Moreover, Ibn ʿAbbād affirms that "the books of the sufis. . .are referred to as *shaykh*

---

of Perfection (Santa Barbara, USA: White Thread, 2005), 30–4. This concise sufic text has good sections on the way of striving for the eradication of bad states and the attainment of noble states.

9 ʿUthmānī, *Sufism & Good Character* 43.

10 ʿAbd al-Fattāḥ Abū Ghuddah, *The Sunnah Way of the Sufis*, trans. Mahomed Mahomedy (Karachi: Zam Zam, 2006), 61.

al-ta'līm."[11] Nevertheless, as with any science, the *shaykh al-taʿlīm* must be knowledgeable in the field that he is being questioned on, as well as fair in his discussion of the matter. To God we ask for success.

Taṣawwuf has been justified by many orthodox scholars as a valid form of Islamic spirituality—and our authors, Ibn ʿAṭā'illāh and Gangōhī, would share in an orthodox reading of the tradition of *taṣawwuf*; and I will only present the most orthodox of sufic thought here. Imām Aḥmad Sirhindī (d. 1624), a Master of the Naqhsbandī Order, wrote: "After one has acquired right beliefs[12] and subjected oneself to the rules of the Sharīʿa,[13] one should, if God so wills, enter the path of the sufis."[14] Moreover, Junayd al-Baghdadī (d. 297/910), one of the foremost sufis of all time and a jurist of Imām Abū Thawr's school of jurisprudence,[15] said, "Whoever has not memorised the Noble Qur'ān or recorded the ḥadīth is not to be taken as a guide in this affair, because this knowledge of ours is tied (*muqayyad*) to the Book [of God] and the Sunna."[16] Therefore, we can summarise *taṣawwuf* in the words of Abū Muḥammad al-Jurayrī (d. 310/923), a student of Junayd al-Baghdadī and companion of Sahl al-Tustarī (d. 283/886),[17] as: "The entering into every exalted trait of character and the leaving of every vile one [as defined in Islam]."[18]

If *taṣawwuf* is thus connected to the Sacred Law and theology of Islam—as both Sirhindī and Junayd al-Baghdadī have mentioned—then it naturally follows that the discipline, in essence, is part of the Prophetic inheritance;

---

11 See ibid. 61–65.

12 *Right beliefs* here refers to orthodox Islamic theology, or tenets of faith, known in Arabic as *ʿaqīda ahl al-sunna wa 'l-jamāʿa*. See Imām Ṭaḥāwī, *Islamic Belief* (*Al-Aqīda al-Ṭaḥāwiyya*] (Leicester: UK Islamic Academy, 2002).

13 For a discussion of legal positions accepted traditionally see Nuh Ha Mim Keller and Ibn Naqīb al-Miṣrī, *Reliance of the Traveller: A Classic Manual of Islamic Sacred Law* (1991; revised edition, Evanston: Sunna Books, 1994), and Ibn Rushd, *Distinguished Jurist's Primer*, trans. Imran Ahsan Khan Nyazee (Reading: Garnet, 1994). Also, see Yusuf al-Qaradawi, *The Lawful and the Prohibited in Islam* (*Al-Ḥalāl wa 'l-Ḥarām fī 'l-Islām*), trans. Kamal El-Helbawy, M. Moinuddin Siddiqi and Syed Shukry (Indianapolis: American Trust, n.d.), for a discussion of the wisdom behind many of these traditional rulings—although the author is prone to a comparative juristic method that is contentious to the conservative. Moreover, there are many works in English that are translations of Taqi Usmani, who is one of the leading conservative jurists of the current time.

14 Ansari, *Sufism and Shari'ah: A Study of Shaykh Ahmad Sirhindi's Efforts to Reform Sufism* (Leicester: Islamic Foundation, 1986), 175.

15 Qushayrī, *Al-Risālah* (Beirut: Dār al-Habil, n.d.) 40–41.

16 Ibid. 431.

17 Ibid. 51.

18 Ibid. 280. In Arabic, the wording of the original is: "*al-dukhūl fī kulli khuluqin saniyy wa al-khurūj min kulli khuluq daniyy.*"

hence it has always been part of the message of Islam. In this regard, we can perceive *taṣawwuf* in the same manner as we view the Sacred Law and orthodox theology of Islam: although all are based upon the reading of the Qur'ān and Sunna by the most advanced scholars throughout Islamic history, a significant amount of the actual nomenclature is not directly taken from those primary sources, despite the fact that their reality, in most cases, is firmly grounded in the Qur'ān and Sunna. It is therefore of no surprise to find ʿAlī Hujwērī quoting the lament of Abū 'l-Ḥasan al-Fūshanjī: "Today Sufism is a name without a reality, but formerly it was a reality without a name."[19] Furthermore, traditionally-read manuals of *taṣawwuf*, such as the *Iḥyā'* of Imām Abū Ḥāmid al-Ghazālī (d. 505/1111) or the *Risāla* of Abū 'l-Qāsim al-Qushayrī, are replete with references from the Qur'ān and Sunna in the course of expounding upon the doctrine—although it must be admitted that ḥadīth deemed *weak* (*ḍaʿīf*) by the scholars of ḥadīth have crept into such manuals.[20]

One cannot deny that *taṣawwuf*—like all other Islamic disciplines, including law, theology, Qur'ānic exegesis and ḥadīth—has suffered from heterodox deviations, as well as controversies amongst the orthodox.[21] The prudent thing is to accept that *taṣawwuf* is the discipline of men, and the way of non-Prophets is to make mistakes—even if the best of men are only prone to the occasional, or least significant, slips. Nevertheless, the acknowledgement of such natural human fallibility should not result in the complete dismissal of the good along with the bad; and this is especially the case with *taṣawwuf*, which has had some of the finest men contribute to its development. Of course, one's conclusions about the acceptable and non-acceptable from the legacy of the sufis will depend on one's methodological leaning—and there are numerous choices to be made from. Nevertheless, one even finds a certain amount of crossover between those scholars of Islamic spirituality who belong to an Order and those who do not. Moreover, one sees great disagreements between varying Orders themselves, with regards to theology, law and spiritual method. Nonetheless, our authors in this work

19 Hujwiri, *Kashf al-Maḥjūb*, trans. Reynold Nicholson, 44.

20 For a discussion on the terminology found in the analysis of ḥadīth literature, one should consult Ibn al-Ṣalāḥ al-Shahrazūrī, *An Introduction to the Science of Hadith* (*Kitāb Maʿrifat Anwāʿ ʿIlm al-Ḥadīth*, but better known as *Al-Muqaddima*], trans. Eerik Dickinson (Reading: Garnet, 2005).

For a discussion of the limited use of weak ḥadīth in the realm of spiritual instruction see Yusuf al-Qaradawi, *Approaching the Sunnah: Comprehension and Controversy*, trans. Jamil Qureshi (London: IIIT, 2006), 66–82.

21 See ʿIsa, *Realities*, 311–325.

would only accept the most orthodox sufi theory as theirs—even if certain aspects of such theory is criticised by those not of the Orders.

THE UNDERSTANDING OF SUFISM IN THE WEST

The normative use of *sufism* in English has not, in many cases, led to an understanding of *sufism* or a *sufi* that conforms to anything even resembling orthodoxy, despite the fact that many past Masters—as quoted earlier—have only striven to be the most orthodox. The principal reason for such mistaken notions is the tendency to view sufism as an entity in itself, separate from Islam, as is the case with much of the literature on "spirituality" that has emerged in the West during the twentieth century. Giles Fraser outlined this twentieth-century trend as follows:

> Spirituality has become the acceptable face of religion. . . And it's not about believing in anything too specific, other than in some nebulous sense of otherness or presence. It offers God without dogma. . . Of course, spirituality has been around for a very long time. With all its beads and symbols, ancient wisdom is part of the appeal to the spirituality shopper. Except what they take to be spirituality is a distinctly 20th century invention. As Professor Denys Turner rightly pointed out: "No mystics (at least before the present century) believed in or practised mysticism. They believed in and practised Christianity (or Judaism or Islam or Hinduism), that is religions that contained mystical elements as parts of a wider whole."[22]

The trend that Fraser speaks of is evident in the *comparative religions* approach of certain Western authors of sufism, whose writings portray sufism as an essentially lawless mysticism that validates "religion" in the plural. Such a liberal tendency is an heterodox assertion that is vehemently and unanimously opposed by the religious authorities of Islam, as expounded in the official religious edict of The Council of Senior Scholars of the Kingdom of Saudi Arabia.[23] The research of Shaykh Nuh Keller (b. 1954) serves as a useful summary of the Saudi Council's ruling:

> That Islam is the only remaining valid or acceptable religion is necessarily

---

22 See Giles Fraser's article in the Comment section of *The Guardian*, 6 June 2005.

23 Included by Abu Aaliyah as an appendix to his translation of Muhammad ibn Saalih al-ʿUthaymeen's *ʿAqīda Ahl al-Sunna wa 'l-Jamāʿa*, entitled *Tenets of Faith* (Birmingham, UK: al-Hidaayah, 2000), 80–92.

> known as part of our religion, and to believe anything other than this is unbelief (*kufr*) that places a person outside of Islam, as Nawawī notes, "Someone who does not believe that whoever follows another religion besides Islam is an unbeliever (like Christians), or doubts that such a person is an unbeliever, or considers their sect to be valid, is himself an unbeliever (*kāfir*) even if he manifests Islam and believes in it (*Rawḍat al-Ṭālibīn*, 10.70)."[24]

Another popular accusation against sufism in general—and not just against the heretics attached to the name of the discipline—is the notion of "union with God" as the perfection of those who have reached the end of the Path. This is such an accepted norm amongst English-speaking authors that it can even be found in Victor Danner's translations of the aphorisms in this publication, which leads the unknowing to conclude that pantheism is perceived by the sufis to be the final achievement in their spirituality. This wording is the result of translating various derivatives from the Arabic root *w-ṣ-l*, such as *wuṣūl*, *wiṣāl*, or *wuṣla*, as *union*; whereas alternative translations could be "arrival (to a deep knowledge of God— *wuṣūl*)," "closeness (to God, that should not be misunderstood as being spatial in any sense—*wiṣāl*)," or "connection (to God, again non-spatial; and conveying a sense of the attachment of a person's heart to the love and obedience of God—*wuṣla*)." Recourse to such a selection would ensure that these derivatives of *w-ṣ-l* are not confused with Arabic terms such as *ittiḥād* or *ḥulūl*, which do have connotations with *union*, but are based on different Arabic root letters to *w-ṣ-l*.

Nevertheless, a case can be made for utilising a figurative understanding of "union" in such circumstances that defends against any charge of heresy. Imām Jalāl al-Dīn al-Suyūṭī (d. 911/1505) has written:

> Know that the expression "union" has appeared in some of the statements of the verifying scholars as an allusion to the reality of Divine Unity. . . It is possible that "union" takes on the meaning of effacing opposition [to the

24 Nuh Keller, *The Shadhili Tariqa* (1999), 23. See *Reliance*, 846-851 (w4), for more details on this theological matter.

Even so, there is a legal process through which people are excluded from Islam, known in Arabic as *takfir*. Again, Imām Nawawī has, elsewhere, concisely expounded the process of *takfir*: "Any Muslim who denies something that is necessarily known to be of the religion of Islam is adjudged a renegade and an unbeliever unless he is a recent convert or was born and raised in the wilderness or for some similar reason has been unable to learn his religion properly. Muslims in such a condition should be informed about the truth, and if they continue as before, they are adjudged non-Muslims, as is also the case with any Muslim who believes it permissible to commit adultery, drink wine, kill without right, or do other acts that are necessarily known to be unlawful." Nawawī, *Ṣaḥīḥ Muslim bi Sharḥ al-Nawawī*, as cited in *Reliance*, 809 (u2.4).

Sacred Law], leaving conformity [to it] to remain, effacement of the soul's portion of the world and keeping one's longing for the Hereafter, effacing the blameworthy qualities and keeping praiseworthy traits, effacing doubt and keeping one's certitude, and effacing heedlessness and keeping one's remembrance. . .[So] the upshot of all of this is that the expression "union" is a homonym. It can be employed according to the blameworthy meaning that is the brother of [akin to] indwelling—which is disbelief—and it can be employed as a word synonymous with annihilation (*fanā'*). There is no harm when it comes to words used in technical nomenclature (*la mashāhata fī 'l-iṣṭilāḥ*); for no one is prevented from using a word if the meaning is correct and it contains nothing blameworthy in the Sacred Law. . .[25]

THE LIFE OF IBN ʿAṬĀ'ILLĀH AND HIS *ḤIKAM*

It is estimated that Ibn ʿAṭā'illāh was born in Egypt around the middle of the thirteenth century, and he is said to have died in Egypt in 709/1309.[26] During his life, Egypt was ruled by the Mamluk regime, and was an important political and religious part of the eastern Muslim world, in which the Mamluks "ushered in an impressive artistic and architectural epoch."[27]

He was born into a family of revered jurists of the Mālikī school of law, who were descendants of an Arab tribe, the Judhām, and had "settled in Egypt during the early Muslim conquests."[28] Ibn ʿAṭā'illāh was to follow the family tradition of excelling in the field of Islamic law, and Danner writes that "all sources are agreed that he was Mālikī, except Subkī, in *Ṭabaqāt*, 5:176, who hesitates between Shāfiʿīsm and Mālikīism."[29] In fact, he was to gain fame as an expert in Islamic law in the city of his birth, Alexandria, before he found similar acclaim in Cairo, where he later taught at the prestigious Al-Azhar, which operated an institution of higher learning for the Islamic disciplines, and other academic institutions in Cairo.[30]

The life of a prominent and recognised jurist did not prevent Ibn ʿAṭā'illāh

---

25 Suyūṭī, *Al-Ḥāwī li 'l-Fatāwī*, as cited in ʿĪsā, *Realities*, 344–5. Also see ʿĪsā, *Realities*, 344–349, for further discussion on the topic, including interesting passages from Ibn Taymiya and his student Ibn al-Qayyim that confirm the understanding highlighted above by Suyūṭī.

26 See Victor Danner's introduction in Ibn ʿAṭā'illāh, *Sufi Aphorisms*, trans. Victor Danner (Leiden: E.J. Brill, 1973), 1, and *Reliance*, 1053 (x156).

27 Danner, in *Sufi Aphorisms*, 1.

28 Ibid. 4–5.

29 Ibid. p. 5, n. 1.

30 Danner, 5 and 9, and *Reliance*, 1053.

from also becoming a leading instructor in the Path of Sufism, while maintaining, contemporaneously, his role as a lecturer in Islamic law.[31] Around 674/1276, he had become a spiritual disciple of Abū 'l-ʿAbbās al-Mursī (d. 686/1288), an Andalusian who had inherited the Path from Abū 'l-Ḥasan al-Shādhilī (d. 656/1258),[32] and he was to be established by Mursī as a Shaykh of the Path in his own right before Mursī's passing away, some twelve years after their initial encounter.[33] Before the latter's death, the *Ḥikam* had been authored by Ibn ʿAṭā'illāh and endorsed by Mursī.[34]

Victor Danner has stated:

> Of all the works written by Ibn ʿAṭā'illāh, the *Ḥikam* is certainly the most admired by later generations of Muslims. . .As it stands, however, the *Ḥikam* was evidently dictated by Shaykh Ibn ʿAṭā'illāh to one of his disciples. . .This disciple was none other than the distinguished Shāfiʿī jurist Taqī al-Dīn al-Subkī (d. 756/1355). The Shādhilī master Aḥmad Zarrūq (d. 899/1493) got five of the works of Ibn ʿAṭā'illāh, including the *Ḥikam*, from the Shafiʿī jurist and historian Shams al-Dīn al-Sakhāwī (d. 902/1497), who also gave him the *isnād*,[35] which begins with Taqī al-Dīn al-Subkī.[36]

Although the subtitle selected for this publication, *A Collection of Sufi Aphorisms*, implies that the *Ḥikam* is a work of aphorisms only, it actually comprises three distinct parts: aphorisms, treatises and supplications.[37] Nevertheless, the subtitle is sufficiently apt because the aphorisms are certainly the most dominant feature of the three, and warrant the most attention. Indeed, the mastering of the aphorisms is likely to bequeath an advanced reading of the treatises and supplications, which are more straight forward in their style; while the aphorisms, due to their concise nature, warrant more analysis, together with an inner perception that is heightened as one's piety and spirituality progresses.

Meanwhile, Victor Danner observes that no other aphoristic work of the sufi Masters—of which numerous examples exist—has "scored with poster-

---

31 Danner, 9.

32 Ibid. 8.

33 Ibid. 9.

34 Ibid.

35 *Isnād* is the chain of transmission for a narration, written or spoken. See M.M. Azami, *Studies in Early Hadith Literature* (Indianapolis: American Trust, 1992), Chapter VI, for a discussion of *isnād* in relation to ḥadīth.

36 Danner, 15.

37 Ibid. 17.

ity so impressively as Ibn ʿAṭā'illāh['s]."[38] He attributes this success to the author's captivating language in the Arabic original, which "not only unfolds the integral Sufi doctrine on all levels, but it does so in a manner calculated to appeal to pious Muslims in general."[39] This appeal to the various ranks of Muslims is surely one of the reasons why scholars, past and present,[40] have attempted to make this work accessible to the general public through their spoken expositions and written commentaries.

SHAYKH ʿABDULLĀH GANGŌHĪ AND HIS COMMENTARY

The commentary of Shaykh ʿAbdullāh Gangōhī was the culmination of various efforts by a group of Indian scholars over a somewhat protracted period of time. We can identify the beginning of this particular process as Shaykh ʿAlī Muttaqī—the sixteenth-century scholar famous for the ḥadīth work *Kanz al-ʿummāl*[41]—who re-arranged the aphorisms into groups under selected titles, which ultimately comprised thirty chapters, entitled *An-Nahj al-Atamm fī Tabwīb al-Ḥikam*. Muttaqī found the *Ḥikam* to be the best of the books detailing the science of *taṣawwuf*, and he felt inclined to make his arrangement as a means of commentary and facilitation towards memorisation.[42]

The resumption of this activity in regards to the *Ḥikam* was to begin at the end of the nineteenth century, when numerous Indian scholars attempted to make the *Ḥikam* accessible to Urdu-speaking people, whose lack of Arabic made it impossible to grasp the work. This endeavour was part of an educational drive that became a focus after the political failure of the 1857 uprising against the British colonial forces. Shaykh Abū 'l-Ḥasan ʿAlī Nadwī (d. 1999) describes how this crushing defeat led these religious scholars to adopt a "defensive role" that manifested a concerted effort of preserving Islamic culture through the development of educational institu-

---

38 Ibid. 19.

39 Ibid. 19–20.

40 Danner lists some of the previous commentators as Shams ad-Dīn Muḥammad ibn ʿAbd al-Raḥmān ibn al-Ṣā'igh (d. 776/1375), ʿAbdullāh al-Sharqāwī, ʿAbd al-Majīd al-Sharnūbī, Aḥmad Zarrūq, Ibn ʿAbbād al-Rundī and Ibn ʿAjība (see ibid. 21–22). Danner also mentions how it is reported that Zarrūq wrote thirty commentaries himself on the *Ḥikam* (see op. cit. 21). Modern commentators, not mentioned by Danner, include Saʿīd Ḥawwā and Ramaḍān Būṭī, both from Syria.

41 *Ikhmalush* [*sic*] *Shiyam* (Port Elizabeth: Mujlisul Ulama of South Africa, n.d.), 60–61.

42 Ibid. 66.

tions of Islamic learning (*madāris*, sing. *madrasa*; or *dār al-ʿulūm*, literally "the place of the sciences").[43] Nadwī identifies Mawlānā Muḥammad Qāsim Nānōtwī as the foremost individual in this task, and he quotes Mawlānā Nānōtwī's biographer, Mawlānā Manāzir Aḥsan Gīlānī, as saying: "After the failure of the upheaval of 1857 his [Nānōtwī's] mind was actively engaged in the establishment of new fronts of resistance and struggle. The educational design of the Dār al-ʿUlūm of Deoband was the most important part of it."[44]

The establishment of Dār al-ʿUlūm Deoband is largely credited to Mawlānā Nānōtwī and Mawlānā Rashīd Aḥmad Gangōhī (d. 1323/1905), both of whom were Islamic scholars tied in spiritual allegiance to Ḥājī Imdādullāh,[45] although others were involved in the creation of the institute in 1867.[46] Metcalf describes the initial syllabus as being essentially the *dars-i niẓāmī* curriculum that had been developed at the Firangi Mahall, but with the ḥadīth content expanded to include the "six classical collections."[47] Even now the institution describes itself in a manner fitting the traditional model: Sunnī in terms of sect; Ḥanafī in jurisprudence; Māturīdī Ashʿarī in theology; and adhering to the main sufi orders of the region, with an emphasis on the Chistī order.[48]

---

43 Nadwī, *Western Civilisation, Islam and Muslims*, trans. Mohammad Asif Kidwai (Lucknow: Academy of Islamic Research and Publications, 1979), 60–62.

44 Gīlānī, *Sawāniḥ-i-Qāsmī*, as cited in Nadwī, ibid. 62. Despite the emphasis being on education, many of the acclaimed graduates of Deoband continued to pursue the eviction of the British from India. In fact, Maḥmūd al-Ḥasan, who was the first student at the Deoband institute and would "become the school's most famous teacher" (according to Metcalf, *Islamic Revival in British India: Deoband, 1860–1900*, 92), was imprisoned in Malta from 1917–20 by the British for his attempt at ousting them with an invasion from the north-west area with the support of the Afghan government and certain notable Turkish leaders, such as Anwar and Jamal Pasha—an event that came to be known as the "silk letter conspiracy," because Ḥasan sent letters to India from his base in Madina (in modern-day Saudi Arabia) containing his plans for revolt concealed in a wooden chest that contained silk; see Nadwī, *Muslims in India*, 116. Furthermore, Ḥusayn Aḥmad Madanī, one of Maḥmūd Ḥasan's famous students, was imprisoned with Ḥasan in Malta, and would later—while still a lecturer at Deoband—become a foremost activist, with other prominent religious scholars, of the Indian National Congress in their efforts to dismiss the British; see Nadwī, *Muslims in India*, 121–22. For a fuller discussion on this struggle against British colonialism, see Farhat Tabassum, *Deoband Ulema's Movement for the Freedom of India* (New Delhi: Manak, 2006).

45 For some details of the lives of these three men, see Metcalf, *Islamic*, 75–80. Nadwī writes of Imdādullāh and Nānōtwī taking part in a "pitched battle against the British forces" in Shamli, a town in the region of Muzaffarnagar (*Islamic Civilisation*, 62 n. 1).

46 See Metcalf, *Islamic*, 88.

47 Ibid. 100–101. The "six classical collections" are held to be those of Bukhārī, Muslim, Tirmidhī, Abū Dāwūd, Nasāʾī and Ibn Māja; see M.Z. Siddiqi, *Hadith Literature: Its Origin, Development & Special Features* (Cambridge: Islamic Texts Society, 1993), for details of these collections.

48 Described online at <http://darululoom-deoband.com/english/index.htm>. The scholarly

Nadwī has written: "Deoband became the forerunner of the new religious trend and the most important seat of traditional Islamic culture and theological learning in India."[49] Moreover, the Dār al-ʿUlūm Deoband has since achieved international fame amongst the Islamic institutes of higher education in the Islamic world.[50] A fame that was helped by the publication of numerous detailed and acclaimed ḥadīth works in Arabic by scholars linked with the school during the twentieth century, such as the shaykhs Anwar Shāh Kashmīrī, Ḥabīb al-Raḥmān al-Aʿẓamī, Ẓafar Aḥmad ʿUthmānī, Zakariyyā Kāndhlawī, Yūsuf Kāndhlawī, Shabbīr Aḥmad ʿUthmānī and Taqi Usmani. While the English-speaking world has received the groundbreaking writings of Dr. Muhammad Mustafa al-Azami,[51] a graduate of Deoband, al-Azhar (M.A.) and the University of Cambridge (Ph.D.);[52] and the multi-volume English translation of the Urdu commentary of the Qur'ān by Muftī Muḥammad Shafī',[53] the former Muftī (juris-consult) of Deoband and then Pakistan.[54]

---

method of Deoband is elaborated in Muḥammad Ṭayyib, *The Maslak of the Ulama of Deoband*, trans. Afzal Hossen Elias (Karachi: Zam Zam, 2005).

See Nadwī, *Saviours of the Islamic Spirit*, trans. Mohiuddin Ahmad (Lucknow: Academy of Islamic Research and Publications, 1986–1993), for the schools of jurisprudence (1:64–66), Māturīdī-Ashʿarī schools of theology (2:87–100) and the sufi orders of India (2:145–341, and volumes 3 and 4). Also, for more information on the sufi orders in India, see Nadwī, Muslims in India, 50-65, and Nadwī, Islam and the World, trans. Mohammad Asif Kidwai (Lucknow: Academy of Islamic Research and Publications, 1980), 160–165.

49 Nadwī, *Western Civilisation*, 63.

50 The Azharī scholar Yusuf al-Qaradawi gave special mention to the "Deoband of Pakistan and India" along with the Azhar in Egypt, Zaytūna in Tunisia and Qarawiyyīn in Morocco as religious institutions that should be sought for endorsement of the Islamic Movement (Qaradawi, *Priorities*, 159). The reason for Qaradawi's mention of Deoband in Pakistan, as well as India, is because the issue of the partition of India after the departure of the British in 1947 was to split the movement, ideologically and then geographically, with some siding with the Deoband scholar Ashraf ʿAlī Thānawī in backing the Muslim League's call for a separate Muslim state called Pakistan; while others remained with Ḥusayn Aḥmad Madanī, who campaigned with the Indian National Congress and favoured a power-sharing solution with the Hindus and other minority groups that would ensure a united India without any provinces being severed off from the national borders as they then existed before the 1947 partition. See Zakariyyā Kāndhlawī, *Aap Beeti* (New Delhi: Idara Isha'at-e-Diniyat, 1996), 4:265–290, for a personalised account of a scholar who possessed close relations with both Deoband factions.

51 M.M. Azami's *Studies in Early Hadith Literature* and *On Schacht's Origins of Muhammadan Jurisprudence* (Oxford Centre for Islamic Studies and Islamic Texts Society, 1996) have been described as "the definitive rebuttal of [Joseph] Schacht's thesis" (Siddiqi, *Hadith Literature*, 131). This latter statement is most likely the comment of Abdal Hakim Murad (AKA T.J. Winter) who edited and updated Siddiqi's original work. Also of interest is Azami's recent *The History of the Qur'ānic Text: A Comparative Study with the Old and New Testaments* (Leicester: UK Islamic Academy, 2003).

52 M.M. Azami's biographical details can be found in his *The History of the Qur'ānic Text*, vi.

53 This work is entitled *Ma'ariful Qur'an*, and consists of eight volumes in English translation.

54 Despite its elevated rank with the best Islamic seats of higher learning in the rest of the

Together with the academic achievements, the leaders of Dār al-ʿUlūm Deoband placed great emphasis on the need for spiritual purity and attaining success in the Path of *taṣawwuf*. Ḥājī Imdādullāh was the "major influence on many *ʿulamāʾ* (religious scholars)"[55] at this time. In particular, he was the "sufi preceptor"[56] of both Mawlānā Nānōtwī and Rashīd Aḥmad Gangōhī, who took him as "their guide in every decision";[57] and Ḥājī Imdādullāh, in time, would grant each of them the rank of *khilāfat*,[58] which is the permission of the Master to his disciple to now guide others along the Path as he had guided them. The leadership of Ḥājī Imdādullāh was to extend to Shaykh ʿAbdullāh Gangōhī and his commentary on the *Ḥikam*. The first event in this process is Ḥājī Imdādullāh's instruction to Mawlānā Khalīl Aḥmad Sahāranpūrī (d. 1346/1927)[59]—who at one time was a lecturer at Deoband, but more famous for being a teacher at Deoband's "sister school in Sahāranpūr, Mazāhir ʿUlūm"[60]—to translate Muttaqī's arrangement of the *Ḥikam* into Urdu from Arabic.[61]

The life of Shaykh ʿAbdullāh Gangōhī is closely related to the spiritual descendants of Ḥājī Imdādullāh and the educational efforts of Dār al-ʿUlūm

world, Nadwī does concede: "But as far as meeting the challenge of the times is concerned, Deoband has failed to make any noteworthy contribution. . .Its graduates have done little to bridge the gulf between the old and the new generations. . .[In] their educational outlook and in the appreciation of the law of social change they have tended, more or less, to be conservative and tradition-bound. The educational system and the syllabus there was [*sic*] outdated" (Nadwī, *Western Civilisation*, 63). Nadwī doesn't just limit this sort of criticism to Dār al-ʿUlūm Deoband; rather, he points to "intellectual sterility and inefficiency of the educational system" to be the state of the "entire Muslim world" from the fifteenth century until our own time; see Nadwī, *Islam and the World*, 108–109, and *Western Civilisation*, 184–5. In the latter work, Nadwī states: "The religious scepticism and waywardness of the modern-educated classes of the Muslim world is, to a certain extent, due also to the intellectual decadence and inertia that has taken hold of the Islamic educational and literary institutions and their representatives."

55 Metcalf, *Islamic Revival*, 76.

56 Ibid. 79.

57 Ibid.

58 Zakariyyā Kāndhlawī, *Masha'ikh-e Chist* (Port Elizabeth: Mujlisul Ulama of South Africa, 1998), 222. See Metcalf, *Islamic Revival*, 364, for her definition of *khilāfat* in the Glossary.

59 See *Masha'ikh-e Chist*, 259–295, for his life details. He was granted *ijāza* (authoritative permission) to be a Master in the sufi Path from both Imdādullāh and Gangōhī, who was his main guide (op. cit. 268).

60 Barbara Metcalf, "Piety, Persuasion and Politics: Deoband's Model of Social Activism," in Aftab Ahmad Malik (ed.), *The Empire and the Crescent: Global Implications for a New American Century* (Bristol, UK: Amal, 2003), 165.

61 This instruction to Sahāranpūrī from Imdādullāh is narrated from Ashraf ʿAlī Thānawī, another spiritual successor to Imdādullāh (*Masha'ikh-e-Chist*, 235), in his Introduction to the publication of Sahāranpūrī's translation (see *Shiyam*, 24). ʿAbdullāh Gangōhī would repeat this claim in his Preface to his commentary of the *Ḥikam* (op. cit. 67).

Deoband and its related institutions. According to Mawlānā Ẓafar ʿUthmānī (former Muftī of Pakistan and a student of Mawlānā Khalīl Sahāranpūrī)[62] and his brother, Shabbīr ʿAlī (a student in both Saharanpur and Deoband),[63] Shaykh ʿAbdullāh Gangōhī received his religious education from Mawlānā Muḥammad Yaḥyā Kāndhlawī, a student of Mawlānā Rashīd Gangōhī,[64] father of Shaykh Zakariyyā Kāndhlawī and a spiritual predecessor to Mawlānā Khalīl Sahāranpūrī.[65] Then, when Mawlānā Ashraf ʿAlī Thānawī requested from Mawlānā Muḥammad Yaḥyā a good teacher for his school in Thana Bhawan, Khānqāh Imdādiyya, he was sent Shaykh ʿAbdullāh Gangōhī.[66] By the accounts of numerous scholars acquainted with him, Shaykh ʿAbdullāh Gangōhī was said to be an excellent religious scholar with a skill for teaching, who eventually became a teacher in Maẓāhir ʿUlūm in Saharanpur and received the rank of Master in the Chistī Path from Mawlānā Khalīl Sahāranpūrī, after initially taking the Path from Mawlānā Rashīd Gangōhī.[67]

Judging by Shaykh ʿAbdullāh Gangōhī's foreword to his commentary of the *Ḥikam*, he undertook this task as a result of being instructed by Mawlānā Khalīl Sahāranpūrī to produce an explanation of the aphorisms in Urdu, so that Mawlānā Khalīl's own Urdu translation might be more fully comprehended by the "laymen."[68] This reference to the "laymen" is, perhaps, very informative about the style of the commentary itself. A reader will be surprised to see very few references to the Qur'ān, ḥadīth or the comments of other scholars in the midst of Shaykh Gangōhī's exposition, which will seem strange for one accustomed to the substantial referencing of sufi theory to such sources by famous authors in the field, like, for example, the previously-mentioned works by Ghazālī and Qushayrī.

Anyhow, the end result is that the position of the reader is like someone in the private lesson of a sufi Master, who aims at guiding the novices to their goal, without being overly verbose, and whose goal is not to merely intellectually stimulate his listeners. Thus the commentary is like a reminder which enhances one's knowledge of the Qur'ānic verses and ḥadīth on topics—like knowledge, repentance, sincerity, the virtue and importance

62 For more on ʿUthmānī, see his *Qawāʿid fī ʿUlūm al-Ḥadīth* (Turath Publishing, 2013), p. 268.
63 *Shiyam*, 13.
64 Kāndhlawī, *Aap Beeti*, 4:122.
65 Kāndhlawī, *Masha'ikh-e Chist*, 268–269.
66 *Shiyam*, 15.
67 Ibid. 7–18.
68 Ibid. 67.

of the remembrance of God, etc.—which one has or should have already been instructed about, because such topics are elementary.

Ultimately, the discipline of *taṣawwuf* must be about a state of being that conforms to the excellences contained in the Qur'ān and ḥadīth, and not something that is memorised and not practised. In this respect, Imām Mālik (d. 179/795) is credited as having said: "Knowledge is a light which Allāh places where He will; it is not much narration."[69] Even so, a firm foundation in Islamic law and orthodox theology, together with a familiarity with Islamic ethics (as contained in works like Imām Nawawī's *Riyāḍ al-Ṣāliḥīn*, Ibn Qudāma Maqdisī's *Mukhtaṣar Minhāj al-Qāṣidīn*, and Ibn Rajab's commentary on Nawawī's *Arbaʿīn*), should assist the reader in a more profound and ultimately more correct reading of the aphorisms as intended by the author, who would have expected his audience to already have a firm foundation of knowledge; for the *Ḥikam* was not expected to be someone's introduction to Islamic spirituality—rather, it is only meant to be an addition to the essential knowledge that a conscientious and learned Muslim should have attained or be in the process of attaining.

A NOTE ON THIS PUBLICATION

This work is a combination of two previous English publications: (1) Ibn Ata'illah, *Sufi Aphorisms* (*Kitab al-Hikam*), trans. Victor Danner (Leiden: E.J. Brill, 1973); and (2) Muḥammad ʿAbdullāh Gangōhī, *Ikhmalush* [*sic*] *Shiyam* (Port Elizabeth: Mujlisul Ulama of South Africa, n.d.). The content of the first publication has been substantially altered in terms of layout, in order to make the aphorisms correspond to the arrangement of ʿAlī Muttaqī. Nevertheless, the actual wording of the original has been left unaltered, and Danner's translations of the aphorisms, treatises and intimate discourses follow the Arabic text. However, most of his footnotes have been omitted.

The South African publication has been edited by myself to try and bring it close to Danner's translation. However, the translations of the aphorisms, treatises and intimate discourses have been omitted in favour of Danner's translations.

Some aphorisms were missing from both the Urdu and South African editions of the *Ikmal*. They were inserted in the relevant places and com-

69 Cited by Abdassamad Clarke, in his Translator's Introduction to Imām Nawawī's *The Complete Forty Ḥadīth* (London: Ta-Ha, 2000), vi.

mentaries were added from Ibn ʿAjība and in one case from Aḥmad Zarrūq. Where there was some confusion in the South African translation, those portions were revised from the original. I translated the section from Zarrūq and checked it with Khalid Williams, and from whom I took the translation of the end poem; and *ustādh* Abdur-Rahman ibn Yusuf Mangera provided the references to the original ḥadīth material therein. Abdur-Rahman also provided the translations from Ibn ʿAjība, as well as all the references for the ḥadīth to original sources, and provided much comparative textual analysis on the *Ḥikam* for the footnotes.

The footnotes in this work are, on the whole, mine; yet I heavily relied upon the identification of Qur'ānic verses in Danner's original work. Explanatory footnotes remaining from Danner's work are identified with (VD) after the note. Comments contained within square brackets in the commentary are from the editor—on occasions, they have been used for additional, clarifying comments. The translations of the Divine Names in the commentary have been largely taken from Imām Abū Ḥāmid al-Ghazālī, *The Ninety-Nine Beautiful Names of God*, trans. David B. Burrell and Nazih Daher (Cambridge, UK: ITS, 1992).

Due to the fact that Danner's text could not be altered, his habit of translating *Allāh* as *God* has been left in tact, despite the fact that the latter is strictly-speaking a translation for *ilāh*. Likewise, whenever I have taken a translation from another copyrighted work, I have left their use of such words as they exist.

ACKNOWLEDGEMENTS

I must thank Ibrar Butt and Rafaqat Rashid for identifying the project, giving it momentum and also allowing me to be involved in such a blessed task. I must also thank Mike Best for reading through the vast majority of the work on two occasions, and making innumerable and detailed suggestions for the improvement of the language to the vast majority of the main text. I must thank my family for their vital support. I would also like to thank those who helped in clarifying certain Arabic passages from various works along the way, in particular Khalid Williams and Joe Bradford; yet I accept any final blame— may Allāh forgive me. Also, I must thank my friend Nazir Joomun for his IT assistance and other deeds of support. Finally, I thank White Thread Press for seeing this project through to the publication stage, after it looked as though the project had died. The acknowledgment to White Thread contains a special appreciation to *ustādh* Abdur-Rahman ibn Yusuf Mangera, whose dedication and skill greatly refined the work.

Jazākumu 'Llāhu khayran. Wa 'l-ḥamdulillāh. Wa mā tawfīqī illā bi 'Llāh.

Andrew Booso
England
July 2010

Introduction

BY SHAYKH AL-ḤADĪTH MAWLĀNĀ
MUḤAMMAD ZAKARIYYĀ KĀNDHLAWĪ

FIRSTLY, MAY ALLĀH BE PRAISED and may salutations be sent upon the Prophet ﷺ. It was mentioned in the foreword of *Irshād al-Mulūk* that this humble one has, since last Ramaḍān, designated that *Irshād al-Mulūk* and *Ikmāl al-Shiyam* be listened to by the numerous sincere friends who spend the blessed month of Ramaḍān here [in the *khānaqāh*].

Details of *Irshād al-Mulūk* have been mentioned in its foreword. *Ikmāl al-Shiyam* is a commentary written by Mawlānā ʿAbdullāh Gangōhī of *Itmām al-Niʿam* by his shaykh and *murshid* Mawlānā Khalīl Aḥmad [Sahāranpūrī] and which he wrote on his shaykh's instructions, as will soon follow in the commentator's foreword. *Itmām al-Niʿam* is the Urdu translation of *Tabwīb al-Ḥikam*, details of which will come in the section regarding it.

Mawlānā ʿAbdullāh Gangōhī was one of the special students of my father, Mawlānā Yaḥyā. He acquired from him all his knowledge, from beginning to end. When my father came to Gangoh in Shawwāl 1311/1893 in the service of Mawlānā Rashīd Aḥmad Gangōhī ﷺ to pursue the final-year studies of the *Ṣiḥāḥ sitta* (six canonical ḥadīth collections), there was in the eastern part of the town a famous mosque known, to this day, as Lāl Masjid. Many new buildings have since been added to the mosque, but at that time it was a simple structure. My father, along with my uncle Mawlānā Riḍā' al-Ḥasan, and some other students, used to stay in one of its rooms. These respected individuals would attend lessons at the *khānaqāh* of Mawlānā Gangōhī, after which they would return to the mosque.

Mawlānā ʿAbdullāh's house was close to that mosque, and at that time he was at least ten to twelve years old. He was very regular with his *ṣalāt*. In spite of his young age, he would offer the five daily prayers with utmost punctuality at the mosque. His behavior greatly impressed my father, who encouraged him to pursue studies in Arabic by studying it a little during the holidays, so that he could become a traditional scholar along with his secular education; at that time, Mawlānā ʿAbdullāh used to attend an English school.

For some time Mawlānā ʿAbdullāh studied Arabic while continuing on with his secular studies. Finally, Allāh Most High aided him to leave aside his secular studies in pursuit of traditional knowledge: he first became an erudite scholar and then, after obtaining *khilāfa* from Mawlānā Khalīl Aḥmad Sahāranpūrī, a shaykh of the order.

Mawlānā ʿĀshiq Ilāhī gives the following account in *Tadhkirat al-Khalīl* of Mawlānā ʿAbdullāh's early period:

> Mōlwī ʿAbdullāh Gangōhī is the *khalīfa* of Mawlānā Sahāranpūrī. He is the student of Mawlānā Muḥammad Yaḥyā and studied in an English school. He frequented the neighborhood mosque for *ṣalāt* where Mawlānā Muḥammad Yaḥyā had taken up a room for living. The Mawlānā observed the young boy's enthusiasm for prayers and concluded that he was not far from being inclined to religious education. He, therefore, created some acquaintance and encouraged him to study Arabic in his free time. Mōlwī ʿAbdullāh complied and commenced the study of *Mīzān* [*al-Ṣarf*].[1] He had some difficulty in learning. Once, Mawlānā Muḥammad Yaḥyā asked him to memorize two verb patterns, which he tried to do till evening. Mawlānā Yaḥyā said, "O slave of Allāh! What injustice is this? You have spent the entire day till evening memorizing one verb pattern." Feeling dejected, Mawlānā ʿAbdullāh responded, "No, Mōlwī Ṣāḥib! It was two verb patterns," and began to cry.
>
> Through such exchanges, Mawlānā Yaḥyā encouraged him to progress in his studies and, as a result, he abandoned the study of English and applied himself to the pursuit of Arabic. Allāh Most High blessed him with good fortune. Thus he first became a scholar who gives practical expression to his knowledge, then progressed to become a *sālik* and attained permission to convey the *ṭarīqa*. Viewing it from this perspective, Mawlānā ʿAbdullāh's righteousness will also be a tribute to Mawlānā Yaḥyā's book of deeds. Had it not been for the good and wise counsel of Mawlānā Yaḥyā, Allāh alone knows where he would have ended up in his pursuit of a secular education.
>
> After Mawlānā Muḥammad Yaḥyā's demise, Mawlānā ʿAbdullāh develM oped increased love for his teacher's son, Mawlānā Muḥammad Zakariyyā. Though older than him, he maintained with him a relationship full of respect and honor. Once he said, "Mōlwī Zakariyyā, I saw a dream. Tell me its

1 *Mīzān al-Ṣarf* is an elementary book in Arabic morphology.

interpretation. The dream goes thus: A huge pomegranate dropped from the sky and, on hitting earth, all of its seeds scattered. Mawlānā Muḥammad Yaḥyā, who was there at the time, said, 'Brother, in this pomegranate one seed belongs to me.'"

After narrating this dream, he insisted Mawlānā Zakariyyā interpret it. When he repeatedly said that he was not versed in the interpretation of dreams, Mawlānā ʿAbdullāh said, "All right, I shall explain its interpretation. The one seed refers to me. I, in fact, belong to Mawlānā Yaḥyā. This is the glad tidings of my death and then of my forgiveness." Indeed, a few months later, Mawlānā ʿAbdullāh died. While afflicted with tuberculosis he would laugh and speak. He departed from this world in this condition. "To Allāh we belong and to Him we shall return" (2:156).

Mawlānā ʿAbdullāh was among the very special and close students of my father. The teacher was proud of his student and vice versa. He was among the senior *khalīfas* of my *shaykh*, Mawlānā Khalīl Aḥmad Sahāranpūrī. Mawlānā ʿĀshiq Ilāhī has recorded in *Tadhkirat al-Khalīl* that Mawlānā ʿAbdullāh obtained *khilāfa* in about 1327/1909. Mawlānā Shabbīr ʿAlī confirms this in his letter. This was the year when the late mawlānā was a teacher at Madrasa Maẓāhir ʿUlūm [Saharanpur]. In spite of this, in Shawwāl 1333/1914 when Mawlānā Sahāranpūrī was travelling to the Hijaz, Mawlānā ʿAbdullāh made a request to renew his *bayʿa*. Coincidentally, this lowly one had also requested *bayʿa* the very same day. Mawlānā Sahāranpūrī instructed us to come on that day after the Maghrib prayer when he had completed his supplementary prayers.

I remained seated at a distance behind Mawlānā Sahāranpūrī immediately after Maghrib. After the supplementary prayers, when he lifted his hands for supplication, I drew close. Mawlānā ʿAbdullāh ﵀, who was sitting further away in another section of the older *madrasa*, also came forward. Mawlānā Sahāranpūrī took hold of our hands and started reciting the *khuṭba*. Mawlānā ʿAbdullāh was overwhelmed by so much emotion that he began sobbing loudly and cried unstoppably until the end. It also affected Mawlānā Sahāranpūrī in such a way that his voice began to tremble; both became very emotional.

In view of the fact that I was unaware of the initial life of Mawlānā ʿAbdullāh, I wrote letters to Mawlānā Ẓafar Aḥmad Thānawī, the Shaykh al-Islām of Pakistan, and Ḥājj Mawlānā Shabbīr ʿAlī Thānawī, the cousin of

Ḥakīm al-Umma Mawlānā Ashraf ʿAlī Thānawī. Both were special students of Mawlānā ʿAbdullāh. I reproduce both their letters here.

Mawlānā Shabbīr ʿAlī's Letter

Respected brother, may Allāh protect you and keep you well. *Al-salāmu ʿalaykum wa raḥmat Allāh wa barakātuh.*

Your letter was received. The great effort that you have expended in the acquisition and, now, dissemination of knowledge is bound to have an effect on your physical health. Allāh Most High will, *inshāAllāh*, reward you in full measure. Your rest and peace are interwoven with the acquisition and dissemination of knowledge and you don't feel at peace or rest without this; hence it would be silly to advise you now to take rest. However, I do fervently supplicate that Allāh bestow safety and complete health to you so that you are blessed with comfort and rest in your pursuit and dissemination of knowledge. *Āmīn.*

On this occasion, our meeting was very short and I was left yearning. If it had not been for my ailment, I would certainly have come as far as the airport to gain some extra time with you. I was, however, helpless. May Allāh Most High once again grant us the fortune of meeting in health and safety. *Āmīn.*

You have requested information about my honorable teacher, Mawlānā ʿAbdullāh 🌸. At the time when I was in his service, I lacked the understanding and it did not occur to me to keep note of the [events of the] different years. In fact, even now I lack such perception, but at that time I was a minor in terms of Sharīʿa. Anyhow, I shall give approximate dates of events by estimating my age. I hope your questions will be answered in this way.

Question 1: When was Mawlānā ʿAbdullāh first appointed in Thana Bhawan? What was so special about him that he was appointed there?
Answer: I was born on 8 Ramaḍān 1312/1894. When I was six, my Barē Abbā and Barī Ammā [Ḥakīm al-Umma and his wife] took me from my late parents; they effectively adopted me and brought me to Thana Bhawan. Barē Abbā became concerned with my education. I now write what I had repeatedly heard from my honorable teacher.

He would say: "Mawlānā Thānawī came to Mawlānā Gangōhī where he met Mawlānā Muḥammad Yaḥyā. Mawlānā Thānawī said to him: 'I require an able student to educate my child. If you have any such student, do assign him to me.' Mawlānā Muḥammad Yaḥyā then assigned me to Mawlānā Thānawī and said: '*Inshā Allāh*, he will teach to your satisfaction. I have confidence in him.'"

Subsequently, Barē Abbā brought my honorable teacher along with him to Thana Bhawan. It is obvious from my age of six years that it was the year 1318/1900. Hence the arrival of my honorable teacher to Thana Bhawan was in 1318/1900 or at the latest in the beginning of 1319/1901. The specialty of my honorable teacher was that his ability and qualifications were attested by his teacher of teachers (i.e., Mawlānā Muḥammad Yaḥyā).

Question 2: His appointment as a teacher at Saharanpur and return from Saharanpur?

Answer: This lowly one again was the reason for these two events. Just as my honorable teacher's teacher had not just taught students all his life, but, rather, with great affection and absorption, fed them knowledge, how could the student not be like his teacher? Thus, when I was entrusted to my honorable teacher, he fed me some Urdu and then began with Persian. During that era, textbooks such as the *Āmad Nāmā* were used for beginners. However, my honorable teacher wanted to feed us knowledge and so he began writing a special book for me, which he named *Taysīr al-Mubtadī*. In its introduction, my honorable teacher, stating the reason for writing the book, writes: "I have to commence the teaching of Persian and Arabic to a beloved child." That "beloved child" is in fact this very lowly one.

This process of affectionate instruction continued until I was fourteen years old and he had taught me the *Hidāya*, *Mishkāt al-Maṣābīḥ*, etc. Then Barē Abbā planned to send me to Saharanpur for the *dawrat al-ḥadīth*.[2] He, therefore, wrote to Mawlānā Sahāranpūrī stating my age and seeking his advice. Mawlānā Sahāranpūrī responded saying that I should be sent and that he would keep me as one of his own children and teach me. After this reply, my going was confirmed. This was in 1326/1908.

My honorable teacher then said to Barē Abbā: "Shabbīr is still young. He has never been out and stayed alone. He will become worried in Saharanpur. I therefore wish that some arrangement be made here (in Thana Bhawan) as I wish to go with him to Saharanpur. He is used to me; hence he will not feel worried in Saharanpur." Barē Abbā asked: "What will you do there for a living?" He replied: "It is a city, I shall try and do some work somewhere. My heart cannot bear Shabbīr going alone."[3]

Barē Abbā wrote to my father: "It has been decided to send Shabbīr

---

2 The final year of the *Dars-i Niẓāmī*, in which students undertake an extensive study of the six major ḥadīth collections.

3 At the time of reading this, I became overwhelmed with emotion and tears flowed from my eyes. What a noble teacher he was. The eyes yearn to see such illustrious men. It is my fervent

to Saharanpur. His teacher insists on accompanying him. Here (in Thana Bhawan) the *madrasa* pays him a wage of 10 rupees a month, it will be good if you undertake this payment." My father replied that he would present fifteen rupees a month to Mawlānā 'Abdullāh.

Thus my honorable teacher took me to Saharanpur in Shawwāl 1326/1908. There a discussion took place with Mawlānā Sahāranpūrī in my presence. My honorable teacher also mentioned the monthly allocation stated by my father. Mawlānā Sahāranpūrī said: "We need a teacher. If you accept, this *madrasa* will pay 20 or 25 rupees a month" (I'm not sure how much). My honorable teacher happily accepted this proposal and added: "I shall keep Shabbīr with me." Mawlānā Sahāranpūrī accepted this condition. According to this, Shawwāl 1326/1908 was the year when my honorable teacher arrived in Saharanpur. In view of my young age, Mawlānā Sahāranpūrī arranged for the *dawrat al-ḥadīth* to be extended to two years for me. Consequently, I accomplished the *dawrat al-ḥadīth* in two years. My honorable teacher also lived in Saharanpur for two years.

After completing the *dawrat al-ḥadīth* I expressed my desire to study ḥadīth under [Shaykh al-Hind] Mawlānā Maḥmūd al-Ḥasan Deobandī and to repeat the *dawra* once more. At that time I was sixteen years old. It was 1328/1910. My honorable teacher said, "Now, *māshā Allāh*, you are big and you have experienced living away from home. I am not worried. By all means go to Deoband."

My honorable teacher said to Mawlānā Sahāranpūrī, "I stayed here because of Shabbīr. Now he is going to Deoband, he no longer needs me. The people of Kandhla are insisting that I come. If you grant permission, I shall go there." Mawlānā Sahāranpūrī happily consented. My honorable teacher left directly for Kandhla (not Thana Bhawan) from Saharanpur in 1328/1910.

Question 3: Where did he undertake the *dawrat al-ḥadīth*?
Answer: There was no specific mention of *dawrat al-ḥadīth*. However, he repeatedly said: "I have studied everything by Mawlānā Kāndhlawī." Therefore, it is most likely that he also studied the *dawrat al-ḥadīth* by him. I have calculated the years from my age being six. It is possible that I have erred in this, I came with Barē Abbā between the ages of five or seven. Therefore, if my estimate (of six years) is not in accordance with my age as recorded in the *madrasa's* register, then the latter is correct.[4]

---

supplication that Allāh bring about my end with true faith so that I attain a place among the shoes of these illustrious souls (sz).

4 The *madrasah* register supports the view that he was seven (sz).

I can also write that my honorable teacher was granted *khilāfa* by Mawlānā Sahāranpūrī during these two years. Finally, I request with utmost humility that you not miss supplicating for my outer and inner reformation and for my end to be with faith. *Wa 'l-salām.* Convey my *salām* to whomever you wish. With requests for supplications.

The lowly MUḤAMMAD SHABBĪR ʿALĪ THĀNAWĪ
Nazimabad, Karachi
30 Rabīʿ al-Awwal 1387 | 9 July, 1967

According to the published *Madrasa* records, Mawlānā ʿAbdullāh ﷺ came to Saharanpur on 12 Shawwāl 1327/1909 and departed for the Ḥajj with the seniors of the *madrasa* in Shawwāl 1328/1910. After his return in Muḥarram 1329/1911, he remained in the service of the *madrasa* from the month of Ṣafar for one month and twenty-four days. He then resigned. He was initially employed at the *madrasa* on a wage of fifteen rupees a month. Mawlānā Shabbīr ʿAlī's final examination was held in Shaʿbān 1331/1912.

The Shaykh al-Islām of Pakistan, Mawlānā Ẓafar Aḥmad Thānawī's Letter

My honorable Mawlānā Muḥammad Zakariyyā, *shaykh al-ḥadīth*, may Allāh keep you safe, and may He honor and protect you. *Al-salāmu ʿalaykum wa raḥmatu 'Llāhi wa barakātuh.*

Your letter was received after a considerable time. I did not receive a reply to the postcard that I had sent after you left Karachi or to the letter that I had sent to the address of beloved Hārūn in Nizamuddin, Delhi. I received your postcard dated 12 Rabīʿ al-Awwal yesterday. I am grieved to learn of your faltering eyesight. May Allāh Most High transform its weakness into strength and may He make widespread and complete the spiritual benefits of your writings. *Āmīn.*

I too am not aware of the correct birth date of Mawlānā ʿAbdullāh Gangōhī. However, I do think that when I started my elementary studies in *ṣarf* (morphology) and *naḥw* (syntax) under him in Thana Bhawan, I was thirteen and he was approximately twenty-five. I was born in Rabīʿ al-Awwal 1310/1892, hence the Mawlānā's birth must have been in 1298/1880.

Mawlānā ʿAbdullāh acquired his full education from Mawlānā Muḥammad Yaḥyā. The Mawlānā's father had him enrolled at an English school, but on the advice of Mawlānā Muḥammad Yaḥyā, he was removed and assigned to him for religious education. Mawlānā Muḥammad Yaḥyā would also financially assist Mawlānā ʿAbdullāh's father to somewhat compensate for his removal from school.

Mawlānā ʿAbdullāh completed his studies in three years. Then, when Ḥakīm al-Umma requested Mawlānā Muḥammad Yaḥyā to arrange for a teacher for Khānaqāh-i Imdādiyya, he sent Mawlānā ʿAbdullāh, who had just completed his studies, to Thana Bhawan. His wage was fixed at nine rupees a month. However, Mawlānā Muḥammad Yaḥyā also advised him to occupy himself in selling books and gave him books from his own bookshop to set up a business. Apparently, he initially gave him a substantial number of books at no charge and thereafter supplied him books at a price. Thanks to this trade, he was not bothered by the low wage. He could fulfill the obligation of teaching with peace of mind. Ḥakīm al-Umma had also entrusted the work of recording his lectures to Mawlānā ʿAbdullāh. This further augmented his monthly income.

Mawlānā ʿAbdullāh was an expert in the elementary subjects of *ṣarf*, *naḥw*, and Arabic literature. In fact, he had written *Taysīr al-Muttaqī* for us. He would write lessons daily and show them to Ḥakīm al-Umma before teaching. In this way, *Taysīr al-Muttaqī* was compiled and published, and received widespread acclaim. He also acquired monetary gain from the publication of this book as he himself had it initially published.

Along with *Mīzān* [*al-Ṣarf*], *Munshaʿib* and *Panj Ganj* [books in Arabic morphology], I studied *Taysīr al-Mubtadī*. After completing the section on *ṣarf*, I studied the section on *naḥw* along with *Naḥw-i Mīr*. During that same period, the mawlānā taught us to translate from Urdu to Arabic and from Arabic to Urdu. After ʿaṣr he would take us for a walk. Along the walk he would recite the Qur'ān and test us on the grammatical construction of Qur'ānic phrases. In this way, during the time of studying *Naḥw-i Mīr*, I acquired practice in writing and speaking Arabic. During this time, in a letter that I had written to a friend in Deoband, I quoted some Arabic poetry, a stanza of which I recollect:

I have not seen you for a while,
  Hence grief has increased in my heart.

On seeing this letter, Ḥakīm al-Umma severely reprimanded me, saying that this was the time for effort and learning, not wasting time in poetry. Nevertheless, he told Mawlānā ʿAbdullāh, "Although I have reprimanded Ẓafar for indulging in poetry, I must say that I am impressed by your excellent teaching. This is clear from the fact that the student of *Naḥw-i Mīr* has gained the ability to compose poetry. In spite of the verses having no poetic value, the grammatical construction is correct."

I learned the following books from Mawlānā: *Mīzān*, *Munshaʿib*, *Panj Ganj*, *Naḥw-i Mīr*, *Sharḥ Mi'at ʿĀmil*, *Hidāyat al-Naḥw* and *Al-Ṭarīf li 'l-Adīb al-Ẓarīf* (a book of literature by Mawlānā ʿAbd al-Awwal Jōnpūrī). Thereafter, I began *Mukhtaṣar al-Qudūrī* and Qur'ān translation. This was in 1323/1905. In the same year, Ḥakīm al-Umma learned through unveiling (*kashf*) that the time of Mawlānā Rashīd Aḥmad Gangōhī's demise was imminent. He advised Mawlānā ʿAbdullāh, who was the *murīd* of Mawlānā Gangōhī, to take leave for six months from Thana Bhawan and stay in the service of his spiritual master.

During this time, Ḥakīm al-Umma repeatedly advised his associates to stay in the service of Mawlānā Gangōhī. My brother Mawlānā Saʿīd Aḥmad and I too were sent to Gangoh to visit him, on the basis that there might not be another opportunity to meet him. We stayed for three days in Gangoh and, by means of Mawlānā Muḥammad Yaḥyā, visited Mawlānā Gangōhī after Fajr in his blessed room. Mawlānā Gangōhī asked, "Who are you?"

"The nephew of Mawlānā Ashraf ʿAlī," I replied.

"The grandson of Shaykh Nihāl Aḥmad?"

"Yes."

I requested Mawlānā Gangōhī to supplicate for me, and he did.

At this time, Mawlānā ʿAbdullāh was resident in Gangoh. He would keep us with him in the spiritual gatherings (*majālis*) of Mawlānā Gangōhī from ẓuhr to ʿaṣr. Although we lacked understanding at that time, we still remember the spiritual light of those sessions. They were gatherings full of light.

In the absence of Mawlānā ʿAbdullāh, I studied Qur'ān translation by Shāh Luṭf-i Rasūl, a part of *Al-Talkhīṣāt al-ʿAshar* by Ḥakīm al-Umma, and the remainder by my elder brother. At this time, Ḥakīm al-Umma told us, "I have now commenced writing *Tafsīr Bayān al-Qur'ān* and will no longer find time for teaching. I shall take you both to my special students in Kanpur, where you will be admitted to Madrasa Jāmiʿ al-ʿUlūm. You can complete your studies there." We were subsequently admitted to the *madrasa* in Kanpur.

When Mawlānā Muḥammad Isḥāq took my entrance examination, he asked, "Which books have you completed so far?" I informed him of the books I have mentioned. He then commented, "You have not studied the *Kāfiya*, *Sharḥ* [*Mullā*] *Jāmī* or *Mukhtaṣar al-Maʿānī*. What do you intend to study now?" I replied, "If my studies had continued in Thana Bhawan I would have studied the *Hidāya*, *Tafsīr al-Jalālayn*, *Mishkāt al-Maṣābīḥ*, and

Taysīr al-Uṣūl." He said, "Without *Nūr al-Anwār* and *Mukhtaṣar al-Maʿānī*, how will you study *Mishkāt al-Maṣābīḥ* and *Tafsīr al-Jalālayn*? Very well. Read from the last two volumes of *Hidāya*, ahead of where the other readers have stopped." After I had recited the Arabic text correctly, he instructed me to translate. I translated correctly. He then told me to explain the meaning. I said that the text that I had read is related to the section above. "Allow me to read the relevant section first," I said. On hearing this, the Mawlānā said, "You may most certainly study the *Hidāya, Mishkāt al-Maṣābīḥ,* and *Tafsīr al-Jalālayn*. These here who are studying the last two volumes of the *Hidāya* are unable to read or translate the text correctly, and have no idea which concept is connected to which." I was thus enrolled at the *madrasa*.

He then said to Hakīm al-Umma, "Indeed this is your miracle. Without having studied *Sharḥ* [*Mullā*] *Jāmī*, *Mukhtaṣar al-Maʿānī,* or *Nūr al-Anwar*, Mōlwī Ẓafar Aḥmad has correctly read the text from the last two volumes of the *Hidāya* and translated it without having studied it or even seeing it before." Ḥakīm al-Umma laughed and said, "This is no miracle. Just excellent teaching. We have Mawlānā ʿAbdullāh, who teaches the foundational subjects brilliantly, so much that the student of *Hidāyat al-Naḥw* is well trained in translating from Arabic to Urdu and Urdu to Arabic."

It was while I was with Ḥakīm al-Umma in Kanpur that news came of Mawlānā Gangōhī's death. "Surely, we belong to Allāh, and to Him shall we return" (2:156). After this event, Mawlānā ʿAbdullāh came to Thana Bhawan while I studied in Kanpur. After Mawlānā Gangōhī's death, Mawlānā ʿAbdullāh turned to Mawlānā Khalīl Aḥmad and in all likelihood had considered it necessary to live with Mawlānā Khalīl in Saharanpur to complete his spiritual and moral reformation. Thus, taking leave for Saharanpur, he took up residence at Madrasa Maẓāhir ʿUlūm. He was appointed a teacher at the *madrasa*.

In 1337/1918, after I had qualified at Madrasa Jāmiʿ al-ʿUlūm, Kanpur, I returned to Thana Bhawan. Mawlānā ʿAbdullāh at that time was already a teacher at Maẓāhir ʿUlūm. I still had to do my studies in logic and philosophy. Although Ḥakīm al-Umma advised me to pursue my studies further at Dār al-ʿUlūm Deoband, Mawlānā Khalīl Aḥmad had sent a message that I should proceed to Maẓāhir ʿUlūm. He said, "Though the lecturer in the rational sciences, Mawlānā Muḥammad Yaḥyā Sahasrāmī, having left for Madrasa ʿĀliya in Calcutta, is not here, another lecturer will be called in his stead." Ḥakīm al-Umma said, "Since Mawlānā Khalīl Aḥmad has taken a special interest in you, it is best that you go in Allāh's name and join Maẓāhir ʿUlūm." I too desired this because Mawlānā ʿAbdullāh was there and I was very attached to him. So, in Muḥarram 1328/1910, I went to Saharanpur. At that time, Mawlānā ʿAbdullāh took me as a partner in the publishing of two letters of the Messenger of Allāh ﷺ. One letter was to Mundhir ibn Sāwā al-ʿAbdī and the other to Emperor Heraclius. They were sold for two or four *anna*[5] each. Each of us made a profit of fifty rupees. This money aided us in our Ḥajj journey, as we had, in Shawwāl of that very year 1328/1910, made it our intention to proceed for the Ḥajj in the company of Mawlānā ʿAbd al-Laṭīf, Mawlānā Thābit ʿAlī, and Mōlwī Fayḍ al-Ḥasan Sahāranpūrī.

Mawlānā ʿAbdullāh had confidence in my dreams. After completing the Ḥajj and having arranged to proceed to Madīna Munawwara, he asked whether I could recall the dream I saw while studying *Naḥw-i Mīr* in which I saw the Messenger of Allāh ﷺ. Mawlānā ʿAbdullāh reminded me that in the dream, the Prophet of Allāh ﷺ, after giving glad tidings of Paradise, informed me that after completion of my studies I would come here to Madīna. In my dream I replied, "I have great yearning to come. Do pray for me." The Prophet ﷺ prayed. Mawlānā ʿAbdullāh commented, "See how your dream has come true. Immediately after completing your studies you have set out for Madīna."

On the journey to Madīna Munawwara, I was seated on a camel, and Mawlānā ʿAbdullāh was on another. On the return journey from Madīna both of us were on one camel. He said, "You had seen a dream that both of us were travelling along the road of Makka and Madīna seated on one camel. Just look how it has come true. We are both on one camel."

On returning from the Ḥajj, Mawlānā ʿAbdullāh requested Mawlānā Khalīl Aḥmad for consent to take up a teaching post in Thana Bhawan. Mawlānā consented. Mawlānā ʿAbdullāh thus went to Thana Bhawan and I was appointed teacher in his place at Maẓāhir ʿUlūm in the month of Rabīʿ al-Awwal 1329/1911. The books that Mawlānā ʿAbdullāh taught—*Sharḥ al-Wiqāya* [a *fiqh* work by Maḥbūbī], *Nūr al-Anwār* [a book in legal theory by Mullā Jīwan], and others—became my responsibility.

In 1334/1915, when Mawlānā Khalīl Aḥmad left for Makka and Madīna with the intention of *hijra*, I took leave from Maẓāhir ʿUlūm to go to Thana Bhawan. When Mawlānā returned from Makka, I too returned to Maẓāhir

5 An *anna* (ānā) was a currency unit formerly used in India, equal to 1/16 rupee. It was subdivided into 4 *paisē* or 12 *pies* (thus there were 64 *paisē* in a rupee and 192 *pies*).

> Ulūm. However, with the permission of the mawlānā, I took up a post at Irshād al-ʿUlūm at Garhi Pukhta.[6] After a stay of approximately two and a half years, I settled permanently in Thana Bhawan.
>
> While I was in Garhi Pukhta, Mawlānā ʿAbdullāh had taken a post in the *madrasa* at Kandhla. I could not establish the reason for this transfer. Anyhow, he remained teaching in Kandhla until his death there. "Surely, we belong to Allāh, and to Him shall we return" (2:156). May Allāh forgive us and him. May He have mercy on us and him, and may He grant us and him Paradise through His mercy and kindness. *Wa 'l-salām*
>
> P.S. Mawlānā ʿAbdullāh had two sons. The name of one is ʿUbaydullāh. I do not remember the name of the other. I have no knowledge of his whereabouts or his condition. Some information about Mawlānā ʿAbdullāh may also be gained from *Tadhkirat al-Khalīl*. 20 Rabīʿ al-Awwal 1387/1967.

The two sons of Mawlānā ʿAbdullāh had gone to stay in the service of my uncle, Mawlānā Ilyās, after their father's death. There they took up permanent residence. The eldest son, Mōlwī Ḥāfiẓ ʿUbaydullāh, died a few years ago on a *tablīghī* journey. The other son, Ḥāfiẓ Inʿāmullāh, appears to be in an enraptured state (*majdhūb*).[7] For many years he has been wandering from city to city and in forests—may Allāh have mercy on him.

*

Besides this work, *Ikmāl al-Shiyam*, Mawlānā ʿAbdullāh has written a variety of other well-known books. Of these, *Taysīr al-Mubtadī* and *Taysīr al-Manṭiq* are the most famous. He had written *Taysīr al-Mubtadī* during his stay at Thana Bhawan with the purpose of teaching it to Mawlānā Shabbīr ʿAlī, as mentioned in his letter. In this regard, Mawlānā Thānawī writes in the introduction of *Taysīr al-Mubtadī*:

> Considering the times, it is essential to keep in mind simplicity and brevity (in methods of tuition) for students pursuing knowledge. The treatise in front of you is a manifestation of this view. The motive for compiling it was a beloved beginner commencing studies in Persian and Arabic for which a short time was allocated.
>
> It is for this reason that I had requested my honorable associate Mōlwī

6 Garhi Pukhta is a town in the Muzaffarnagar district of the north-Indian state of Uttar Pradesh.

7 A Sufi whose mental faculties are paralyzed or confused.

> Ḥāfiẓ Muḥammad ʿAbdullāh Gangōhī, who I have presently engaged to teach students, to compile in simple language a treatise consisting of a few concise rules of Persian and Arabic grammar that are in common use and that will facilitate the understanding of books that students have to study subsequently. Mōlwī ʿAbdullāh, in compliance with my request, devoted a portion of his precious time for this purpose and compiled the desired treatise.
>
> Purely on account of the good esteem he held me in, he submitted every word of the treatise for my review. On various occasions he accepted my suggestions. The benefit of this book does not require any elaboration. Its benefit could be ascertained by teaching it to a beginner. The date of this foreword is 14 Dhū 'l-Ḥijja, 1321/1903.

Taysīr al-Manṭiq was written by Mawlānā ʿAbdullāh during his stay in Kandhla. In the introduction to this treatise, the Mawlānā writes:

> In this age, the ability of students has become very weak. Logic (*manṭiq*) is a science which is related only to the intellect and understanding. For this reason, there is generally very little affinity with it. Furthermore, all the books on the laws of logic are in foreign languages, such as Persian or Arabic. It is for this need that the essential laws of logic have been translated into Urdu. This compilation has been named *Taysīr al-Manṭiq*. This treatise was presented for checking to Mawlānā Ṣiddīq Aḥmad, the *muftī* of Malerkotla[8] and *khalīfa* of Mawlānā Gangōhī. He was also the patron and examiner of the primary classes at Dār al-ʿUlūm Deoband and Maẓāhir ʿUlūm Saharanpur. This treatise was completed on 25 Dhū 'l-Ḥijja, 1336/1917.

According to the *madrasa* records, Mawlānā Ḥājj ʿAbdullāh Gangōhī was appointed at Maẓāhir ʿUlūm on 12 Shawwāl 1327/1909. During the month of Shawwāl 1329/1911, he accompanied the *madrasa's* elders for the Ḥajj. After returning from the journey, he was in the service of the *madrasa* for one month and twenty-four days.

After serving this period, as far as I can remember, he stayed for some time in Thana Bhawan. He then proceeded to Kandhla. According to the letter of Mawlānā Shabbīr ʿAlī, he went directly from Saharanpur to Kandhla. Mawlānā Shabbīr ʿAlī is three years older than me. He also lived in Thana Bhawan. His recollection, therefore, has preference. However, Mawlānā Ẓafar Aḥmad, who is two years older than Mawlānā Shabbīr ʿAlī, wrote

8 Malerkotla was a princely state founded and ruled by Sherwani Pathans in the Punjab during the British Raj.

that Mawlānā ʿAbdullāh proceeded from Saharanpur to Thana Bhawan. Be that as it may, the fact remains that he went to Kandhla at the insistence of its people and on the instruction of Mawlānā Sahāranpūrī.

As a result of Mawlānā ʿAbdullāh's settling in Kandhla the existing *madrasa* progressed immensely. He continued to teach until the end of his stay. He lived with his family in a rented house in the town. On the night of Saturday 15 Rajab 1329 (26 March 1921), he died in Kandhla and was buried in our ancestral cemetery, which is adjacent to the *ʿīdgāh* (place where ʿīd prayers are performed). In this cemetery lie Muftī Ilāhī Bakhsh[9] and other senior *ʿulamāʾ* and *shaykhs* of our family—may Allāh enlighten and cool his resting place.

Whatever Mawlānā Ẓafar Aḥmad and Mawlānā Shabbīr ʿAlī have said regarding his style of teaching is absolutely correct. His methodology was influenced by the teaching style of my father, Mawlānā Muḥammad Yaḥyā, who was a true *mujtahid* in the way he taught, especially the elementary stages. He would teach every student according to his ability with methods he pioneered. He would make a point not to teach the non-core books that are customarily taught. He would, instead, after making students carry out extensive practice, listen to [the student read from memory] *Ṣarf-i Mīr* and *Panj Ganj* within a day or two.

This also happened with this lowly one. He explained the rules relating to *mithāl*, *muḍāʿaf*, *ajwaf* of the *wāw* and the *yāʾ*, and *nāqiṣ* of the *wāw* and the *yāʾ* [root letter paradigms of Arabic verbs], and had me write them in a notebook. He then asked me to write the letters *bāʾ* and *tāʾ* and instructed me to conjugate verbs from them according to these rules and would check each verb in my notebook along with the morphophonemic rules (*taʿlīl*). I will always remember the verb *batta*, as I conjugated so many series of verbs from it. Likewise, he would tell me the rules of *naḥw*, have them written down and then ask us to parse sentences according to these rules. I can still remember the [unusual] syntactic structure of *Yūsu fi Zulaykha* that he made us do. *Yūsu* is a clipped form of the vocative ("O Yusuf"), *fi* is the imperative form of the verb *wafā* ("be faithful") and *Zulaykhā* is the object of the verb. [Therefore, "Yūsuf, be faithful to Zulaykha!"] I remember many other such verb patterns and grammatical structures.

9 Muftī Ilāhī Bakhsh Kāndhlawī (1162/1748–1245/1829) was a celebrated scholar and *murīd* of Shāh ʿAbd al-ʿAzīz Dihlawī. He was an erudite jurist, physician, poet and author of many books, the most famous being his completion of Mawlānā Jalāl al-Dīn Rūmī's *Mathnawī* as foretold by the Mawlānā toward the end of his *magnum opus*.

He was well acquainted with literature. In this also, after making the student practice, he would listen to the widely taught books, such as *Maqāmāt al-Ḥarīrī* and *Dīwān al-Mutanabbī*, in the same way that ḥadīth is listened to in the *dawrat al-ḥadīth*. He had the habit of teaching [various] Forty Ḥadīths along with *Naḥw-i Mīr*; he would teach the *Majmūʿa Chihil Ḥadīth*, which is a collection, published by himself, of the forty ḥadīths of Imām Shāh Walī Allāh, Mullā *Jāmī* and Qāḍī Thanā Allāh Pānipatī.

Along with the *Kāfiya* he would teach the translation of the last chapter of the Qur'ān. He would say, "There are two things in literature: words and meanings. Muslim children know the last chapter of the Qur'ān; they only need to learn the meanings, because the words are from the last chapter and they are always remembered. He had the habit of teaching the *Kāfiya* along with *Hidāyat al-Naḥw*. He would, in the order in which chapters are set in The *Kāfiya*, teach *Hidāyat al-Naḥw* in the morning and then repeat the same lesson from the *Kāfiya* in the evening. Likewise, he would teach *Mukhtaṣar al-Qudūrī* and *Kanz al-Daqā'iq* in the order in which lessons in *Kanz al-Daqā'iq* were set; the *Kanz al-Daqā'iq* lessons would be foundational, and *Mukhtaṣar al-Qudūrī* would be taught to complement it as supplementary reading. He would teach so much of *Talkhīṣ al-Miftāḥ* on a Friday to allow that much subject matter to be covered in *Mukhtaṣar al-Maʿānī* by the next Friday. He would teach *Mukhtaṣar al-Maʿānī* for the entire week and then teach *Talkhīṣ al-Miftāḥ* the next Friday. This would be the situation with *Kitāb al-Manār* and *Nūr al-Anwar*. Because *Kitāb al-Manār* is not published individually, it would be necessary to copy its text (*matn*) from [its commentary] *Nūr al-Anwar* before Friday. He would listen to the lessons of *Alfiyya Ibn Mālik* by rote.

This lowly one began *Mīzān al-Ṣarf*, etc., in Rajab 1328/1910, and started *Naḥw Mīr* in Ramaḍān. By Shaʿbān 1329/1911, I had completed *Naḥw-i Mīr*, *Sharḥ Mi'at ʿĀmil* along with its textual analysis (*tarkīb*), *Hidāyat al-Naḥw*, *Kāfiya*, *Kubrā*, *Īsāghūjī*, *Sharḥ al-Tahdhīb*, *Mufīd al-Ṭālibīn*, some poems from *Nafḥat al-Yaman*, *Alfiya Ibn Mālik*, *Fuṣūl-i Akbarī*, *Majmūʿa Chihil Ḥadīth* and the translation of the last two parts, or *ajzā'*, of the Qur'ān.

He loved to teach the elementary books. He repeatedly requested the *madrasa* authorities to allow him to teach the primary classes, saying that others are available to teach ḥadīth. This influence extended over all his students and hence Mawlānā ʿAbdullāh Gangōhī was so eager to teach the primary class; the same eagerness and absorption he had for teaching the elementary books, he did not have for the advanced ones.

My uncle, Mawlānā Muḥammad Ilyās, similarly took great care in teaching the elementary books. It was the opinion of my honorable father that a fully qualified *m*ōlwī should never be engaged to teach the primary classes. His view was that intelligent students, after completing *Sharḥ Jāmī* and *Mukhtaṣar al-Maʿānī*, should be appointed to teach the primary classes. He would often say, "A fully qualified mawlānā will always be concerned with his own progress. He will, therefore, teach the elementary books with very little care. On the other hand, whoever has not studied the higher books will not be concerned with further progress." He was very critical of the contemporary style of teaching in *madrasas*. He would say, "What sort of mastery can be gained from the current style of teaching in the *madrasas* in which the teacher lectures and it is the kindness of the student if he listens or not?" This lowly one remembers many incidents from his education.

The discussion is, however, getting lengthy, something that was not intended. I will, nevertheless, mention one incident relating to the teaching of *Mishkāt al-Maṣābīḥ* in that I studied it without translation. I was, however, permitted to ask the meanings of whichever words I wished. If my father felt it apt to provide the meaning then he would, or else he would rebuke me. He, in turn, was allowed to ask me the translation whenever he wished; if I told him the correct answer then it would be "*al-ḥamdu li 'Llāh*" or else he would reprimand me for not asking. Once the ḥadīth had been read, it would be the responsibility of this lowly one to say whether the ḥadīth is in harmony with or contrary to the juridical doctrine of the Ḥanafīs. If it is contrary, then it would be necessary to furnish the Ḥanafī proof and provide an explanation of the ḥadīth. I was also not permitted to read [the Urdu commentary] *Maẓāhir-i Ḥaqq* when studying *Mishkāt al-Maṣābīḥ*. It was, however, necessary to study the *Hidāya* and [Ṭaḥāwī's] *Sharḥ Maʿānī 'l-Āthār*. I was also permitted to look at the marginal gloss on *Mishkāt al-Maṣābīḥ* and the gloss of any other ḥadīth book I wished. I remember this very well.

I also remember once—and will always remember it—that at the end of one ḥadīth this lowly one explained it saying that [the contents] were said as a severe reprimand (*taghlīẓan*). I received a smack and he said, "Then that means that the Prophet ﷺ—we seek refuge with Allāh—spoke a lie to only scare." He then added, "The explanation of *taghlīẓ* is only done in relation to rulings (*aḥkām*) in the way it has been narrated regarding thieves and people who drink alcohol that on the fourth occasion execute them. This explanation cannot be given in relation to ḥadīths detailing historical events (*akhbār*)." It is because of this that I remember that smack whenever I see the explanation of *taghlīẓ* in *akhbār* in the major commentaries.

My father initiated the teaching of *Mishkāt al-Maṣābīḥ* to this lowly one with utmost care. Straight after the ẓuhr prayer, he performed *ghusl*, offered two units of optional prayers and, turning toward me, recited *bismi 'Llāh* and read the book's introduction. He then faced the *qibla* and with a great sense of begging and crying supplicated. Mawlānā Mīrathī has mentioned this incident with much detail in *Tadhkirat al-Khalīl*.

My father was also very keen to teach Arabic to those pursuing a Western education. He would say to them, "Give me seventy-two hours and I shall, *inshā Allāh*, teach you Arabic." Those seventy-two hours, however, consisted of two hours every Sunday within which he would teach so many rules and principles that it would take a lot from the students to learn them by the following Sunday. Mōlwī Manfaʿat ʿAlī—who was the former advocate (*wakīl*) of Saharanpur and, after the partition, went to Karachi, where he died—studied Arabic like this from my father. He was after this able to read the first two parts of the *Hidāya* very quickly and easily. There are many others who pursued a secular education and were taught Arabic. However, on account of their jobs and their moving towns, they did not proceed further.

It was his rule that students should strive hard, and that teachers are only responsible for listening.—If what is read to them is correct they should acknowledge it, and if it is wrong they should point it out. If the student was to continually speak incoherently then he would act on the verse: "And We sent down iron, in which there is strong power and benefits for the people" (57:25). He would say that Allāh Most High has revealed four books to read and one of these to act upon and that this [verse] has also been revealed from the heavens.

He also disliked teaching books of literature that had marginal gloss or were voweled. He would make the students write out the *Sabʿa Muʿallaqāt* and *Dīwān al-Mutanabbī* from memory, and when this lowly one studied *Maqāmāt al-Ḥarīrī* he specially ordered a copy that did not have the marginal notes and had been published in Calcutta. He was against students reading books that had translations in them. He used to take so much work out of students that it's hard to believe it these days.

He would also not be too bothered with completing textbooks, except in the case of ḥadīth books, which he would finish to the end. In fact, he would become worried if a student missed a ḥadīth during lessons. It was his principle in regard to books, apart from ḥadīth books, that when eight to ten lessons are completed in such a way that the teacher is able to ask what he wishes and the student does not ask anything, it is as if he has read the book and there is no need to read further. When studying *Dīwān al-Mutanabbī*, I remember that he very quickly asked me to stop and said there was no need to study further and commenced with the *Ḥamāsa*. These incidents require much more detail. I do not wish to write my biography, nor that of my father. The aim was to mention the source of Mawlānā ʿAbdullāh Gangōhī's style of teaching as explained by Mawlānā Ẓafar Aḥmad and Mawlānā Shabbīr ʿAlī.

ITMĀM AL-NIʿAM

Ikmāl al-Shiyam is the commentary of *Itmām al-Niʿam*, which was written by my shaykh and guide, Mawlānā Khalīl Aḥmad Sahāranpūrī. *Itmām al-Niʿam* in turn is the Urdu translation of *Tabwīb al-Ḥikam*, the translation of which was done by Mawlānā Khalīl Aḥmad on the instruction of Ḥājī Imdādullāh Muhājir Makkī. Mawlānā Khalīl Aḥmad did not, however, designate a name for the translation but, on the instructions of Ḥājī Imdādullāh, handed it to Ḥakīm al-Umma Mawlānā Ashraf ʿAlī Thānawī for publishing. Mawlānā Thānawī was, on the instruction of Ḥājī Imdādullāh, the first to publish the book. He named it *Itmām al-Niʿam* as stated by himself in his foreword, which will appear later.

Itmām al-Niʿam was written at the time when Mawlānā Sahāranpūrī was a lecturer at Dār al-ʿUlūm Deoband, before his engagement at Maẓāhir ʿUlūm. Thus he wrote at the end of *Itmām al-Niʿam*, "This translation was completed on 27 Ramaḍān 1313/1895, after the Friday prayer in Masjid Maḥālla Khānaqāh, in the town of Deoband, district Saharanpur. All praise is for Allāh, the Lord of the worlds, and peace and blessings on our master Muḥammad, his family, companions and followers, all together."

Ḥakīm al-Umma Mawlānā Ashraf ʿAlī Thānawī first published it on the instruction of Ḥājī Imdādullāh and wrote the following foreword:

> In the name of Allāh, the Compassionate and Merciful. All praise is for Allāh, the Bestower of bounties and the Limitless in grace and kindness. Peace and blessings on His Messenger Muḥammad who was given concise speech and on his family and companions who were the fountains of wisdom.
>
> Glory to Allāh; the love and concern of the accepted servants of Allāh is such that, night and day, they think of ways to deliver benefit to the slaves of Allāh. In fact, these are the illustrious souls who represent the exegesis of the verse "You are the best of nations ever raised for mankind" (3:110).

The effect of our shaykh and guide Sayyidunā Mawlānā Ḥājj Ḥāfiẓ Shāh Muḥammad Imdādullāh's concern [for the Umma] is that his blessed self has written, translated, and published extremely beneficial books. Among the beneficial and essential books is a book called the *Ḥikam*, aphorisms of the pole of his time (*quṭb al-waqt*) and proof of Allāh (*ḥujjatullāh*) Shaykh Ibn ʿAṭā' Iskandarī who is the author of *Al-Tanwīr fī Isqāṭ al-Tadbīr*. Truly, the spiritual style of moral training and firmness in gnosis (*maʿrifa*) that exude from the words of this saint has seldom been found in the words of others. Its exotic beauty and esoteric excellence need no description. As someone said, "Once you have gold bangles what need is there for imitation bangles."[10]

However, on account of the topics of discussion being scattered, a reader would find it difficult to understand the topic in which each discussion falls. Thus Shaykh ʿAlī Muttaqī arranged the topics of this work in a very beautiful and systematic order. This systematic arrangement became known by the name *Al-Nahj al-Atamm fī Tabwīb al-Ḥikam*. For the benefit of the people of India, our master and guide Ḥājī Imdādullāh instructed Mawlānā Khalīl Aḥmad, the former lecturer at Dār al-ʿUlūm Deoband and present lecturer at Madrasa Islāmiyya, to translate this book. Mawlānā Khalīl Aḥmad subsequently translated it in very simple language and in an elaborate form full of meaning. In accordance with Ḥājī Imdādullāh's instructions, he handed the translation to me for publishing.

It is purely out of extreme humility and sincerity that the honorable translator has not given a name to his translation, let alone mention his name. I have, therefore, named it *Itmām al-Niʿam*: *Tarjama Tabwīb al-Ḥikam*. My beloved and honorable benefactor, who is an embodiment of virtue and grace, Ḥāfiẓ Muḥammad Abū Saʿīd Khān, the manager of Niẓāmī Printers, has, on account of the sincerity that he has for our Ḥājī Imdādullāh, enthusiastically and with utmost care arranged for its printing, bestowing spiritual light to the eyes of devotees and pleasure to their hearts. After numerous dives into the depths of the hidden ocean, this priceless pearl has finally been brought to the surface. For those who even now hesitate in accepting it, what can be said of them save that they are unable to recognize true value.

Written by Muḥammad Ashraf ʿAlī
May He forgive him

10 Women in the subcontinent, before marriage, would wear fake jewelry, which would be replaced with gold and silver jewelry after marriage. Hence, when one has something advanced, what need is there for the elementary.

THE AUTHOR OF *ITMĀM AL-NIʿAM*

The biography of Mawlānā Khalīl Aḥmad Muhājir Madanī (Emigrator to Madīna) has been narrated by Mawlānā ʿĀshiq Ilāhī in *Tadhkirat al-Khalīl.* A brief biography of his life has also been given by me in the introduction of the commentary of *Muwaṭṭa' Imām Mālik, Awjaz al-Masālik.*

The exemplar of the *sāliks*, the best of gnostics (*ʿārifs*), the *Ḥāfiẓ* of the Qur'ān and Ḥadīth, my master and guide Ḥājj Abū Ibrāhīm Khalīl Aḥmad ibn Shāh Majīd ibn Shāh Aḥmad ʿAlī ibn Shāh Quṭub ʿAlī Ayyūbī Anṣārī Ambhētwī was born in Ambheta in the district of Saharanpur toward the end of Safar 1269/1852.

He studied the primary Urdu and Persian textbooks by his paternal uncle, Shaykh Anṣārī ʿAlī, as well as other local *ʿulamā'*. Thereafter, he went to his father in Gwalior. He provides this information himself in his writings that will follow later. In 1283/1866, when the foundation of Dār al-ʿUlūm Deoband was laid, he enrolled at the *madrasa*. However, in the same year, the foundations for Maẓāhir ʿUlūm were laid in Saharanpur, and the maternal uncle of Mawlānā Khalīl, Mawlānā Muḥammad Maẓhar Nānōtwī, was appointed the head lecturer. He was also the *khalīfa* of Mawlānā Gangōhī. With the appointment of Mawlānā Muḥammad Maẓhar, Mawlānā Khalīl Aḥmad left Deoband and came to Saharanpur that very year.

At this time, Mawlānā Khalīl was studying the *Kāfiya*, etc. All of the rational and religious sciences after this, including *fiqh*, *tafsīr*, and ḥadīth, he completed at Maẓāhir ʿUlūm and was appointed lecturer at the same *madrasa* with a wage of three rupees a month. This was the year 1288/1871, and he was nineteen. He thus attained qualifications in all branches of academic religious knowledge within five years after the *Kāfiya.*

He was, however, very enthusiastic about mastering Arabic literature, and so, after having been appointed as lecturer at Saharanpur, went into the service of Mawlānā Fayḍ al-Ḥasan Sahāranpūrī, who was at that time a famous expert in literature and was working in Lahore. Mawlānā Fayḍ al-Ḥasan was, in fact, a commentator of the *Sabʿa Muʿallaqāt*, *Dīwān al-Ḥamāsa,* and *Dīwān al-Mutanabbī.*

This humble one had himself posed many questions to Mawlānā Sahāranpūrī regarding his employment. Out of his affection, Mawlānā would always provide answers. Some of my writings in this regard were in the possession of Mawlānā ʿĀshiq Ilāhī. He has narrated most of these in *Tadhkirat al-Khalīl* in his own words.

At this juncture, I wish to present the statement of Mawlānā Sahāranpūrī. On 23 Jumādā 'l-Ūlā 1240/1824, I asked him if he had studied all his books at this *madrasa* (Maẓāhir ʿUlūm). In reply he said:

> My father was employed in Gwalior. My paternal uncle, Anṣār ʿAlī, too was somewhere nearby. Coincidentally, he too came to Gwalior and began teaching me Arabic. When I began Arabic, I was studying [Saʿdī's] *Bustān*. After beginning Arabic studies, when I completed *Ṣarf-i Mīr* and *Panj Ganj*, my father left his job and went to Ambheta. I too accompanied him. There was no *madrasa* in Ambheta. Nevertheless, while I was superficially studying the *Kāfiya* and had reached *Sharḥ Jāmī*, the foundations of the *madrasa* in Deoband were laid.

In answer to another question that I asked on 12 Rabīʿ al-Awwal 1344/1924, the Mawlānā replied:

> In Ambheta there was a pious man, Mawlānā Sakhāwat ʿAlī, who was an ardent follower of the Sunna. In following the Sunna he was very, very strict and stringent. Prior to my admission to the *madrasa* of Deoband, I had studied some primary books by him. Mōlwī ʿAbdullāh, Mōlwī Ṣiddīq Aḥmad, and I took admission at the *madrasa* of Deoband. Although we had completed *Sharḥ Jāmī*, Mawlānā Yaʿqūb ﵀ arranged for us to be admitted into the *Kāfiya* class.
>
> Six or seven months later, on 1 Rajab 1283/1866, the foundations of Maẓāhir ʿUlūm were laid. Since I could not adapt to the climate of Deoband, I took admission at Maẓāhir ʿUlūm. It was through the blessings and kindh ness of Mawlānā Maẓhar ﵀ that he said although there is no class for *Sharḥ Jāmī* at the *madrasa*, admit yourselves into the *Mukhtaṣar al-Maʿānī* class.

After returning from Lahore, Mawlānā Sahāranpūrī himself said:

> I went to Lahore and stayed there a few months. After studying *Maqāmat al-Ḥarīrī* and *Dīwān al-Mutanabbī* under Mawlānā Fayḍ al-Ḥasan ﵀, I returned to Deoband. Mawlānā Yaʿqūb employed me for ten rupees a month to translate the *Qāmūs* into Urdu and sent me to a mountain to execute this duty. I returned after about two months.

Thereafter, he was sent as a teacher to the Arabic *madrasa* of Mawlānā Manglore (*Tadhkirat al-Rashīd*, vol. 1). It was during this time that Mawlānā Khalīl Aḥmad gave his *bayʿa* to Mawlānā Gangōhī. The episode of his *bayʿa* is mentioned later.

During the same time an offer of employment from Bhopal came for Mawlānā Yaʿqūb for a salary of three hundred rupees a month. Much pressure was put on him to accept. However, in spite of him earning at that time thirty rupees a month, he declined the offer. The Madār al-Mahām[11] pressed him to send another reliable person to take up the post. Mawlānā Yaʿqūb sent his nephew, Mawlānā Khalīl Aḥmad. Thus, having been chosen by his honorable uncle and approved by Mawlānā Gangōhī, he left during 1293/1876 to take up the post in Bhopal at a salary of fifty rupees a month.

His residence was in the mansion of the Madār al-Mahām at the Mōtī Mahāl (Pearl Palace) and every arrangement was made for his comfort and wants. However, the flood of spiritual effulgence that he experienced in the former places (Saharanpur and Deoband) was lacking here. Furthermore, the weather did not agree with him. Mawlānā Khalīl Aḥmad Sahāranpūrī therefore handed in his resignation to his shaykh, Mawlānā Gangōhī, and requested permission to return. The reply that Mawlānā Gangōhī wrote is recorded in *Tadhkirat al-Khalīl* and is reproduced here:

> Brother Mōlwī Khalīl Aḥmad, may your spiritual grace and outpouring (*fayḍ*) endure for a long time. After the *sunna* greeting, your letter was received today and your condition was learned. In view of the weather there not agreeing with you, your return is necessary. Relocating on account of the weather is confirmed in the ḥadīth. However, since it involves livelihood, the matter is somewhat delicate. Therefore, until alternate arrangements are not made, leaving is not appropriate. It is therefore advisable to stay there for a while. You were much in demand in Moradabad. However, Mōlwī ʿAbd al-Ḥaqq Pūrī has now taken up the post there, but he is unable to fulfill his duties as required. If it becomes advisable, I shall endeavor (to acquire a post for you) there or elsewhere. I shall inform you after arrangements are made, Allāh-willing. 18 Rabīʿ al-Awwal 1293/1876 on the day of Friday.

In accordance with the instructions of Mawlānā Gangōhī, Mawlānā Sahāranpūrī stayed on in Bhopal until the Ḥajj season dawned. The urge to go for Ḥajj became overpowering. According to the law of that state, employees wishing to embark on the Ḥajj would be granted leave without a deduction in salary and would be given a few months' salary in advance. Mawlānā Khalīl asked for leave and, although the money he received

11 Madār al-Mahām was the title given to the prime minister in Mughal India; it was a term that remained in use in the various princely states of British India, such as in Bhopal.

was insufficient, his enthusiasm impelled him to proceed. This episode is described in detail in *Tadhkirat al-Khalīl.*

On reaching Makka Mukarrama, he presented himself at the residence of Ḥājī Imdādullāh. What can be said about that place! The pleasure felt from the spiritual light there was most wonderful. This was Mawlānā Khalīl Aḥmad's first Ḥajj.

After completing the Ḥajj, his intention was to proceed to Madīna Munawwara. However, the road to Madīna was at that time very dangerous. Even those people who had already commenced the journey to Madīna were returning because of danger. Killings and anarchy were rampant. Ḥājī Imdādullāh said, "Mōlwī Khalīl Aḥmad, what do you intend? I have heard the pilgrims are returning home in large numbers on account of the dangers on the road to Madīna." Mawlānā Khalīl Aḥmad replied, "Shaykh, I have firmly resolved to go to Madīna. The appointed time of death cannot be delayed anywhere. If it comes on this road, then what greater fortune could a Muslim wish for? It is by the grace of Allāh Most High that he has brought me thus far. If I were to now abandon the journey to Madīna for fear of death, who could be more unfortunate than me?" Ḥājī Imdādullāh's face brightened with pleasure, and he said, "Enough! Enough! For you the advice is that you should certainly go. Allāh-willing, you will reach." Thus Mawlānā Khalīl took leave and set out for Madīna Munawwara. He said, "Only I know of the great peace and comfort I experienced along the journey. I stayed about two weeks in the sacred precincts and reached home safely and arrived in the service of Mawlānā Gangōhī."

In this journey, Mawlānā Sahāranpūrī received authorization (*ijāza*) in ḥadīth from the Shaykh of the Ḥaram, Shaykh Aḥmad [Zaynī] Daḥlān, and the shaykh of the shaykhs Shāh 'Abd al-Ghanī Mujaddidī Naqshbandī Dihlawī, who had taken up residence in Madīna. This is recorded in detail in the beginning of his *Musalsalāt.*[12] The authorization from Shaykh Aḥmad Daḥlān was acquired in Makka Mukarrama, while that of Shāh 'Abd al-Ghanī was obtained in Madīna Munawwara after the Ḥajj in the year 1294/1877.

After returning from the Ḥajj, Mawlānā Sahāranpūrī had no intention of returning to Bhopal because the weather conditions there were not favorable. After staying a few days in his hometown of Ambheta, he left in Jumādā

12 The *musalsalāt* (sing. *musalsal*) are ḥadīths transmitted over the generations through narrators with a common attribute such as each narrator smiling when transmitting the ḥadīth or shaking hands. A famous collection of this genre is by Shāh Waliyyullāh Muḥaddith Dihlawī.

'l-Ūla 1294/1877 for Sikandrabad in the district of Bulandshahr, where he took up a post as a lecturer at the Madrasa 'Arabiyya Jāmiʿ Masjid. However, here the people of innovation (*bidʿa*) vehemently opposed him. They left no stone unturned to harm him, and so he sought permission from Mawlānā Gangōhī to return. Mawlānā Gangōhī, however, refused permission and wrote the following letter:

> Mōlwī Khalīl Aḥmad: *Al-salāmu ʿalaykum wa raḥmatu 'Llāhi wa barakātuh.*
>
> Your letter has been received and contents noted. Do not permit the latest developments to alarm you. In this world, events occur which please and displease. Continue with your work. If the opponent is bent on harming you, know that the Supporter is protecting you. As far as possible do not resort to abandonment.
>
> Accepting a gift from a child is permissible and accepting the gift of those who inherit from a child is also permissible. There is no problem in this. What was written in the letter before was a mistake.
>
> If deemed appropriate, raise and highlight the falsity of that complaint with Mīr Qādir 'Alī via somebody else, even if it may not be beneficial. It is better to keep all happy. Perhaps it will prove beneficial. Allāh Most High has said, "Thus because of the mercy of Allāh are you affectionate towards them" (3:159) However, there is no hope that this sect will become pleased, especially when they are exhorted by their preachers [to oppose you]. *Wa 'l-salām.* Friday 16 Jumādā al-Thāniya 1294 (29 June 1907)

However, despite Mawlānā Sahāranpūrī's affection and affability, the intransigence of the people there went on increasing, so, with the permission of Mawlānā Gangōhī, he finally handed in his resignation and returned.

In that very year, Shawwāl 1294/1877, an august group consisting of the senior scholars of India departed for the Ḥajj. In this group were illustrious stars of knowledge and piety such as Mawlānā Gangōhī, Mawlānā Nānōtwī, Mawlānā Muḥammad Maẓhar, Mawlānā Muḥammad Yaʿqūb (the chief lecturer at Dār al-ʿUlūm Deoband), as well as other senior *ʿulamā'*. With immense eagerness and yearning, Mawlānā Sahāranpūrī also requested to accompany this august caravan of seniors. However, Mawlānā Gangōhī did not consent, on account of some difficulties regarding travel arrangements and because the Mawlānā had just returned from the Ḥajj. This illustrious group returned from the pilgrimage in Rabīʿ al-Awwal 1295/1878.

On their return, Mawlānā Muḥammad Yaʿqūb had received a letter from

Mōlwī Shams al-Dīn, Chief Justice of Bahawalpur, requesting a highly qualified teacher. Many qualities were stipulated in the letter: the teacher had to be a young man, extremely intelligent, an expert in all branches of knowledge, well-mannered, organized, and an embodiment of virtue and character who could be an example for students. Mawlānā Yaʿqūb selected Mawlānā Khalīl Aḥmad for the post. Mawlānā Khalīl would often say he had declined the offer, saying he was not adequately qualified. But Mawlānā Muḥammad Yaʿqūb said, "The people of knowledge usually consider themselves in this way. You consider yourself unqualified because you still have your seniors above you. But when you go outside you will not find anyone as qualified as yourself."

Finally, with the unanimous support of Mawlānā Yaʿqūb and Mawlānā Gangōhī, Mawlānā Khalīl Aḥmad took up the post in Bahawalpur for a monthly salary of 30 rupees. While in Bahawalpur, he undertook his second Ḥajj journey which he himself describes in his diary. This journey is also described in *Tadhkirat al-Khalīl*. It took place in the month of Shawwāl 1297/1879. The year 1296/1881, as mentioned in part two of *Tadhkirat al-Rashīd*, is a printing error. It was on this blessed journey that Ḥājī Imdādullāh bestowed the mantle of *khilāfa* on Mawlānā Sahāranpūrī and presented him with his blessed turban. This is mentioned in the second volume of *Tadhkirat al-Rashīd* as follows:

> When the honorable mawlānā made the Ḥajj to Makka for the second time, Imām Rabbānī [Mawlānā Gangōhī] wrote to Ḥājī Imdādullāh requesting him to confer the mantle of *khilāfa* to Mawlānā Khalīl Aḥmad. On seeing the mawlānā, Ḥājī Imdādullāh became extremely happy. During Muharram 1297/1879 he presented the document of *khilāfa* adorned with his seal, and in a state of elation he removed his blessed turban from his head and placed it on the Mawlānā's head.
>
> The honorable mawlānā presented both gifts to Mawlānā Gangōhī and said, "I am not deserving of these. This is only your affection and kindness to me." Mawlānā Gangōhī replied, "May these be blessed for you." He then signed the authorization letter and handed it together with the turban to the mawlānā. The respect of Mawlānā Khalīl was such that whenever he would take *bayʿa*, he would instruct the *murīd*, after having repented for past sins, to say, "I have made *bayʿa* to Mawlānā Rashīd Aḥmad at the hands of Khalīl Aḥmad."

In this account, the date Muḥarram 1297/1879 is a printing error. The mawlānā's departure for the Ḥajj was in Shawwāl 1297/1897. The turban mentioned above is the same blessed turban that Mawlānā Sahāranpūrī presented to my father, Mawlānā Muḥammad Yaḥyā, when he granted him *khilāfa*. This episode is narrated by Mawlānā ʿĀshiq Ilāhī in *Tadhkirat al-Khalīl*. He writes:

> The late Mōlwī Muḥammad Yaḥyā was my benefactor and sincere friend. His hidden excellences and auspicious states require a separate volume. After all, he must have been a someone for Imām Rabbānī to love him more than his own children. Mawlānā Gangōhī often said that he was the staff in old age and the eyes in blindness. If he were to disappear for a few minutes for some work, Imam Rabbani would become perturbed and restless. Until Mawlānā Gangōhī's death he spent twelve years in such love and affection for which there is no parallel.
>
> Mawlānā Khalīl Aḥmad, whose foresight had discerned the worth and value of Mawlānā Muḥammad Yaḥyā twelve years ago, went specially to Gangoh to present with his own hands the turban which Ḥaji Imdādullāh had presented to him and which had been stitched according to its original folds and preserved. While placing the blessed turban on Mawlānā Muḥammad Yaḥyā's head with his blessed hand, he said, "You are deserving of this. Until this day, I was its protector and trustee. All praise is for Allāh. Today I have handed the right to the rightful one and I am now relieved of the responsibility of this trust. I authorize you to initiate any seeker into the four paths and to show him the Name of Allāh."

This was Mawlānā Sahāranpūrī's second Ḥajj. His third and subsequent Ḥajj journeys were undertaken from Saharanpur. The third Ḥajj was after the heart-rending demise of Mawlānā Gangōhī. Consolation for the immense grief which he suffered as a result of this event could only be obtained from his presence at the Holy Grave of the Prophet of Allāh ﷺ.

His fourth Ḥajj was in 1328/1910. In this year, Mawlānā Shāh ʿAbd al-Raḥīm Rāipūrī went for Ḥajj accompanied by a large group of his *murīds* and companions. Mawlānā Sahāranpūrī accompanied Mawlānā Rāipūrī as far as Delhi to see him off. On his return from Delhi, Shāh Zāhid Ḥusayn, the head of the village of Bahat, prevailed on Mawlānā Sahāranpūrī to also proceed for the Ḥajj and that he would also accompany him. Perhaps this insistence was the effect of the yearning and enthusiasm which overwhelmed Mawlānā Sahāranpūrī's heart as a consequence of Mawlānā Rāipūrī's departure. Hence he accepted the offer after much pressure from

Shāh Zāhid Ḥusayn. He thus left Saharanpur during the middle of Dhū 'l-Qaʿda and reached Makka Mukarrama on 6 Dhū 'l-Ḥijja. After Ḥajj he went to Madīna Munawwara via Yanbu. He stayed twenty-two days there. He returned to Saharanpur at the end of Ṣafar 1329/1911. It was also during this journey that my father taught all of Mawlānā Sahāranpūrī's lessons.

The fifth Ḥajj was that contentious journey which took place in Shawwāl 1333/1914 in the company of Shaykh al-Hind Mawlānā Maḥmūd Ḥasan. Mawlānā Sahāranpūrī did not obtain the companionship of Shaykh al-Hind from the beginning of the journey. However, a week before the journey, four illustrious personalities—Mawlānā Sahāranpūrī, Shaykh al-Hind, Mawlānā Shāh ʿAbd al-Raḥīm Rāipūrī, and Mawlānā Ḥājj Ḥakīm Aḥmad Rāmpūrī ﵏—gathered for secret discussions in the library of Maẓāhir ʿUlūm. No one else besides these four was allowed to participate in the talks. After the ishrāq prayers each day, they would go into privacy. At midday, word would repeatedly come from the home of Mawlānā Sahāranpūrī announcing that meals were ready; they would reply, "We are coming." They would descend from upstairs just before the *adhān* of the ẓuhr prayer and, after quickly eating, would perform their prayers and then immediately seclude themselves to continue talks until after the *adhān* of the ʿaṣr prayer. After ʿaṣr there would be no gathering where religious instructions would be given. There would, however, sometimes be such a gathering after Maghrib prayer. Everyone was curious to know what was being said during these lengthy and secret talks which lasted for a whole week, but nobody had any idea. At the time, I was a child and would ask all of my seniors about these talks. My father had some idea what these discussions were about and made some allusions which would satisfy my curiosity.

This journey, which was decided in those lengthy consultations, took place in Shawwāl 1333/1914. During the absence of Shaykh al-Hind, the responsibility of his duties was assumed by Mawlānā Rāipūrī. Although these personalities held high aspirations [of carrying out *jihād* to free India from colonial rule], fate did not permit their attainment. On account of the excess and oppression of Sharīf Ḥusayn in Makka, Mawlānā Sahāranpūrī was compelled to return before the Ḥajj during Shawwāl 1334/1915, while Shaykh al-Hind ﵀ was imprisoned in Malta.

Although it is mentioned in *Tadhkirat al-Khalīl* that Mawlānā Sahāranpūrī returned from this journey in Shaʿbān, he in fact departed from Makka Mukarrama at the end of Shawwāl and his ship reached Bombay on 8 Dhū 'l-Qaʿda. As he alighted from the ship, he was handed a telegram announcing the demise of my honorable father, Mawlānā Muḥammad Yaḥyā. This news aggravated the grief he suffered as a result of the difficult events that transpired during the year he was resident in Makka Mukarrama. For an entire year he had faced anxiety and difficult events in the Hijaz, and then after he received this telegram informing of this major loss we heard that he fell silent for a short while. To compound all this, as he disembarked from the ship in Bombay, he was taken into custody along with his respected wife and brother, Ḥājī Maqbūl Aḥmad, who was like his right-hand man. Together with their luggage, the three were taken to Nainital. The whole story is quite long. But they were interrogated for several days, after which, through the favor of Allāh, they were eventually freed.

His sixth Ḥajj took place in 1338/1914. He left Saharanpur on 2 Shaʿbān; this sinner also accompanied him on this journey. There was some delay in finding a ship in Bombay because Mawlānā Sahāranpūrī's retinue consisted of approximately three hundred people and he disliked travelling ahead without them all. They allowed two ships to sail without them neither had enough to room to give the entire group passage. Tickets for the entire group were purchased well in advance for the journey on a third ship. Those were very difficult days in Bombay, where it was extremely difficult for Deobandīs to live publicly. Some sincere friends had therefore arranged accommodation for the group in a tent pitched in a field on the outskirts of the city. The group reached Makka Mukarrama on 11 Ramaḍān.

In spite of Mawlānā Sahāranpūrī's weakness and old age, and the dizziness he felt as a result of the ship's motions, he himself led the tarāwīḥ prayers standing. He would recite half a chapter in eight units of prayer and I would lead the remaining twelve units reciting a three quarters of a chapter. On reaching Makka Mukarrama, Mawlānā Sahāranpūrī offered the tarāwīḥ prayers behind an excellent reciter who would recite two parts a night from the beginning of the Qur'ān and completed his own Qur'ān in *nafl* prayers.

On reaching Makka Mukarrama, Mawlānā Muḥibb al-Dīn Wilāyatī Muhājir Makkī—who was among the *khalīfas* of Ḥājī Imdādullāh and a man of great inspirations—said the following while embracing Mawlānā Sahāranpūrī: "Mawlānā, how have you come here? The Day of Judgment is about to be enacted here. Return to India immediately after Ramaḍān." Mawlānā Sahāranpūrī told us, "It was my intention to take up residence in Madīna Ṭayba, but Mawlānā Muḥibb al-Dīn vehemently forbids it. I have already visited Madīna Ṭayba several times. Since this is your first Ḥajj and it is not known if you will again get this opportunity, proceed to Madīna."

Those times were so unsafe and dangerous that some people would hazard the trip to Madīna before the Ḥajj and very few would venture after Ḥajj. Neither lives nor people's property were safe. The government of Sharīf Ḥusayn had no control beyond the four walls of Makka. Killing and plundering were rampant and people were only permitted to stay in Madīna for three days. If anyone wished to stay more than three days, a daily fee of one guinea had to be paid to the bedouin in charge of your caravan as long as he was in agreement with you staying. A few of us *murīds*, with the blessings of Mawlānā Sahāranpūrī and the grace and favor of Allāh, finally reached Madīna Ṭayba, travelling initially along the coast and then, in a clandestine fashion, through the valleys of Mount Ghā'ir. The story of this journey is indeed long and interesting.

One of the small manifestations of the innumerable bounties and grace of Allāh Most High that have always been with this humble one was that, instead of just three days in Madīna, I was able to spend forty. This is truly an example of the bounties mentioned in the Qur'ānic verse "And if you count the bounties of Allāh, never will you be able to enumerate them" (14:34). On reaching Madīna, one of the camels in our caravan died due to exhaustion. Neither did the camel owner have sufficient funds to purchase another mount, nor did we possess enough money to advance a loan with which another camel could be purchased. Mawlānā Sahāranpūrī had calculated our expenses for a return journey and three-day stay in Madīna. Thus we were only given a small sum of money for this. The rest of our funds were left at Ḥājī 'Alī Jān's shop in Makka. Whenever the camel owner would ask us for a loan to enable him to purchase a camel, we would in turn ask him for a loan to buy food, saying that we had only made arrangements for three days. As a result, the poor man (may Allāh Most High reward him well) would repeatedly ask to be pardoned for the delay and his shortcomings. When one of our associates would sometimes complain to the amīr of Madīna, he too would apologize and instruct us to be patient, and rebuke the bedouin.

These are very unique and wonderful incidents, but it is not my intention to write my autobiography here. These lines have been written without original intent. Anyway, after Ḥajj, we returned [to India] with Mawlānā Sahāranpūrī and reached Saharanpur in Ṣafar 1339/1920.

The seventh Ḥajj was the journey in which Mawlānā Sahāranpūrī bid his final farewell to India. On the insistence of the *murīds* of Hyderabad, it was arranged for Mawlānā Sahāranpūrī to stay one week in Hyderabad. The departure from Saharanpur for Hyderabad was on 16 Shawwāl 1344/1925.

It was agreed that I accompany Mawlānā Sahāranpūrī as far as Hyderabad. However, after arriving at the station, and precisely at the moment of departure after taking up seats in the carriage, it was discovered that Mawlānā's main item of luggage was left behind in his room; the case contained all his items of trust, as well as money for the journey. So I returned as the train departed and reached Hyderabad the next day with it.

After staying about a week in Hyderabad, Mawlānā Sahāranpūrī left for Bombay. According to plan, the rest of the group together with Ammājī (his wife) left from Saharanpur directly for Bombay on 23 Shawwāl, while Mawlānā Sahāranpūrī departed from Hyderabad at 9 a.m. on Saturday 25 Shawwāl. He reached Bombay on Sunday morning. From Bombay, the ship sailed on 7 Dhū 'l-Qaʿda (20 May). The ship docked on the 17th at Kamaran[13] for quarantine, and sailed from there on the 18th, reaching Jeddah on the 21st. From Jeddah the journey to Makka Mukarrama was by camel. The group reached Makka on the 25th. Mawlānā Sahāranpūrī had rented a house in a narrow street opposite Bāb Ibrāhīm; he stayed there along with three or four of us attendants.

On the 8th we left for Mina. Mawlānā Sahāranpūrī and Ammājī were on one camel. Some other close companions were nearby on other camels, while some of us attendants walked on foot alongside his blessed camel. In Mina we stayed in the tent of a Ḥajj caravan organizer (*muṭawwif*). One tent was for the ladies, in which Ammājī and a female attendant stayed. The other was for the men, and Mawlānā Sahāranpūrī and we stayed in it. Likewise, we travelled from Mina to ʿArafāt, and from there to Muzdalifa, Mina, and Makka for the *ṭawāf al-ziyāra*. From Makka we returned to Mina and returned once more from Mina on 13 Dhū 'l-Ḥijja. After completing the Ḥajj, we stayed in Makka Mukarrama for a few days and then decided to proceed to Madīna.

On 22 Dhū 'l-Ḥijja (2 July 1926), the process of *tabrīz* began. *Tabrīz* was a well-known practice associated with travel by camels. Caravans would halt for a night about a mile or two outside Makkah to enable people to return to Makkah to bring any goods or persons left behind and then the journey would continue. Nowadays, in view of motor transport, people are no longer aware of this practice. A few camels would leave at a time and

13 Kamaran is an island in the Red Sea off the coast of Yemen. The Ottomans used the island during the nineteenth century as a quarantine station for Ḥajj pilgrims travelling to Jeddah. It came under British control in June 1915 during the First World War.

stop at Jarwal.[14] The departure was planned for the 24th, but the government confiscated twenty-three camels. This resulted in a delay of two days. Therefore we left Jarwal two days later after ʿaṣr prayer at nine o'clock Arabian Time.[15] Some had left and performed ʿaṣr in Tanʿīm. At six o'clock Arabian Time we reached Wādī Fāṭima,[16] where there were many long orchards of date trees; these orchards were not so wide, but very long. There was also a small stream of very sweet water in which we bathed; we also ate dates.

From here we left at ẓuhr on Thursday and reached Usfan[17] on Friday morning at twelve o'clock. The camels from the caravan trailed in until two. Here was a well; it is said that the saliva of the Messenger of Allāh ﷺ had mingled in the water of this well. Here there were also many gardens full of date trees; they weren't laid out systematically but scattered in groups of two or four. There were also several wells, the water of which was very sweet. Dates, hens, goats, and sheep were in abundance and very cheap.

We left Usfan at eight. We accomplished the long and arduous mountain climb before Maghrib and reached Daff[18] at six on Saturday night. However, on account of the steep mountain climb, the camels trailed in until nine at night. Here, too, dates were in abundance. Thin bread drenched in ghee was being sold very cheap. Milk was also available in abundance.

We departed from here after ʿaṣr prayer and reached Qadimah[19] on Sunday morning at nine Arabian Time. Qadimah was a big town where a government court, officials, and police were much in view. The different routes from Makka converged here. Those coming from Jeddah would also arrive here. There was a shortage of water, and the water available was brackish. We left after ẓuhr prayer at six o'clock and reached Rabigh[20] at two on Monday morning. Rabigh used to be a pleasant and large town. However, on account of the war between the Najdīs and Sharīf Ḥusayn, the city had

---

14 With the expansion of Makkah today, Jarwal is now situated within the city.

15 This refers to a system of timekeeping that was widely used under different names across the world for many centuries. It remained in use in Saudi Arabia until the late 1960s. According to this system, every day at sunset people would adjust their watches and clocks to 0 hours (or 12 o'clock). They would then allow their clocks to run normally for almost 24 hours until sunset, when clocks would then be adjusted once more.

16 Wādī Fāṭima, or Valley of Fāṭima, is an area that lies between Makkah and Jeddah. It is one of the main tributaries in the Jeddah-Makkah region and drains into the Red Sea.

17 Usfan is situated east of north Jeddah along the Makkah-Madinah highway.

18 Daff is also situated east of the Makkah-Madinah highway.

19 Qadimah is located north of both Jeddah and the old fishing town of Thuwal along the Red Sea coast. It is south of Yanbu and is the *iḥrām* boundary (*mīqāt*) of Juḥfa.

20 Rabigh is situated along the Red Sea coast just outside the *mīqāt* of Juḥfa.

been deserted and buildings had fallen over. There was also a market there where food, drink, clothes, etc., could be purchased. Some traders here offered a postal service where they would arrange for pilgrims' letters to be delivered to post offices in Yanbu or Jeddah. All caravans were required to stop here for one night. Mawlānā Sahāranpūrī, along with his companions, stayed the night here.

We departed from Rabigh on Tuesday evening after ʿaṣr at nine o'clock Arabian Time and reached Mastūra[21] on Wednesday morning at twelve. All of the wells here were salty. Whatever was cooked with this well water also became bitter. But through the blessings of Mawlānā Sahāranpūrī we located some very sweet water. It was learned that the government had just recently dug a few wells from which sweet water was, through the grace of Allāh Most High, obtainable. This water was even sweeter than the water of Rabigh and Qadimah.

On Wednesday evening at nine o'clock after ʿaṣr, we departed and reached Bi'r al-Shaykh on Thursday morning at eleven. Although there was a market here, milk was unavailable. After ʿaṣr we left and reached Bi'r Banī 'l-Ḥisān on Friday before dawn. This place was also known as Bi'r Shaykh ʿAbdullāh at the time. It is said that Ḥisān was a famous chief who had seven children and was very wealthy. The settlement is named after him and several roads from here lead to Madīna Ṭayba. Some caravans accomplish this journey in three halts (*manzils*), while most do it in four: Shufay, Khalas Watr, Bi'r Rāḥa and Bi'r ʿĀmir, Furaysh (also known as Bi'r Darwish), Dhū 'l-Ḥulayfa (which is also called Bi'r ʿAlī) and then Madīna Ṭayba. These halts don't all come on one road; some are on one side of a mountain and some on the other.

Mawlānā Sahāranpūrī's caravan left Bi'r Banī al-Ḥisān on Friday after ẓuhr and reached Khalas[22] on Saturday morning, leaving again after ẓuhr. On Sunday morning, the caravan reached Furaysh where several caravans had gathered. From Furaysh we left on Sunday evening and reached Madīna Munawwara (may Allāh increase it in dignity and honor) on Monday mid-morning. If Dhū 'l-Qaʿda had thirty days, then the date on this day would have been 8 Muḥarram and if Dhū 'l-Qaʿda had twenty-nine, the date would have been the 9th. The late Uncle ʿAzīz al-Ḥasan Kāndhlawī, whose camel at some stop would separate from our caravan and halt elsewhere, writes in his diary that the date of arrival in Madīna Ṭayba was the morning

21 Masturah is also situated along the Red Sea coast north of Rabigh and south of Yanbu.

22 Khalas is situated east of Badr and west of the Makka-Madīna highway.

of Monday 19 July. According to the common Islamic calendar, 19 July is Tuesday 8 Muharram. In Arabia a difference of a day in dates is common; hence 19 July corresponds with 8 Muharram (Tuesday).

Mawlānā Ḥājj Sayyid Aḥmad (the elder brother of Shaykh al-Islām Mawlānā Sayyid Ḥusayn Aḥmad Madanī) had rented a house at the old Madrasa Sharʿiyya. The word *old* is mentioned here in relation to the present new building, which was erected as a consequence of the changes and development projects undertaken by the Saudi government. The old *madrasa* building was very simple and had an appealing structure. Its main entrance was located on the main road facing the Bāb al-Nisā' [of the Ḥaram]. The small door was on the southern side opening into a narrow street. The ground floor of this house was occupied by Mawlānā Sayyid Aḥmad. Mawlānā Sahāranpūrī took up residence on the second floor, where he also wrote *Badhl al-Majhūd,* his commentary of *Sunan Abī Dāwūd.* The third floor was occupied by the womenfolk of Mawlānā Sayyid Aḥmad's household. Adjacent to this, toward the side of the Bāb al-Nisā', was the residence of the womenfolk from Mawlānā Sahāranpūrī's group.

After the ishrāq prayer,[23] Mawlānā Sahāranpūrī would go to the study, where he would write his commentary and remain there until eleven o'clock Indian time in complete solitude, engrossed in writing *Badhl al-Majhūd.* He would thereafter have his meals in the same room. His meals would come from his household and upstairs would come meals from the household of Mawlānā Sayyid Aḥmad. Both these seniors regarded me as their guest, and so I partook in the meals. This became apparent when only once during my yearlong stay I had a severe fever and could not join them. Meals were diligently sent to me by both seniors separately after ẓuhr. Throughout my entire stay, I did not have to make my own arrangements for food.

After meals, Mawlānā Sahāranpūrī would go to the women's quarters. After a short siesta, he would leave for the Prophet's Mosque before noon. The ẓuhr *adhān* would be called soon after noon. Mawlānā Sahāranpūrī would recite the Holy Qur'ān for about an hour after ẓuhr. Thereafter, he would become occupied in studying [Samhūdī's] *Wafā' al-Wafā'.* After ʿaṣr, which would be offered when the shadow was only a length, he would proceed to the home of Mawlānā Sayyid Aḥmad, which was on the ground floor, and remain there until Maghrib. Here, Mawlānā Sahāranpūrī would

---

23 Ishrāq prayer is a supererogatory prayer offered ten to twenty minutes after sunrise consisting of two or more *rakʿas.*

hold his gathering, which would be open to the public. Both local residents and visitors to the Prophet's Mosque would attend. On these occasions, Mawlānā Sayyid Aḥmad would take great delight in serving green tea to those present. In one large spoon he had kept a mixture of ambergris and musk that had been boiled together and which was called *chamchā-i-qudrat* (spoon of power). He would add this to the cups of special guests. Mawlānā Sahāranpūrī would only drink one cup, but this sinful one would drink eight to ten cups and would add the mixture himself.

In Rabīʿ al-Awwal 1345/1926, Mawlānā ʿAbd al-Qādir Rāipūrī arrived in Madīna Ṭayba with several close associates. Despite his illness, he would regularly attend Mawlānā Sahāranpūrī's gathering after ʿaṣr. Some of Mawlānā Rāipūrī's associates, however, would not attend. One day, as an apology for their absence, he said to Mawlānā Sahāranpūrī, "Insensitivity is becoming predominant. First, these people should have realized that when I am attending regularly, they too should ensure their attendance. Second, I have even reprimanded them for their absence." Mawlānā Sahāranpūrī responded forcefully, "Never! I feel very embarrassed about this. I have never exhorted anyone to take *bayʿa* to my shaykh. I consider my shaykh to be the sun [of spiritual guidance and illumination]. Whoever is not keen to derive illumination from him, the loss is his own." Mawlānā Sahāranpūrī then pointed to me and said, "It is the habit of this father and son [referring to myself and my father] to cling to the person who offers even the slightest attention to them." I had for several days repeatedly said the following to Mawlānā Sahāranpūrī, "A certain person is very sincere. Although he is devoted to yourself, he completely abstains from [a prescribed regimen of] *dhikr* and spiritual exercise. You should write instructing him to observe *dhikr*." Each time Mawlānā Sahāranpūrī's response would be, "When he asks, I will instruct. Why should I show him when he does not inquire?" A day before the episode with Mawlānā Rāipūrī, I said to Mawlānā Sahāranpūrī, "If you permit me, I shall myself write to that person." "Don't write anything on my behalf," he replied. "You may write whatever you wish from yourself."

As mentioned earlier, on arrival in Madīna Ṭayba, Mawlānā Sahāranpūrī engrossed himself in the completion of his commentary, *Badhl al-Majhūd*, of which he had reached volume four, the chapter on funeral rites (*janāʾiz*), before arriving to the holy city. On reaching Madīna, Mawlānā Sahāranpūrī began this chapter. In the beginning of the manuscript of *Badhl al-Majhūd* that was written in Madīna, the following is recorded: "13 Muḥarram 1345/1926, Saturday, in Madīna Munawwara." The solitude that Mawlānā

Sahāranpūrī experienced, coupled with the blessings of Madīna Ṭayba, enabled him to complete one and a half volumes in seven and a half months, while the previous three and a half volumes were completed in about nine and a half years. The work was written in Mawlānā Sayyid Aḥmad's room, as mentioned earlier. But for the acquisition of blessings, its completion was rendered in the Prophet's Mosque in the blessed place known as the "garden from the gardens of Paradise" (*rawḍa min riyāḍ 'l-Janna*). Thus, at the end of *Badhl al-Majhūd*, Mawlānā Sahāranpūrī writes:

> With the accordance and strength granted by Allāh Most High, it has been completed in Madīna Munawwara, in *rawḍa min riyāḍ al-Janna,* near to the grave of the leader of the progeny of Ādam, the leader of the creation and the universe, on 21 Shaʿbān 1345/1926 since the migration of the trustworthy prophet. O Allāh! accept it from us as you accept from Your close and pious servants. Make it purely for Your gracious sake and forgive us for our mistakes and lapses and those acts that are not pleasing to you. Surely, You are most forgiving and gracious. You are the Cherisher who is oft-forgiving and merciful.

Mawlānā Sahāranpūrī was extremely delighted with the completion of *Badhl al-Majhūd* and held a lavish feast on its completion. He had invitation cards printed in Arabic and invited the *ʿulamā'* of Madīna. He also sent cards to some close individuals in India, such as Mawlānā ʿĀshiq Ilāhī, solely as a means to include them in the joy. The original printed invitation is together with the manuscript of *Badhl al-Majhūd* in the *madrasa* library. It is reproduced hereunder:

> In the Name of Allāh, the Most Compassionate, the Most Merciful. All Praise is due to Allāh alone, and peace and blessings on him after whom there is no messenger.
>
> Lofty and honorable Shaykh (may your spiritual blessings endure). *Al-salāmu ʿalaykum wa raḥmat Allāh wa barakātuh.*
>
> Allāh Most High has favored the one extending this invitation with the compilation of *Badhl al-Majhūd fī Ḥall Abī Dāwūd.* Allāh Most High has granted its completion in the city of the Performer of Miracles (may the best of praise and purest of peace be on him and his family). May Allāh Most High make it purely for his gracious pleasure, and benefit Islam and Muslims by way of it. *Āmīn.*
>
> We desire your presence after Friday prayer on 23 Shaʿbān 1345/1926,

at Madrasat al-ʿUlūm al-Sharʿiyya, which is situated on al-Budūr Street, and to participate in meals; [our] happiness would be complete with your presence. Thanks are for Allāh Most High. *Wa 'l-Salām.*

Your host and the servant of students of religious knowledge,
Khalīl Aḥmad (may he be forgiven).

Mawlānā Sahāranpūrī's schedule until the completion of *Badhl al-Majhūd* was as mentioned above, spending the morning writing the book, reciting the Qur'ān after ẓuhr, and so forth. After completing *Badhl al-Majhūd*, the morning part was now also utilized for studying *Wafā' al-Wafā'* and other books on Madīna that had piled up during his stay there.

A few days later, the blessed month of Ramaḍān commenced. During the Holy Month, Mawlānā Sahāranpūrī would engage in recitation of the Qur'ān for a considerable time from after ishrāq. Then, after a short nap, he would return to the Holy Mosque before noon. He would return home after ẓuhr. Ammājī, together with me, would listen to his Qur'ān. After ẓuhr, I would present myself at Mawlānā Sahāranpūrī's place of residence at the appointed time. According to the usual practice, Mawlānā Sahāranpūrī would proceed after ʿaṣr to the residence of Mawlānā Sayyid Aḥmad. He would leave for the Prophet's Mosque a short while before Maghrib and make *ifṭār* there with dates and Zamzam water. After Maghrib, Mawlānā Sahāranpūrī would recite two parts of the Qur'ān in supererogatory prayers, sitting down on the roof of Madrasa al-ʿUlūm al-Sharʿiyya; I would listen to his recitation.

After ʿishā' prayers in the Prophet's Mosque, Mawlānā Sahāranpūrī would return to the madrasa and perform tarāwīḥ behind Qārī Muḥammad Tawfīq, who would recite two parts with utmost reverence and tranquility. The tarāwīḥ would end at five o'clock Arabian Time (or about twelve-thirty a.m.). He would then retire for a rest at about six. I was instructed to wake him at eight. Besides on one or two occasions, I cannot remember finding him asleep. Thereafter, Mawlānā Sahāranpūrī would listen to two parts of the Qur'ān in supererogatory prayers recited separately by two students of the madrasa. The Mawlānā had, for some time, been eager to listen to the recitation in the reading of Imām Nāfiʿ. Both these students were Mālikīs from the Maghrib and recited according to Nāfiʿ's reading.

Toward the end of the Holy Month, the effect of paralysis began appearing on Mawlānā and he found it difficult to move. The paralysis had, in fact, begun after the completion of *Badhl al-Majhūd*, when he became afflicted with severe fever and colds. However, as a result of the blessings of the Holy Month, these illnesses disappeared with the dawn of Ramaḍān. The illness, however, reappeared two or three days before ʿīd and then paralysis set in. It remained like this till the end; the illness would disappear and reappear return until he died, as will be explained later.

Bayʿa and Traversing the Path

The incident of Mawlānā Sahāranpūrī's *bayʿa* and traversal, or *sulūk*, of the path is something that occurred very early on. Mawlānā ʿĀshiq Ilāhī has described it in detail in *Tadhkirat al-Khalīl.* A detailed account is also given in a separate chapter in *Tadhkirat al-Rashīd* (part one). He writes that it can be understood from the anecdotes of Mawlānā Gangōhī that just as he was the first among the *ʿulamāʾ* to take the *bayʿa* to Ḥājī Imdādullāh, so too was Mawlānā Khalīl Aḥmad the first among the contemporary *ʿulamāʾ* to take the *bayʿa* at the blessed hands of Mawlānā Gangōhī ﵀. This is in line with a dream in which the Prophet of Allāh ﷺ told Ḥājī Imdādullāh's sister-in-law, "Get away! The guests of Ḥājī Imdādullāh are *ʿulamāʾ*. I shall bake their bread." The manifestation of this dream is that the first "guest," without any intermediary, was Imām Rabbānī Mawlānā Gangōhī, and the first "guest" via an intermediary was Mawlānā Sahāranpūrī.

After this, the author of *Tadhkirat al-Rashīd* quotes a piece of writing that Mawlānā Sahāranpūrī wrote himself; I have quoted this below with changes to make it brief:

> Prior to entering into the order, I had no special connection with Mawlānā Gangōhī, nor were there any close family ties between us. During my student days I had a slight acquaintance with the mawlānā and we would only regard him as a pious scholar. One day my paternal uncle, Mōlwī Anṣār ʿAlī, said to me when I was studying by him, "After your studies, you should pursue *taṣawwuf* from Mawlānā Gangōhī."
>
> Once during Ramaḍān—it was most likely when I was between twelve and fourteen—I went to Gangoh and at night went to the *khānaqāh* to listen to Mawlānā Gangōhī's Qur'ān. I stood under the Indian lilac tree, or *neem*, to listen to his recitation. He was offering the tarāwīḥ prayers. He was a ḥāfiẓ with an exceptionally beautiful voice. He was reciting with such beauty that its sweetness remains in my heart till this day. I remember the words "greed for wealth [from the spoil]" (33:19). I can now say he was reciting Sūrat al-Aḥzāb at the time.

I got married in Gangoh during my student days and as a result had greater occasion of staying in Gangoh. During my stay in Gangoh, I would spend time in the blessed company of Mawlānā Gangōhī. I remember well that at that time I had the feeling of a spiritual light and peace and serenity in my heart in that blessed confine [the *khānaqāh*] despite not being a *murīd*, a devoted follower. Second, I found the souls of those who were constantly in attendance, such as Ḥāfiẓ ʿAbd al-Raḥmān and Mōlwī Alṭāf al-Raḥmān, had been purified from lowly traits and adorned with praiseworthy traits on account of the spiritual outpouring (*fayḍ*) and association (*suḥba*). Their moral character, simplicity, love for the *sunna* and dislike for innovation (*bidʿa*) had in a way made them copies of the Companions. Nevertheless, the thought of approaching the mawlānā for *bayʿa* did not occur to me.

After completing my studies, when I was sent as a teacher to Madrasa Mangalore in the district of Saharanpur, there developed in me a peculiar condition and an inclination to immerse in worship. At that time, the following of Qāḍī Muḥammad Ismāʿīl was in great prominence. The thought of joining his group occurred to me. However, I also felt that I should first consult my seniors and seek their permission. Thus I consulted Mawlānā Muḥammad Yaʿqūb, who wrote in response, "The paths to Allāh are as many as there are souls of people. Reaching Allāh is not confined to this way that you are following. Although it is also a way of reaching Allāh, right now it is not appropriate for you to join it."

About this time (1288/1871 or 1289/1872) the idea of *bayʿa* occurred to me. Coincidentally, Mawlānā Muḥammad Qāsim Nānōtwī happened to come to Roorkee. On my invitation he stayed at Mangalore on his return. At night, in privacy, I said to him, "He who is consulted is held in trust. I would like counsel as I have the thought of offering *bayʿa*. In our surroundings are several saintly personalities: you, Mawlānā Rashīd Aḥmad, Mawlānā Shaykh Muḥammad, and Qaḍī Muḥammad Ismāʿīl. I do not know what is best for me. If you feel that it is best for me to enter into the association of your attendants, then do accept me. If not, instruct me in whatever you feel best for me." In reply, Mawlānā Nānōtwī delivered a long speech, the essence of which was that there is none better at the time than Mawlānā Rashīd Aḥmad. "He is extremely reluctant regarding *bayʿa*," I said. "If you intercede in my behalf, the matter will be done." He responded, "Very well. When I go to Gangoh, be there."

I thus waited anxiously for the opportunity. When I was informed a few days later that the mawlānā was going to Gangoh, I immediately went and

> said to him, "When a gracious man promises, he fulfills." He smiled and said, "Well and good." During the morning, after he had discussed with Mawlānā Gangōhī, he called me. I entered, made salaam, and sat down. Mawlānā Nānōtwī was silent. With a slight smile on his face, Mawlānā Gangōhī said, "These weavers become my *murīds*. You are already the son of a shaykh and this and that. Why do you want to enter into *bayʿa* with me?" I was already awestruck when I had entered his august presence. This statement further froze my senses. I could only stammer, "Shaykh, I am worse, more contemptible, and useless than them." He responded, "Enough! Enough! Make *istikhāra*. I am coming to the mosque." I proceeded immediately to the mosque, made *wuḍū'*, performed two units of prayer and recited the sunna supplication for *istikhāra*. On Mawlānā Gangōhī's arrival, he asked, "How do you feel?" I said, "I feel the same. Accept me in your service." It chanced that Mōlwī Muḥammad Isḥāq Ambhētwī, who was the son of brother Ḥamīd ʿAlī, who was studying under and being looked after by Mawlānā Gangōhī, also came and sat down to offer *bayʿa*. Mawlānā Gangōhī instructed us both to repent and entered us into the order of servitude. All praise for that is due unto Allāh.

In the above narrative of Mawlānā Sahāranpūrī, the intercession of Mawlānā Nānōtwī is mentioned. It is, however, mentioned in *Tadhkirat al-Khalīl* that Mawlānā Sahāranpūrī had appointed as intercessor his maternal uncle Mawlānā Yaʿqūb, who, as the son of Mawlānā Gangōhī's teacher, was given a lot of attention:

> Mawlānā Sahāranpūrī had written to him: "Intercede on my behalf so that Mawlānā Gangōhī accepts me in *bayʿa*." Thus Mawlānā Yaʿqūb wrote a letter of intercession and sent it to Mawlānā Sahāranpūrī, who went with it to Gangoh.

Since the information in *Tadhkirat al-Rashīd* is from the writing of Mawlānā Sahāranpūrī himself, it will have preference. This was the initial stage of the bond of love with his shaykh. Regarding what happened thereafter can only be described in the words that Mawlānā Gangōhī used to describe himself [when he himself took *bayʿa*]: "Then I was as nothing."[24] In this regard, it is recorded in *Tadhkirat al-Rashīd* that Mawlānā Gangōhī would say:

---

24 This means wholehearted and complete engrossment in the process of achieving moral purification (trans.).

> When the time came to take *bayʿa* at the blessed hands of Ḥājī Imdādullāh, I said, "Shaykh, I am unable to apply myself to a regimen of *dhikr*, spiritual exercise, and struggle, nor am I able to wake up at night." Ḥājī Imdādullāh smiled and said, "Well, what wrong is there in that?" An attendant then asked, "Shaykh, what happened then?" Mawlānā Gangōhī gave a wonderful reply. He said, "Then I was as nothing."

Thus in 1288/1871 Mawlānā Sahāranpūrī took the *bayʿa*, and in Shawwāl 1288/1871 Mawlānā Gangōhī requested his shaykh in Makka Mukarrama, Ḥājī Imdādullāh, to appoint Mawlānā Sahāranpūrī as a *khalīfa*. As a result of this intercession, Ḥājī Imdādullāh bestowed Mawlānā Sahāranpūrī with the *khilāfa* in Muharram 1289/1872. He also presented him with a blessed turban.

Mawlānā Sahāranpūrī's spiritual condition can be appreciated from those twelve letters that appear in volume three of *Tadhkirat al-Rashīd* under the title *Makātīb-i-Rashīdiyya* and also from the five letters in *Tadhkirat al-Khalīl*. Among my friends, those who follow a regimen of *dhikr* in general, and those whom I have authorized to initiate *murīds* in particular, should repeatedly read these letters with great attention. For the sake of blessings, I reproduce here one of the letters which Mawlānā Sahāranpūrī wrote to Mawlānā Gangōhī and the latter's reply from *Tadhkirat al-Rashīd* and another one of Mawlānā Gangōhī's letters from *Tadhkirat al-Khalīl*.

Mawlānā Sahāranpūrī's Letter

> My master and lord, the medium of my day and night. May Allāh perpetuate the shadow of your blessings.
>
> The lowliest slave, the smallest of those who pay homage and the worst of the *murīds*, the disgraced Khalīl—after offering his salutations and *salāms*—wishes to say that for some time I have intended to inform you of my lowly and sorrowful condition. However, fear of being audacious and the anxiety relating to not having means became a misfortune for the self and an impediment.
>
> First, after the *bayʿa* and by virtue of [your] spiritual attention (*tawajjuh*), I felt the consolation that is felt by a child. However, since the blessed days of fasting I have been thrown into an abyss of confusion. What can I say? Instead of proximity (*qurb*) and attainment (*wiṣāl*), I am experiencing distance and feeling forsaken. It is not just loss of that spiritual state (*ḥāl*), but there is also a feeling of the matter being strait in that there is no way of proximity, joining and witnessing Him (*mushāhada*). What do I possess

with respect to the Lord of Lords, who is Most High. From the beginning until the present time, this useless one has been unable to do anything. Nevertheless, the grace of Allāh Most High has been with me by virtue of your spiritual attention. Although I have always been deficient in the fulfillment of commands, you have not curtailed me of your benevolence. As a result, I have always mustered courage [to continue]. My courage, however, is now breaking; in fact it has now broken. We have not recognized you as you deserve.

Whatever I think about, I see "the other" (*ghayr*),[25] the different types of *nūr* are *ghayr*, existence (*wujūd*) is *ghayr*, and bewilderment (*ḥayra*)[26] is *ghayr*. The heart yearns for the perception of the Divine (*idrāk*) in a formless state; this, however, appears impossible. There is no formless *idrāk*. Whatever *idrāk* occurs is coupled to some form.

The search is for You; tell us where.

The point is that my temperament remains in strange thoughts. There was, at the beginning, hope of a gracious gaze which could be seen; now it cannot be seen even when searching for it. It is as if it were something never mentioned. Along with this bewilderment, darkness can be felt which seems to be from one side. Nevertheless, all praise is for Allāh and again all praise is for Him that [the feeling of] *ḥuḍūr*[27] is intact and there is a feeling of consolation in the interior of the heart. To be more audacious and write further would be disrespectful. If there is a blessed prayer for this servant in this respect, then do instruct, as it will be a means for contentment and peace.

Let it enlighten the various sections of the heart and soul
  So that you may become a coveted full moon,
It is heard that with your light you
  Enlighten the fourteen worlds at once.

The most contemptible servant who is hopeful for your gracious gaze.

KHALĪL AḤMAD (may he be forgiven)
Saharanpur
Friday 9 Dhū 'l-Qaʿda 1315 AH

25 *Ghayr* is used by the sufis to mean things apart from Allāh Most High. Only when the heart is removed from all sorts of *ghayr* will it be in a position to be for Allāh.

26 A spiritual state of ecstatic bewilderment in Divine Presence (trans.).

27 The sense of the presence of Allāh Most High toward which sufis aspire.

Mawlānā Gangōhī's Reply

From the slave Rashīd Aḥmad (may he be forgiven).

After the sunna greeting, know that your letter has reached me. Your condition has been understood. Whatever you have written in regard to bewilderment is, in fact, divine proximity. The saints have said that those in close divine proximity dwell in bewilderment.

The essence (*dhāt*) of Allāh is beyond comprehension (*idrāk*) as is said [in the Qur'ān]: *Eyes cannot comprehend Him* (6:103). In fact, even the heart and intelligence of man cannot comprehend Him.

Other than those who have been granted the spiritual foresight of the Realm of Alast,
None else can even imagine the reality of the True Existence.[28]

That essence is absolute (*muṭlaq*). In fact, He is above absoluteness (*iṭlāq*); there is no scope for even any sense of absoluteness. Whatever has entered one's heart or mind is all *ghayr*; the Pure Being is free of all that. Hence, in such a condition, what possibility is there for a formless state? The lot of the slave is only *ḥuḍūr* and that is all. All praise is for Allāh that you have acquired a portion of this. The ḥadīth "That you worship your Lord as you are seeing Him" is everyone's purpose, and this is the claim of the Messenger of Allāh ﷺ. Fortunate is he who attains whatever amount of it.

All other spiritual conditions besides this are not the purpose. Thus, on the basis of [the Qur'ānic verse] *If you are grateful, I shall certainly increase (my bounties) for you* (14:7), continue to strive in [developing] the relationship (*nisba*) of presence *ḥuḍūr* and do not seek anything else. Hope for the kindness of Allāh.

Whatever little water the cupbearer pours us is exact kindness.

Wa 'l-salām. Pray for this slave who will also supplicate for you. 14 Dhū 'l-Qaʿda 1315

28 The translation of the Persian poems in the introduction have been kindly provided by Mawlānā Tameem Ahmadi. He provides here a brief explanation of the above poem. He says, "No human being can ever comprehend the true reality of Allāh Most High's sublime Being. The only thing that can ever perceive His existence is the heart of the gnostic (*ʿārif*) who has been endowed with the recognition (*maʿrifa*) of Allāh Most High and remembers the ancient covenant from the World of Souls (*ʿālam al-arwāḥ*) when the souls answered the call of their Sustainer saying "Of course!" The ancient covenant is referred to as the *ʿahd-i alast*, a name with roots in the Qur'ān (see 7:172).

Mawlānā Gangōhī's Second Letter

Mōlwī Khalīl Aḥmad, peace be upon you.

Your letter has arrived. I am extremely pleased to learn of the said [condition of] *ḥuḍūr* and your inability to express gratitude [for this state]—all praise for this is due unto Allāh. If every particle and hair of man were to be transformed into thousands and thousands of tongues and then one were to wish for a lengthy period of time of this world to give thanks for the most insignificant favor [of Allāh], then thanking Allāh Most High would not be possible. In fact, every intention to express thanks is also a great blessing. Who is there who can express gratitude for being accorded the condition of *ḥuḍūr*?

Yes, if Allāh accepts man's inability of giving thanks in lieu of thanks, then it would not be too remote to say that the slave is under divine favor in that such a worthless and incapable one has had dealings with the Eternal Benefactor. He should thus completely annihilate himself and become shameful. The shame of one's shortcomings and His favors should make one feel as if one is nothing. What else can be done?

It is of great thanks that you have been bestowed with this station (*maqām*) which, in the nomenclature of the Naqshbandīs, is known as *yād-dāsht*. Now, along with this *yād-dāsht*, it is essential to have shame for Allāh who is the true sovereign. Just as one will not commit a displeasing, degrading act in the presence of some senior benefactor of standing, so too should be one's attitude in privacy with that ever-present and ever-seeing (*ḥāẓir wa nāẓir*) Lord, so that the reality of *ḥuḍūr* can be complete.

Measure and weigh every act of yours, while keeping in view the Master Most High, according to the scale of the Sharīʿa, which is the law by which to acquire [His] pleasure. This meditation (*murāqaba*) should be practiced constantly. In short, one should contemplate every action in front of that Being; every action should be done or abandoned on the basis of His pleasure and displeasure. This is *iḥsān* (may Allāh grant us it). Pray for this incapable one that he also be bestowed with this. Alas, life has been wasted and the actual goal has not been attained. However, the good opinion (*ḥusn al-ẓann*) of friends can be of use so I have hope in [the ḥadīth] "I am according to the opinion which My servant has of Me."

Regarding the issue of marriage, what advice can I give? It is my firm belief that there is no freedom in anything the way there is in remaining unmarried. However, from among those necessary needs there is also marriage and to fulfill one necessity one needs to tolerate many difficulties. If there is no urge to fulfill this need then I do not feel having a family is better than remaining single. However, if the intention is to increase the Umma, then this is a different matter. Hence, I am unable to write anything clear and decisive on this issue. You know your situation more than me.

Regarding your desire to take up residence in Gangoh, what objection do I have? What else can I say? I have no objection regarding this. If you feel that it will be beneficial for you, then that is better. . .[29]

It is not my intention to write Mawlānā Sahāranpūrī's biography, for that is a massive treasure trove and *Tadhkirat al-Khalīl* is a brief sample of it. Nevertheless, as an example, I shall reproduce from *Tadhkirat al-Khalīl* some episodes relating to his knowledge, spiritual strength, and *taṣarruf* (effect):

1. [Mawlānā Ẓafar Aḥmad Thānawī relates:] On the occasion of Mawlānā Sahāranpūrī's fifth Ḥajj, when he went to the Ḥaram for the *ṭawāf al-qudūm*, this lowly one[30] was sitting by Mawlānā Muḥibb al-Dīn (who was among the senior *khalīfas* of Ḥājī Imdādullāh and a well-known man of *kashf*). At that time, Mawlānā was reciting his *wird* (daily regimen of invocation) from a book containing *ṣalāt* and *salām* when he suddenly turned to me and said: "Who has entered the Ḥaram at this time? The entire Ḥaram has all of a sudden become filled with light." I remained silent and by then Mawlānā Sahāranpūrī had just completed his circumambulation and was heading toward the Ṣafā gate for the *saʿy*. He came close to Mawlānā Muḥibb al-Dīn as his seating area was there, and the Mawlānā stood up, smiled, and said, "I can say who has today come to the Ḥaram." He then shook hands and embraced Mawlānā, who then proceeded for the *saʿy*. Mawlānā Muḥibb al-Dīn returned to his place and said to me, "Brother Ẓafar, Mawlānā Khalīl is an embodiment of light. He is nothing besides light. I did not see Mawlānā Rashīd Aḥmad but I was told that he was a *quṭb al-irshād* (pole of guidance). Having seen Mawlānā's *khalīfas* I can say that truly he was a *quṭb al-irshād* and produced such accomplished men." I then plucked up the courage and asked him what Mawlānā ʿAbd al-Raḥīm [Rāipūrī][31] is like. He replied, "He

---

29 The meaning of the next sentence here has been left untranslated as its meaning was unclear.

30 This was the fourth Ḥajj of 1328/1910 and not the fifth as Mawlānā Ẓafar Aḥmad was in Dālē in 1328/1910 (sz).

31 Mawlānā ʿAbd al-Raḥīm Rāipūrī was also one of the senior *khalīfas* of Mawlānā Gangōhī and the later shaykh of Mawlānā ʿAbd al-Qādir Rāipūrī.

is a man of very strong spiritual connection (*nisba*). It doesn't matter what type of heart one brings to him, he will purify it at once."

2. [Mawlānā ʿĀshiq Ilāhī writes:] Mawlānā Sahāranpūrī rarely employed the power of his heart for *taṣarruf*. He would only resort to it on special occasions of need. There was a debate in Saharanpur between Muslims and the [Hindu] Arya [Samaj];[32] the debate began in [the village of] Roopri and then came to Saharanpur. Mawlānā Sahāranpūrī was present in the gathering. Mōlwī Kifāyatullāh and Mōlwī Aḥmadullāh were, on behalf of the Muslims, appointed to record the proceedings. Mōlwī Aḥmadullāh became tired and Mōlwī Kifāyatullāh completed this duty.

He writes that in the debate, on the side of the Arya, was a young *sadhu* dressed in beautiful red and reclining in an armchair. When a Muslim speaker began his speech, the *sadhu* would sit up and lower his head [most likely in some type of meditation and hypnotism]. As a consequence, the speeches of the Muslim speakers were extremely disjointed and poorly delivered. Even Mawlānā ʿAbd al-Ḥaq Ḥaqqānī was unable to present his arguments on infinite regress (*tasalsul*) and circular reasoning (*dawr*) well.

I [Mawlānā ʿĀshiq Ilāhī] wrote a note to the head of the event, Mirzā ʿAzīz Baig, informing him that when a Muslim speaker takes the stand this yogi casts his hypnotizing influence and Mawlānā Khalīl Aḥmad should be notified. He passed the note to the Mawlānā. On reading the note, Mawlānā Sahāranpūrī immediately lowered his head and thus commenced the battle of truth and falsehood between the spiritual hearts of the two. Two minutes had not passed before the *sadhu* stood up from the armchair, looking restless, and departed. Thereafter, the speeches of the Muslim speakers were like a dam had been opened. Ultimately, even though there were many unseemly occurrences at that debate, eleven people were blessed with Islam.

During the afternoon meals on the same day, Mawlānā Sahāranpūrī said, "I firmly believed that Islam would remain dominant. Truth dominates and cannot be dominated. But Allāh Most High is without need. His fear should be at all times and with everyone."

3. After the annual graduation ceremony of Maẓāhir ʿUlūm, the out-of-town guests left. The train for the Punjab arrived first and guests heading

32 The latter part of 19th century and the early part of 20th century in India saw the launch of the Shuddhi movement by the Arya Samaj, a move to convert, among several other groups, Muslims to Hinduism. The Shuddhi campaign was considered a grave challenge at the time and led to Muslim scholars carrying out intense *daʿwa* work.

there took their seats. A *sadhu* was seated in a carriage having come from Hardwar.[33] Seeing the crowds at the station he enquired where they had come from. One of Mawlānā Sahāranpūrī's attendants, who was in that carriage, informed him that there was a great shaykh in Saharanpur that people from various places had come to meet and they were now returning home. He asked further regarding Mawlānā Sahāranpūrī and then sat down silently. The attendant explained, "After a while, I experienced an alien feeling and severe pressure on my heart. I could not fathom what the reason was for this; my heart was gripped by fear from within and was becoming blocked. I was in bewilderment. Was it day or night? Was I in a gathering or alone? Was I in a full carriage or in the wilderness? I wondered why this bewilderment and worry had overcome me. I was losing myself and had gone dumb, unable to speak. I suddenly saw the resemblance of Mawlānā Sahāranpūrī, whose reflection began to fall on my heart. He commanded me to read: *ḥasbiya 'Llāhu wa niʿma 'l-wakīl* (Allāh is sufficient for me, and he is the best disposer of affairs).

Although my tongue was numb, I began the litany with my heart and the clouds of fear and restlessness began to disperse. Within a few minutes, the terrible condition disappeared and my heart was at peace. I then heard the *sadhu* saying, "Truly, your guru is highly qualified and very powerful." I understood that he had been influencing me and so I said, "Do you only have this much ability? You could have at least demonstrated a little better." The *sadhu* seemed close to tears. He turned away and never spoke again to me.

How much of Mawlānā Sahāranpūrī's perfect qualities should I keep writing, especially in this brief piece?

The extent of my sight is limited and the flowers of your beauty are too many,
The flowers of your spring (garden) complain of the incapacity of my (limited) sight.
It (the praise of your excellent qualities) cannot be cut short, thus I have abandoned the attempt to expound,
The story (of your genius and brilliance) is never-ending, thus I have chosen to adopt silence.

It has already been mentioned that Mawlānā Sahāranpūrī's illness began with the completion of *Badhl al-Majhūd*. Sometimes he would be well and

33 Hardwar (or Haridwar) is a town located close to Saharanpur. The River Ganges, a popular site of Hindu pilgrimage, flows through the town.

sometimes he would be in difficulty. In reality, his health and strength were founded on the eagerness and desire to complete *Badhl al-Majhūd.* At the end of Ramaḍān he experienced the effects of partial paralysis. This too would sometimes disappear, only to reappear later. Even on ʿĪd al-Fiṭr, the effect of the paralysis was predominant. Therefore he was unable to attend the ʿĪd prayers in the Prophet's Mosque ﷺ. However, he regained some strength later and would go to the mosque with the aid of a cane. In the month of Rabīʿ al-Thānī 1346/1927, his illness intensified: sometimes it would be fever, sometimes colds, and sometimes paralysis. When the illness would be severe, it would be difficult to go to the Prophet's Mosque. When he felt somewhat better, he would go to the mosque with the support of a stick and an assistant.

After we had returned from Madīna Ṭayba, Mawlānā Sahāranpūrī would continue attending the Noble Ḥaram, albeit with some difficulty. In the first week of Rabīʿ al-Thānī 1346/1927 he experienced chest pain, which would disappear when massaged. In the second week, on the request of some *ʿulamāʾ* of Madīna, he began delivering lessons on *Sunan Abī Dāwūd* after ʿaṣr at the residence of Mawlānā Sayyid Aḥmad. After imparting lessons for two days, Saturday and Sunday, he mentioned while returning from ẓuhr on Monday that he was once again experiencing chest pains. He added that he had felt similar pain three or four days earlier, which disappeared within two or three hours after being massaged. On reaching the house, he was massaged. At the time of ʿaṣr, although the pain had decreased, he was very weak and was not able to go to the Noble Ḥaram. He therefore performed ʿaṣr at home behind Mōlwī Sayyid Aḥmad and, in spite of his weakness, stood and offered the prayer. His weakness increased and instead of feeling feverish he started to feel cold and sweaty. He could not perform Maghrib standing and instead sat and requested Mōlwī Sayyid Aḥmad to make the prayer short and quick. He was unable to get down for ʿIshāʾ and prayed on his bed. Despite the weakness, restlessness, and increased pain, he spent the night reciting the formula [of *tawḥīd*, *Lā ilāha illa 'Llāh*], invocations of forgiveness, and invocations of blessing and peace on the Messenger of Allāh ﷺ. He did not sleep even a little.

On Tuesday morning, he again performed Fajr sitting in bed. His cold sweat continued to increase, and it was clear this would be his last morning. His attendants continued to administer medication during the day, but he was unable to urinate or digest the medicine. He was overcome with so much weakness at the time of ẓuhr that he was unable to make ablution. He offered the prayer on the bed sitting down, having performed *tayammum* (dry ablution). Movement then became very difficult and he was in need of someone to help him. By ʿaṣr, his sense of awareness had further deteriorated; he did not perform the *rukūʿ* when the imām said *Allāhu Akbar*, but only did so when Ḥājī Maqbūl said the word *rukūʿ* and gestured. The same happened when it came to the *sajda*. He completed the four *rakʿas* like this with much difficulty and was then made to lie down. His silence then increased; before this he understood what was being said and was able to answer and speak for himself. At Maghrib time, when Mawlānā Sayyid Aḥmad arrived to lead the prayer, Mawlānā Sahāranpūrī was in total oblivion; he did not give an answer and did not have the strength to lift himself. His attendants offered their prayers separately and waited for the mawlānā to recover slightly so he might be informed about Maghrib prayer. His relationship with the world was now completely severed. Besides *pās anfās*,[34] there was no other movement. He did not ask for anything or respond. During the night, Zamzam water was given, but it passed his throat with much difficulty.

Twenty-four hours had passed in complete silence, and on Thursday 16 Rabīʿ al-Thānī 1346/1927 in Arabia, 15 Rabīʿ al-Thānī in India, Mawlānā Sahāranpūrī went to his final abode, proclaiming aloud "Allāh! Allāh!" His eyes then closed and he was silent.

In spite of the short time available, speedy burial arrangements were made with divine assistance. The pilgrim guide Sayyid Aḥmad Tawwāb washed the body while Abū Saʿūd poured water. Mōlwī Sayyid Aḥmad and Mōlwī ʿAbd al-Karīm assisted. The body was quickly prepared and brought outside the Prophet's Mosque and placed near Jibrīl Gate for the funeral prayer. After Maghrib prayer, Mawlānā Shaykh Ṭayyib, the rector of Madrasat al-ʿUlūm al-Sharʿiyya, led the funeral prayer, after which the body was taken to Jannat al-Baqīʿ. Even though there was very little time to spread the news of the mawlānā's demise, the crowd was so large that many did not receive the opportunity to carry the bier, despite their best efforts to do so. It was considered a great blessing to be able to simply touch the bier.

> O the one whose countenance is a sight of wonder to behold for all the worlds!
> To which sight are you headed toward to behold?

Finally, his enlightened body, which had been dissolved by the burning of divine love, was committed to its grave before ʿIshā', next to the dome of

34 *Pās anfās*, a Persian term meaning "guarding the breath," is a method of *dhikr* through a breathing exercise that consists of concentrating on the word *Allāh* when inhaling and on the syllable *-hū* when exhaling.

the Ahl al-Bayt. That night was a night of extreme happiness, for that desire was fulfilled that he had repeatedly expressed in both speech and writing: "Would that my remains be mingled with the holy sand of Baqīʿ." All praise is for Allāh. "Surely, we belong to Allāh, and to Him shall we return" (2:156). "To Allāh belongs that which He takes and that which He gives. Everyone who is on it [the earth] has to perish. And your Lord's Countenance will remain, full of majesty, full of honor" (55:26–27).

Mawlānā's Dream

The day before his illness, Mawlānā Sahāranpūrī said:

> In a dream, I saw myself in a building beneath which is a basement. The ceiling was made of wooden boards, of which two were loose and hanging down. I descended very easily into it [through them] and discovered that it was a very large, solidly built, and well-lit structure. On the one side was a door from which a light and some other illuminated objects shone. I intended to return via the opening in the ceiling where the two boards were hanging. My mind then drifted from there and my eyes opened.

He then interpreted the dream thus: "The final moment will come at its time. However, in this dream is the glad tiding that there will be, Allāh-willing, ease for me in the grave. The illuminated door indicates the door of Paradise, as is confirmed in the ḥadīth." After Mōlwī Sayyid Aḥmad heard the interpretation and left, Mawlānā Sahāranpūrī called his wife and, in beseeching fashion, said, "Whatever your rights are over me, even if I had spoken harshly to you, for Allāh's sake forgive me." He then addressed his brother, Ḥājī Maqbūl Aḥmad, who had been living with him for many years: "I was angry with you many times and had spoken harshly to you. Do forgive me." (*Tadhkirat al-Khalīl*)

It is possible that Mawlānā ʿĀshiq Ilāhī has narrated this dream in a shortened form or that it is another dream that Mawlānā Sahāranpūrī saw after my return from Madīna Ṭayba. The latter is more likely. In my presence, Mawlānā Sahāranpūrī had mentioned a similar dream. He said that after the removal of the loose boards, he reached Jannat al-ʿAdn and then Shaykh Rashīd Aḥmad appeared. Mawlānā Sahāranpūrī then asked me to interpret the dream, but I declared my inability to do so. He then said: "In the dream, Allāh-willing, are the good tidings of Jannat al-ʿAdn." It is my understanding that Shaykh Rashīd Aḥmad refers to his shaykh, Mawlānā Gangōhī. The meeting of souls after death has been transmitted [in ḥadīth].

May Allāh Most High bestow even a small part of the spiritual outpouring (*fayḍ*) of these seniors to this humble one, for this is not far from His Grace. Verily, He is Magnanimous, Gracious, Affectionate and Merciful.

TABWĪB-ḤIKAM

Tabwīb al-Ḥikam, the translation of which is *Itmām al-Niʿam*, is the work of Mawlānā Shaykh ʿAlī Muttaqī Burhānpūrī. This in turn is a rearrangement (*Tabwīb*) of the *Ḥikam* of the shaykh of shaykhs and the pole (*quṭb*) of the world, Shaykh Ibn ʿAṭā'illāh al-Iskandarī. The *Ḥikam* is a famous work on *taṣawwuf*. It is unparalleled in the mysteries and secrets of the science, but it is not chaptered or arranged in some other systematic way. This is why Shaykh ʿAlī Muttaqī arranged it in a systematic order [of topics] and divided it into thirty chapters.

A brief life sketch of the author of the *Ḥikam* and the author of *Tabwīb al-Ḥikam* has been given by Mawlānā Muḥammad Ḥayāt Sambhalī, the chief administrator of Madrasa Ḥayāt al-ʿUlūm Moradabad. His writing appears at the beginning of some editions of *Ikmāl al-Shiyam*. I shall here record something of the biographies of these two authors, a portion of which is from Mawlānā Sambhalī's writings and the other from elsewhere.

SHAYKH IBN ʿAṬĀ'ILLĀH AL-ISKANDARĪ THE AUTHOR OF THE *ḤIKAM*

His name is Aḥmad ibn Muḥammad ibn ʿAbd al-Karīm ibn ʿAṭā'illāh al-Iskandarī. His title is Tāj al-Dīn and teknonym is Abū 'l-Faḍl. He belonged to the Shādhilī order and followed the Mālikī school. He is the student of Shaykh Taqī [al-Dīn] al-Subkī. Among his teachers is Shaykh Abū 'l-ʿAbbās al-Mursī, who was among the select pupils of the Shaykh of the Group (*shaykh al-ṭā'ifa*), Abū 'l-Ḥasan al-Shādhilī. It is well known that Shaykh Abū 'l-ʿAbbās was the sole inheritor of the knowledge of Shaykh Abū 'l-Ḥasan al-Shādhilī.

Shaykh Ibn ʿAṭā'illāh was among the great ascetics and top-ranking people of his time. His speech produces [spiritual] sweetness in souls. He passed away from this transitory abode to the eternal abode of bliss in the year 709/1309 at Qarāfa, near Cairo (see *Al-Ṭabaqāt al-Kubrā* of Shaykh ʿAbd al-Wahhāb al-Shaʿrānī). Some of his works include *Al-Tanwīr fī Ithbāt al-Taqdīr*, *Al-Ḥikam al-ʿAṭā'iyya* and *Laṭā'if al-Minan*. When he composed the *Ḥikam* he showed it to his teacher, Shaykh Abū 'l-ʿAbbās al-Mursī, who read it with attention and said, "My son, in this treatise you have discharged the aims of all friends and even more." This book has been greatly accepted by the elite; hence the many commentaries that have been written on it. Shaykh [Aḥmad] Zarrūq wrote three. Besides this, Shaykh Muḥammad ibn Ibrāhīm [ibn ʿAbbād al-Rundī] wrote *Ghayth al-Mawāhib* [*al-ʿAliyya*] and his son, ʿAlī ibn Muḥammad ibn Ibrāhīm, wrote the *Tanbīh.* A number of other commentaries have also been written, as recorded by the author of *Kashf al-Ẓunūn.*

Mawlānā Ḥayāt has reported two of his miracles from *Jāmiʿ Karāmāt al-Awliyā'* of Shaykh Yūsuf ibn Ismāʿīl al-Nabahānī who cites them on the authority of Shaykh ʿAbd al-Ra'ūf al-Munāwī al-Miṣrī, a commentator of the *Ḥikam.*[35] These miracles are as follows:

1. ʿAllāma Kamāl Ibn al-Humām, the author of *Fatḥ al-Qadīr*, visited the grave of Shaykh Ibn ʿAṭā'illāh al-Iskandarī; while reciting Sūra Hūd, when he reached the verse "Among them are the unfortunate and fortunate ones" (11:105), the shaykh's voice came from the grave, saying, "O Kamāl, among us are no unfortunate ones." It was for this reason that, at that time of his death, he instructed that he be buried close to the grave of Shaykh Ibn ʿAṭā'illāh. In addition to being an imām of fiqh and ḥadīth, Allāh Most High had granted Shaykh Ibn al-Humām al-Ḥanafī a high rank in unveilings (*kashf*) and miracles. He died on Friday 7 Ramaḍān 861/1456; *nūr-i Khūdā* (light of Allāh) was the date of his death [according to the Abjad Notation system].[36] According to some *ʿulamā'* he was among the *ʿabdāl* (substitutes). Imām Suyūṭī states in *Bughyat al-Wuʿā* [*fī Ṭabaqāt al-Lughawiyyīn*] that Ibn al-Humām was a powerful debater who would often say that in the rational sciences (*maʿqūlāt*) he was not *muqallid* of anyone.

2. One of Shaykh Ibn ʿAṭā'illāh's students had gone for the Ḥajj. Although he had left his *shaykh* in his place at home, he was astonished to see him on the *maṭāf* (around the Kaʿba), the Maqām of Ibrahim and other places. On his return, he inquired from others if the *shaykh* had gone for the Ḥajj after his departure. People replied in the negative. When he went to meet his *shaykh*, he narrated the several occasions they had met during the Ḥajj. On hearing this the *shaykh* smiled. Similar episodes relating to other *walīs* appear in my book *Faḍā'il-i Ḥajj.*

---

35 His commentary is *Al-Durar al-Jawhariyya fī Sharḥ Ḥikam al-ʿAṭā'iyya.*

36 The Abjad Notation is a numeral system in which the twenty-eight letters of the Arabic alphabet are assigned numerical values that are then aggregated to assign numerical values to Arabic words; the system can also be used in a reverse fashion to create words from numbers.

MAWLĀNĀ ʿALĪ MUTTAQĪ
AUTHOR OF *TABWĪB AL-ḤIKAM*

His lineage in *Nuzhat al-Khawāṭir*[37] is as follows: "The shaykh, the imām, the great *ʿālim*, the ḥadīth scholar ʿAlī ibn Ḥusām al-Dīn ibn ʿAbd al-Malik ibn Qāḍīkhān Muttaqī al-Shādhilī al-Madīnī al-Chishtī al-Burhānpūrī." His ancestors were from Jaunpur [U.P. India]. For some reason, Mawlānā's father, Ḥusām al-Dīn, migrated to Burhanpur, where Mawlānā ʿAlī Muttaqī was born during the year 885/1480. In some books the erroneous date of 857/1453 is given. I have explained this error in detail in the introduction of *Lāmiʿ al-Darārī*.

At the age of eight, his father had him offer *bayʿa* to Shāh Bājin, whose proper name is Bahā' al-Dīn Chishtī. Shāh Bājin was a renowned *ʿālim* and a great *walī* of his time. Mawlānā ʿAlī Muttaqī acquired his knowledge at the primary level from him. After Shāh Bājin's death in 912/1506, Mawlānā ʿAlī Muttaqī became a *murīd* of his son, Shāh ʿAbd al-Ḥakīm, and for a considerable time he remained in his company in acquisition of the exoteric and esoteric sciences. He also acquired *khilāfa* from him in the Chishtī order.

He then went to Multan, where he remained for some time in the service of Shaykh Ḥusām al-Dīn Muttaqī and derived much benefit from him. In 952/1545, with the intention of proceeding to Makka Mukarrama, he left Multan and arrived in Gujarat. During that time, Indian Ḥajj pilgrims would travel to the Arab lands from Gujarat, which was under the reign of Sultan Maḥmūd III.[38] The sultan met the shaykh with great honor and respect. He hosted the shaykh for several months as his guest. Thereafter, he left for Makka Mukarrama.

In Makka he studied ḥadīth and *taṣawwuf* under the Egyptian Shaykh Abū 'l-Ḥasan al-Bakrī al-Shāfiʿī, on whose *wilāya* there exists the consensus of all the *ʿulamā'*, and Shaykh Muḥammad ibn Muḥammad al-Sakhāwī, who was a great Arabian scholar. The benefit which Mawlānā ʿAlī Muttaqī derived from these august personalities was in the field of ḥadīth and *taṣawwuf*. He also acquired *khilāfa* in the Qādirī, Shādhilī, and Madīnī Sufi orders.

Since it was difficult to use and benefit from ʿAllāma Suyūṭī's *Jamʿ al-Jawāmiʿ*, which is written in alphabetical order according to the *masānīd*

---

37 This is *Nuzhat al-Khawāṭir wa Bahjat al-Masāmiʿ wa 'l-Nawāẓir* (or *Al-Iʿlām biman fī Tārīkh al-Hind min al-Aʿlām*), an eight-volume biographical work on the luminaries of the Indian subcontinent.

38 Sultan Mahmud III was a sultan of the Muzaffarid dynasty that ruled Gujarat from 793/1391 until 991/1583. Mahmud III was sultan of Gujarat from 944/1537 until 961/1554.

genre of ḥadīth writing, Shaykh ʿAlī Muttaqī simplified it by rearranging it into chapters and paragraphs and named it *Kanz al-ʿUmmāl*. This is now a famous book of ḥadīth published in Hyderabad and is known throughout the world; it is an extremely beneficial book. Besides *Kanz al-ʿUmmāl*, the shaykh wrote many other books which, according to the author of *Abjad al-ʿUlūm*,[39] number more than a hundred.

Shaykh ʿAbd al-Wahhāb Muttaqī, who was the close student of Shaykh ʿAlī Muttaqī, records many wonderful episodes and miracles of his shaykh in his book *Itḥāf al-Taqī fī Faḍl al-Shaykh ʿAlī al-Muttaqī*. One of these episodes, he writes, was when the shaykh's death drew close. He was overwhelmed by enthusiasm on the night. He called Shaykh ʿAbd al-Wahhāb and instructed, "Recite that poem." Shaykh ʿAbd al-Wahhāb said, "I understood the poem he was referring to and so recited [the following in Persian]:

> Never will come to (my) sight a better countenance than your face.
> Not the sun, nor the moon, not the nymph, nor the fairy.

"On hearing the poem, the shaykh went into a state of ecstasy and instructed me to repeat it. I repeated it several times. By that time, an attendant announced that meals were ready and so the shaykh said, 'Make it into a *kuchwandā*.' It was the shaykh's practice to mix all foods together before eating. He then instructed the attendant to mix the food such that it became one and there remained no trace of another in the way it has been said in another couplet. . . ."[40]

Regarding the mixing of different foods, as mentioned above, it was also the practice of my honorable father, Mawlānā Muḥammad Yaḥyā. When my father's food, and that of Mawlānā ʿAbd al-Laṭīf (the ex-chief administrator of Madrasa Maẓāhir ʿUlūm), Mawlānā Ẓafar Aḥmad Thānawī (a teacher at the madrasa) and other teachers and students would arrive from their respective homes, all of their curries would be mixed in a large plate and they would eat together. Sometimes chapatti would be added to the mixture; meat would also be cooked and added to the stew, which was called *tharīd*. It was very delicious.

Shaykh ʿAbd al-Wahhāb said that Shaykh ʿAlī passed the entire night in this state of enthusiasm. At the time of death, his blessed head was resting on the thighs of Shaykh ʿAbd al-Wahhāb while he was engrossed in the *dhikr* of Allāh. He died, aged ninety, on 2 Jumādā al-Ūlā 975/1567. Shaykh ʿAbd

39 That is, Nawāb Ṣiddīq Ḥasan Khān.

40 We were unable to work out the meaning of the couplet here.

al-Ḥaqq, the ḥadīth scholar of Delhi, gives a lengthy account of Shaykh ʿAlī Muttaqī in five chapters of his book *Zād al-Muttaqīn*. Mawlānā Ḥayāt also narrates many miracles of Shaykh ʿAlī Muttaqī, of which is the following:

> Approximately twelve or fourteen years after the death of Shaykh ʿAlī Muttaqī, his paternal cousin's son, Aḥmad, died. Before dying, Aḥmad had expressed the wish to be buried in the grave of a saintly person. Since it is the practice in Makka to open up old graves to bury others, it was decided to bury the deceased in the grave of Shaykh ʿAlī Muttaqī. When the grave was opened up, the shaykh's blessed body was discovered intact with the shroud in the same way in which it had been buried years ago, despite the fact that bodies disintegrate and transform into earth within a short while on account of the peculiar characteristics of the sand of Makka Mukarrama.

It is recorded in *Abjad al-ʿUlūm* that Shaykh ʿAbd al-Wahhāb said, "I saw the Messenger of Allāh ﷺ in a dream. I asked, 'O Messenger of Allāh, who is the noblest in this age?' The Prophet of Allāh replied, 'Your shaykh, then Muḥammad Ṭāhir.'" This anecdote is narrated in greater detail in *Nuzhat al-Khawāṭir*, and it is a wonderful incident. The author of *Nuzhat al-Khawāṭir* has narrated on the authority of *Al-Nūr al-Sāfir*[41] and mentions the following:

> On the night of 27 Ramaḍān, Shaykh ʿAlī Muttaqī saw the Messenger of Allāh ﷺ in a dream and inquired, "O Messenger of Allāh, who is the noblest in this age." The Messenger of Allāh replied, "You." The shaykh then asked, "O Messenger of Allāh, then who?" He replied, "Muḥammad Ṭāhir Hindī." The very same night, Shaykh ʿAbd al-Wahhāb saw the dream which was mentioned earlier. In the morning he presented himself in the service of Shaykh ʿAlī Muttaqī to relate his dream. However, before he had even spoken, Shaykh ʿAlī Muttaqī said, "Last night, I also saw a dream similar to the dream you saw."

The author of the *Nuzha* has elaborately written the biography of Shaykh ʿAlī Muttaqī. Mawlānā Ḥayāt has also recorded the following testament *waṣiyya* of the shaykh:

> In the name of Allāh, Most Compassionate, Most Merciful. Peace and blessings on our master Muḥammad and on all his family and companions.

41 *Al-Nūr al-Sāfir fī Akhbār al-Qarn al-ʿĀshir* is an index of major events and people of note in 10th century Hijaz, Yemen and Gujarat by Shaykh ʿAbd al-Qādir al-ʿAydarus (d. 1038/1628), who was born in Ahmedabad of mixed Haḍramī-Gujarati lineage.

This is the testament written by the one who is entirely dependent on Allāh, ʿAlī ibn Ḥusām, who is known as Muttaqī. This testament has been written on the day which was the day of departure from this world and the day of entry into the Hereafter.

When this lowly one was a child, my father (may Allāh be pleased with him) had me initiated as a *murīd* of the illustrious Shaykh Bājin (may his secret be sanctified). His order was the way of loftiness, purity, and ecstasy. When I attained the age of discernment between right and wrong, I chose and was pleased with him as my shaykh. They [the Sufis] have said that when a child is made the *murīd* of a shaykh, after reaching maturity, he has the option of remaining a *murīd* of his shaykh or of entering the association of another shaykh of his choice. I agreed with my father in what he had chosen for me.

After the death of my father and my shaykh (may Allāh be pleased with them both), I acquired the mantle of the Chishtī shaykhs from Shaykh ʿAbd al-Ḥakīm, the son of Shaykh Bajin (may his secret be sanctified). Thereafter, I yearned for such a shaykh who would guide me along the lofty and precarious stages of the Path of Truth. I therefore turned my gaze to Multan and stayed in the service of the gnostic (*ʿārif*) of Allāh Shaykh Ḥusām al-Dīn Muttaqī ﷺ for some time.

I then journeyed to the two Noble Sanctuaries [Makka and Madīna]. There I chose the companionship of the *ʿārif* of Allāh Shaykh Abū ʾl-Ḥasan al-Bakrī (may his secret be sanctified). From him I acquired *khilāfa* in the Qādirī, Shādhilī and Madīnī orders. I also gained *khilāfa* in these three from Shaykh Muḥammad bin Muḥammad al-Sakhāwī (may his secret be sanctified).

His Students

Shaykh ʿAlī Muttaqī had numerous students. Mawlānā Ḥayāt has mentioned some of them:

Shaykh ʿAbd al-Wahhāb Muttaqī was born in Burhanpur. His father passed away while he was in early childhood. At the age of twelve he was sent to Gujarat, the Deccan, and other cities to acquire knowledge. At twenty, in 963/1555, he went to Makka Mukarrama, where he stayed in the service of Shaykh ʿAlī Muttaqī and attained accomplishment in both the exoteric and esoteric sciences. Shaykh ʿAlī Muttaqī appointed him as his *khalīfa* on the day of his death. After the demise of his shaykh, he spent thirty-six years in Makka imparting the knowledge of ḥadīth and fiqh. He died in

1001/1592. He wrote a biography of his teacher entitled *Itḥāf al-Taqī fī faḍl al-Shaykh ʿAlī al-Muttaqī*. The famous ḥadīth scholar of India Shaykh ʿAbd al-Ḥaqq Muḥaddith Dihlawī is one of his students.

Shaykh Muḥammad Ṭāhir Patnī, whose actual name is Muḥammad ibn Ṭāhir, as he himself states in the introduction of his book *Tadhkirat al-Mawḍūʿāt*. However, in Gujarat, the father's name is made part of the son's name. The author of *Nuzhat al-Khawāṭir* states his lineage as follows: The shaykh, the great *ʿālim*, ḥadīth scholar, lexicographer, the *ʿallāma*, the reviver of the faith, Muḥammad ibn Ṭāhir ibn ʿAlī al-Ḥanafī Patnī al-Gujarātī. He was born in Patan [Gujarat] in 913/1507 as part of the Bohra community, which is a prominent community of Gujarat. This community had embraced Islam at the hands of Shaykh Mullā ʿAlī Ḥaydarī, whose grave is in Khambat, a well-known place in Gujarat. According to the author of *Nuzhat al-Khawāṭir*, this community accepted Islam approximately seven centuries before his time.

In the time of Shaykh Muḥammad Ṭāhir, the heresy of Muḥammad Jōnpūrī[42] was fast spreading in the Indian subcontinent and the Bohra community was following him. Muḥammad Jōnpūrī had proclaimed himself the Mahdī, and it is because of this that his sect is called the Mahdawī. When Shaykh Muḥammad Ṭāhir returned to Gujarat from Makka, and saw the deplorable condition of his people, he removed his turban from his head and pledged, "As long as this heresy has not been eradicated, I shall not don a turban."

In 980/1572, Akbar Shāh conquered Gujarat and met Shaykh Muḥammad Ṭāhir in Patan. The king tied the turban with his hands and pledged, "The eradication of this *bidʿa*, in accordance with your wish, is my responsibility." Appointing Khān Aʿẓam Mirzā ʿAzīz the governor of Gujarat, the king instructed him to eliminate this heresy in fulfillment of the command of the shaykh. The governor gave full assistance to the shaykh. However, in 985/1577, ʿAbd al-Raḥīm [Mirzā] Khān, who was a Shiite, was appointed governor. He aided the Mahdawī sect, and so the shaykh set out on a journey to Akbarabad to lodge a complaint about the new governor. Muḥammad Jōnpūrī's disciples martyred him along the way in the year 986/1578. His body was transported to Patan. Among his writings, the book *Majmaʿ Biḥār* [*al-Anwār fī Gharāʾib al-Tanzīl wa Laṭāʾif al-Akhbār*] is famous in the field

42 Muḥammad Jōnpūrī (d. 911/1505) claimed to be the awaited Imām Mahdī and created a large following in Gujarat. He died in the town of Farah, Afghanistan.

of ḥadīth. His other well-known books are *Al-Mughnī fī Ḍabṭ Asmā' al-Rijāl*, *Qānūn al-Mawḍū'āt* and *Tadhkirat al-Mawḍū'āt*. It is also necessary to point out that he was a follower of the Ḥanafī school. He himself explicitly mentions this in both his *Tadhkirat al-Mawḍū'āt* and *Qānūn al-Mawḍū'āt*, in which he writes:

> Thus the lowliest of the slaves of Allāh Most High, Muḥammad ibn Ṭāhir ibn 'Alī, al-Hindī by ethnicity, Patnī by parentage, Bohra (that is, traders) by cultural heritage, and Ḥanafī in legal doctrine.

Such has also been written in *Tadhkirat al-Mawḍū'āt*; those who have written that he was a Shāfi'ī have erred.

Shāh Muḥammad ibn Faḍlullāh Burhānpūrī Ṣiddīqī was initially the *murīd* of Shaykh Ṣafī Gujarātī. Thereafter, he went to Makka Mukarrama and spent approximately twelve years in the service of Shaykh 'Alī Muttaqī, achieving accomplishment in both the exoteric and esoteric sciences. After his return from Makka, he continued teaching and imparting knowledge. He died in 1029/1619 in Burhanpur.

Shaykh Shihāb al-Dīn ibn Ḥajar al-Makkī was among the distinguished *'ulamā'* of Arabia. He is the author of numerous well-known books, including *Al-Khayrāt al-Ḥisān fī Manāqib al-Nu'mān*, *Al-Fatāwā al-Kubrā*, *Sharḥ Shamā'il al-Tirmidhī*, *Sharḥ al-Mishkāt*, *Al-Zawājir 'an Iqtirāf al-Kabā'ir*. Regarding the last book, it is said that there is no better book on the subject of major sins. In refutation of the Rawāfiḍ, he wrote *Al-Ṣawā'iq al-Muḥriqa*, which is well-known. Besides these, he has written many other books, which are mentioned in *Abjad al-'Ulūm*.

He was initially Shaykh 'Alī Muttaqī's teacher; he later became his student. He also acquired *khilāfa* from Shaykh 'Alī Muttaqī. His lineage is Aḥmad ibn Muḥammad ibn 'Alī ibn Ḥajar. He was an *imām* in both *fiqh* and ḥadīth. He was born in the month of Rajab 909/1503 and his father passed away when he was an infant. He studied the primary books by the shaykhs of the time. In 924/1518 he enrolled at Azhar University, where he acquired knowledge from the famous shaykhs of Egypt. Toward the end of 933/1526, he moved to Makka Mukarrama, where he became occupied with issuing *fatwas* and teaching and later died there. He travelled to Egypt once or twice during his stay in Makka.

Among his books is *Tuḥfat al-Muḥtāj Sharḥ Minhāj al-Nawawī*, a voluminous work on Shāfi'ī *fiqh*. Apart from this, numerous other books that he authored are mentioned in the notes on *Al-Fawā'id al-Bahiyya*. According to the author of *Abjad al-ʿUlūm*, on the authority of Shaykh ʿAbd al-Ḥaqq, he died in 975/1567. However, the year 995/1586 is mentioned in the notes on *Al-Fawāʾid al-Bahiyya*.

Since the translation of the introduction of *Tabwīb al-Ḥikam*, which appears at the beginning of *Itmām al-Niʿam*, was not included in *Ikmāl al-Shiyam*, I am reproducing it here.

> In the name of Allāh, Most Merciful, Mercy Giving. All praises are for Allāh, who lifts the veil from subtleties and secrets for His elect servants. Peace and blessing be upon our Master, Muhammad, who is the chosen one of that auspicious group to whom wisdom and prophecy were bestowed. Furthermore, may peace and blessings be upon his progeny and Companions, who are the founts and resorts in the fields of spiritual subtleties and mysteries.
>
> To proceed: this humble servant dependent on the benevolence of the Independent One, ʿAlī ibn Ḥusām al-Dīn, known by the title Muttaqī Hindī (May Allāh forgive him, his parents and all the believers), says: When I saw the book, the *Ḥikam*, which is the work of the imām, specialist and gnostic Abū ʾl Faḍl Tāj al-Dīn Aḥmad ibn ʿAbd al-Karīm ibn ʿAṭāʾ al-Iskandarī, and found it to be the most excellent of all books in the science of the of knowledge of the sufis, then even though the early sufis did embark on writing commentaries on it, they did not, to the best of my knowledge, attempt to systematically arrange it in the form of chapters. It occurred in my heart that I would arrange the aphorisms into chapters under relevant headings to facilitate the learning of the words of wisdom and their meanings. This arrangement would then also act as a concise commentary. I name it *Al-Nahj al-Atamm fī Tabwīb al-Ḥikam* (The best approach in the arrangement of the aphorisms) and set it out in thirty chapters.

This completes the introduction of this humble one. Now, in the name of Allāh, the actual book *Ikmāl al-Shiyam* commences.

ZAKARIYYĀ KĀNDHLAWĪ
Friday 4 Jumādā ʾl-Ūlā 1387

THE BOOK *of* WISDOMS

KITĀB AL-ḤIKAM

A Collection of Sufi Aphorisms

Shaykh Ibn ʿAṭāʾillāh al-Iskandarī

Translated by Victor Danner

With commentary Ikmāl al-Shiyam by

SHAYKH ʿABDULLĀH GANGŌHĪ

Forewords

After praising Allāh and sending peace and blessing on the Prophet, I would like to submit that this unworthy and sinful one is completely incapable of writing a commentary of *Itmām al-Ni'am* the translation of *Tabwīb al-Ḥikam*. The task of explaining such subject matters is of those individuals who are acquainted with this science. This sinful one has obeyed the instructions of our master and *murshid*, the medium of my days, Mawlānā Khalīl Aḥmad (may the Most High lengthen his shadow), and with the use of commentaries I have written whatever has come to mind in any which way. There might be, rather, there will be, many mistakes in this. Wherever the people of insight see a mistake, let them rectify them and let them do so with discretion. If this commentary—through the blessings of Mawlānā Sahāranpūrī—is of any benefit, then please remember me in your prayers.

Muḥammad 'Abdullāh [Gangōhī]
(may he be forgiven)
Wednesday 12 Rabī' al-Thānī 1337/1919

All praises are for Allāh. We praise Him, seek His aid, and seek His forgiveness. We believe in Him and trust in Him. We take protection with Allāh from the evils of ourselves and from the evils of our deeds. Whomever Allāh guides, none can lead astray; and whomever He leads astray, none can guide. We bear witness that there is no deity but Allāh and that Muḥammad is His servant and Messenger.

To proceed: Sometime ago my guide and master, the honorable ḥājī and ḥāfiẓ Khalīl Aḥmad, on the instruction of our guide and master, the shaykh Ḥājī Imdādullāh the emigrator to Makka (may his soul be sanctified), had translated the *Tabwīb al-Ḥikam* into Urdu. It was published under the title *Itmām al-Ni'am Tarjuma Urdū Tabwīb al-Ḥikam* (completing the blessings: an Urdu translation of the arrangement of the *Ḥikam*) and was published several times.

Since the translation in most places was beyond the comprehension of laymen, the honorable [shaykh] instructed me to write a commentary of it in Urdu. Obeying his command, I took aid from an Arabic commentary of the *Ḥikam* of Ibn 'Atā' ﷺ and wrote whatever was grasped by my weak comprehension.[1]

I have named it *Ikmāl al-Shiyam Sharḥ Itmām al-Ni'am, Tarjuma Urdu Tabwīb al-Ḥikam* (perfecting character: an exposition of completing the blessings: an Urdu translation of the arrangement of the *Ḥikam*).

If I have achieved rectitude it is from Allāh, and then through the blessing of my guide. If I have erred, it is from my self.

May Allāh accept it and make it beneficial. I do hope that those who study it will remember in his prayers this weak one, my honorable shaykh (Sahāranpūrī) (may Allāh extend his outpouring), the original author (Ibn 'Aṭā'illāh), and the one responsible for its arrangement ('Alī Muttaqī).

The writer, the weak servant
MUḤAMMAD 'ABDULLĀH GANGŌHĪ
(May Allāh forgive him and his parents)
Lecturer, Madrasa 'Arabiyya Kāndhla, Muzaffarnagar
Ṣafar 1338/1919

1 In light of a comment by Gangōhī in chapter twenty-six we can surmise that the commentary referred to is the one of Ibn 'Abbad.

PART I

الحكم

Aphorisms

I

ON KNOWLEDGE

اَلْعِلْمُ النَّافِعُ هُوَ الَّذِي يَنْبَسِطُ فِي الصَّدْرِ شُعَاعُهُ، وَيَنْكَشِفُ بِهِ عَنِ الْقَلْبِ قِنَاعُهُ.

Beneficial knowledge is the one whose ray of light expands in the breast[2] and uncovers the veil over the heart. [231]

Beneficial knowledge (*ʿilm nāfiʿ*) refers essentially to the knowledge of Allāh's essence (*dhāt*) and His attributes (*ṣifāt*), and this is the knowledge that man needs as a foundation for travelling the path of worshipping the Lord. The similitude of this knowledge is that of a lamp or candle: when it is cast into the heart of a servant [of Allāh], its rays illumine his heart and all vestiges of doubt and suspicion pertaining to either the religion (*dīn*) or the world (*dunyā*) are eliminated. Then one proceeds to the doors of certainty (*yaqīn*) and higher spiritual realities open up before one, and the darkness of lowly desire (*shahwa*) is dispelled from the heart: this state of spiritual being is the meaning of the "Reality of Knowledge" (*ḥaqīqat al-ʿilm*). In fact, any knowledge that is devoid of this quality and effect is not, in truth, knowledge; rather, it is merely verbal information.

2 Danner has "mind" here for *ṣadr*, while breast is more appropriate.

خَيْرُ الْعِلْمِ مَا كَانَتِ الْخَشْيَةُ مَعَهُ.

The best knowledge is the one accompanied by fear. [232]

Fear [of Allāh] is to perceive, so to speak, the grandeur of Allāh in the heart. When knowledge is accompanied by this quality, it is the highest and most beautiful form of knowledge, as praised in Allāh's speech: *Indeed among His servants, it is but the learned who fear Allāh* (35:28). In order to be a possessor of knowledge, and not merely a carrier of information, one must be characterized by this fear. The sign of this spiritual state is a strict obedience to the Sacred Law. One must understand that fear, in the absence of obedience to the Sacred Law, is in reality non-existent.

A contrasting state of being is when one acquires "knowledge" while accompanied by worldly desire, such as the yearning for the flattery of wealthy people, or pride or neglect of the Hereafter. When this pitiful spiritual state is found in a person who is taken to be a religious scholar (*ʿālim*), then such a person is not to be counted among the inheritors of the Prophets.[3]

اَلْعِلْمُ إِنْ قَارَنَتْهُ الْخَشْيَةُ .. فَلَكَ، وَإِلَّا فَعَلَيْكَ.

If fear is united with knowledge, then it is for you; if not, then it is against you. [233]

Knowledge that is accompanied with fear of Allāh is beneficial in both this world and the next, while "knowledge" that lacks such a quality will be harmful in both abodes.

True religious scholars are distinguished from pseudo-scholars by this inner quality of fear. The latter are devoid of fear on account of their pride, which is the result of having gained superficial "knowledge": superficial, that is, due to the lack of spiritual purity.

3 A famous ḥadīth transmitted by Abū Dāwūd and Tirmidhī includes the statement: "The religious scholars are the heirs of the Prophets." See Ibn Rajab al-Ḥanbalī's detailed exposition of this ḥadīth in *The Heirs of the Prophets*, trans. Zaid Shakir (Chicago: Starlatch, 2001).

2

ON REPENTANCE

كَيْفَ يُشْرِقُ قَلْبٌ صُوَرُ الْأَكْوَانِ مُنْطَبِعَةٌ فِي مِرْآتِهِ؟ أَمْ كَيْفَ يَرْحَلُ إِلَى اللّٰهِ وَهُوَ مُكَبَّلٌ بِشَهَوَاتِهِ؟ أَمْ كَيْفَ يَطْمَعُ أَنْ يَدْخُلَ حَضْرَةَ اللّٰهِ وَهُوَ لَمْ يَتَطَهَّرْ مِنْ جَنَابَةِ غَفَلَاتِهِ؟ أَمْ كَيْفَ يَرْجُو أَنْ يَفْهَمَ دَقَائِقَ الْأَسْرَارِ وَهُوَ لَمْ يَتُبْ مِنْ هَفَوَاتِهِ؟

How can the heart[4] be illumined while the forms of creatures are reflected in its mirror? Or how can it journey to God while shackled by its passions? Or how can it desire to enter the presence of God while it has not yet purified itself of the stain of its forgetfulness? Or how can it understand the subtle points of mysteries while it has not yet repented of its offenses? [13]

How can a heart become illumined when it has been consumed by love of worldly wealth, worldly reputation, offspring, property, idle thoughts and false hopes? A heart that is fettered night and day with the chains of base desires—such as constant and excessive preoccupation with food, garments, or family—cannot advance to Allāh Most High and the divine presence. Is it possible that a soiled heart can be permitted entrance into a pure court? A diseased heart is prohibited such an entry in the same way that a person in a major state of ritual impurity is not permitted into the pure arena of a mosque (*masjid*).[5] Furthermore, a heart that has been afflicted in this manner cannot hope to comprehend mysteries and divine subtleties.

---

4 References to the "heart" in these contexts are allusions to the spiritual heart.

5 See Ibn Rushd's *Distinguished Jurist's Primer*, 1:49–50, for a discussion of the verdicts of various Islamic jurists on this issue.

For a spiritual light to settle in the heart, the darkness of illusions must be dispelled. When the diseased one has repented of his futility, then he may progress to a stage where he is endowed with the ability to understand divine mysteries.

لَا صَغِيرَةَ إِذَا قَابَلَكَ عَدْلُهُ، وَلَا كَبِيرَةَ إِذَا وَاجَهَكَ فَضْلُهُ.

There is no minor sin when His justice confronts you; and there is no major sin when His grace confronts you. [50]

Should Allāh's attribute of justice (*ʿadl*) be manifested on earth, dealing with us according to the strict criteria of such equity, the smallest of sins (*ṣaghīra*) would be treated as an enormity (*kabīra*). In truth, a minute action of disobedience to such a majestic and great Lord and Benefactor, whose grandeur is infinite and bounties are incalculable, justifies the application of complete punishment upon the disobedient one.

If, on the other hand, His grace is manifested, then our greatest sins wane into oblivion, after becoming insignificant due to His magnanimous forgiveness.

إِذَا وَقَعَ مِنْكَ ذَنْبٌ .. فَلَا يَكُنْ سَبَبًا لِيَأْسِكَ مِنْ حُصُولِ
الْإِسْتِقَامَةِ مَعَ رَبِّكَ، فَقَدْ يَكُونُ ذٰلِكَ آخِرَ ذَنْبٍ قُدِّرَ عَلَيْكَ.

When you commit a sin, let it not be a reason for your despairing of attaining to righteousness before your Lord, for that might be the last decreed for you. [148]

When one commits some sin, as the result of human nature, one should never allow the sin to bring about the slightest change in one's determination to remain steadfast upon the religion. Do not permit it to slacken one's bond with Allāh Most High. Do not be deceived by the thought "I am unable to remain steadfast on the religion, hence my sinning; therefore I might as well give up!" Never think that steadfastness is impossible in the aftermath of committing a sin. Rather, one must hope—as the aphorism suggests—that maybe Allāh will not destine another sin for one.

With this hope, one must be very careful to not become audacious in sin. Indeed, a sin committed spontaneously due to temporary human weakness is not in conflict with steadfastness upon the religion; however, persistence in sins without constant recourse to repentance, whereby one engages in a prolonged and deliberate commission of sins, is a complete negation of steadfastness.

مِنْ عَلَامَاتِ مَوْتِ الْقَلْبِ عَدَمُ الْحُزْنِ عَلَى مَا فَاتَكَ مِنَ الْمُوَافَقَاتِ، وتَرْكُ النَّدَمِ عَلَى مَا فَعَلْتَهُ مِنْ وُجُودِ الزَّلَّاتِ.

A sign of the heart's death is the absence of sadness over the acts of obedience that you have neglected and the abandonment of regret over the mistakes that you have made. [48]

Know that just as the life of the physical body is dependent on food, the life of the spiritual heart is dependent on faith (*īmān*) and righteous deeds (*aʿmāl ṣāliḥa*). In the same way as the physical body would perish if deprived of nourishment, the spiritual heart dies without its own sustenance. Thus if one is unconcerned with acts of disobedience—such as the neglect of the ritual prayer (*ṣalāt*), fasting (*ṣawm*), or actions of disobedience committed by others—then this spiritual state is clearly indicative of the fact that one's spiritual heart is dead, and devoid of the states of faith.

Yet when the heart derives pleasure from acts of obedience, and grieves when afflicted with sin, then the indication is that the light of faith (*nūr al-īmān*) is radiating.

لَا يَعْظُمِ الذَّنْبُ عِنْدَكَ عَظَمَةً تَصُدُّكَ عَنْ حُسْنِ الظَّنِّ بِاللّٰهِ تَعَالَى .. فَإِنَّ مَنْ عَرَفَ رَبَّهُ اسْتَصْغَرَ فِي جَنْبِ كَرَمِهِ ذَنْبَهُ.

Let no sin reach such proportions in your eyes that it cuts you off from having a good opinion of God, for, indeed, whoever knows his Lord considers his sin as paltry next to His generosity. [49]

One should not hold one's sins in such a grave light that one loses hope in the grace and mercy of Allāh Most High. One should not think "The gravity of my sin is so great that there is no forgiveness for it, and I have, on account of this sin, now reached a stage where I am unfit for His grace and mercy." Such despair is the consequence of an unawareness of the attributes of Allāh Most High.

One who has recognized the Creator and is aware of His attributes will be acquainted with His attributes of forgiveness and grace. He will thus understand that in the presence of these infinite attributes, his sins are insignificant. In such a state, a servant will always have hopes of being forgiven.

3

ON SINCERITY

اَلْأَعْمَالُ صُوَرٌ قَائِمَةٌ، وَأَرْوَاحُهَا وُجُودُ سِرِّ الْإِخْلَاصِ فِيهَا.

Actions are lifeless forms, but the presence of an inner reality of sincerity within them is what endows them with life-giving Spirit. [10]

THE RIGHTEOUS DEEDS of the servant that are devoid of sincerity are like the dead body without the soul. However, if action is accompanied with sincerity, the body will have life. Insincere actions are lifeless and will bring no benefit in the Hereafter.

مَا أَرَادَتْ هِمَّةُ سَالِكٍ أَنْ تَقِفَ عِنْدَ مَا كُشِفَ لَهَا إِلَّا وَنَادَتْهُ هَوَاتِفُ الْحَقِيقَةِ: الَّذِي تَطْلُبُ أَمَامَكَ، وَلَا تَبَرَّجَتْ ظَوَاهِرُ الْمُكَوَّنَاتِ إِلَّا وَنَادَتْهُ حَقَائِقُهَا: ﴿إِنَّمَا نَحْنُ فِتْنَةٌ فَلَا تَكْفُرْ﴾.

Hardly does the intention of the initiate want to stop at what has been revealed to him, than the voices of Reality call out to him: "That which you are looking for is still ahead of you!" And hardly do the exterior aspects of created beings display their charms, than their inner realities call out to him: "We are only a trial, so disbelieve not!" [Q. 2:102] [20]

A servant, while traversing the Path and engaging in invocation (*dhikr*), reflection (*fikr*) and contemplation (*murāqaba*), might receive numerous kinds of mysteries and realities in his heart. The spiritual ecstasy experienced as a result can lead to one becoming engrossed in these states, to the extent that one begins to think that this is the goal, whereas it is most certainly not.

Yet such an afflicted person can rejoice in the hope of divine guidance where the accomplished Shaykh's shadow is over the seeker [to inspire him on toward the goal of divine pleasure]. This can happen with the inspiration in the heart: "Your goal is ahead. Don't halt here. Advance! These conditions and states that you are experiencing are creations like yourself. They are not the Creator. Your goal is the Creator Most High."[6]

Similarly, the external beauty of worldly objects can be revealed to the traveler during the course of his journey, and he can become excessively attracted to them. If deviation has been decreed for him—which can be in the form of being attached to an unaccomplished guide—he becomes entrapped in these worldly objects. He regards these worldly allurements as the medium for the attainment of the goal.

If divine guidance comes to his aid, the reality of the objects of the transitory world become manifest to him and they call out to him loudly: "We have been created by Allāh Most High as a trial for you. Do not be ungrateful to your Creator by engrossing yourself in us.'

لَا تَرْحَلْ مِنْ كَوْنٍ إِلٰى كَوْنٍ .. فَتَكُونَ كَحِمَارِ الرَّحٰى؛ يَسِيرُ وَالَّذِي ارْتَحَلَ إِلَيْهِ هُوَ الَّذِي ارْتَحَلَ عَنْهُ، وَلٰكِنِ ارْحَلْ مِنَ الْأَكْوَانِ إِلَى الْمُكَوِّنِ ﴿وَأَنَّ إِلٰى رَبِّكَ الْمُنْتَهٰى﴾، وَانْظُرْ إِلٰى قَوْلِهِ صَلَّى اللّٰهُ عَلَيْهِ وَسَلَّمَ: «فَمَنْ كَانَتْ هِجْرَتُهُ إِلَى اللّٰهِ وَرَسُولِهِ .. فَهِجْرَتُهُ إِلَى اللّٰهِ وَرَسُولِهِ، وَمَنْ كَانَتْ هِجْرَتُهُ إِلٰى دُنْيَا يُصِيبُهَا أَوِ امْرَأَةٍ يَتَزَوَّجُهَا .. فَهِجْرَتُهُ إِلٰى مَا هَاجَرَ إِلَيْهِ.» فَافْهَمْ قَوْلَهُ عَلَيْهِ الصَّلَاةُ وَالسَّلَامُ، وَتَأَمَّلْ هٰذَا الْأَمْرَ إِنْ كُنْتَ ذَا فَهْمٍ .. وَالسَّلَامُ.

6 Aḥmad Sirhindī deals with these matters in his *Maktūbāt*: "Forms, these or others, and lights, physical or spiritual, are all created by God. He transcends them altogether; they are nothing but His signs and proofs" (Ansari, *Sufism and Shari'ah*, 175). Elsewhere in the *Maktūbāt*, the author states: "For the vision of God is promised in the next life and cannot be had in this life. . .God transcends them [revelations and visions of the sufis] absolutely" (op. cit. 177).

Travel not from creature to creature, otherwise you will be like a donkey at the mill: roundabout he turns, his goal the same as his departure. Rather, go from creatures to the Creator: "And that the final end is unto thy Lord." [Q. 53:42] Consider the Prophet's words (God bless him and grant him peace!): "Therefore, he whose flight is for God and His Messenger, then his flight is for God and His Messenger; and he whose flight is for worldly gain or marriage with a woman, then his flight is for that which he flees to."[7] So understand his words (upon him peace!) and ponder this matter, if you can. And peace on you! [42]

The true goal of the seeker of Allāh is Allāh Himself. The seeker's gaze must be focused on his Master in everything. The purpose of all the acts of worship, invocation and effort is the diversion of the seeker's gaze from all things besides Allāh, so that the heart becomes absorbed in the invocation of Allāh Most High. Although the seeker's goal of reward, lofty ranks and acquisition of spiritual pleasure is lawful, he has not attained the true rank of a complete spiritual aspirant, because he is still not totally focused on his Lord. Yet if he abandons everything and fixes his spiritual gaze on Allāh Most High, then this will be the goal that he attains.

If a man of the world abandons the world, engrossing himself in a variety of spiritual efforts, to convey to others that he is a man of piety and a saint, he has in fact abandoned one object of creation to involve himself in another. In other words, he has abandoned wealth for the sake of name and fame. It is clear that those whose acclaim he seeks are all creation.

لَا عَمَلَ أَرْجَى لِلْقُلُوبِ مِنْ عَمَلٍ يَغِيبُ عَنْكَ
شُهُودُهُ وَيُحْتَقَرُ عِنْدَكَ وُجُودُهُ.

No deed is more fruitful for the heart than the one you are not aware of and which is deemed paltry by you. [51]

The deed that has the greater acceptance by Allāh Most High is an act that the servant understands to be from Allāh. He discerns it with his heart and

7 For commentary upon this famous ḥadīth see Ibn Rajab, *Compendium*, 1–26.

does not attribute it to himself. By viewing with the heart's eye, he says: "If Allāh Most High does not wish that I render this deed, never will I be able to accomplish it." He should, subsequently, not regard this deed as being of such significance whereby he guarantees for himself the attainment of divine proximity. On the contrary, [from his perspective] he should consider it unworthy of acceptance since it has emanated from himself. When deeds possess such a balance [between hope and fear] they readily find acceptance in the Divine Court.

لَا تُفْرِحْكَ الطَّاعَةُ لِأَنَّهَا بَرَزَتْ مِنْكَ، وَافْرَحْ بِهَا
لِأَنَّهَا بَرَزَتْ مِنَ اللّٰهِ إِلَيْكَ، ﴿قُلْ بِفَضْلِ اللّٰهِ وَبِرَحْمَتِهِ
فَبِذٰلِكَ فَلْيَفْرَحُوا هُوَ خَيْرٌ مِمَّا يَجْمَعُونَ﴾

Let not obedience make you joyous because it comes from you, but rather, be joyous over it because it comes from God to you. "Say: In the grace of God and in His mercy, in that they should rejoice. It is better than that which they hoard." [Q. 10:58] [58]

When the servant gives vent to exhilaration and feels proud of his acts of worship, thinking that he has rendered these by virtue of his choice and will, then he will be guilty of displaying ingratitude. The happiness of the servant on account of having practiced righteousness should be because he knows that he was able to render the deed by virtue of Allāh's grace, mercy and aid. He thus expresses his gratitude (*shukr*) to Allāh Most High, who enabled him to execute the deed of virtue.

جَلَّ رَبُّنَا أَنْ يُعَامِلَهُ الْعَبْدُ نَقْدًا فَيُجَازِيَهُ نَسِيئَةً.

Far be it for our Lord to recompense with credit the servant who deals with Him in cash. [89]

It is not the attitude of a generous person to extract work and delay payment of the wages; thus He who is truly generous, to the greatest degree, will not act ungenerously. He does not delay compensation to the next world for the servant's deeds. Rather, He grants the reward for obedience here in this world. Such a reward comprises the sweetness the heart tastes while engaged in worship and invocation, together with the variety of secrets, mysteries and subtleties that He bestows. In comparison to this reward, the servant regards the kingdom of the world as dust. Yet this immediate reward is insignificant in comparison to the reward one will receive in the next world. The reality of the gifts of the Hereafter is beyond description.

كَفَى مِنْ جَزَائِهِ إِيَّاكَ عَلَى الطَّاعَةِ أَنْ رَضِيَكَ لَهَا أَهْلًا.

Suffice it as a recompense to you for obedience that He has judged you worthy of obedience. [90]

The worldly reward for spiritual purity is also limitless. Among these, the greatest reward for the traveler is that the Ruler of Rulers, and King of Kings, has selected one for rendering obedience to Him. One is, in fact, nothing. One is a contemptible slave and a pure non-entity [metaphorically speaking]. Similarly, when a king in the world extracts some service from a man, the latter feels proud of it because he has gained a rank. Whether or not he receives anything more is not of importance. The attainment of a rank in proximity to the king is adequate for him.

كَفَى الْعَامِلِينَ جَزَاءً مَا هُوَ فَاتِحُهُ عَلَى قُلُوبِهِمْ فِي طَاعَتِهِ، وَمَا هُوَ مُورِدُهُ عَلَيْهِمْ مِنْ وُجُودِ مُؤَانَسَتِهِ.

It suffices as a reward for the doers of good that He has inspired obedience to Him in their hearts and brought upon them the existence of His reciprocal intimacy. [91]

The bounties that are bestowed here in this world to those who practice virtue are the variety of inspirations that cascade into their hearts from the Divine Court at the time of enacting righteousness. They experience spiritual pleasure from these inspirations. Furthermore, vistas of the pleasure of supplication are opened in their hearts. As a result of the bond of love that Allāh Most High bestows upon them, the bounties of the world recede into oblivion.

مَنْ عَبَدَهُ لِشَيْءٍ يَرْجُوهُ مِنْهُ أَوْ لِيَدْفَعَ بِطَاعَتِهِ وُرُودَ الْعُقُوبَةِ عَنْهُ .. فَمَا قَامَ بِحَقِّ أَوْصَافِهِ.

Whoever worships Him for something he hopes for from Him, or in order to stave off the arrival of chastisement, has not concerned himself with the real nature of His Attributes. [92]

If the servant's purpose in rendering worship is the acquisition of Paradise and salvation from Hell, then—Allāh-willing—he will achieve these goals. However, [in this scenario] he has desired personal pleasure by way of worship. He thus remains trapped in the web of the ego; he has not discharged the right of Allāh's lofty attributes.

The servant's attribute of excellence is that his worship should be purely for Allāh's greatness and glory, not because of the sole desire for Paradise or fear of Hell. The duty of the slave is to serve, whether the Master favors or rebuffs him.

مَتَى طَلَبْتَ عِوَضًا عَنْ عَمَلٍ .. طُولِبْتَ بِوُجُودِ الصِّدْقِ فِيهِ، وَيَكْفِي الْمُرِيبَ وِجْدَانُ السَّلَامَةِ.

When you seek a recompense for a deed, the existence of sincerity in it is demanded of you in return. As for the insincere, the feeling of security from chastisement suffices him. [121]

If the intention underlying worship and other virtuous deeds is solely the acquisition of compensation from Allāh Most High, then Allāh will show him that only a deed accomplished by sincerity is worthy of reward. If sincerity truly existed in one, one would not have rendered the deed in expectation of compensation. For such a person it will suffice that he is not punished by Allāh Most High.

لَا تَطْلُبْ عِوَضًا عَنْ عَمَلٍ لَسْتَ لَهُ فَاعِلًا .. يَكْفِي مِنَ الْجَزَاءِ لَكَ عَلَى الْعَمَلِ أَنْ كَانَ لَهُ قَابِلًا.

Do not seek recompense for a deed whose doer was not you. It suffices you as recompense for the deed that He accepts it. [122]

It should be understood that Allāh is the True Doer of all actions.[8] Therefore, in worship the servant's gaze should be on Allāh Most High. He should understand that Allāh Most High has created the act of worship in him and that it is His favor.

Since the servant is not the creator of his good deeds, it is highly improper for him to desire compensation [as though it is his right]. Therefore, if he is only in the pursuit of reward, sincerity will be negated. In fact, the servant deserves to be apprehended [on account of his deficiency].

أَنْتَ إِلَى حِلْمِهِ إِذَا أَطَعْتَهُ أَحْوَجُ مِنْكَ إِلَى حِلْمِهِ إِذَا عَصَيْتَهُ.

You are more in need in His forbearance when you obey Him than you are when you disobey Him. [132]

The excellence and loftiness of the servant are in his awareness that the actual goal of all worship is only Allāh Most High; thus, at all times and in all acts, his gaze must remain focused on Allāh Most High, as a beggar might solicit food from his benefactor. His actions, deeds and even his existence are completely out of his sight [when in this excellent spiritual state]. His reliance is only on Allāh Most High. The heart derives solace from only Him, and the direction of his heart is only focused on Him. There remains absolutely no trust in one's efforts and plans.

8 It states in *Al-ʿAqīda al-Ṭaḥāwiyya*: "People's actions are created by Allāh but earned by people" (point 86). Islamic orthodoxy does not, however, contend that humans are forced to act; and it affirms human free-will, which, at the same time, is not absolute. Thus one will be judged for one's works.

The contemptibility and destruction of the servant are brought about when his attention turns to his ego and he becomes pleased with his deeds [as though he is, in reality, responsible for their creation] and where he begins to value himself. When the servant develops this disposition, he is expelled from the Divine Court and becomes accursed.

Now understand that when the servant sins, he is in need of Allāh's kindness, for if he is denied divine kindness, Allāh's punishment will overtake him. He therefore requests divine kindness to avoid being apprehended, and to secure pardon for his sins.

Since obedience and worship are, in fact, divine pleasure, the issue of kindness does not arise [in the servant's mind]. Kindness is [perceived as] necessary when an act is rendered in conflict with divine pleasure. However, very often the opposite [should occur to the servant], i.e., the need for divine kindness at the time of obedience is greater than at the time of sin. The explanation of this [paradoxical] claim is as follows: It is the natural disposition of the believer (*mu'min*) to be racked by remorse after commission of a sin. He becomes overwhelmed by regret, grief and self-contempt. He despises and detests his own self. He gains greater humility and he hastens to supplicate for forgiveness in the Divine Court. In this pitiful state, his gaze is not on his effort and deed [of repentance]; the attitude of complete dependence on Allāh's kindness becomes ingrained in his heart; he is fully aware that apart from Allāh's grace, mercy and kindness there is no other refuge for him. This attribute that he has subsequently developed is the objective that he is supposed to cultivate as the state of excellence [as a believer].

On the other hand, sometimes after obedience and worship the servant's gaze falls on his deeds. He then becomes vain, considering himself an obedient servant and a pious worshipper (*'ābid*). He feels that he has discharged Allāh's rights. Hence, he believes that he must be rewarded [as though his worship was characterized by excellence]. In this state his gaze is on his own effort and he ceases to rely on Allāh's grace and mercy. Therefore, it will not be surprising if Allāh's wrath settles on him [on account of his vanity and pride] and he thus becomes the object of divine displeasure. On the occasion of this type of obedience, the servant is in greater need of divine kindness than his need at the time of sinning.

رُبَّمَا دَخَلَ الرِّيَاءُ عَلَيْكَ مِنْ حَيْثُ لَا يَنْظُرُ الْخَلْقُ إِلَيْكَ.

Sometimes ostentation penetrates you in such a way that no one notices it. [160]

Ostentation is to render an act of worship or some other virtuous deed with the motive of creating an impression on others, in order that they consider one a pious and saintly person.

If a person commences an act of worship in the presence of people, or in the absence of people who later arrive, with the sole desire to create the impression of piety—such as performing the ritual prayer in a beautiful manner [which is not one's normal practice]—then this servant has committed an act of ostentation [which is clear to almost anyone].

Sometimes, however, a person renders an act in private; yet, notwithstanding this privacy, ostentation enters his heart. This kind of ostentation is very subtle. The sign of this type of ostentation is a man's desire to be honored when he meets others: that he be appointed to a position of prominence and leadership, with others serving him. When he is honored, he becomes elated. When such honor is not forthcoming from people, he is stung with surprise. This attitude indicates that the person's efforts and deeds are motivated by the desire for name and fame, and to gain service from people.

اِسْتِشْرَافُكَ أَنْ يَعْلَمَ الْخَلْقُ بِخُصُوصِيَّتِكَ دَلِيلٌ
عَلَى عَدَمِ صِدْقِكَ فِي عُبُودِيَّتِكَ.

Your desire that people know your particular distinction is a proof of insincerity in your servanthood. [161]

Truth in the state of worship is the diversion of the gaze from all things except Allāh. The attention of the servant should turn solely to Allāh Most High. If the servant possesses this, then he is true [to his servanthood].

If he desires people to become informed of his pious acts and his special spiritual conditions, and he adopts various methods for publicizing these, then he should know that he is not sincere.

غَيِّبْ نَظَرَ الْخَلْقِ إِلَيْكَ بِنَظَرِ اللّٰهِ إِلَيْكَ، وَغِبْ
عَنْ إِقْبَالِهِمْ عَلَيْكَ بِشُهُودِ إِقْبَالِهِ إِلَيْكَ.

Make mankind's looking at you disappear by being content with God's looking at you! Slip away from their approach to you by contemplating His approach to you! [162]

The disposition of the sincere servant is such that the pleasure and displeasure of people are irrelevant to him. He has no care for either reaction. Since the gaze of divine mercy is perpetually on him, he is oblivious to the attention others accord him. To him it is irrelevant whether people honor or dishonor him, or whether they respect or despise him. His heart attaches no importance to their attention. On the contrary, he contemplates the divine attention that is on him at all times, considering it an invaluable treasure. Being in possession of this great treasure, he can never [truly] divert his attention to others.

It is simple to understand that if a man is under the care and protection of the King who caters for all his requirements, then this person will have no care for the attention of others. The gaze of the Ruler of Rulers is with us every moment of our lives. Every minute He showers on us a variety of bounties. Therefore to avert our gaze from Him would make us from the ungrateful. In consequence of such ingratitude, the punishment of such behavior should be the snatching away of all bounties; yet, because of His boundless mercy, He overlooks our ingratitude.

كَمَا لَا يُحِبُّ الْعَمَلَ الْمُشْتَرَكَ كَذٰلِكَ لَا يُحِبُّ الْقَلْبَ الْمُشْتَرَكَ؛
اَلْعَمَلُ الْمُشْتَرَكُ لَا يَقْبَلُهُ، وَالْقَلْبُ الْمُشْتَرَكُ لَا يُقْبِلُ عَلَيْهِ.

Just as He does not love the deed possessed of associationism,[9] so similarly He does not love the heart

9 "Associationism" (*shirk*) is the gravest of errors in Islam. It consists in associating something or someone with Allāh, as if there were two or more Gods. On the plane of the virtues, associationism is the opposite of sincerity (*ikhlāṣ*), and that is hypocrisy (*nifāq*). The affirmation of the Oneness of Allāh (*tawḥīd*) demands increasing sincerity in the *faqīr*: the false gods in him must go. The deed

possessed of associationism. As for the deed possessed of associationism, He does not accept it; and as for the heart possessed of associationism, He does not draw near to it. [203]

Associationism in worship is a deed contaminated with ostentation: Allāh does not love such a deed. Similarly, the heart of associationism is a heart in which is found the love of others [besides Allāh]; and Allāh does not love such a heart. Allāh Most High loves the heart that contains only His love.

When deeds are performed solely for the pleasure of others, they are not acceptable to Allāh Most High. Only deeds devoid of ostentation are acceptable to Him.

مَا أَحْبَبْتَ شَيْئًا .. إِلَّا كُنْتَ لَهُ عَبْدًا، وَهُوَ
لَا يُحِبُّ أَنْ تَكُونَ لِغَيْرِهِ عَبْدًا.

You have not loved anything without being its slave, but He does not want you to be someone else's slave. [210]

When man loves, on this earth, anything besides Allāh, he becomes its slave because of the deep relationship that develops. This object of love can be love of wealth, or enslaving love of spouses and children. Separation from such an object of love produces grief. This, then, is the meaning of enslavement to the object of one's love.

It should, however, be understood that the love of worldly objects that is detestable is such a love that induces the slave to ignore the Sacred Law: where the lover devotes himself to the object of love even if the love leads to the violation of the Law. If priority is accorded to the Sacred Law, thus keeping the love subservient, then the natural love one has for certain matters, such as children or relatives, is not abominable. In fact, this love is part of the Prophetic Practice (Sunna) in such instances.

that is associationist is the one performed without Allāh in view; the heart that is associationist is the one that loves other than Allāh (VD).

لَيْسَ الْمُحِبُّ الَّذِي يَرْجُو مِنْ مَحْبُوبِهِ عِوَضًا أَوْ يَطْلُبُ مِنهُ غَرَضًا، فَإِنَّ الْمُحِبَّ مَنْ يَبْذُلُ لَكَ، لَيْسَ الْمُحِبُّ مَنْ تَبْذُلُ لَهُ.

The lover is not the one who hopes for a recompense from his beloved or seeks some object. The lover is indeed the one who spends generously on you; the lover is not the one on whom you spend generously. [243]

The object of love of all [true] servants is The Truth (*al-Ḥaqq*—one of the Names of Allāh). The believer is His lover; hence Allāh Most High has spoken of those with faith possess deep love for Him.

The true lover of Allāh desires nothing but the pleasure of his Beloved; and love of Paradise, states of spiritual ecstasy, mysteries and subtleties are not given priority over one's love of Allāh. In fact, the true lover sacrifices his life and body for the pleasure of his Beloved.

كَيْفَ تَطْلُبُ الْعِوَضَ عَلَى عَمَلٍ هُوَ مُتَصَدِّقٌ بِهِ عَلَيْكَ، أَمْ كَيْفَ تَطْلُبُ الْجَزَاءَ عَلَى صِدْقٍ هُوَ مُهْدِيهِ إِلَيْكَ؟

How can you seek recompense for a deed He bestowed upon you out of charity? Or how can you seek recompense for a sincerity He gave you as a gift? [252]

Acts of virtue, rectitude and sincerity are all gifts conferred upon the servant by the Gracious Master—there is absolutely no benefit in them for Him; He is entirely independent [of any need]; hence the notion of Him benefiting from the worship of a servant is preposterous.

It is absurd to expect [in the sense of demand] to be remunerated for the gifts that He bestows upon one. How can a pauper (*faqīr*) who receives charity from someone turn around and demand his benefactor to compensate him? The absurdity is self-evident.

4

ON THE RITUAL PRAYER

اَلصَّلَاةُ طُهْرَةٌ لِلْقُلُوبِ مِنْ أَدْنَاسِ الذُّنُوبِ، وَاسْتِفْتَاحٌ لِبَابِ الْغُيُوبِ، اَلصَّلَاةُ مَحَلُّ الْمُنَاجَاةِ ومَعْدِنُ الْمُصَافَاةِ، تَتَّسِعُ فِيهَا مَيَادِينُ الْأَسْرَارِ، وَتُشْرِقُ فِيهَا شَوَارِقُ الْأَنْوَارِ.

Ritual prayer is a purification for hearts [from the impurities???? of sins] and an opening-up of the door of the invisible domains. Ritual prayer is the place of intimate discourses and a mine of reciprocal acts of purity wherein the domains of the innermost being are expanded and the rising gleams of light ray out. [119–120]

The hearts of the chosen servants of Allāh are perpetually absorbed in His invocation. However, association with people and tending to natural needs produce a kind of forgetfulness (*ghafla*) and a relationship with beings other than Allāh. As a result, hearts become contaminated.

Yet, when servants become engrossed in the ritual prayer (*ṣalāt*), their hearts are cleansed of the foreign pollution and the "divine perception" is again restored to their hearts in accordance with their respective ranks. When the foreign veils are removed from their hearts during the ritual prayer, thus eliminating any impediments, the doors of hidden divine mysteries and the secrets of divine knowledge open up in their hearts. Thus their ritual prayer becomes the substratum for communion with their Lord. Their hearts become imbued with sincerity and love, leaving no room whatsoever for anything besides Allāh. There remains, then, not the slightest vestige of fear or constriction in their hearts as they expand for the intake of divine mysteries. For these illustrious servants, celestial illuminations (*anwār*) glitter like stars in their ritual prayer. They perceive this illumination with the eyes of the heart.

Every believer should strive to perform such a prayer [as described above].

لَمَّا عَلِمَ الْحَقُّ مِنْكَ وُجُودَ الْمَلَلِ .. لَوَّنَ لَكَ الطَّاعَاتِ، وَعَلِمَ مَا فِيكَ مِنْ وُجُودِ الشَّرَهِ .. فَحَجَرَهَا عَلَيْكَ فِي بَعْضِ الْأَوْقَاتِ، لِيَكُونَ هَمُّكَ إِقَامَةَ الصَّلَاةِ لَا وُجُودَ الصَّلَاةِ، فَمَا كُلُّ مُصَلٍّ مُقِيمٌ.

Since God knows of the existence of weariness on your part, He has varied the acts of obedience for you; and since He knows of the existence of impulsiveness in you, He has limited them to specific times, so that your concern be with the performance of the ritual prayer, not with the existence of the ritual prayer. For not everyone who prays performs well. [118]

Man is, by nature, of a weak constitution, and thus tires of doing the same act for a length of time. Prolonged performance makes the act difficult. Yet, his heart feels no strain in a variety of acts, and he is therefore better equipped to accomplish them all. Nevertheless, it should be understood that it is incumbent on the servant to perpetually apply himself to the worship of Allāh [as ordered].

In view of this disposition of man, Allāh Most High designed a variety of acts of worship for him. He has not decreed perpetual observation of any one act of worship, because the servant would tire of it. For example, had a perpetual state of ritual prayer been decreed, the servant would certainly be exhausted. The heart of the servant now remains in worship on account of the variety, such as the ritual prayer, recitation of the Qur'ān, the pilgrimage to Mecca (*ḥajj*), the poor-due tax (*zakāt*), sacrifice, fasting, invocation, etc. His heart does not become bored because the "taste" of each worship is different. In this way, the entire time [of the dedicated servant] is spent in worship without the servant tiring and becoming bored. He does not, therefore, abandon worship.

In contrast to the condition of tiring and becoming bored is the trait of [misjudged] greed and enthusiasm. When this trait exceeds the limit, the act is corrupted. For example, when there is extreme enthusiasm for the ritual prayer, it will be difficult to discharge it with all its rights. Such extreme enthusiasm will cause one to refrain from ablution [so that one remains engrossed in the ritual prayer), or one will recite the Qur'ān hastily without humility and reflection. In view of this disposition in man, Allāh Most High has forbidden him from the ritual prayer and other worship at certain times so that man does not plunge headlong into any deed in haste and with excessive enthusiasm. He has decreed ritual prayer at appointed times so that the servant resolves to execute it with perfection. Haste and enthusiasm lead to only the external form of ritual prayer. Between the form and the perfect prayer there is a great difference.

عَلِمَ وُجُودَ الضَّعْفِ مِنْكَ فَقَلَّلَ أَعْدَادَهَا،
وَعَلِمَ احْتِيَاجَكَ إِلَى فَضْلِهِ فَكَثَّرَ أَمْدَادَهَا.

He knew of the existence of weakness in you, so
He made the number of ritual prayers small;
and He knew of your need of His grace, so
He multiplied their fruitful results. [120]

On the night of the Prophet's Ascension to the heavens (*miʿrāj*),[10] fifty daily ritual prayers were initially made obligatory. Upon the repeated request of the Messenger of Allāh ﷺ, the number was reduced to five. The reduction was granted on account of our weakness and our inability to perform fifty daily prayers steadfastly. Since man is in need of Allāh's grace, the reward of fifty prayers was retained.

قَيَّدَ الطَّاعَاتِ بِأَعْيَانِ الْأَوْقَاتِ كَيْ لَا يَمْنَعَكَ عَنْهَا وُجُودُ
التَّسْوِيفِ، وَوَسَّعَ عَلَيْكَ الْوَقْتَ كَيْ تَبْقَى لَكَ حِصَّةُ الْإِخْتِيَارِ.

He laid down specific times for acts of obedience so that
procrastination not divert you from them, and He made

10 See Abu 'l-Ḥasan A. Nadwī, *Muhammad Rasulullah: The Apostle of Mercy* ﷺ, trans. Mohiuddin Ahmad (Karachi: Haji Arfeen Academy, n.d.), 134–136, for details of this miraculous night journey.

each time span ample so that you would have a share in making the choice. [194]

Allāh Most High has fixed times for certain acts of worship which He has decreed obligatory, such as ritual prayer and fasting, for example. If these acts are performed within the prescribed limits of the time, they will be fulfilled. If the time lapses, the worship is lost.

If fixed times were not prescribed for worship, and if its performance was left to our discretion and choice, laziness would have set in. We would have said: "As soon as I am over with this work, I shall perform the ritual prayer." Or we would have performed the ritual prayer of several months in a couple of days. In this way the worship would be lost.

The time fixed for the ritual prayer is not so short that one is obliged to perform it immediately on the entry of the time, otherwise it would become a make-up prayer. On the contrary, the time has been so extended as to permit one's free choice: one may perform it at any time during the duration of the valid time. The benefit and wisdom for this is to ensure our serenity for the worship. At the approach of the time, we may make preparations for the act in peace and without haste. The extended time enables us to terminate our other activities in an orderly manner in preparation. These benefits would have been lost if extended times were not granted. The ritual prayer would then have been performed hastily and without peace of mind, and the soul of the ritual prayer—which is presence of the heart—would then have been non-existent.

عَلِمَ قِلَّةَ نُهُوضِ الْعِبَادِ إِلٰى مُعَامَلَتِهِ، فَأَوْجَبَ عَلَيْهِمْ
وُجُودَ طَاعَتِهِ، فَسَاقَهُمْ إِلَيْهِ بِسَلَاسِلِ الْإِيْجَابِ، «عَجِبَ
رَبُّكَ مِنْ قَوْمٍ يُسَاقُونَ إِلَى الْجَنَّةِ بِالسَّلَاسِلِ».

He knew of the irresolution of servants in dealing with Him, so He made obedience to Him obligatory for them. Thus, He drove them to obedience with the chains of obligation. Your Lord is amazed at people who are driven to Paradise with chains! [195]

In every state and circumstance, the worship of Allāh Most High and the display of one's servanthood (*ʿubūdiyya*) are imperative and incumbent on the servants of Allāh. This is the demand of intelligence—whether Allāh Most High decrees that worship is obligatory on us or not—because the duty of the slave is servanthood, regardless of whether his master commands him or not. But, on account of man's indolence and defects regarding the rendition of worship, and out of His boundless mercy, Allāh Most High decreed the duties of worship obligatory on His servants. Along with this He notified them of His promise of Paradise for obedience. He further warned the transgressors of the chastisement of Hell.

The similitude of this imposition [of worship as an obligatory duty) is like a chain that is tied around the neck of a prisoner: the prisoner is taken by means of the chain in any desired direction, irrespective of his wishes. Similarly, by decreeing obedience obligatory, Allāh Most High draws the indolent ones toward worship and obedience.

Another example of mercy and love is a guardian who trains and punishes his ward who perpetrates wrong. He does not permit unbridled freedom to the child, so that he can do as he pleases. The child is thus compelled to do duties he dislikes and to abandon detestable characteristics, whether he likes it or not.

It is maybe surprising that some servants have to be drawn toward Paradise by means of chains. However, because these deeds have been imposed on them as compulsory duties, they oppose their desires in the execution of righteousness and gain entry into Paradise.

أَوْجَبَ عَلَيْكَ وُجُودَ خِدْمَتِهِ، وَمَا أَوْجَبَ عَلَيْكَ .. إِلَّا دُخُولَ جَنَّتِهِ.

He made the service of Him obligatory upon you, which is as much as to say that He made entry into His Paradise obligatory for you. [196]

Allāh Most High has made obedience and service to Him compulsory. This conveys the impression to the ignorant person that Allāh Most High derives benefit from the servant's obedience and service. However, such an understanding is false: He is independent and is in no need of anything. The benefit of worship is ours alone. The imposition of worship on us is in actual fact ensuring our entry into Paradise. Glory is to Allāh! How boundless is His mercy!

5

ON SOLITUDE & DETACHMENT

مَا نَفَعَ الْقَلْبَ شَيْءٌ مِثْلُ عُزْلَةٍ يَدْخُلُ بِهَا مَيْدَانَ فِكْرَةٍ.

Nothing benefits the heart more than a spiritual retreat wherein it enters the domain of meditation. [12]

Association with people in general and unnecessary association in particular keeps the focus of the heart on people; in such a situation the heart's gaze is diverted from The Creator—Most High—and forgetfulness increases further. In most cases, the cause of forgetfulness is mingling with people.

When the spiritual traveler takes to solitude, people are out of his sight. The seeker of Allāh then necessarily turns his gaze toward Allāh Most High. Hence, nothing is more efficacious than solitude for the heart to gain divine proximity (*qurb*). However, it is necessary in this solitude to meditate on the attributes and bounties of Allāh Most High.

اِدْفِنْ وُجُودَكَ فِي أَرْضِ الْخُمُولِ، فَمَا نَبَتَ مِمَّا لَمْ يُدْفَنْ لَا يَتِمُّ نِتَاجُهُ.

Bury your existence in the earth of obscurity, for whatever sprouts forth, without having first been buried, flowers imperfectly. [11]

The dearest wish of man's ego is to be held in honor and esteem by others. Man thus pursues name and fame. This characteristic is a highway robber in the path leading to Allāh and negates sincerity and truthfulness. The aim of obedience should be the pure worship of and servitude to Allāh. Greatness is the right of only Allāh Most High. Therefore, the duty of the servant is to humble himself and hold himself in contempt in the Divine Court.

Therefore, the Shaykh ﵀ says that you should bury yourself in anonymity, which is like the ground, i.e., make yourself lost, unknown and humble. The seed that is not planted under the soil will not grow and flourish. Similarly, if man does not bury himself in the field of anonymity, but remains in the pursuit of name and fame, he will not attain spiritual excellence and perfection. He will remain defective.

سَتَرَ أَنْوَارَ السَّرَائِرِ بِكَثَائِفِ الظَّوَاهِرِ إِجْلَالًا لَهَا أَنْ تُبْتَذَلَ بِوُجُودِ الْإِظْهَارِ، وَأَنْ يُنَادٰى عَلَيْهَا بِلِسَانِ الْإِشْتِهَارِ.

By way of honoring them, He veiled the lights of the innermost hearts with the opacities of exterior phenomena so they would not be abused when expressing themselves nor be accused of seeking renown. [155]

The hearts of those who are blessed with divine proximity and divine presence are radiant with innumerable rays of invocation and worship. Their hearts are illumined with these celestial rays. However, Allāh Most High has concealed the illuminated states of their hearts with dense veils of materialism, like eating, drinking, walking, sitting, etc.

Externally, He has made them to resemble the masses by their indulgence in worldly activities. Thus, the difference between these Friends of Allāh (*awliyā'*) and the masses is indiscernible. These external worldly states act like thick veils that conceal the celestial and internal illumination of Allāh's Friends from the eyes of men. But those whose spiritual gaze is sharp recognize these inner spiritual lights even behind the veils, while the general public do not discern these rays of celestial illumination because their physical vision cannot penetrate these veils. They therefore echo the statement that the non-Muslims made to the Prophet: "You are but a man like us."[11]

Allāh has hidden the inner lights of His Friends so that their honor is maintained. He has protected them from the disgrace of publicity. If their illuminated state had become known to the general public, then [word of] it would have been on the tongues of all and sundry. Mentioning in public even the name of a modest, chaste and beautiful lady protected behind her

11 This accusation against the Prophet ﷺ is discussed in Muḥammad ʿĀshiq Ilāhī, *Illuminating Discourses on the Noble Qur'ān*, 5:516 (Karachi: Zam Zam, 2001).

veil is dishonorable on account of her high degree of modesty and honor. This, then, is the similitude for the inner illuminations of the Friends concealed behind dense worldly veils.

If this system of concealment did not exist, these inner lights of the Friends would have become fully manifest. Their radiant illumination would have predominated to such a degree that the external material veils would disappear from even the physical vision of worldly people.

سُبْحَانَ مَنْ سَتَرَ سِرَّ الْخُصُوصِيَّةِ بِظُهُورِ الْبَشَرِيَّةِ،
وَظَهَرَ بِعَظَمَةِ الرُّبُوبِيَّةِ فِي إِظْهَارِ الْعُبُودِيَّةِ.

Praise be to Him who has hidden the inner reality of holiness by manifesting the quality of human nature, and who has appeared in the sublimity of Lordship by manifesting servanthood! [108]

The meaning of this statement is similar to the aforementioned observation.

People are unaware of the mysteries and subtleties that Allāh Most High reveals to His close servants. This spiritual treasure is concealed from the gaze of the public. The veils of physical attributes have been cast over these spiritual lights.

Concealing these inner lights is an extremely marvelous act. These lights are infinite in number and are of such supreme quality that if a single spark appeared on earth, then the light of the sun and moon would become dull and the light of this single spark would permeate from East to West. In spite of their infinity and quality, Allāh Most High has concealed this vast, boundless ocean of illumination in a cup. In other words, He has concealed these boundless lights in man who is constituted of a handful of dust. Therefore the physical gaze of [a normal and heedless] man [when he looks at such a saint] is only on this handful of dust and its physical effects, such as the man's movement and rest, his eating, sleeping and working. In view of this marvelous act of Allāh, the author expresses his wonder and amazement by glorifying Allāh by uttering *Subḥān Allāh* (Glory be to Allāh)!

His power is indeed wonderful and marvelous. When He desires to display the greatness and splendor of His Lordship to His servants, then He does so by revealing the effects of servanthood. The effects of servanthood are those states of the servants that draw their attention to Allāh Most

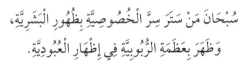

High. Such states are sickness, poverty, hardships, etc. When the servant is afflicted with these conditions, he is compelled to turn toward his Creator. He supplicates for the removal of the hardships and humbles himself. In such circumstances, he develops firmness in faith and understands well that he, most certainly, has a Creator who is All-Powerful.

In the absence of these effects, the greatness of Allāh would not have become manifest for His servants, because they would be perpetually dwelling in their personal whims and fancies. The servants of Allāh would then have been deprived of this inner knowledge.

سُبْحَانَ مَنْ لَمْ يَجْعَلِ الدَّلِيلَ عَلَى أَوْلِيَائِهِ إِلَّا مِنْ حَيْثُ الدَّلِيلُ عَلَيْهِ، وَلَمْ يُوْصِلْ إِلَيْهِمْ إِلَّا مَنْ أَرَادَ أَنْ يُوصِلَهُ إِلَيْهِ.

Glory be to Him who has not made any sign leading to His saints save as a sign leading to Himself, and who has joined no one to them except Him who God wants to join to Himself. [156]

Allāh Most High conceals Himself from our gaze, behind the veils of His creation. The earth, the heavens, the moon, the sun, the stars, the animal kingdom, the plant kingdom, man, etc. are all His creation (*makhlūqāt*). While the Pure Being of The Creator is conspicuously manifest, He is hidden from our sight. In fact, He remains so concealed that some brainless people even deny His existence. Those on whom the grace of Allāh has settled acknowledge His Unity and have accepted belief in the message (*risāla*) of His Messengers.

Allāh bestows a deep recognition of Himself on those whom are favored by His grace. The medium for the acquisition of this special knowledge and the path leading to the Divine Court is this special grace. There is no other way or method for this attainment.

The author then expresses his amazement saying that He is pure and that, in fact, purity belongs only to Him. The cause of the author's amazement is the fact that the method that Allāh has fixed for His recognition has also been fixed for the recognition of His saints. Just as Allāh Most High has concealed Himself in the veils of His physical creation, so too has He hidden His Friends behind the veils of their mundane conditions. Moreover, just as Allāh has fixed His special grace as the way for attaining Him, He has fixed His special grace as the way of recognizing His saints. Only those who are favored with divine grace will recognize the saints.

Only a blessed few are blessed with the special recognition of Allāh. Likewise, very few are guided to the saints. Some saints even aver that it is more difficult to recognize the saints than Allāh Most High: in view of Allāh's attributes of beauty (*jamāl*) and splendor (*jalāl*) being conspicuously manifest in creation, it is relatively easier to recognize Him than to recognize a saint (*walī*). A saint resembles all others in mundane acts and attributes; hence it is difficult to recognize him.

The author then says that Allāh leads to His saints those whom He will lead to Himself. In other words, when Allāh Most High wills a man to reach Him, He blesses him with the love, recognition and special companionship of the saints. The wisdom underlying this system is that the saints are Allāh's beloved ones. Those who love one's beloved are also beloved. Thus, when a person loves the saints it indicates that Allāh loves him.

6

ON TIME AND ITS IMPORTANCE

مَا مِنْ نَفَسٍ تُبْدِيهِ .. إِلَّا وَلَهُ قَدَرٌ فِيكَ يُمْضِيهِ.

Not a breath do you expire but a decree of destiny has made it go forth. [22]

Man is perpetually in a state that is either pleasing or displeasing to his ego. If it is pleasing [to Allāh], it will be a blessing (*niʿma*) on condition that it is not a sin. If it is displeasing [to Allāh], it will be a calamity on condition that it is not the effort of an act of obedience.

Every state (*ḥāl*) has a right (*ḥaqq*). It is incumbent on man to discharge these rights. The right of a blessing is gratitude (*shukr*); and the right of the state of calamity is patience (*ṣabr*). It is, therefore, imperative for the servant to be patient or grateful for every moment of his life. Thus, he should not destroy even one minute of his life.

لَا تَتَرَقَّبْ فُرُوغَ الْأَغْيَارِ .. فَإِنَّ ذٰلِكَ يَقْطَعُكَ عَنْ
وُجُودِ الْمُرَاقَبَةِ لَهُ فِيمَا هُوَ مُقِيمُكَ فِيهِ.

Do not look forward to being free of alterities for that is indeed what cuts you off from vigilant attention to Him in that very state He has assigned to you. [23]

When the grace (*faḍl*) of Allāh Most High focuses on the spiritual traveler, his heart establishes a connection with the invocation of Allāh. Thereafter, sometimes the condition of his engrossment in invocation is such that his heart becomes completely emptied of all things besides Allāh. However, sometimes the alterities of mundane affairs and activities dominates him.

Due to involvement in worldly affairs, the original state of invocation in the heart is overshadowed. The spiritual traveler becomes terrified and desires to extricate himself from this state of perplexity. Much of his time is then spent in this desire. He waits in anticipation of a time that will make him free from all this activity so that he can engage peacefully in invocation.

The Shaykh ﵀ advises the spiritual traveler not to wait for such a free time in order to resume invocation. Even the state of spiritual darkness and spiritual pollution, into which the True Lord has cast one, is a time granted to one by Him. Involving the heart excessively with the need to eliminate this pollution—before actively engaging in invocation—will in fact prevent one from meditation and invocation of Allāh Most High; such time is thus to be defined as negligent squandering. Consequently, the idea of waiting for a time devoid of activity should be abandoned. Think that this is the only available time and that there is no other time because one has no certainty regarding the future. Thus, become engrossed with your Master in this very time of pollution and darkness.

Someone asked Sahl[12] ﵀ "When does the *faqīr* attain comfort?" He replied "The *faqīr* attains comfort when he knows that the time which has passed over him is the only time.'

When this knowledge becomes grounded in the spiritual traveler, the pollution and the confusion will be dispelled. In reality, this advice of the Shaykh is the remedy for these alterities.

The aforementioned discussion will apply if the Shaykh's advice is intended for the spiritual traveler who is involved in invocation and spiritual exercises. Nevertheless, this advice can also apply to people who are ensnared in the world. Generally, people involved in the world wait for a time when they will be freed from the encumbrances of a certain activity. They deceive themselves by believing that on the accomplishment of a particular activity they will be free to apply themselves to the invocation of Allāh. After accomplishing one worldly activity, however, they commence another. There is no end to the hopes and desires of the ego. One's entire life is squandered without achieving a time to devote to the invocation of Allāh.

For such people of the world, the Shaykh's advice will also be applicable.

12 This is Sahl ibn ʿAbdillāh al-Tustarī (d. 283/896), a famous sufi. See Abū ʿAbd al-Raḥmān al-Sulamī, *Ṭabaqāt al-Ṣūfiyya;* Ibn al-Mulaqqin, *Ṭabaqāt al-Awliyāʾ;* and Dhahabī, *Siyār Aʿlām al-Nubalāʾ.*

They should not wait for a time when they will be free of worldly encumbrances. They should immediately engage themselves in the invocation of their Master (*mawlā*), regardless of worry and disturbance. Allāh Most High can Himself dispel the state of worry and agitation from the heart [despite one's apparent worldly preoccupations].

إِحَالَتُكَ الْأَعْمَالَ عَلَى وُجُودِ الْفَرَاغِ مِنْ رُعُونَاتِ النَّفْسِ.

Your postponement of deeds till the time when you are free is one of the frivolities of the ego.[13] [18]

This statement is similar to the aforementioned advice.

When man becomes involved in worldly affairs, there is no end to its ramifications. When there is no end to man's worldly indulgences, it is simply the indolence and stupidity of his ego to postpone righteous deeds, moral reformation and spiritual uplifting for the future, under the notion of obtaining a time devoid of worldly affairs.

Man [in this sense] destroys his present time and in his stupidity waits to acquire a time of which he is uncertain. Life can come to an end without a servant ever obtaining a period of free time—for death often makes a sudden appearance.

---

13 Victor Danner alternates the translation of *nafs* between *ego* and *soul*. The understanding of ego is clear from the context in which it is used, i.e. in the negative sense. This latter negative sense is given more lucidity through the explanation of the *soul* by ʿAbd al-Khāliq al-Shabrāwī. Firstly, he writes of "the Passional Soul (*al-nafs al-shahwāniyya*)": "that subtle vapour that exists behind life, sensory perception, and voluntary movements, which exists in the form of a 'waking state', 'sleep' or 'death.'" Secondly, "the Rational Soul (*al-nafs al-natiqa*)": "unrelated to matter, but is connected to it inasmuch as it acts upon it. This soul is that which is termed either 'Inciting', 'Reproachful', 'Inspired', 'Serene', 'Contented', 'Found Pleasing', or 'Perfect.' Whenever it acquires an attribute it acquires the name that designates it. When it befriends the. . .passional soul and submits to it it is called 'Inciting' (to evil) (*ammāra bi 'l-sū'*). When it submits to the dictates of *shari'a* and agrees to follow the truth but still harbours some attraction to passional pleasures it is called 'Reproachful' (*lawwāma*). When this attraction disappears, and it acquires strength in opposing the passional soul and is attracted to the World of Sanctity (*ʿālam al-quds*) and begins to receive inspirations, it is then called 'Inspired' (*mulhama*). When its agitation quietens and the passional soul loses all power over it and it forgets its pleasures altogether it is termed 'Serene' (*muṭma'inna*). When it ascends higher than this and the (spiritual) stations themselves lose importance in its sight and it becomes extinct to all [its own] wishes it is called 'Contented' (*rāḍiya*). When this state increases, it is termed 'Found Pleasing' (*marḍiyya*), that is, to both the Real and created beings. When it is commanded to return to created beings to guide and perfect them it is called 'Perfect' (*kāmila*)." See ʿAbd al-Khāliq al-Shabrāwī, *The Degrees of the Soul*, trans. Mostafa al-Badawi (London: Quilliam, 1997), 1–2.

An intelligent man, therefore, is the one who values the time he has obtained [in the very moment that it exists]. He does not postpone the work [of the religion] for a later time; nor does he wait in anticipation of free time, the attainment of which is improbable.

If, however, the worldly affairs [that occupy one] are permissible activities, one should continue therewith and involve oneself simultaneously in invocation and righteous actions. If these affairs are unlawful, one must abandon them.

حُقُـوقٌ فِي الْأَوْقَاتِ يُمْكِنُ قَضَاؤُهَـا، وَحُقُوقُ الْأَوْقَاتِ لَا يُمْكِنُ قَضَاؤُهَـا، إِذْ مَا مِنْ وَقْتٍ يَرِدُ.. إِلَّا وَلِلهِ عَلَيْكَ فِيهِ حَقٌّ جَدِيدٌ وَأَمْرٌ أَكِيدٌ، فَكَيْفَ تَقْضِي فِيهِ حَقَّ غَيْرِهِ وَأَنْتَ لَمْ تَقْضِ حَقَّ اللّٰهِ فِيهِ؟

It is possible to fulfill some obligations at times, but it is impossible to fulfill the obligations of every moment, for there is no moment wherein God does not hold against you a new obligation or a definite matter. So how can you fulfill someone else's obligation when you have not fulfilled God's? [208]

There are two kinds of obligations upon the servant. The first kind pertains to worship. These rights [of Allāh] become obligatory at fixed times, such as the daily ritual prayer or fasting in the month of Ramadan. If these obligations are not discharged at their appointed times, it is possible to redeem them by executing these acts of worship at some other time [by way of make-up (*qaḍā'*)].

The second kind of obligation concerns time. These obligations apply at every moment. There is no separate fixed time set out for them, since these are the rights of time itself and the existence of time is perpetual.

Time in this context refers to the states that continually occur to the servant. These states are of four kinds: bounty (*niʿma*), calamity (*muṣība*), obedience (*ṭāʿa*) and sin (*maʿṣiya*). At any given time, the servant will certainly be in one of these four states.

These states also have obligations that are due during their presence: the obligation of bounty is gratitude (*shukr*); the obligation of calamity is patience (*ṣabr*); the obligation of obedience is perception of Allāh's grace; the obligation of sin is repentance (*tawba*).

It is imperative that the servant observes the obligations of time. At every breath, he should be mindful of this duty. It is for this reason that the righteous scholars have said "The sufi is the son of the moment (*ibn al-waqt*)." In other words, he is fully and perpetually engrossed in the discharge of the obligations of time.

مَا فَاتَ مِنْ عُمُرِكَ لَا عِوَضَ لَهُ، وَمَا حَصَلَ لَكَ مِنْهُ لَا قِيمَةَ لَهُ.

That part of your life that has gone by is irreplaceable, and that which has arrived is priceless. [209]

No compensation can ever be offered for man's time that has expired. Therefore, the time that one obtains at present is priceless. The entire earth with all its possessions cannot buy such a thing, which has the potential to bring everlasting happiness for one who uses it wisely. It is precisely for this reason that the pious predecessors (*salaf ṣāliḥīn*) treasured their breathing, taking a constant reckoning of every breath. Never would they destroy a single moment.

According to a ḥadīth, the moment that a servant spends in forgetfulness will be a cause of regret for him, but at that time [in the future, once one has passed from this world] remorse will be of no avail.

اَلْخِذْلَانُ كُلُّ الْخِذْلَانِ أَنْ تَتَفَرَّغَ مِنَ الشَّوَاغِلِ ثُمَّ لَا تَتَوَجَّهَ إِلَيْهِ، وَتَقِلَّ عَوَائِقُكَ ثُمَّ لَا تَرْحَلَ إِلَيْهِ.

It would be disappointing—really disappointing—if you were to find yourself free of distractions and then not head toward Him, or if you were to have a few obstacles and then not move on to Him! [259]

It does not matter to what extent man is involved in worldly affairs and in the execution of his family duties, he is under obligation at all times to turn to Allāh and remember Him. Worship is obligatory on him in all circumstances. It is, therefore, essential that he casts aside the redundant affairs of the world and contents himself with basic needs.

If all his time is consumed in worldly matters, leaving no time for building up a capital for the next world, then indeed the servant will find himself in complete disgrace and total loss. It will be his greatest misfortune. His excuse of not being able to find the time [to obey Allāh] will not be acceptable.

Yet if a man has sufficient wealth to free himself of excessive involvement in worldly affairs, but fails to apply himself to obeying Allāh, then he ruins his life in forgetfulness, play and amusement; his disgrace, misfortune and destruction are multiplied manifold. Indeed, his plight is most pitiful. He had acquired the priceless treasure of time and then destroyed it [i.e., destroyed any benefit it potentially offered]. Alas, for such a one!

7

ON INVOCATION

لَا تَتْرُكِ الذِّكْرَ لِعَدَمِ حُضُورِكَ مَعَ اللّٰهِ فِيهِ، لِأَنَّ غَفْلَتَكَ عَنْ وُجُودِ ذِكْرِهِ أَشَدُّ مِنْ غَفْلَتِكَ فِي وُجُودِ ذِكْرِهِ.. فَعَسٰى أَنْ يَرْفَعَكَ مِنْ ذِكْرٍ مَعَ وُجُودِ غَفْلَةٍ إِلٰى ذِكْرٍ مَعَ وُجُودِ يَقَظَةٍ، وَمِنْ ذِكْرٍ مَعَ وُجُودِ يَقَظَةٍ إِلٰى ذِكْرٍ مَعَ وُجُودِ حُضُورٍ، وَمِنْ ذِكْرٍ مَعَ وُجُودِ حُضُورٍ إِلٰى ذِكْرٍ مَعَ وُجُودِ غَيْبَةٍ عَمَّا سِوَى الْمَذْكُورِ، ﴿وَما ذٰلِكَ عَلَى اللّٰهِ بِعَزِيزٍ﴾.

Do not abandon the invocation because you do not feel the Presence of God therein. For your forgetfulness of the invocation of Him is worse than your forgetfulness in the invocation of Him. Perhaps He will take you from an invocation with forgetfulness to one with vigilance, and from one with vigilance to one with the Presence of God, and from one with the Presence of God to one wherein everything but the Invoked is absent. "And that is not difficult for God." [Q. 14:20] [47]

Many people complain of a lack of concentration in their invocations[14] and the incidence of stray thoughts (*waswasa*). Some even abandon invocation on account of this. The Shaykh ﷺ therefore advises such people that one should not abandon invocation because of a lack of concentration. The lack of concentration is only one calamity, but at least the existence of invocation

14 A comprehensive English resource on the topic of invocation is Ibn al-Qayyim al-Jawziyya, *The Invocation of God*, trans. Michael Abdurrahman Fitzgerald and Moulay Youssef Slitine (Cambridge, UK: ITS, 2000).

is with one, even though it is accompanied by forgetfulness. Yet in the event of abandoning invocation altogether, it will not be simply invocation without concentration, but the loss of invocation itself. This state of abandoning invocation is, therefore, extremely grave. Invocation with forgetfulness is far superior to the total abandonment of invocation.

In the state of invocation with a heart that is negligent, at least the tongue is involved with invocation. However, in contrast to the state where both tongue and heart are inert, having abandoned the invocation of Allāh Most High, even mere verbal invocation is a valuable treasure. Providing encouragement, the Shaykh ﵀ further adds that it is quite possible that Allāh Most High may improve the quality of one's invocation. The initial invocation without concentration can progress to the stage where concentration will be achieved and stray thoughts cease. It will then be the invocation of wakefulness and concentration. In this stage of invocation, the heart will not drift toward the stray thoughts of the ego. The verbal invocation at this time will keep the heart alert; and one will then taste pleasure in this very invocation.

The progress will then continue to the stage where the spiritual presence [of the heart] accompanies the invocation. This is the achievement of the heart's attention to the verbal invocation. In a state of spiritual presence, invocation becomes the attribute of the heart, just as seeing is the attribute of the eye. Thus, invocation becomes the permanent attribute of the heart.

However, in this latter stage the heart does perceive itself to be in possession of the attribute of invocation. Here, the spiritual traveler is conscious of his invocation being with concentration. Perception of even such a presence is a kind of forgetfulness, because the perception itself is an object besides Allāh. Hence, there is an even higher stage of invocation, where this inner perception of concentration perishes and is assigned to the realm of oblivion; it enters the domain of other deities that are negated in the invocation of the One True Allāh. At such a juncture, everything else is annihilated. In other words, invocation predominates one to such an extent that the servant's entire being is permeated by the invocation of Allāh.

If someone expresses amazement, thinking that such a lofty stage is unattainable, the Shaykh ﵀ provides the answer for this doubt: he says that the attainment of this stage will be impossible by one's own efforts. This spiritual station is the consequence of Allāh's bounty; it is not difficult for Him to bestow His bounty to anyone, therefore never despair.

ـہؔ

أَكْرَمَـكَ بِكَرَامَاتٍ ثَلَاثٍ: جَعَلَكَ ذَاكِرًا لَهُ، وَلَوْلَا فَضْلُهُ .. لَمْ تَكُنْ

أَهْلًا لِجَرَيَانِ ذِكْرِهِ عَلَيْكَ، وَجَعَلَكَ مَذْكُورًا بِهِ إِذْ حَقَّقَ نِسْبَتَهُ لَدَيْكَ،

وَجَعَلَكَ مَذْكُورًا عِنْدَهُ فَتَمَّمَ نِعْمَتَهُ عَلَيْكَ.

He ennobled you with three charismatic gifts: He made
you an invoker of Him, and had it not been for His
grace, you would not have been worthy of the flow of the
invocation of Him in you; He made you remembered by
Him since He confirmed His relationship to you; and
He made you remembered by those with Him, thereby
perfecting His grace upon you. [256]

Here the Shaykh 🙠 is addressing the obedient person of invocation. He
says that Allāh Most High has conferred three honors upon such a person.
These honors collectively constitute a limitless treasure of goodness and
excellence for one, and are from the immense mercy of Allāh.

The very first of these honors is that He has enabled one to invoke Him;
hence one is able to engross oneself in His invocation, with tongue, limbs
and heart. If not for His bounty, the tongue, heart and limbs would never
have been able to render the invocation of the Ruler of Rulers; one would
not have been qualified [through one's own efforts] to worship the King of
Kings, because deficiency, inertia and indolence are inherent in one's nature.
It is through nothing other than His mercy and grace that, while keeping
millions of His creation in forgetfulness, He applied you to His invocation.

The second honor is that He Himself remembers one. Allāh says in
the Qur'ān: *Remember Me and I shall remember you* (2:152). What greater
honor can there be than the servant, constituted of a handful of dust, being
remembered by the True King, the Lord of all Lords, the Sovereign of all
Creation? In this state, people regard one as a saint of Allāh, and as a chosen
one of Allāh. Indeed, this is a very high honor to be bestowed upon a person.
In this day and age, if some puny worldly king confers a title on a man, he
becomes bloated with happiness, his pleasure boundless. Now, imagine the
high state of the honor conferred on one when the True and Eternal King
proclaims one to be His friend?

The third honor is highlighted in a ḥadīth, where the Messenger of

Allāh ﷺ said: "Allāh said: 'Whoever remembers Me in his heart, I too remember him in My Heart; and whoever remembers Me in a gathering, I remember Him in a gathering which is nobler than his gathering'"[15] [i.e., the gathering of the angels].

مَا كَانَ ظَاهِرُ ذِكْرٍ .. إِلَّا عَنْ بَاطِنِ شُهُودٍ وَفِكْرٍ.

The outer aspect of an invocation would not be save for the inner aspect of contemplation and meditation. [254]

The worship, obedience and invocation of the servant, which become manifest in this world, are in a certain sense a return to the inner witnessing experienced by the spirit (*rūḥ*) prior to its entry into this world. They are thus connected to the effects of that earlier spiritual perception, even though the servant is unaware of it.

The reason for this unawareness is the domination of the effects of the physical body over the spirit. However, Allāh Most High bestows the knowledge of even that spiritual realm to whomever He pleases, whereby He eliminates all impediments to this awareness.

15 This ḥadīth is part of a longer narration that has been transmitted in *Ṣaḥīḥ al-Bukhārī* and *Muslim*.

8

ON MEDITATION

اَلْفِكْرَةُ سَيْرُ الْقَلْبِ فِي مَيَادِينِ الْأَغْيَارِ.

Meditation is the voyage of the heart in the domains of alterities. [260]

ALL OF CREATION, from the heavens to the earth, has been portrayed or compared to the domains of alterities. The reality of meditation is the wandering of the heart in these domains. Wandering in these domains, in this context, means to meditate on the wonderful manifestations of Allāh's power (*qudra*) that reveals itself, perpetually, in His creation. For instance, some are born, while others die; some are poor, while others are wealthy. There are innumerable marvels in His creation inhabiting the heavens and the earth. Man is required to derive lessons from these marvelous objects of creation and meditate on Allāh's attributes of beauty, excellence and splendor. This meditation will lead him to [recognizing] the Creator Most High. He will firmly believe that his Creator is Most Wise, Most Gracious, Most Majestic and Most Splendid. This is the type of meditation that we are commanded to observe.

We have been forbidden to meditate on the Essence (*dhāt*) of the Creator, because our limited minds cannot comprehend the Infinite, Eternal Being. In such meditation lurks the danger of renouncing the religion—and we seek Allāh's protection. Belief in the Creator should be confined to the limits indicated to us.

Furthermore, one should meditate on obedience and sin—that for a certain act of obedience there is a particular reward and for a sin there is a certain degree of punishment.

We should also meditate on the bounties of Allāh. His bounties are innumerable and He is the true Benefactor. We should also meditate on the perishable nature of the world and its objects. These various types of meditation are praiseworthy and we have been instructed to observe them.

اَلْفِكْرَةُ سِرَاجُ الْقَلْبِ، فَإِذَا ذَهَبَتْ .. فَلَا إِضَاءَةَ لَهُ.

Meditation is the lamp of the heart; so when it goes away, the heart has no illumination. [261]

This aphorism means that bereft of meditation the heart resembles a dark room in which there is no light-giving lamp. One does not know what lurks in that dark room as nothing is visible. Similarly, without meditation the reality and true nature of an object will not be fathomed.

When man meditates, the inner nature and reality of things will be revealed to him. He will see with open eyes [i.e., his spiritual eyes] the realities of truth, falsehood, the perishable nature of the world and the everlasting nature of the Hereafter. The glory, splendor, power and wrath of Allāh, as well as His being the True Benefactor, will become vivid realities. Man will also become aware of his own hidden defects, the schemes and deceptions of his ego, and that the world is the abode of futility and deception.

If the servant refrains from meditation, his heart will become like a dark room. He will then be unable to differentiate the various things outlined above.

اَلْفِكْرَةُ فِكْرَتَانِ: فِكْرَةُ تَصْدِيقٍ وَإِيمَانٍ، وَفِكْرَةُ شُهُودٍ وَعِيَانٍ، فَالْأُوْلَى لِأَرْبَابِ الْإِعْتِبَارِ، وَالثَّانِيَةُ لِأَرْبَابِ الشُّهُودِ وَالْإِسْتِبْصَارِ.

Meditation is of two kinds: the meditation of belief and faith, and the meditation of contemplation and vision. The first is for the adepts of reflective thoughts, the second is for the adepts of contemplation and intellectual vision. [262]

The select servants of Allāh are of two kinds: the traveler to Allāh (*sālik*) and the ecstatic (*majdhūb*). The one who logically deduces the Cause from the effects is a traveler; he meditates on the effects and arrives at the knowledge of the Cause. His heart initially wanders in the objects of creation. From these meditations he reaches the way to the divine attributes. For example, he sees people transgressing without Allāh Most High punishing them, and from this the traveler appreciates Allāh's attribute of patience (*ḥilm*), where He refrains from punishing despite having the power. Moreover, from the beauty, excellence and perfection of objects, he infers that Allāh is All-Wise. By means of prolonged meditation on the names and attributes of Allāh, the heart finally discovers the way leading to Allāh Himself. Thus, by meditating on the effects, he ultimately reaches the Cause: Allāh Most High.

On the other hand, the one who acknowledges effects after meditating on the Cause is the ecstatic. Initially, his heart becomes imbued with the spiritual perception, figuratively speaking, of the Being. He then dwells in the names and attributes of Allāh. Finally, he enters into meditating on creation.

Thus the traveler is taken from the bottom to the top, so to speak, and the ecstatic is brought down from the top to the bottom. However, this is the state of those whose perfection Allāh Most High desires, since some of these attracted ones remain in the state of attraction (*jadhb*), while some travelers remain suspended without attaining accomplishment.

The Shaykh ﵁ says that there are two kinds of meditation: the first form is known as belief and faith, while the second is contemplation and vision.

In the first kind of meditation the travelers reach [the knowledge of] Allāh by their meditative study of His created objects. They utilize their physical senses in the observation of creation to conclude the greatness of the Creator. The aim of this meditation is the spiritual perception (*mushāhada*) of the Pure Being of Allāh Most High. Its motivating force is not only belief—because progression is not, in this instance, essentially from the Creator to the creation—but, in this case, the progression, so to speak, is from the creation to the Creator. Thus the gaze of the traveler's heart in this state is more focused, concentrated on creation, then ultimately on the Creator.

On the other hand, the knowledge possessed by the ecstatic dictates to him the reality of the existence of creation on account of the existence of the Creator. The focus of his heart is initially on the Creator, later reaching creation. For this reason, the traveler is one whose senses and intellect are intact, whereas the ecstatic acts, generally, in conflict with [customary] intelligence.

It should be understood that the knowledge derived from [both types of] meditation is inspired. It is a bestowal from Allāh Most High.

9

ON ABSTINENCE

مَا قَلَّ عَمَلٌ بَرَزَ مِنْ قَلْبٍ زَاهِدٍ، وَلَا كَثُرَ عَمَلٌ بَرَزَ مِنْ قَلْبٍ رَاغِبٍ.

No deed arising from a renouncing heart is small, and no deed arising from an avaricious heart is fruitful. [45]

As long as love for the world and love for fame dominate, sincerity in actions will not develop. Worldly motives and lustful desires will appear in every place and in every deed of such a person.

Acceptance of deeds in the Divine Court occurs only when these deeds are devoid of such calamities. On the contrary, the servants upon whom Allāh's grace settles, and whose egos are purified from love of the world—all their actions, whether pertaining to the religion or the world, are based on sincerity. The aim of such a person is solely Allāh, because the world has been expelled from his heart. Hence, a deed rendered by an abstinent one is not insignificant, even if in quantity it appears slight. Although his deed may be quantitatively little, it is imbued with a true spirit and is accepted by Allāh Most High; consequently, it is very significant.

On the other hand, the actions of a man whose heart is greedily set on the world and who is forgetful of Allāh Most High are insignificant, even if in appearance they are considerable and great. This is because the aim of these deeds is not proper. Such a heart is contaminated with falsehood; therefore his deeds are not free of the calamities of show and the base motives of the ego and the devil, even if he considers himself to be free of such ailments.

It is of utmost importance to cleanse the heart of all things besides Allāh Most High. The heart should be purified and adorned with lofty attributes so that the righteous deeds rendered are full of life and soul. Then, even if the deed is ostensibly small, in reality it will be great.

It is essential to understand that righteous deeds should not be abandoned on account of the existence of these spiritual calamities in one. After all, rendering the deeds is better than abandoning them. Moreover, righteous deeds, if practiced constantly, will ultimately produce sincerity.

لِيَقِلَّ مَا تَفْرَحُ بِهِ يَقِلَّ مَا تَحْزَنُ عَلَيْهِ.

So that your sadness over something be little, let your joy in it be little. [226]

In most cases, the cause of man's grief and worry is the loss of worldly objects: the loss of wealth and property is one example. The possession of such objects, on the other hand, produces pleasure and comfort.

If anyone wishes to decrease grief and worry, he should decrease his worldly possessions. He will not then possess the things that cause him grief. The greater man's worldly possessions, the greater will be his grief and sorrow. The heart will not find peace. Thus the intelligent man will content himself with necessary requirements and eliminate superfluous possessions. In this way he acquires the peace and comfort of both worlds.

إِنْ أَرَدْتَ أَنْ لَا تُعْزَلَ .. فَلَا تَتَوَلَّ وِلَايَةً لَا تَدُومُ لَكَ.

If you do not want to be dismissed, then do not take charge of a post that will not always be yours. [227]

This aphorism is an example of the former statement. The kingdom of the world has no true existence [of its own]; it is transitory and perishable [and only sustained by Allāh]. Do not acquire it [in abundance] because you will be confronted with the grief of being dismissed from it. Even if you are not dismissed in worldly terms, death will ultimately tear you away from this kingdom. You will then suffer the grief of dismissal. Hence, abstain from the acquisition of this perishable kingdom.

إِنْ رَغَّبَتْكَ الْبِدَايَاتُ .. زَهَّدَتْكَ النِّهَايَاتُ، إِنْ دَعَاكَ إِلَيْهَا ظَاهِرٌ .. نَهَاكَ عَنْهَا بَاطِنٌ.

If beginnings make you desirous, endings will make you abstinent: if their exteriors invited you, their interiors will hold you back. [228]

Initially, the pomp and pleasure of the worldly kingdom appear magnificent and pleasing. Those who possess such wealth appear honorable and noble in the estimate of others; even their own egos bask in delight. This initial pomp draws people into trying to acquire the wealth of the world. Ultimately, however, the result is that the owner is either dismissed during his lifetime or is separated from it by death.

When dismissed, an ex-ruler will be overwhelmed with grief. When he is separated from his kingdom by death, sorrow will be his lot on account of his oppression and denial of the rights of people. Thus sorrow and regret will be his end. This regrettable end will disenchant him from his worldly kingdom, but by then it will be too late.

While the outer form of the worldly kingdom is alluring with its ranks, wealth and comforts, its inner reality diverts man from the invocation of Allāh Most High. It is, therefore, absolutely disastrous for one's happiness and success in the next world. This ultimate fate of the worldly kingdom should thus prevent one from hankering after it.

The intelligent man is far-sighted; he is not deceived by the external façade of anything. His sight is set on reality and the ultimate result.

إِنَّمَا جَعَلَهَا مَحَلًّا لِلْأَغْيَارِ وَمَعْدِنًا لِوُجُودِ الْأَكْدَارِ تَزْهِيدًا لَكَ فِيهَا.

He only made the world the place of alterities and the mine of impurities by way of inducing detachment in you toward it. [229]

Allāh Most High has made the world a place from which man should derive lesson and experience. He has also made it an abode of pollution and worries. From the awful and awesome episodes enacted night and day on earth, the intelligent man takes a lesson and gains experience. From the terrible calamities and upheavals happening in the world, man gains admonition. No one is able to attain fulfillment of his wishes and goals. In short, the world is the abode of worry and pollution.

In the hardships, trials, tribulations and experiences of man there is considerable mercy of Allāh Most High. As a result of these trials, man [as truly defined] becomes disenchanted from the world. By means of this disinclination, Allāh Most High separates him from this carrion that is the world.

عَلِمَ أَنَّكَ لَا تَقْبَلُ النُّصْحَ الْمُجَرَّدَ، فَذَوَّقَكَ مِنْ ذَوَاقِهَا مَا يُسَهِّلُ عَلَيْكَ وُجُودَ فِرَاقِهَا.

He knew you would not accept mere counsel, so He made you sample the world's taste to a degree that separation from it would be easy for you. [230]

The Qur'ān, ḥadīth and counsel of the learned are adequate for a man devoid of the love of the world and whose intelligence is sound. However, Allāh knows that the love of worldly pleasures and pollution is firmly entrenched in the hearts of numerous people. The intelligence of such people is deficient; hence, good counsel alone is not sufficient for them. He gives them a taste of worldly hardships and trials so that they become disillusioned with this carrion. Abandoning the world, therefore, becomes a matter of ease.

There are also such people who fail to gain any lesson from difficulties and hardships. Nevertheless, numerous Muslims do turn toward Allāh Most High in consequence of the calamities that befall them. Thus, in relation to their former state of degeneration, they progress in the direction leading to Allāh Most High.

اَلطَّيُّ الْحَقِيقِيُّ أَنْ تُطْوٰى مَسَافَةُ الدُّنْيَا عَنْكَ حَتّٰى تَرَى الْآخِرَةَ أَقْرَبَ إِلَيْكَ مِنْكَ.

The real journey is when the world's dimension is rolled away from you so that you see the Hereafter closer to you than yourself. [87]

Miracles (*karāmāt*) that Allāh Most High awards to His saints, such as traversing huge distances in a minute, are not what one aims for [in the Path], nor something to hanker after. Traversing distances miraculously is not necessarily the trait of the accepted servants. In other words, if someone possesses the ability of travelling huge distances in minutes, it does not follow that he is necessarily an accepted saint of Allāh Most High. It is quite possible that a man can acquire such powers by exercises, even while he is not obedient to the Sacred Law. A seemingly miraculous deed displayed by an irreligious person is an act that leads that person further astray (*istidrāj*).

The true journey is to wrap up the distance of the world from in front of one's heart, i.e., not only to expel the love of the world from the heart, but not to permit it even to pass near to the heart. One should eliminate the love of the world so that the Day of Judgment appears to be nearer to one than one's own self.

The heart gains the ability to traverse the distance of the world when Allāh Most High inspires the servant's heart with the light of certainty. With the inner illumination of this light of certainty, one will gain the reality of the Qur'ānic expression: *Say: Truth has arrived and Falsehood has perished* (17:81). At such a time, the world will be completely annihilated from the heart: *And that is the Bounty of Allāh. He grants it to whomever He wishes* (57:21). *And that is not difficult for Allāh* (14:20).

May Allāh bestow [all of] this upon us. May He accept our prayer.

لَوْ أَشْرَقَ لَكَ نُورُ الْيَقِينِ .. لَرَأَيْتَ الْآخِرَةَ أَقْرَبَ إِلَيْكَ مِنْ أَنْ تَرْحَلَ إِلَيْهَا، وَلَرَأَيْتَ مَحَاسِنَ الدُّنْيَا قَدْ ظَهَرَتْ كِسْفَةُ الْفَنَاءِ عَلَيْهَا.

Were the light of certitude to shine, you would see the Hereafter so near that you could not move toward it, and you would see that the eclipse of extinction had come over the beauties of the world. [136]

Allāh and His Prophet ﷺ have informed us that this world is a transitory abode of falsehood and deception, while the next world is everlasting and is the abode of truth. If one had firm belief in these truths and the light of this certitude permeated the heart, enabling one to see that the promises of Allāh and His Prophet ﷺ are brighter than the sun, then the next world would be actually present in the heart.

The discernment of reality is the result of the light of certitude, which is inspired in the heart. When it is inspired in the heart, it makes the realities of things conspicuous. Every Muslim knows that the world is perishable and the next world is everlasting. Every Muslim believes in the promises of Allāh and His Messenger ﷺ. Yet, when the light of certitude dawns in the heart these objects of faith become as visible as the things seen by the physical eyes.

The effect of this discernment is that such a man will cast the world behind his back and all his efforts will be for the next world, the inordinate desires of his ego will dissipate, and he will treasure time.

May Allāh bestow this to us. May Allāh accept our prayer. *Āmīn.*

اَلْأَكْوَانُ ظَاهِرُهَا غِرَّةٌ وَبَاطِنُهَا عِبْرَةٌ، فَالنَّفْسُ تَنْظُرُ إِلٰى ظَاهِرِ غِرَّتِهَا، وَالْقَلْبُ يَنْظُرُ إِلٰى بَاطِنِ عِبْرَتِهَا.

Outwardly, creatures are an illusion, but, inwardly, they are an admonition. Thus, the soul looks at the illusory exterior while the heart looks at the admonitory interior. [85]

The soul is ensnared into excessive love of this world by the external beauty and glitter of worldly things. Consequently, the person in this condition pursues these worldly objects. In this pursuit, man forgets the next world. But the inner realities of these things are an admonition. While every earthly object is initially beautiful and pleasurable, its ultimate end is distasteful and disgusting. As an example, consider the beginning and the end of food.

The worldly allurements cause man even to turn his back on the religion. If Allāh's granting of success (*tawfīq*) is at hand and He bestows sound intelligence, the soul is prevented from [falling victim to] the superficial beauty and glitter of the world. The [essential] nothingness and ultimate extinction [of them] are kept in sight and man does not plunge into these deceptions. He contents himself with needs. He leaves everything else and goes in search of the everlasting treasure.

إِنْ أَرَدْتَ أَنْ يَكُونَ لَكَ عِزٌّ لَا يَفْنَى .. فَلَا تَسْتَعِزَّنَّ بِعِزٍّ يَفْنَى.

If you want a glory that does not vanish, then do not glory in a glory that vanishes. [86]

Worldly honor is wealth and fame. Both of these are snatched away from man here in this earthly life; or, ultimately, man is separated from them by death. Thus, this honor will end. If one acquired this honor while remaining forgetful of the Master, then one's honor will not endure, because the basis of such honor is perishable.

True and everlasting honor is that the heart establishes no [unhealthy] relationship with worldly objects. Hence, the heart is truly enriched by establishing a bond with the Eternal Being. If the kingdom of the world is presented to an individual with a heart imbued with the divine bond, the heart will not be attracted to the worldly kingdom. Compared to the kingdom of the Ruler of Rulers, the kingdom of the world is not equal to the wing of a mosquito.

Whoever desires the true and everlasting honor then let him abandon the perishable honor of the world. This true honor will be with man even in this life, while its full and perfect manifestation will be after death.

10

ON POVERTY

وُرُودُ الْفَاقَاتِ أَعْيَادُ الْمُرِيدِينَ.

The feast-days of novices are when states of need arrive. [174]

The feast-days are the days of celebration and happiness. The happiness of man is in the attainment of his objects of desire. While the happiness of laymen is in food, garments, wealth and worldly honor, the happiness of the selected servants of Allāh—those who have established a true bond with Allāh—is in the denial of the desires of their egos. When the objects of desire of the ego are denied to it, it is the feast-day of the novices.

The basis of this happiness is a heart purified of the contaminations of all aliens—that is, of all things besides Allāh Most High. Whenever the ego acquires things of its desire, it turns toward them. Contamination then affects its purity. On the other hand, when the desires of the ego are denied, the ego runs toward Allāh Most High. It then experiences peace and pleasure in this condition.

Poverty is in conflict with the desire of the ego. Poverty is a festive occasion for those who are in the state of climbing the ladder of spiritual progress. Although [in the early stages of the Path] they have created a bond with Allāh Most High, they have not yet attained firmness and steadfastness; lower urges still remain in them. However, after perfection, when the ego has mounted the stage of being serene (*mutma'inna*), every moment and condition is its feast-day. Adversity and prosperity are then equal.

رُبَّمَا وَجَدْتَ مِنَ الْمَزِيدِ فِي الْفَاقَاتِ مَا لَا تَجِدُهُ فِي الصَّوْمِ وَالصَّلَاةِ.

Sometimes you will find more benefit in states of need than you find in fasting or ritual prayer. [175]

The basis for the incidence of celestial lights, inspirational knowledge, divine mysteries and subtleties is denial of the desires of the ego. Therefore, if the ritual prayer and fasting are executed after the desires of the ego have been satisfied, as in breaking the fast with delicious food or performing the ritual prayer in [extravagantly] fine garments, then in such a prayer and fast there will not be such abundance of inner illumination and spiritual mysteries as would cascade into the heart at the time of starvation and during conditions that are in conflict with the desires of the ego.

اَلْفَاقَاتُ بُسُطُ الْمَوَاهِبِ.

States of need are gift-laden carpets. [176]

Poverty is a divine bestowal that is like a carpet. During periods of starvation the carpet is filled with gifts in the form of inner illumination, gnosis and mystical secrets (*asrār*). Thus, the selected servants of Allāh are not scared by poverty and starvation. On the contrary, their happiness is boundless [in this state].

إِنْ أَرَدْتَ وُرُودَ الْمَوَاهِبِ عَلَيْكَ .. صَحِّحِ الْفَقْرَ
وَالْفَاقَةَ لَدَيْكَ، ﴿إِنَّمَا الصَّدَقَاتُ لِلْفُقَرَاءِ﴾.

If you want gifts to come your way, then perfect the spiritual poverty you have. "Alms are only for the poor." [Q. 9:60] [177]

The attribute of want and need is poverty. Cultivation of poverty thus means to cultivate the attribute of need and want in relation to the Master, Allāh Most High. Dependence must be on Allāh at all times. The heart should not develop independence on account of worldly possessions. Man's heart should not feel satisfied and independent because of wealth and children. Independence of the heart should be only by virtue of the divine bond.

If one desires the torrents of divine effulgence to rain down on one, then one must become wholly dependent on Him. When this state of need has become entrenched in one's self, one will experience the wonder of His mysteries cascading on one. An ocean of inner knowledge will flood upon one. The proof for this claim is Allāh's statement: *Alms are only for the poor (fuqarā')*.

One will, therefore, only receive the charity of His spiritual gifts when one has become imbued with the attributes of poverty. At all times, even if one possesses an abundance of worldly wealth, one should ingrain in oneself the attribute of dependence on Him. One should always remain a beggar at His door.

فَاقَتُكَ لَكَ ذَاتِيَّةٌ، وَوُرُودُ الْأَسْبَابِ مُذَكِّرَاتٌ لَكَ بِمَا خَفِيَ
عَلَيْكَ مِنْهَا، وَالْفَاقَةُ الذَّاتِيَّةُ لَا تَرْفَعُهَا الْعَوَارِضُ.

Your indigence belongs to you essentially, for accidents do not abolish essential indigence: the trials that arrive in this world are but reminders to you of what you ignore of indigence. [99]

O Mankind! In your present existence and in your next existence after death, you are and will be perpetually dependent on your Creator and Lord. Therefore, remember that your poverty and dependence are natural to your constitution. Not even for a second are you free from this dependence.

However, here on earth, on account of the health, wealth and freewill granted to you, you have developed an independent attitude, forgetting your Creator and Sustainer. You have thus become oblivious of your natural and inherent dependency on Allāh Most High. It is only on account of divine mercy that you are reminded of your natural attribute by way of the imposition of circumstances of difficulty and trial, which constrain you to turn in supplication to your Creator. These conditions of hardship imply: "o Mankind! Why have you forgotten your origin?'

The selected servants of Allāh always keep in mind this natural attribute of man's dependence on Allāh Most High. The difficulties and trials that come their way are not for reminding them of their dependence, but are for the elevation of their ranks.

All things that have deceived one into a false state of independence are temporary. Allāh Most High is at all times capable of snatching away these material possessions that are keeping one in deception. When it happens, as it often does, man's original state of dependence is exposed. He should, therefore, understand that his temporary and superficial façade of independence does not eliminate his natural and inherent state of absolute dependence. One should thus employ one's intelligence and remember one's origin. One's welfare is in this.

خَيْرُ أَوْقَاتِكَ وَقْتٌ تَشْهَدُ فِيهِ وُجُودَ فَاقَتِكَ،
وَتُرَدُّ فِيهِ إِلَى وُجُودِ ذِلَّتِكَ.

The best of your moments is the one wherein you witness the existence of your indigence and, through it, arrive at the existence of your lowliness. [100]

O searcher of the Truth! The best moments in your life are the times that you spend in the contemplation of your actual and natural dependence. Taking lesson from this perception, you will return to your original state of humility that has become obscure to your heart.

Since man and the entire creation are perpetually under divine domination and subjugation, man should understand his lowliness. Allāh Most High manipulates creation at His will. True power, beauty and splendor belong only to Him. If, therefore, the servant gains the impression that he too possesses respect and honor, he will become a rebel. Chastisement for rebellion is self-evident [as necessary for such behavior].

It is not sufficient that man only acknowledges his dependence and humility, because this mere knowledge is with everyone. The recognition of one's dependence should become a perpetual state permeating one's heart. The effect should at all times be on the heart. It should reach the stage of certainty that precludes all doubt.

On the contrary, man's vilest time will be the moments in which he feels that he possesses the attributes of independence, excellence, rank and honor.

لَا تَمُدَّنَ يَدَكَ إِلَى الْأَخْذِ مِنَ الْخَلَائِقِ .. إِلَّا أَنْ تَرَى أَنَّ الْمُعْطِيَ
فِيهِمْ مَوْلَاكَ، فَإِنْ كُنْتَ كَذٰلِكَ .. فَخُذْ مَا وَافَقَكَ الْعِلْمُ.

Do not stretch out your hand to take from creatures unless you see that the Giver amongst them is your Lord. If such is your case, then take what knowledge says is suitable for you. [190]

O servant of Allāh! Gifts awarded to you by people may be accepted on two conditions.

Firstly, you have reached such a state [of spiritual elevation] that you firmly believe that the actual Giver is Allāh Most High and creation is the medium only. Mere knowledge of this fact is not adequate, because both Muslims and non-Muslims believe that Allāh is the Giver. Rather, the state of your heart should be such that you consciously feel that creation is not the giver under any circumstances. The gaze of the heart should not be on creation.

Secondly, when you have imbued in yourself the aforementioned condition, then accept the gift according to your outer and inner knowledge. Outer knowledge refers to the Sacred Law: in other words, if it permits acceptance of the gift, accept it, otherwise refrain. For example, if the gift is presented to one by a person whose earnings are unlawful, then refrain from accepting it.

Inner knowledge refers to the knowledge of your inner condition. If you have need for the object presented, accept only what you need and leave the excess. If, however, it is your intention to give the excess to others, you may accept it. Moreover, do not accept something that you have abandoned in the process of training your ego for the sake of Allāh Most High, for perhaps Allāh Most High is sending it to you by way of trial.

Do not accept the gifts of proud people and of those who advertise their favors. Similarly, do not accept a gift from such a person whose presentation of a gift produces pressure on your heart for some reason.

11

ON DISCIPLINING THE EGO

تَشَوُّفُكَ إِلَى مَا بَطَنَ فِيكَ مِنَ الْعُيُوبِ خَيْرٌ مِنْ
تَشَوُّفِكَ إِلَى مَا حُجِبَ عَنْكَ مِنَ الْغُيُوبِ.

Your being on the lookout for the vices hidden within you is better than your being on the lookout for the invisible realities veiled from you. [32]

O SEEKER! You are eager to discover hidden matters. You desire to know of the divine mysteries, secrets and subtleties. You consider these matters to be the goal. Remember that to incline the heart in this direction and pursue these hidden entities is not for your welfare. This attitude is in fact harmful for you. It is better for you to view your spiritual defects, such as showing-off, envy, pride, etc. and to concern yourself with their elimination.

If, in the course of your spiritual journey, some mystery is revealed to you, do not attach significance to it. Keep in mind that your purpose is the purification of your ego from evil attributes.

أُخْرُجْ مِنْ أَوْصَافِ بَشَرِيَّتِكَ عَنْ كُلِّ وَصْفٍ مُنَاقِضٍ
لِعُبُودِيَّتِكَ لِتَكُونَ لِنِدَاءِ الْحَقِّ مُجِيبًا، وِمِنْ حَضْرَتِهِ قَرِيبًا.

Amongst the attributes of your human nature, draw away from every one that is incompatible with your servanthood, so that you may be responsive to the call of God and near His Presence. [34]

There are two kinds of human attributes: vice and virtue. The virtuous attributes are: obedience, faith, humility, contentment, patience, etc. The evil attributes are classified into two categories: the first class is related to the physical limbs, such as backbiting, injustice, theft, etc; and the second class is related to the heart, such as pride, vanity, jealousy, etc.

The evil attributes are in conflict with worship and obedience. It is imperative to strive to eliminate these evil attributes. The heart will become adorned with the virtuous attributes after it has been purified of the evil ones. Only then will man accept the inner call of Allāh Most High.

Allāh Most High constantly calls you to His obedience. The Qur'ān says that Allāh calls one to the Abode of Peace. One should truthfully acknowledge this divine call. One will then attain divine proximity. Without purification of the ego from the evil qualities, one will not be able to truthfully answer His call. One will be deprived of divine proximity as a consequence. A man who is soiled with impurities is unfit for presentation in a royal court.

٣٥

أَصْلُ كُلِّ مَعْصِيَةٍ وَغَفْلَةٍ وَشَهْوَةٍ الرِّضَا عَنِ النَّفْسِ، وَأَصْلُ كُلِّ طَاعَةٍ وَيَقَظَةٍ وَعِفَّةٍ عَدَمُ الرِّضَا مِنْكَ عَنْهَا، وَلَئَنْ تَصْحَبَ جَاهِلًا لَا يَرْضَى عَنْ نَفْسِهِ .. خَيْرٌ لَكَ مِنْ أَنْ تَصْحَبَ عَالِمًا يَرْضَى عَنْ نَفْسِهِ، فَأَيُّ عِلْمٍ لِعَالِمٍ يَرْضَى عَنْ نَفْسِهِ؟ وَأَيُّ جَهْلٍ لِجَاهِلٍ لَا يَرْضَى عَنْ نَفْسِهِ؟

The source of every disobedience, indifference, and passion is self-satisfaction. The source of every obedience, vigilance, and virtue is dissatisfaction with one's self. It is better for you to keep company with an ignorant man dissatisfied with himself than to keep company with a learned man satisfied with himself. For what knowledge is there in a self-satisfied scholar? And what ignorance is there in an unlearned man dissatisfied with himself? [35]

When a man is pleased with his condition, then he is in fact pleased with his own ego, whether his state is good or bad. This pleasure with the ego is the root of every evil, negligence and lowly desire. When a man is pleased with his ego, its defects and evils will be concealed from his gaze, and his own evil will also appear pleasing. His heart will feel safe and satisfied with his ego. He will then become forgetful of Allāh Most High. In the wake of forgetfulness, stray satanic thoughts and lustful desires will strike one with force. Sin will then be the result.

Being displeased with the state of one's ego is the root of obedience, alertness and purity. When man is displeased with his ego, he will always be alert. He will understand every trick and desire of this enemy. He will examine intelligently every demand of the ego by the standards of the Sacred Law; and any demand that he finds in conflict with the Law will be shunned.

In the initial stage [of the Path], the struggle against the ego is difficult; sometimes the ego will emerge victorious and sometimes it will be defeated. However, if the struggle (*mujāhada*) is maintained, the power of the ego will gradually be neutralized and it will become content with the Sacred Law. It will then refrain from rebellion. Purity and obedience will become its nature. Sin and inertia will be banished.

Since the benefits of a knowledgeable one's company and the harm of an ignorant one's company are acknowledged facts, the Shaykh ﵀ says that the company of a man who is ignorant of book [external] knowledge, but displeased with his own ego, is superior to the company of a learned man satisfied with his ego. The ignorant man [mentioned in this context], though lacking in academic knowledge, understands with conviction that his ego is the embodiment of evil and defect. He does not commit the error of believing in himself as having any excellences. Such a man is spiritually perfect. He is not an ignoramus.

Conversely, association with a man who is content with his ego—despite his qualifications in academic knowledge—will prove harmful. In him is the root of every evil; hence even if his academic knowledge induces one to obey the Sacred Law, his moral state is dangerous, and hence, one cannot place confidence in him. His spiritual disease will most certainly exercise its influence at some time. His companionship will harm whomsoever is in his association, because the influence of companionship is an acknowledged fact. Such a person will be enamored by his academic research and pleased with his own self. This is precisely what forgetfulness is.

The disease of being satisfied with one's ego is extremely subtle. The one in whom it lurks is himself unable to detect it. The man who is always displeased with the state of his ego, regardless of how beautiful the condition of the ego may appear, will not be harmed by ignorance. On the other hand, the knowledge of a man of learning who is content with his ego, but who endeavors to acquire the pleasure of the people for his acts—this man's knowledge is of no benefit.

كَيْفَ تُخْرَقُ لَكَ الْعَوَائِدُ وَأَنْتَ لَمْ تَخْرِقْ مِنْ نَفْسِكَ الْعَوَائِدَ؟

How can the laws of nature be ruptured for you so that miracles result, while you, for your part, have yet to rupture your bad habits? [127]

Miraculous demonstrations (or supernatural acts) displayed by a man who is meticulous in his obedience to the Sacred Law are called miracles (*karāmāt*); however, if these same acts are demonstrated by an irreligious person, they will be states that are a means of leading further astray one who has already rejected the way of the Prophets.

Many spiritual travelers suffer from the ailment of the desire for fame and hanker after miracles. Consequently, the Shaykh ﷺ asks: when the seeker has not eliminated "bad habits" [i.e., evil attributes], how can he expect to display miracles? Miracles are a testimony of the sainthood (*wilāya*) of a person. When the seeker is shackled by lowly attributes, how can he expect the rank of sainthood?

تَمَكُّنُ حَلَاوَةِ الْهَوٰى مِنَ الْقَلْبِ هُوَ الدَّاءُ الْعُضَالُ.

Incurable sickness results when the sweetness of passion takes possession of the heart. [201]

Some physical ailments deteriorate to the degree of incurability and the patient is rendered terminally ill. The case of spiritual ailments is similar.

Everyone is plagued with lowly desires and the desires for worldly pleasure, but when the pleasure of some lowly desire becomes ingrained in the heart, the disease becomes incurable. Faith, obedience and the seeking of forgiveness (*istighfār*), although these are remedies for spiritual ailments, are efficacious as long as the disease has not become ingrained in the heart. After entrenchment in the heart, only the grace of Allāh Most High can eliminate it.

It is therefore essential that the traveler prevent spiritual ailments from becoming ingrained in the heart.

لَا يُخَافُ عَلَيْكَ أَنْ تَلْتَبِسَ الطُّرُقُ عَلَيْكَ، وَإِنَّمَا يُخَافُ عَلَيْكَ مِنْ غَلَبَةِ الْهَوٰى عَلَيْكَ.

It is not feared that the ways leading to God be confusing to you, but rather, it is feared that passion overcome you. [107]

There is not much fear of the paths of worship becoming obscure and confusing for one, because the Qur'ān, ḥadīth, and the books of Sacred Law (*fiqh*) have explicitly explained these acts. The scholars have simplified these with their expositions. However, there exists the danger of passion [i.e., lowly desire that leads to opposing the law] overwhelming one at the time of executing the commands of Allāh. Such desire will prevent one from obeying the teachings of Allāh and His Messenger ﷺ; thus plunging one into sin: becoming proud of the attainment of some bounty, hence forgetting the True Benefactor; or, at the time of calamity, the ego overwhelming one and inducing an act that conflicts with the Law.

It is therefore of the utmost importance to remain submissive to Allāh Most High in every circumstance and condition, and to suppress the rebellion of the ego.

اَلنَّاسُ يَمْدَحُونَكَ لِمَا يَظُنُّونَهُ فِيكَ، فَكُنْ أَنْتَ ذَامًّا لِنَفْسِكَ لِمَا تَعْلَمُهُ مِنْهَا.

People praise you for what they suppose is in you; but you must blame your soul for what you know is in it. [142]

Man is deceived by the praises which people laud on him on account of some attribute of excellence. Such praise produces vanity (*ʿujb*) in him. He then tends to forget his reality. It is for this reason that the Shaykh ﷺ says that people praise one for virtuous attributes that they imagine are in one, but they in fact do not know if these imagined lofty attributes actually exist in one or not. If one is intelligent, then caution will not allow this praise to deceive one.

One should attribute praises to the imagination of the one who praises, while criticizing and reviling one's self on account of the presence of evil attributes and bad habits—for one possesses irrefutable evidence, knowledge and experience of one's own shortcomings and evil qualities. When praised by others, the knowledge of one's evil attributes should be recalled to mind, thus making one doubt the veracity of such praises.

اَلْمُؤْمِنُ إِذَا مُدِحَ اسْتَحْيَا مِنَ اللّٰهِ تَعَالَى أَنْ يُثْنَى
عَلَيْهِ بِوَصْفٍ لَا يَشْهَدُهُ مِنْ نَفْسِهِ.

When the believer is praised, he is ashamed before God that he should be lauded for an attribute he does not see in himself. [143]

At all times, the close servants of Allāh have the perception of Allāh Most High. They believe themselves to be embodiments of deficiencies and evils. In view of this conception they feel highly embarrassed if praised, since they are aware of the non-existence of the attributes for which they are complimented.

On the occasions when he is praised, however, the man who is heedless [of Allāh] becomes puffed up with vanity, and believes that the praise is on account of some excellence that he most certainly possesses.

أَجْهَلُ النَّاسِ مَنْ تَرَكَ يَقِينَ مَا عِنْدَهُ لِظَنِّ مَا عِنْدَ النَّاسِ.

The most ignorant of all people is the one who abandons the certitude he has for an opinion people have. [144]

Generally, when people entertain a good opinion of a man, they praise him. They conclude the existence of lofty attributes in a man from his behavior, states and actions. When they see a man performing the ritual prayer with great care, for example, they infer that he is a pious man, even if all the attributes of sainthood are not found in him, and even if his prayer abounds with satanic and lowly thoughts [imperceptible to the observer of the external]. Thus, the person who is delighted with the praise of imagined virtues in him, while being blind to his defects, is a great ignoramus.

The stench of inner (*bāṭin*) evils is worse than the stench of physical putrefied matter. O ignoramus! How can you be pleased with such a stench?

إِذَا أَطْلَقَ الثَّنَاءَ عَلَيْكَ وَلَسْتَ بِأَهْلٍ .. فَأَثْنِ عَلَيْهِ بِمَا هُوَ أَهْلُهُ.

When He lets praise of you burst forth, and you are not worthy of it, praise Him for what He is worthy of. [145]

When people praise one, in reality it is the effect of Allāh Most High activating their tongues. If Allāh Most High employs the tongues of people to laud on one praises that are undeserved, then it behooves one to offer such praise to the Pure Being as befits Him. Do not praise those who are praising you, for their praise in reality is Allāh's veil of concealment that hides one's defects from others. Therefore, do not become trapped by the praise of people.

حَظُّ النَّفْسِ فِي الْمَعْصِيَةِ ظَاهِرٌ جَلِيٌّ، وَحَظُّهَا فِي الطَّاعَةِ بَاطِنٌ خَفِيٌّ، وَمُدَاوَاةُ مَا يَخْفَى صَعْبٌ عِلَاجُهُ.

The ego's share in disobedience is outwardly clear, while its share in obedience is inwardly hidden. To cure what is hidden is hard indeed! [159]

As long as the ego has not reached the stage of being serene, it will interfere in every act, be it obedience or sin. Its interference in sin is plainly evident. The ego derives full pleasure in sin. Despite its knowledge of divine chastisement, the ego perpetrates the sin because of the pleasure it derives.

The ego does not refrain from staking its claim of pleasure even in obedience. But it is difficult to understand this plot of the ego: it is generally understood that the ego has no share in obedience, because obedience is supposed to be difficult and detestable to the ego, hence in conflict with its wishes. It should be well understood that in spite of the difficulty of obedience, the ego can also derive pleasure therein. In some people love of fame can be found; in some is love of showing-off. Even if the worship is performed initially with sincerity, the ego can contaminate it with showing-off and love of fame.

Some people believe that the feeling of pleasure and sweetness experienced in worship is the goal to strive for. The sign of this misconception is that the ego induces man to rush toward the form of worship in which it derives greatest pleasure. It will constrain one to refrain from other types of worship, even if these are obligatory, since it does not derive pleasure therein. For example, a man performs supererogatory prayer in abundance but refrains from paying *zakāt*: he experiences pleasure in the former, not so in the latter. This indicates that in his performance of supererogatory prayer the ego derives some pleasure and that this person searches for the pleasure of the ego, not for the pleasure of Allāh Most High. If he was truly interested in Allāh's pleasure, he would not abstain from paying *zakāt*.

Thus the ego has its share of pleasure, even in worship. Although the operation of the ego in worship is extremely well concealed, the people of insight (*ahl al-baṣīra*) are able to fathom it.

When an ailment is concealed, its remedy is difficult on account of diagnosis being difficult. When even awareness of the existence of the disease is lacking and the person is considered to be spiritually healthy, then the disease is incurable.

إِذَا الْتَبَسَ عَلَيْكَ أَمْرَانِ .. فَانْظُرْ أَثْقَلَهُمَا عَلَى النَّفْسِ
فَاتَّبِعْهُ، فَإِنَّهُ لَا يَثْقُلُ عَلَيْهَا .. إِلَّا مَا كَانَ حَقًّا.

When two matters seem confusing to you, see which is heavier on the ego and follow it through. For, indeed, nothing weighs on the ego but that which is true. [192]

When one experiences uncertainty in the choice of one of two meritorious (*mustaḥabb*) or permissible (*jā'iz*) acts, then it is necessary to reflect in order to establish which act is more difficult and displeasing to the ego. One should then adopt the act that is more displeasing to the ego. The act that is better for this person will be more difficult on the ego.

The nature of the ego is ignorance. Therefore, it always searches for things that are pleasurable to it, while it flees from things that are beneficial for it.

اَلْمُؤْمِنُ يَشْغَلُهُ الثَّنَاءُ عَلَى اللّٰهِ عَنْ أَنْ يَكُونَ لِنَفْسِهِ شَاكِرًا،
وَتَشْغَلُهُ حُقُوقُ اللّٰهِ عَنْ أَنْ يَكُونَ لِحُظُوظِهِ ذَاكِرًا.

The believer is he who is diverted from extolling himself by the praise of God, and who is diverted from remembering his good fortune by the fulfillment of God's rights. [242]

Beautiful habits and virtuous attributes are purely by the grace of Allāh Most High. When the servant attributes his virtuous state to his ego, he will be guilty of showing gratitude to his ego, thereby honoring it. It does not behoove the true believer to do so.

The true and perfect believer will recite the praise of Allāh when goodness emanates from him because Allāh Most High is the True Actor. He is the Creator of all actions of man. The servant is only the means of manifestation of Allāh's acts of creation. He should therefore not attribute his virtuous deeds to his ego.

When he offers praise and thanks to Allāh Most High [on account of being given acts of obedience], he will not view his virtues as the deeds of his ego. Man should therefore engross himself in proclaiming the praises of Allāh Most High and perpetually keep in mind the fulfillment of His rights. He should not heed the pleasure of the ego, i.e., in worship and obedience. The desire for Paradise, salvation from Hell and sweetness in worship should not be fixed as the [only] goals of one's pursuit. If these are one's [sole] goals, then one's sincerity will be contaminated. The duty of the slave is to serve his Master. He should not be motivated [only] by personal pleasure and desires.

لَوْلَا مَيَادِينُ النُّفُوسِ .. مَا تَحَقَّقَ سَيْرُ السَّائِرِينَ،
إِذْ لَا مَسَافَةَ بَيْنَكَ وَبَيْنَهُ حَتَّى تَطْوِيَهَا رِحْلَتُكَ، وَلَا
قُطْعَةَ بَيْنَكَ وَبَيْنَهُ حَتَّى تَمْحُوَهَا وُصْلَتُكَ.

Were it not for the arenas of the soul, the progress of the adepts could not be realized: there is no distance between

you and Him that could be traversed by your journey, nor is there any particle between you and Him that could be effaced by your union with Him. [244]

The literal meaning of *sulūk* is to traverse a physical distance. In the terminology of the sufis, *sulūk* means to overcome and abandon the emotional and bestial attributes and desires by means of the following: struggling against the ego (*mujāhada*); specially designed devotional exercises (*riyāḍa*); acts of obedience; and invocation of Allāh. Man's domination over his ego should reach such a degree [in the Path] that observance of the laws of the Sacred Law becomes his nature, and his heart remains engrossed in the invocation of Allāh Most High. This stage of control and domination over the ego is also called *waṣl*, which means "having reached Allāh Most High.'

The desires and pleasures of the soul have been described as "arenas," because the soul runs and operates in them. If man did not possess lowly desires, there would not be the spiritual journey for the travelers (*sālikīn*, singular *sālik*), since the objective of *sulūk*, or journeying to Allāh (*sayr ila 'Llāh*), is to subjugate the desires of the ego to the Law of Allāh by way of battling (*mujāhada*) against base urges. The meaning of *sulūk* here is the spiritual flight toward Allāh, not a physical journey. The literal meaning could only be applicable if there was physical distance between man and Allāh, but Allāh is not material or a physical body or form.

Similarly, the meaning of *waṣl* also means the subjugation of the lowly promptings and desires. The Qur'ānic verse *We are nearer to man than his jugular vein* (50:16) negates any idea of *sulūk* being a journey in which the traveler (*sālik*) has to traverse a physical distance to reach Allāh Most High.[16]

16 Abū Ḥanīfa is recorded as having said: "The closeness and distance of Allāh is not in terms of long and short distances; rather, it is in terms of honor and humiliation. The obedient is close to Him without description and the disobedient is far from Him without description. Closeness, distance, and turning toward are applied to a servant who converses intimately with Allāh. Likewise without modality are the servant's closeness to Allāh in Paradise and his standing before Him." See Abū 'l-Muntahā al-Maghnīsāwī, *Imām Abū Ḥanīfa's Al-Fiqh al-Akbar Explained*, trans. Abdur-Rahman ibn Yusuf (Santa Barbara, USA: White Thread, 2007), 201–2.

12

ON MODERATION IN FEAR AND HOPE

مِنْ عَلَامَاتِ الْإِعْتِمَادِ عَلَى الْعَمَلِ نُقْصَانُ الرَّجَاءِ عِنْدَ وُجُودِ الزَّلَلِ.

One of the signs of relying on one's own deeds is the loss of hope when a downfall occurs. [1]

In every single act, the reliance of those who are experientially aware of Allāh (*ʿārifīn*, singular *ʿārif*; the "gnostic") is only on Allāh Most High. They do not rely on their spiritual states, knowledge and righteous deeds.

When these saints of Allāh render virtuous deeds, their hopes do not rise; they do not feel that they have acquired elevation in their ranks on account of their pious deeds. They perpetually dwell in the hope of Allāh's mercy. Their gaze is never on their righteous deeds.

On the other hand, the one who is yet to become an *ʿārif* reposes confidence in his good acts. When he practices virtue, his hopes rise and he feels pleased with himself, thinking that he has now become deserving of forgiveness and Paradise. Yet, when he sins, his hopes diminish. Since his reliance is on his own deeds, he labors under the impression that his sins constitute an obstacle in the path of ultimate divine mercy. In consequence, such a person often abandons righteous deeds and takes to the road of sin. This is plain stupidity and ignorance.

Although righteous actions have been commanded and sins are forbidden, they do not constitute the basis of forgiveness [by themselves]. The basis is solely Allāh's mercy. Thus, the sinner should not despair. He should advance along the Path and turn the gaze of his heart away from his deeds, relying solely on the mercy of Allāh.

The aforementioned explanation should not be misconstrued. It should not be understood to mean abstention from regret and repentance after commission of sin. Regret and repentance are essential. The believer will most assuredly repent. However, he will not despair of Allāh's mercy.

لَا نِهَايَةَ لِمَذَامِّكَ .. إِنْ أَرْجَعَكَ إِلَيْكَ، وَلَا تَفْرُغُ مَدَائِحُكَ .. إِنْ أَظْهَرَ جُودَهُ عَلَيْكَ.

Were He to make you go back to yourself, there would be no end to the reasons for blaming you; and were He to manifest His beneficence to you, there would be no end to the reasons for praising you. [124]

The natural propensity of the ego is toward evil and vice. Whatever virtue emanates from the ego is purely by the grace of Allāh Most High. If Allāh Most High allows one to remain enslaved to the ego, and withholds His grace and kindness from one, then there will be no end to the evil [wrought by the ego], because the ego is the root of all evils and mischief.

On the other hand, if Allāh Most High directs His grace and kindness to one, then one's virtues will be limitless—on account of His grace being limitless. Thus, when goodness emanates from the servant, he should reflect on the grace of Allāh Most High and refrain from attributing the virtue to his ego. Yet, if he perpetrates transgression, he should know that it is from his ego.

مَنْ عَبَّرَ مِنْ بِسَاطِ إِحْسَانِهِ .. أَصْمَتَتْهُ الْإِسَاءَةُ، وَمَنْ عَبَّرَ مِنْ بِسَاطِ إِحْسَانِ اللّٰهِ إِلَيْهِ .. لَمْ يَصْمُتْ إِذَا أَسَاءَ.

He who holds forth from the standpoint of his own virtuous behavior will be silenced by misbehavior toward God; but he who holds forth from the standpoint of God's virtuous behavior toward him will not be silenced when he misbehaves. [181]

If the propagator of advice (*naṣīḥa*) to people or the one who expounds spiritual realities and subtleties labors under the impression that the knowledge which he is expounding is the consequence of his uprightness and good deeds, then he will be silenced if he commits a sin. Since his gaze is riveted on his uprightness, shame will overwhelm him. He will feel his discourses to be hypocrisy, and will, consequently, abandon his duty of propagating the truth.

This is not the state of the *ʿārif*, however, who believes that whatever knowledge and virtue he possesses to be by the grace of Allāh Most High. Since this is his constant perception, he never attributes anything of his excellences to himself. Should he commit a sin, he will not abandon the duty of proclaiming Allāh's Law. He will continue to proclaim the Law with the same confidence and eloquence with which he rendered his duty before the sin.

إِذَا أَرَدْتَ أَنْ يَنْفَتِحَ لَكَ بَابُ الرَّجَاءِ .. فَاشْهَدْ مَا مِنْهُ إِلَيْكَ، وَإِذَا أَرَدْتَ أَنْ يَنْفَتِحَ لَكَ بَابُ الْخَوْفِ .. فَاشْهَدْ مَا مِنْكَ إِلَيْهِ.

If you want the door of hope opened for you, then consider what comes to you from Him; but if you want the door of sadness opened for you, then consider what goes to Him from you. [149]

The *sālik* maintains a perception of the state of his ego and the evils perpetrated by him. As a result, his heart suffers grief and despondency. Sometimes he is overwhelmed by despair and he loses hope in the mercy of Allāh. At times, when the despair becomes excessive, the *sālik* will even abandon the ritual prayer, fasting, etc. It is therefore essential that the aspect of divine mercy be kept in view.

When despair sets in, the *sālik* should employ his intelligence. He should bring into contemplation all the bounties and favors that Allāh Most High has conferred on him. He should then convince himself that if Allāh was about to destroy him, He would not have blessed him with so many outer and inner favors. He should meditate for a considerable time on this aspect. Allāh Most High will hopefully open the door of hope for the *sālik* and the state of despair will be dispelled.

Sometimes the opposite condition settles over the *sālik*: perceiving his good deeds, he develops vanity and self-esteem. On such occasions, the *sālik* should call to memory his acts of disobedience and transgression. This contemplation will engender fear in him.

In conclusion, the *sālik* should not be overwhelmed by despair, nor should he have excessive hope that will render him audacious. He should adopt moderation.

اَلرَّجَاءُ مَا قَارَنَهُ عَمَلٌ، وَإِلَّا فَهُوَ أُمْنِيَّةٌ.

Hope goes hand in hand with deeds, otherwise it is a wish. [78]

The hope that is genuine is the hope that the *sālik* entertains when practicing righteousness. Along with his practice of virtue, he hopes for the mercy of Allāh Most High. The farmer that has hope of reaping the fruits of his labors on his farm will expend full effort in ploughing and caring for his fields. Similarly, the *sālik* who has hope of acquiring Allāh's mercy will diligently involve himself in practicing virtuous deeds. His hope can then be said to be justified and true.

If one acts in conflict with the Sacred Law and refrains from righteous actions, his hope for divine mercy and Paradise will be vain and false. It is false to describe such wishful thinking as *rajā'*: such a person is like one who does not plough his land, but expects to reap a crop.

إِنْ لَمْ تُحْسِنْ ظَنَّكَ بِهِ لِأَجْلِ وَصْفِهِ .. فَحَسِّنْ ظَنَّكَ بِهِ لِوُجُودِ مُعَامَلَتِهِ مَعَكَ، فَهَلْ عَوَّدَكَ إِلَّا حَسَنًا؟ وَهَلْ أَسْدَى إِلَيْكَ إِلَّا مِنَنًا؟

If you have not improved your thinking of Him because of His nature, improve it because of His treatment of you. For has He accustomed you to anything but what is good? And has He conferred upon you anything but His favors? [40]

A true believer is he who holds a high opinion of His Lord. He believes that whatever treatment his Creator metes out is for his own benefit and welfare, regardless of it being pleasing or displeasing. Do you not acknowledge His boundless favors upon you? He created you in perfect form. He bestowed a variety of innumerable bounties upon you. You are, in fact, drowned in the abundance of favors. This wonderful relationship that Allāh Most High has with you should be sufficient to induce a good opinion of Him.

Having a good opinion of Allāh is the rank of Allāh's elect servants. Those who lack this rank should reflect on the bounties of Allāh Most High, as a means of cultivating this beautiful perfection.

مَنِ اسْتَغْرَبَ أَنْ يُنْقِذَهُ اللّٰهُ مِنْ شَهْوَتِهِ، وَأَنْ يُخْرِجَهُ مِنْ وُجُودِ غَفْلَتِهِ
.. فَقَدِ اسْتَعْجَزَ الْقُدْرَةَ الْإِلٰهِيَّةَ، ﴿وَكَانَ اللّٰهُ عَلَى كُلِّ شَيْءٍ مُقْتَدِرًا﴾.

Whoever finds it astonishing that God should save him from his passion or yank him out of his forgetfulness has deemed the divine Power to be weak. "And God has power over everything." [Q. 18:45] [197]

When people lost in worldly affairs and forgetfulness of Allāh Most High see a pious man, they sometimes yearn to be like him. They momentarily wish to be free from worldly encumbrances in order that they too could take to the path of piety. But the ego immediately raises its head and neutralizes their eagerness for piety. The ego leads them to believe that it is not possible for them to adopt piety, on account of their numerous mundane involvements. Their initial desire for piety then seems impossible to realize.

Similarly, some people of invocation (*dhākirūn*, singular *dhākir*), despite their invocation and spiritual efforts, do not discern any improvement in their moral and spiritual condition. They then labor under the notion that their reformation is impossible.

There are also *dhākirūn* in whose hearts invocation has taken effect, but has not yet become entrenched. Consequently, they sometimes experience forgetfulness and at other times they dwell in the state of invocation. This fluctuating state can remain for years. They therefore begin to believe that it is impossible to eliminate their forgetfulness and improve their condition.

The Shaykh ﵀ says that those who feel that it is difficult for Allāh Most High to extricate them from the grip of their ego are in reality attributing weakness to Allāh Most High. They are implying by their attitude that the infinite power of Allāh Most High is defective—and we seek refuge in Allāh [from such a belief]!

It is easy for Allāh Most High to deliver one from the grip of the ego and bless one with His invocation. There is, therefore, no need for despair. Many saints were involved in sin and transgression in their initial stage, but later Allāh Most High elevated them to the noble ranks of the saints and the shaykhs.

لَا يُخْرِجُ الشَّهْوَةَ مِنَ الْقَلْبِ .. إِلَّا خَوْفٌ مُزْعِجٌ أَوْ شَوْقٌ مُقْلِقٌ.

Only an unsettling fear or a restless desire can expel passion from the heart. [202]

It was explained earlier that when a lowly desire becomes grounded in the heart, it is most difficult to remedy it. The Shaykh ﵀ informs of its remedy. There are two treatments for such a severe disease: fear (*khawf*) and desire (*shawq*).

Fear of Allāh is either [dread] of the terrifying episodes of the Day of Judgment or of the majestic attributes of Allāh Most High, such as Him being The Dominator (*al-Qahhār*), The Compeller (*al-Jabbār*), or The Avenger (*al-Muntaqim*). The former state of fear is for the masses; the latter kind is for the élite.

By meditating on these issues for some time, fear will be cultivated. Gradually, it will permeate the heart and eliminate the domination of emotional desires.

An initial state of desire is achieved by contemplating the pleasures of Paradise, which is the level of desire that laymen striving for piety have. The second kind of desire is achieved by meditating on Allāh's attributes of beauty (*jamāl*), such as Him being The Infinitely Good (*al-Raḥmān*) and The All-Forgiving (*al-Ghafūr*). This kind of desire is for the élite.

It should, however, be understood that fear and desire of a low level will not eradicate lust from the heart. To eliminate the entrenched disease of lust, a strong state of either fear or desire is essential. In view of the essentiality of a high degree of these states, the Shaykh ﵀ qualifies fear with "unsettling" and desire with "restless."

لَا تَيْأَسْ مِنْ قَبُولِ عَمَلٍ لَمْ تَجِدْ فِيهِ وُجُودَ الْحُضُورِ ..
فَرُبَّمَا قَبِلَ مِنَ الْعَمَلِ مَا لَمْ تُدْرِكْ ثَمَرَتَهُ عَاجِلًا.

Do not lose hope in the acceptance of an act of yours wherein you found no awareness of the Divine Presence. Sometimes He accepts an act the fruit of which you have not perceived right away. [219]

Perfect concentration is to perform worship with such focus of mind and heart as if one is seeing Allāh Most High: where not a vestige of satanic and lowly thoughts of desire remains to distract the heart from Allāh Most High. The pleasure of such presence of heart permeates the entire being of the servant. If, by the grace of Allāh Most High, the servant gains such a high degree of concentration, it indicates the acceptance of his worship by Allāh Most High.

If the servant fails to attain this high degree of concentration, he should not despair, nor interpret it as a rejection of his worship. While presence of heart is the sign of acceptance, it is not conditional for acceptance of worship. Thus, the absence of a sign does not indicate rejection of the act. It frequently happens that Allāh Most High accepts a deed while such effects are withheld here on earth: the reward is reserved for the Hereafter.

13

ON THE ETIQUETTE OF SUPPLICATION

لَا يَكُنْ تَأَخُّرُ أَمَدِ الْعَطَاءِ مَعَ الْإِلْحَاحِ فِي الدُّعَاءِ مُوْجِبًا لِيَأْسِكَ، فَهُوَ ضَمِـنَ لَكَ الْإِجَابَةَ فِيمَا يَخْتَارُهُ لَكَ لَا فِيمَا تَخْتَارُهُ لِنَفْسِـكَ، وَفِي الْوَقْتِ الَّذِي يُرِيدُ لَا فِي الْوَقْتِ الَّذِي تُرِيدُ.

If, in spite of intense supplication, there is a delay in the timing of the Gift, let that not be the cause for your despairing. For He has guaranteed you a response in what He chooses for you, not in what you choose for yourself, and at the time He desires, not the time you desire. [6]

MANY PEOPLE CONTEND that despite making abundant supplications their entreaties are not answered. Some who have inculcated in themselves a degree of piety usually say that their supplications are not accepted because of their sins. They believe sin to be an impediment to the acceptance of supplication. Some of the people who engage in the invocation of Allāh are also trapped in this thought, which is an inspiration of the devil. They feel that despite years of spiritual effort and invocation their spiritual condition remains unchanged. They earnestly supplicate, but see no change in their moral or spiritual state. This attitude produces in them despair. The Shaykh ﵀ answers these misgivings by saying that if the supplication does not materialize—despite earnestness and apparent humility being present during supplication—one should not interpret this as rejection by Allāh Most High.

Although Allāh Most High has promised to accept supplication, He has not promised to grant whatever is supplicated for. Our knowledge and intelligence are not always adequate to comprehend what is beneficial and harmful for us. Sometimes the object requested is not for our good. Allāh

Most High is Most Merciful to us. He knows our needs more than we do. He withholds the object we are supplicating for in view of it being harmful. Instead, something better and beneficial will be given.

The meaning of the divine promise of accepting supplication is that Allāh Most High will grant supplications and fulfill supplications according to His wisdom and choice. Sometimes the object requested is awarded and sometimes withheld. Perhaps something better will be awarded, either in this world or in the next, or some earthly disaster is averted. Sometimes the very object supplicated for is given, but at some time in the future. The reason for delaying the fulfillment of the supplication is that in the divine wisdom the immediate awarding of the object requested is fraught with either a religious or worldly harm.

The servant should, therefore, refrain from employing his intelligence in issues that Allāh Most High decides. He should be constant in his supplication and not despair of acceptance.

لَا يُشَكِّكَنَّكَ فِي الْوَعْدِ عَدَمُ وُقُوعِ الْمَوْعُودِ بِهِ وإِنْ تَعَيَّنَ زَمَنُهُ،
لِئَلَّا يَكُونَ ذٰلِكَ قَدْحًا فِي بَصِيرَتِكَ وإِخْمَادًا لِنُوْرِ سَرِيرَتِكَ.

If what was promised does not occur, even though the time for its occurrence had been fixed, then that must not make you doubt the promise. Otherwise, your intellect will be obscured and the light of your innermost heart extinguished. [7]

Sometimes a servant of Allāh is informed inspirationally of the occurrence of a future event at a stipulated time. Such news may be transmitted to him by way of a dream, inspiration or the voice of an angel. The information may be, for example, rainfall on a particular date or the ending of famine on a certain date, etc.[17] If the appointed day arrives without the promise materializing, the servant should not doubt the truth of the promise. It is

17 See *Reliance*, 1015–1016, for a discussion of knowledge of the unseen and miracles by Ibn Ḥajar Haytamī. In summary, Haytamī quotes Nawawī, from his *Legal Rulings*, as saying: "[. . .] no one except Allāh knows this [the "unseen"] independently and with full cognizance of all things knowable. As for . . . inimitable prophetic miracles (*muʿjizāt*) and divine favors (*karāmāt*) it is through Allāh's giving them to know it that it is known; as is also the case with what is known through ordinary means."

quite possible that the materialization of the prediction depends on some conditions that were absent on the stipulated day; or the matter was a test for the servant, hence the requisite conditions were not revealed to him.

Thus the servant should not commit the fatal error of doubting the truth of the divine promise, for doubting is a grave act of disrespect, ignorance and stupidity. It is also a sign of pride. Such an attitude will blind the intelligence, because violation of the divine promise is impossible. Allāh Most High has declared that He does not dishonor a promise.

There is the grave danger of this disrespect extinguishing the light of the heart. Thus, one's inner treasure will be snatched away. At no stage should the servant abandon respect and his state of servanthood.

The servant should attribute all defects and vice to himself and believe that his insight and understanding are deficient. The statement of the Shaykh ﷺ pertains to valid unveiling (*kashf*) and inspiration (*ilhām*), not to mere thoughts and imagination.

طَلَبُكَ مِنْهُ اتِّهَامٌ لَهُ، وَطَلَبُكَ لَهُ غَيْبَةٌ مِنْكَ عَنْهُ، وَطَلَبُكَ لِغَيْرِهِ
لِقِلَّةِ حَيَائِكَ مِنْهُ، وَطَلَبُكَ مِنْ غَيْرِهِ لِوُجُودِ بُعْدِكَ عَنْهُ.

Your requesting Him is suspecting Him. Your seeking Him is due to your absence from Him. Your seeking someone else is because of your immodesty toward Him. Your requesting someone else is on account of your distance from Him. [21]

At this juncture, it is essential to understand a few important facts. Firstly, it is of utmost importance for the spiritual traveler whose heart has been impacted upon by his invocation to perpetually engross himself in invocation with his heart, after rendering the obligatory duties. He should eliminate all vestiges of satanic whisperings and keep the heart's attention engrossed with Allāh Most High, until he gains complete mastery of his heart. Secondly, the saints have summarized *taṣawwuf* as: "*Taṣawwuf* is the maintaining of proper manners (*adab*)." Finally, as long as lowly desires have not been eliminated and one has not annihilated the ego, all of one's deeds—supplication, ritual prayer or fasting, etc.—will be contaminated by the ego. Of great importance, therefore, is the engrossment of the heart, so that invocation permeates it and egotistic contamination is eliminated from one's righteous actions. Sincerity will then be achieved.

Now understand the gist of the Shaykh's statement. He is actually saying that the supplications of the traveler are of four kinds, and that they are in conflict with the proper manners necessary for the Divine Court.

Firstly, your supplication is for things that He has undertaken the responsibility for giving, such as sustenance. Since your ego is still alive, its interference will certainly be in this supplication. By implication it means: "If I ask, He (Allāh) will give, otherwise perhaps not." This is to accuse Allāh of withholding. Moreover, the traveler, in this situation, is in doubt regarding an issue (e.g., sustenance) on which there is absolute certitude [due to the divine promise]. Your request, therefore, implies doubt [on your part]; hence abstain from such a supplication. Apply yourself to your occupation, which is invocation. If one had been an *ʿārif*, one's supplication would have been sincere and one would not have regarded the supplication to be a determinant. The aim of supplication, then, would not have been for the acquisition of the object requested, because Allāh Most High has already promised to bestow it upon one. The *ʿārif's* supplication is simply to profess his weakness, humility and dependence on Allāh Most High. Since one is not an *ʿārif*, the supplication is not free of egotistic contamination.

Secondly, you are supplicating for His proximity (*qurb*) and spiritual perception (*mushāhada*) and this is against your [current] rank, because proximity and spiritual perception for you are actually involvement with your own state. When you concern yourself with the request for proximity and spiritual perception, then that proximity and spiritual perception that one had possessed disappears; hence, this supplication is not appropriate. One should not divert one's attention for even a second from Allāh Most High.

Thirdly, supplicating for anything besides your True Master—whether a mundane need or a spiritual rank or state—is on account of one's audacity, because one professes to be a searcher of the Master while seeking something other than Him. If one had any shame, one would not have asked Him for anything. Rather, one would have remained in full concentration [upon Allāh].

Fourthly, to ask from anyone besides one's Master is because of one's remoteness from Him. If one were near to Him, one would never ask from others.

The *ʿārifīn* believe that their supplication is by virtue of Allāh's aid. They do not attribute it to themselves. Hence, their supplication is for Allāh, with His aid.

لَا تَتَعَدَّ نِيَّةُ هِمَّتِكَ إِلَى غَيْرِهِ .. فَالْكَرِيمُ لَا تَتَخَطَّاهُ الْآمَالُ.

Let not the intention of your aspiration shift to what is other than He, for one's hopes cannot outstrip the Generous. [38]

An honorable person will place his needs in front of a gracious benefactor. He does not go to a dishonorable person for his needs. The True, Gracious Benefactor is none besides Allāh Most High: Allāh forgives a criminal, despite possessing the power to punish him; when He makes a promise, He honors it; and when He gives, He gives more than expected. Whoever comes within the confines of His refuge, He does not destroy him. He has no need for intercessors. These attributes par excellence exist only in Allāh Most High. Hence, the Shaykh ﷺ instructs the traveler to direct his attention only to Allāh Most High for his needs.

When asking someone for something, if reliance is on that person and Allāh Most High is forgotten, then such asking will be a negation of the rank of servanthood. However, if the person is considered only as the external or mundane means created by Allāh Most High, but complete reliance is only on Allāh, then such asking will not be in conflict with servanthood.

لَا تَرْفَعَنَّ إِلَى غَيْرِهِ حَاجَةً هُوَ مُورِدُهَا عَلَيْكَ .. فَكَيْفَ يَرْفَعُ غَيْرُهُ مَا كَانَ هُوَ لَهُ وَاضِعًا؟ مَنْ لَا يَسْتَطِيعُ أَنْ يَرْفَعَ حَاجَةً عَنْ نَفْسِهِ .. فَكَيْفَ يَسْتَطِيعُ أَنْ يَكُونَ لَهَا عَنْ غَيْرِهِ رَافِعًا؟

Appeal to no one but Him to relieve you of a pressing need that He Himself has brought upon you. For how can someone else remove what He has imposed? And how can he who is unable to free himself of a pressing need free anyone else of one? [39]

O traveler! Turn only to Allāh Most High for the fulfillment of any need or for the removal of a calamity that He has imposed on you. Do not turn to anyone else. Who can fulfill the need or remove the calamity He has imposed on you. Consider if the ruler of the day was to afflict someone with a problem, who from among his subjects would be able to remove it. The solution would be to plea with the ruler himself and try to convince him. The [created] person to whom you are turning is himself overwhelmed with needs and problems. If he had power, he would firstly have relieved himself of his own problems. When a man is unable to resolve his own situation, how can he resolve yours? The only solution is to direct your need to your True Master.

لَا تُطَالِبْ رَبَّكَ بِتَأَخُّرِ مَطْلَبِكَ وَلٰكِنْ طَالِبْ نَفْسَكَ بِتَأَخُّرِ أَدَبِكَ.

Do not press claims against your Lord because your request has been delayed; instead, press claims against yourself for slackening in your behavior. [109]

If when supplicating to your Lord for some worldly or otherworldly need there is a delay in the response from Him, then do not complain against Him by saying, "We supplicated but did not receive a response?" or "Why is it not quickly forthcoming." This is against the etiquette and has also been prohibited in ḥadīth. How do you know whether or not your supplication has been accepted? It is possible that it has indeed been accepted but you are unaware, since it is not necessary for the acceptance of a supplication that you receive exactly what you ask for, as has been discussed before. It is possible that it is not in your interests to receive it at this time and you will receive it later. Besides, His transcendence is such that *He cannot be questioned for His acts* (Qur'ān 21:23). Therefore do not complain nor rush Him nor weaken in your supplication, since this is the role and responsibility of the suppliant, and do not abandon the etiquette.

مَا الشَّأْنُ وُجُودُ الطَّلَبِ؛ إِنَّمَا الشَّأْنُ أَنْ تُرْزَقَ حُسْنَ الْأَدَبِ.

The point at issue is not the existence of searching. The point at issue is only that you be provisioned with virtuous conduct. [128]

According to the noble ḥadīth, supplication is the essence of worship.[18] On account of having heard of this significance of supplication, the traveler

18 Ibn Rajab writes: "Tirmidhī narrated a ḥadīth of Anas ibn Mālik from the Prophet ﷺ, 'Supplication is the marrow of worship.' So, these words comprise that Allāh Most High is asked

who has as yet not attained freedom from his ego thinks that the goal is supplication. In so doing, he errs.

There will be contamination of the ego as long as the reign of the ego exists, even in the supplication. The ego will supplicate for its desires and pleasures, and the attention of the heart will be on the need for which the supplication is being made, not on Allāh Most High. On the other hand, the supplication of the *ʿārifīn* is undoubtedly the essence of their worship, because the purpose of their worship is expression of their weakness and dependence on Allāh Most High.

The ego of the *ʿārif* is annihilated and his gaze is perpetually on Allāh Most High, not on his supplication, which he makes on account of his servanthood and the Lordship of Allāh Most High.

Since the supplication of the non-*ʿārif* is for the sake of his ego, the Shaykh ﷺ says that such a supplication does not reflect a beautiful state, even though it is good (and permissible). A beautiful condition of the traveler is *adab*. The *adab* for him is to resign himself to Allāh Most High in all his affairs, and engross himself in the invocation and spiritual perception of his Lord.

مَا طَلَبَ لَكَ شَيْءٌ مِثْلُ الْاِضْطِرَارِ، وَلَا أَسْرَعَ
بِالْمَوَاهِبِ إِلَيْكَ مِثْلُ الذِّلَّةِ وَالْاِفْتِقَارِ.

Nothing pleads on your behalf like extreme need, nor does anything speed gifts to you quicker than lowliness and want. [129]

O traveler! Allāh Most High demands from you worship and that you remain His slave. The most perfect attributes of servanthood are weakness and restlessness. There is nothing superior to your weakness and the restlessness of your heart in your yearning for Allāh Most High at all times. Your condition should be like that of a drowning man who sees no succor other than the help of Allāh Most High; or like a man lost in a desolate wilderness with no one to show him the road. Just as the heart of this lost person will be engulfed by anxiety and restlessness, so too should be the state of your heart in your yearning for Allāh Most High.

---

and no other than Him is asked, and that Allāh is sought help from and no other." See Ibn Rajab, *Compendium*, 324.

When your heart is overcome with the feeling of helplessness and dependence, the bounties of Allāh Most High will be showered upon you. There is no better state for the attraction of divine favors, both outer and inner, than the sad and forlorn state of your heart.

رُبَّمَا دَلَّهُمُ الْأَدَبُ عَلَى تَرْكِ الطَّلَبِ اعْتِمَادًا عَلَى
قِسْمَتِهِ وَاشْتِغَالًا بِذِكْرِهِ عَنْ مَسْأَلَتِهِ.

Sometimes good behavior leads some to abandon asking because of confidence in His Providence or because concern for the invocation of Him stymies their asking of Him. [172]

The gnostics are of a variety of dispositions. Some are overwhelmed by being completely resigned and contented with whatever their lot is. In this state, their hearts are absolutely resigned to the eternal predestined Decree of Allāh Most High. Whatever has been predestined will come their way. In this condition, they consider supplication to be in conflict with *adab* and a negation of their disposition of resignation (to the divine will). Furthermore, their complete engrossment in invocation does not allow them any time whatsoever for supplication.

However, it will be evident that the best and most perfect state is the one that resembles the state of the Messenger of Allāh ﷺ. The disposition of the Messenger of Allāh ﷺ was to make supplication in every affair, despite his state of being pleased with Allāh Most High, and having resigned himself to Allāh Most High in a manner that was the highest standard possible. Thus, the most perfect state is undoubtedly to verbally proclaim one's weakness and dependency while the heart remains in the state of pleasure in all matters.[19]

---

19 A number of wonderful books highlight the truth of the Prophet Muḥammad ﷺ turning to Allāh in all his states. In Arabic, *Al-Adhkār* by Nawawī is a great and comprehensive resource. Nevertheless, works which effectively work as abridgements of Nawawī's great aforementioned work can be found in English; namely: *Fortification of the Muslim through Invocation and Supplication from the Qur'aan and Sunnah* by Sa'eed Ibn 'Ali Ibn Wahf al-Qahtaani; *The Noble Words: Invocation and Prayers of the Prophet Muhammad* ﷺ (Leicester: UK Islamic Academy, 2003); *Radiant Prayers: A Collection of Easy Prayers from the Qur'ān, Sunnah and from Sahabah and Tab'in* by Muhammad Taqi Usmani, trans. Muhammad Shameem (Karachi: Idaratul-Ma'arif, 2001); and *Reflections of Pearls* by Inam Uddin and Abdur-Rahman ibn Yusuf (Santa Barbara, USA: White Thread, 2005). For the etiquette of supplication, one can consult Abū Ḥāmid al-Ghazālī, *Invocations and Supplications*, trans. K. Nakamura (Cambridge, UK: The Islamic Texts Society, 1990), 32–46.

إِنَّمَا يُذَكَّرُ مَنْ يَجُوزُ عَلَيْهِ الْإِغْفَالُ، وَإِنَّمَا يُنَبَّهُ مَنْ يُمْكِنُ مِنْهُ الْإِهْمَالُ.

Only he to whom forgetfulness is possible is to be
reminded; and only he to whom inattention is possible
is to be warned. [173]

This is mentioned by way of proof of the previous statement of the Shaykh
🕮. Some people of spiritual ecstasy feel that abstention from supplication is
proper manners because it appears as if one is reminding Allāh Most High
of one's needs; others think if one does not ask, He will not give. Yet both of
these understandings are incorrect with regards to the Divine Being, because
reminding is proper only where the possibility of forgetfulness exists. But Allāh
Most High is The Knower of the Unseen and Seen. There is no need to draw
His attention to anything since He is neither forgetful nor unmindful of the
one in need. He has already predestined everything for the servant, while at
the same time His boundless mercy engulfs all things whether one asks or not.

رُبَّمَا اسْتَحْيَا الْعَارِفُ أَنْ يَرْفَعَ حَاجَتَهُ إِلَى مَوْلَاهُ اكْتِفَاءً بِمَشِيئَتِهِ، فَكَيْفَ
لَا يَسْتَحْيِي أَنْ يَرْفَعَهَا إِلَى خَلِيقَتِهِ؟

Sometimes the gnostic is ashamed of submitting his
urgent need to his Lord, being content with His Will. So
why should he not be ashamed of submitting his urgent
need to a creature of His? [191]

Since it is a known fact that all things will happen according to the divine
decree, in accordance with Allāh's will, the *'ārif* is content with letting these
decrees manifest themselves in whatever way they are decreed. Thus he feels
ashamed of presenting his needs in the Divine Court. Yet his shame would
be greater if he was to then ask for the fulfillment of his needs from other
people, whom are themselves paupers and helpless.

لَا تَسْتَبْطِئْ مِنْهُ النَّوَالَ، وَلٰكِنِ اسْتَبْطِئْ مِنْ نَفْسِكَ وُجُودَ الْإِقْبَالِ.

Do not deem His giving to be slow; but rather, deem
your approaching to be slow. [207]

The ego generally believes everyone else is like itself. Sometimes, when the traveler does not experience the effects of his abundance of spiritual effort, he begins, on account of the ignorance of the ego, to think that he will not achieve any spiritual progress and the delay is from Allāh's side—and we seek refuge in Allāh! The Shaykh ﷺ thus says that the traveler should not think that there is a delay in the bestowal of Allāh Most High. Delay in giving is the act of a miser: this is not possible in regard to Allāh Most High.

The ocean of divine grace flows perpetually. The cause of the delay is because of the deficiency of the traveler, who lacks in perfect concentration. His attention is not fully toward Allāh Most High. False images are engraved in his mind, hence the delay. It is essential that he erases these images from his heart and applies his attention fully to Allāh. He will then see divine forgiveness every moment.

خَيْرٌ مَا تَطْلُبُهُ مِنْهُ مَا هُوَ طَالِبُهُ مِنْكَ.

The best that you can seek from Him is that which He seeks from you. [75]

Man has been created for worship and obedience. Allāh states in the Glorious Qur'ān: *I have not created jinn and man except that they worship Me* (51:56).

Allāh Most High, therefore, demands worship of Him from the servant. Thus, the best thing that the traveler can ask Allāh is steadfastness in worship and obedience. All other things -whether worldly or pertaining to the religion—are not the best, because there is some desire and pleasure of the ego in these things; yet worship and slavery (to Allāh Most High) do not give any pleasure to the ego. To ask for something that gives pleasure to the ego is in conflict with the state of servanthood.

لَا يَكُنْ طَلَبُكَ تَسَبُّبًا إِلَى الْعَطَاءِ مِنْهُ .. فَيَقِلَّ فَهْمُكَ عَنْهُ، وَلْيَكُنْ طَلَبُكَ لِإِظْهَارِ الْعُبُودِيَّةِ وَقِيَامًا بِحُقُوقِ الرُّبُوبِيَّةِ.

Let not your asking be the cause of His giving, for then your understanding of Him might diminish. Let your

asking be for the sake of showing servanthood and fulfilling the rights of Lordship. [166]

O traveler! The objective of your engrossment in supplication and worship should not be the acquisition of some worldly or religious bounty. If your purpose is only that, then you have failed to understand the essence and wisdom of supplication. The purpose of your supplication and worship should only be the demonstration of your state of servanthood, in order that you fulfill the rights of His Lordship. In fact, Allāh Most High has instructed the observance of supplication and worship so that the servant presents his appeal, dependency and supplication in His Court.

If this is the aim underlying the servant's supplication, he will never relent in supplicating—even if all his wishes are continuously being fulfilled—because his aim is to display Allāh's Lordship and his own servanthood. On the contrary, if one supplicates without these dual purposes, then he will cease to supplicate once his need has been fulfilled—such an abstention from supplication is abominable, because it is as though one is manifesting an independence from Allāh.

The true servant is the one who at all times proclaims his need for the bounties and mercy of Allāh Most High.

كَيفَ يَكُونُ طَلَبُكَ اللَّاحِقُ سَبَبًا فِي عَطَائِهِ السَّابِقِ؟

How can your subsequent asking be the cause of His prior giving? [167]

In the previous aphorism it was mentioned that it behooves the believer to engage in supplication for the sake of displaying his dependency on Allāh Most High, and not for anything else. In the aphorism under discussion it is posited that supplication should not be regarded as the cause for acquisition (of needs and wants). Whatever one will obtain has already been predestined, while the supplication for that object of need or desire came later. A later development cannot be a cause for an earlier existent. The Shaykh ﵁ therefore tells the traveler to eliminate the idea of his supplication being the cause of his needs being fulfilled.

In the next aphorism, the Shaykh ﵁ draws the mind to the same issue, in a different style. The statement is also proof of the assertion that is made here.

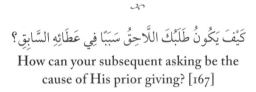

جَلَّ حُكْمُ الْأَزَلِ أَنْ يَنْضَافَ إِلَى الْعِلَلِ.

Far be it for the decree of the Eternal to be subject to contingent causes! [168]

O traveler! How is it possible for you to regard your supplication as being the cause of the bestowal! The dignity of the divine, eternal decree is far above this idea. The eternal decrees are not in need of any causes and reasons. The acts of the Creator are far above such needs. There is, therefore, no [necessary] cause or reason for the bounties that He bestows on anyone. His bestowals were decreed in eternity, while the request for them developed much later.

After having learnt this truth, it will be in conflict with the rank of servanthood to abandon supplication.

مَتَى أَطْلَقَ لِسَانَكَ بِالطَّلَبِ .. فَاعْلَمْ أَنَّهُ يُرِيدُ أَنْ يُعْطِيَكَ.

When He loosens your tongue with a request, then know that He wants to give you something. [102]

"When He loosens your tongue with a request" for the objective of servanthood or other than it through spontaneous outburst, "then know that He wants to give you something." [In such a case,] what you want is what He wants. It has been narrated on the authority of ʿAbdullāh ibn ʿUmar ﷺ that the Messenger of Allāh ﷺ said that whoever is permitted to make supplication, the gates of mercy are opened up for him. Allāh is never asked for a thing more beloved to Him than being asked for forgiveness and well being.

With this meaning it is said [in a poem]:

If You did not will that I receive what I hope for of Your bounty,
You would not have taught me how to ask.[20]

20 Both the aphorism and commentary are missing at this point in the original Urdu and the South African translation of Gangōhī's work. The commentary has therefore been taken from Aḥmad Zarrūq's commentary entitled *Al-Ḥikam al-ʿAṭā'iyya bi-sharḥ* (Beirut: Dār al-Kutub al-ʿIlmiyya, 1424/2003), 116. The words attributed to the Prophet ﷺ in Zarrūq's commentary have been left without inverted commas, because it seems that the narration is quoted in meaning and not word-for-word. A similar narration in *Sunan al-Tirmidhī* (no. 3548) reads: "Whomever of you has the door of supplication opened for him, the doors of mercy have been opened for him. Allāh

14

ON ACCEPTING THE DIVINE DECREE AND ABANDONING CHOICE

إِرَادَتُكَ التَّجْرِيدَ مَعَ إِقَامَةِ اللّٰهِ إِيَّاكَ فِي الْأَسْبَابِ مِنَ الشَّهْوَةِ الْخَفِيَّةِ، وَإِرَادَتُكَ الْأَسْبَابَ مَعَ إِقَامَةِ اللّٰهِ إِيَّاكَ فِي التَّجْرِيدِ انْحِطَاطٌ عَنِ الْهِمَّةِ الْعَلِيَّةِ.

Your desire for isolation, even though God has put you in the world to gain a living, is a hidden passion. And your desire to gain a living in the world, even though God has put you in isolation, is a comedown from supreme aspiration. [2]

O TRAVELER! If Allāh Most High has granted you fortitude in your religion while keeping you engaged in mundane activities—such as farming, trade, employment, etc.—and you are blessed with steadfastness in the outer and inner aspects of worship, then your desire to abandon worldly means for the sake of gaining freedom from the mundane encumbrances is the deceptive desire of the ego, which is concealed and suppressed in the innermost recesses of the ego. Although superficially this thought appears good—on account of the idea of complete renunciation of worldly attachment bringing greater divine proximity—it is in reality a very sinister plot of the ego that prompts this idea.[21]

is not asked for anything more beloved to Him than well being (*ʿāfiya*)." Another narration with variant wording can be found in *Mustadrak al-Ḥākim*.

21 The word *tajrīd* carries with it the implication of withdrawing from society for contemplative purposes, the one doing so being called a *mutajarrid*. On the other hand, the one who carries on his contemplative life within society is the *mutasabbib* (VD).

Name and fame ensue in the wake of renunciation. The ego desires to be known as a great saint so that people become followers. If you, O traveler, act according to this egotistic prompting, you will lose the present state of spiritual fortitude that you have gained, because the inclination of people toward a person is a fatal poison for him—even though complete renunciation is not harmful for one who has reached spiritual perfection.

O traveler! It is best for you to remain in whatever condition Allāh Most High has chosen for you. Do not choose another condition for yourself.

On the other hand, if Allāh Most High has granted one renunciation and steadfastness in the religion, without the need for involvement in mundane activities, one would have fallen from a lofty state to a degenerate state if one then desired to return to the pursuit of worldly means of acquisition. After having established your bond with Allāh Most High—such a bond which has set you free from people and which has completely eliminated your trust in them, and developed in you perfect reliance [upon Allāh]—your abandonment of that lofty state to cultivate a link with created beings is to degenerate, to fall from the top to the bottom. Therefore, ignore the prompting of the ego and be pleased with the condition in which your Master is keeping you.

"*Tajrīd*, linguistically, is to scrape off and remove (something). You say, *jarrattu 'l-thawb*, 'I removed the garment from myself' . . .and *jarrattu 'l-jilda*, 'I removed the skin.' According to the sufis there are three types of *tajrīd* (isolation): (1) external isolation, (2) spiritual isolation, and (3) the two combined. External isolation is to abandon the adoption of worldly means and to rend bodily habits, while spiritual isolation is to abandon the attachments of the ego and delusive impediments. The two combined is to abandon the attachments of the ego and bodily habits.

"Alternatively, you can say that the external isolation is to abandon all that occupies the limbs from obedience to Allāh, and spiritual isolation is to abandon all that occupies the heart from presence with Allāh. The isolation of both is to devote the heart and form entirely to Allāh. A complete external isolation is to abandon adopting means and to denude the body of customary clothing, while complete spiritual isolation is to rid the heart from every blameworthy trait and embellish it with every noble quality. . .

"The one who achieves external isolation but not spiritual isolation is a flagrant liar similar to the one who plates copper with silver. He is spiritually ugly though externally pretty. Whoever achieves spiritual isolation but does not [conform to the dictates of] the external [Sacred Law], then he is beautiful like the one who plates silver with copper. However, this is rare, because the one whose external state is firm, then likewise his spiritual state [becomes]; and whoever's external becomes occupied with this sensation, then so does his spiritual, but the strength will not be equivalent in both. However, whoever combines between external and spiritual isolation, then he is the complete friend and is the pure refined gold worthy of the treasure houses of kings." See Ibn 'Ajība, *Īqāẓ al-Himam fī Sharḥ al-Ḥikam* (Damascus: Dār al-Khayr 1426/2005), 23–24.

لَا تَطْلُبْ مِنْهُ أَن يُخْرِجَكَ مِنْ حَالَةٍ لِيَسْتَعْمِلَكَ فِيمَا سِوَاهَا، فَلَوْ أَرَادَ لَاسْتَعْمَلَكَ مِنْ غَيْرِ إِخْرَاجٍ.

Do not request Him to get you out of a state to make use of you in a different one, for, were He to desire so, He could make use of you as you are, without taking you out! [19]

It is not proper for a man involved in an activity, such as employment, to supplicate to be extricated from his involvement so that he can apply himself fully to the invocation of Allāh Most High. If his involvement is not in conflict with the Sacred Law, there is no valid reason for abandoning it.

Frequently, we find that abandoning the occupation leads to worry and frustration. If Allāh Most High wishes, He can grant the other state that is desired, without the need for renouncing the existing state (in which the traveler is involved). Since He has not done so despite His power [to do so], it clearly indicates that it is in your best interests to remain in your present state. Thus, do not abandon your existing condition voluntarily. When He wills, He will deliver you to the stage that is your objective. When He wills, He will remove you from your existing state.

سَوَابِقُ الْهِمَمِ لَا تَخْرِقُ أَسْوَارَ الْأَقْدَارِ.

Antecedent intentions cannot pierce the walls of predestined Decrees. [3]

The ability of the ego to influence the heart, with the permission of Allāh Most High, is termed *himma* in the language of the sufis.

Despite the abilities of the people of spiritual effort stepping ahead of everything and exercising their influence swiftly on anything toward which they direct their attention, these *himam* [plural of *himma*] cannot act in conflict with the "predestined Decrees."

If such an effective ability as *himma* is impotent and of no significance in front of the wall of destiny, then the effect of the employment of mundane means has absolutely no recognition. It is, therefore, incumbent on the believer to refrain from reposing trust in mundane means and agencies.

He should not regard them as effective. The gaze should be on the decree of Allāh Most High.

أَرِحْ نَفْسَكَ مِنَ التَّدْبِيرِ، فَمَا قَامَ بِهِ غَيْرُكَ عَنْكَ لَا تَقُمْ بِهِ لِنَفْسِكَ.

Rest yourself from self-direction for what Someone Else has carried out on your behalf, do not you yourself undertake to do it. [4]

For the purpose of earning a livelihood, a little worldly involvement that does not put pressure and strain on the ego is sufficient. Only such a degree of worldly involvement should be adopted which does not form an impediment to one's obedience to Allāh. The reliance of the heart should not be on the means; reliance should be only on the Providence of Allāh Most High.

However, a means that strains the ego with an abundance of unnecessary encumbrances, overwhelming it with worry and a multitude of satanic whisperings, should be abandoned. It does not behoove the traveler to burden his ego with unnecessary strain and pressure in the pursuit of a livelihood. He should give his ego rest by releasing it from unnecessary mundane pressure.

When the responsibility of something is undertaken by a stronger, more experienced and kinder person than oneself, it is logical to feel relieved and to rely on him. Do not assume the responsibility. Leave it to the plan of your Master and set your mind at rest.

اِجْتِهَادُكَ فِيمَا ضُمِنَ لَكَ وَتَقْصِيرُكَ فِيمَا طُلِبَ مِنْكَ دَلِيلٌ عَلَى انْطِمَاسِ الْبَصِيرَةِ مِنْكَ.

Your striving for what has already been guaranteed to you, and your remissness in what is demanded of you, are signs of the blurring of your intellect. [5]

O traveler! Your Master has already assumed the responsibility for your sustenance (*rizq*) and the means of your livelihood. Declaring this responsibility, He says that there is not a living creature on earth whose sustenance is not His responsibility.

Have you then no trust in His Providence? You labor and toil to acquire sustenance that is the responsibility of Allāh Most High. On the other hand, you are lax and deficient in worship and obedience that He demands of you and for which purpose He has created you. This attitude clearly proves that the light of your intelligence has been extinguished; hence you are devoid of intellect. If your intellect functioned correctly, you would have been unconcerned regarding the issue of sustenance, whose responsibility has been assumed by Allāh Most High; at the same time, you would have applied your full attention and effort toward the fulfillment of Allāh's demand of worship.

The use of the word "striving" by the Shaykh ﵀ implies that a little effort for the acquisition of sustenance will not be misplaced. However, engrossment in its pursuit is improper.

مَا تَرَكَ مِنَ الْجَهْلِ شَيْئًا مَنْ أَرَادَ أَنْ يَحْدُثَ
فِي الْوَقْتِ غَيْرُ مَا أَظْهَرَهُ اللّٰهُ فِيهِ.

He who wishes that at a given moment there appear other than what God has manifested in it, has not left ignorance behind at all! [17]

It is imperative for the believer to confront every situation that is not in conflict with the Sacred Law with pleasure and resignation, whether the situation is a calamity pertaining to life and property or whether it is a state (emotional or spiritual) of the heart. The attitude of pleasure and resignation is the demand of dignity, knowledge, gnosis and recognizing Lordship.

If a person wishes that the condition that Allāh Most High has imposed on him be substituted with another condition, i.e., adversity with prosperity or despondency with elation, then he displays complete ignorance. The basis of such wishes and regrets is the ignorance of his ego. If he had truly possessed the gnosis of Allāh Most High, he would have understood that these predestined conditions will never be displaced, hence regret and wish would not have occurred to him. He would have been content with every circumstance and have observed respect. Now, he is clashing with the preordained, divine decrees.

مَا تَوَقَّفَ مَطْلَبٌ أَنْتَ طَالِبُهُ بِرَبِّكَ، وَلَا
تَيَسَّرَ مَطْلَبٌ أَنْتَ طَالِبُهُ بِنَفْسِكَ.

No search pursued with the help of your Lord remains at a standstill, but any search pursued by yourself will not be fruitful. [25]

O traveler! Regardless of how difficult the object of your desire may seem, be it a mundane object or a religious matter, as long as your sight is set on your Creator and you repose absolute trust in Him its acquisition is not difficult.

On the other hand, no matter how easy the acquisition of your desired object appears, if your gaze is on the ability of your ego and on your plans—thereby forgetting Allāh Most High—then its achievement will become difficult. In fact, failure is almost certain.

It is necessary, therefore, that reliance be placed on Allāh Most High, and that trust be completely shifted from one's own strength, intelligence and plans.

إِلَى الْمَشِيئَةِ يَسْتَنِدُ كُلُّ شَيْءٍ، وَلَا تَسْتَنِدُ هِيَ إِلَى شَيْءٍ.

Everything depends on the Divine Will, but It Itself depends on nothing at all. [171]

Allāh's eternal will has already decided and predestined all occurrences in the universe, be it good or evil, guidance or deviation. The manifestation of occurrences is by divine will alone.

The divine will is an eternal attribute of Allāh Most High, and is therefore not dependant on any created being or thing. To say otherwise would be to attribute a defect to the Divine Being—and we seek refuge in Allāh from such an evil claim. Indeed, Allāh Most High is perfect, and thus independent of need.

It is essential for the believer to ensure that this knowledge of the divine will becomes his permanent state (*ḥāl*). He should abandon ignorance, and never cast his gaze on his means and plans.

اَلْغَافِلُ إِذَا أَصْبَحَ يَنْظُرُ مَاذَا يَفْعَلُ، وَالْعَاقِلُ يَنْظُرُ مَاذَا يَفْعَلُ اللّٰهُ بِهِ.

When the forgetful man gets up in the morning, he reflects on what he is going to do, whereas the intelligent man sees what God is doing with him. [114]

Know that the True Actor in every act is Allāh Most High. The true belief of the *Ahl as-Sunna wa 'l-Jamāʿa* is that the Creator of all actions is Allāh Most High. Man is only the substance of manifestation for the divine acts of creation.

The person whose affirmation-of-Oneness (*tawḥīd*) is imperfect will attribute actions to himself. Hence when the new day dawns his mind dwells on different activities. But, the *ʿārif* who possesses correct knowledge, whose affirmation-of-Oneness is sound and from whose ego ignorance has been eliminated, ponders on the treatment Allāh Most High will be meting out to him on this day. He is not concerned with what he should do, because he attributes all actions to Allāh Most High. This attitude has become his state. His insignificance is clear to him.

Since the forgetful man's gaze is on his own capability, he attributes all his actions to his own self. Allāh Most High, therefore, assigns him to his ego. Thus, all his affairs become difficult and he becomes entrapped in numerous problems. But, for the true believer in Allāh's Oneness, the most difficult task does not overwhelm him because his gaze is fixed on Allāh Most High. He acquires aid openly from Allāh Most High.

15

ON PATIENCE THROUGH ADVERSITY

إِذَا فَتَـحَ لَكَ وِجْهَةً مِنَ التَّعَرُّفِ فَلَا تُبَالِ مَعَهَا إِنْ قَلَّ عَمَلُكَ، فَإِنَّهُ مَا فَتَحَهَا لَــكَ إِلَّا وَهُوَ يُرِيدُ أَنْ يَتَعَرَّفَ إِلَيْكَ؛ أَلَمْ تَعْلَمْ أَنَّ التَّعَرُّفَ هُوَ مُــوْرِدُهُ عَلَيْكَ وَالْأَعْمَالَ أَنْتَ مُهْدِيهَا إِلَيْـهِ، وَأَيْنَ مَا تُهْدِيهِ إِلَيْهِ مِمَّا هُوَ مُورِدُهُ عَلَيْكَ؟

If He opens a door for you, thereby making Himself known, pay no heed if your deeds do not measure up to this. For, in truth, He has not opened it for you but out of a desire to make Himself known to you. Do you not know that He is the one who presented the knowledge of Himself to you, whereas you are the one who presented Him with deeds? What a difference between what He brings to you and what you present to Him! [8]

AMONG ALL THE GOALS of *taṣawwuf*, the greatest aim and bounty is the gnosis of Allāh Most High, hence the Shaykh ﷺ says: O traveler! When Allāh Most High has opened up an avenue of His gnosis for you, do not be concerned if you are rendering only a small amount of acts of worship. Do not become despondent on account of this paucity. The aim of additional voluntary worship, verbal invocation and abundance of meditation is the acquisition of gnosis. When you have acquired this aim, then a decrease in your deeds due to a valid reason will not adversely affect your progress in the acquisition of higher ranks of gnosis. For the purpose of maintaining firmness in obedience, continue with acts of worship as much as you are able to render with ease.

The Shaykh ﷺ then states a subtle reason for this advice: there should be no regret on account of paucity of righteous deeds, because the very fact that Allāh Most High has opened up for one an avenue of His gnosis indicates that He wills one to progress higher than one's external deeds; hence the bestowal of the elevated stage of gnosis. [In this case,] Allāh Most High wills to manifest the spiritual illumination of His beautiful names and attributes to one. This blessing is immeasurably superior to an abundance of physical acts of worship [without the same gnosis].

You, the traveler, should also understand that the blessing of gnosis has been divinely conferred upon you, whereas the acts of worship are your presentations. There is absolutely no comparison between Allāh's bestowal and your presentations. Thus, the blessing of gnosis is immensely superior to physical acts of worship. Although in reality the divinely-granted success (*tawfiq*) of performing physical acts of worship is also the effect of Allāh's grace, the servant is the medium for these acts, and the blessing of gnosis is inspired directly into the servant's heart. Thus, from this angle, the deeds of virtue are related to the servant, while the blessing of gnosis is from Allāh in every aspect. The effort of the servant is not the cause of the acquisition.

لَا تَسْتَغْرِبْ وُقُوعَ الْأَكْدَارِ مَا دُمْتَ فِي هٰذِهِ الدَّارِ .. فَإِنَّهَا مَا أَبْرَزَتْ إِلَّا مَا هُوَ مُسْتَحَقٌّ وَصْفِهَا وَوَاجِبُ نَعْتِهَا.

So long as you are in this world, be not surprised at the existence of sorrows. For, truly, it manifests nothing but what is in keeping with its character or its inevitable nature. [24]

As long as you are in this world, do not be surprised at difficulties, misfortunes and sorrows. O traveler! While you are in this earthly abode, do not feel surprised if clouds of contamination settle over you. An amazing and surprising event is something that is not expected to transpire. Regarding the misfortunes and calamities of this world, nothing surprising happens. Such events are merely the natural manifestations of the attributes of the world.

Contamination and pollution are the natural and necessary characteristics of the world, since Allāh Most High has created it as a trial and a test to distinguish between the patient and the impatient, and between the grateful and the ungrateful.

لِيُخَفِّفْ أَلَمَ الْبَلَاءِ عَلَيْكَ عِلْمُكَ بِأَنَّهُ سُبْحَانَهُ هُوَ الْمُبْلِي لَكَ، فَالَّذِي وَاجَهَتْكَ مِنْهُ الْأَقْدَارُ هُوَ الَّذِي عَوَّدَكَ حُسْنَ الْإِخْتِيَارِ.

To soften for you the suffering of affliction, He has taught you that He is the One who causes trials to come upon you. For the one who confronts you with His decrees of Fate is the same who has accustomed you to His good choice. [105]

When you keep in mind that the misfortunes that befall you are from Allāh Most High, the worldly causes having absolutely no significance in this regard, then grief and sorrow will be lessened. You will realize that the Being who has afflicted you with the misfortune is the same Being who has always acted for your welfare in all your affairs. He has always treated you with love and kindness.

In view of Allāh's kind and loving treatment in all your affairs, you will understand that there most certainly is some benefit for you in the hardship. While ostensibly the hardship appears to be a misfortune, in reality it is for your benefit. In fact, it is a mercy for you.

When this knowledge develops into a state in you, your worry and grief will disappear. Although the hardship will produce pain to your physical body or to your physical heart, your spiritual heart will be contented and delighted.

مَنْ ظَنَّ انْفِكَاكَ لُطْفِهِ عَنْ قَدَرِهِ .. فَذٰلِكَ لِقُصُورِ نَظَرِهِ.

Whoever supposes that His gentleness is separate from His decree of Fate does so out of shortsightedness. [106]

The idea that Allāh's gentleness is only with the servant in the state of pleasure and prosperity, not in the state of difficulty and hardship, is the product of deficiency of the intellect. The believing servant who holds this notion is lacking in insight, because his gaze is limited to the external circumstances. In difficulties and hardships the believer achieves inner bounties that he does not acquire in prosperity. In fact, in the luxuries and the state of prosperity are numerous calamities, because when the ego acquires the objects of its pleasure it gains strength; hence its rebellion will increase. It will thus become involved in sin. If not sin, then at least it will certainly fall into forgetfulness.

On the contrary, the power of the ego weakens in difficulties and hardships. Since faith exists, the servant turns his gaze toward Allāh Most High. He supplicates to Allāh Most High and adopts patience. He turns away from the world and cultivates the attribute of contentment with the divine decree. These attitudes are the acts of the heart, which are superior to the outward acts of worship executed by a healthy person in a state of peace.

Thus, it is deficiency in one's intelligence to believe that Allāh Most High's mercy is lifted during difficulties and hardships.

16

ON THE BENEFICENCE OF ALLĀH UPON HIS SERVANTS

إِنَّمَا جَعَلَ الدَّارَ الْآخِرَةَ مَحَلًّا لِجَزَاءِ عِبَادِهِ الْمُؤْمِنِينَ؛ لِأَنَّ هٰذِهِ الدَّارَ لَا تَسَعُ مَا يُرِيدُ أَنْ يُعْطِيَهُمْ، وَلِأَنَّهُ أَجَلَّ أَقْدَارَهُمْ عَنْ أَنْ يُجَازِيَهُمْ فِي دَارٍ لَا بَقَاءَ لَهَا.

He made the Hereafter an abode to reward his believing servants only because this world cannot contain what He wishes to bestow upon them and because He deemed their worth too high to reward them in a world without permanence. [71]

Allāh Most High has fixed the abode of the next world for rewarding the deeds of His believing servants. He did not establish this world for this purpose. There are two wisdoms for this choice of Allāh. Firstly, this world does not contain the rewards that He desires for His servants. According to the ḥadīth, the extent of the Paradise that the lowest-ranking Muslim will receive will be a distance of seven hundred years.[22] Another ḥadīth states that the Paradise of the Muslim entering into Paradise last will be equal to ten times the size of the earth. This vastness is in regard to quantity and size.[23]

22 For the joys and delights of Paradise see Ghazālī, *The Remembrance of Death and the Afterlife*, trans. T.J. Winter (Cambridge, UK: ITS, 1995), 232–251. The description of Paradise mentioned by Gangōhī can be found in Ghazālī's aforementioned work. Ḥasan al-Baṣrī relates, "The last man to enter Heaven, who is the least of them in degree, will be given to see all that he owns for the distance of a hundred years journey, all of which is gold and silver palaces, and tents of pearls. . ." (op. cit. 249). Another saying is related on the authority of Mujāhid: "The lowliest of Heaven's people shall travel a thousand years in his kingdom, beholding its farthest parts just as he beholds its nearest. . ." (op. cit.).

23 This ḥadīth is narrated from ʿAbdullāh ibn Masʿūd ﷺ in both *Bukhārī* (no. 6571) and *Muslim* (no. 359).

Even in terms of quality, this world does not contain the rewards of a believer. The world is the place of pollution, while the rewards of the Hereafter are pure and holy. According to the ḥadīth, if a bangle of a *houri* of Paradise appeared on earth its glitter would overshadow the light of the sun and the moon.[24]

Secondly, Allāh Most High has elevated the ranks of His believing servants immensely. It is not, therefore, in accord with their lofty ranks to reward them in this perishable and transitory world; hence the abode of the next world has been created for rewarding the believers.

The believer should not forget the Hereafter through involvement in the bounties of this world. Neither should he regard worldly hardships as misfortunes, as such pleasures are being prepared there for him that would not have crossed his mind.[25]

رُبَّمَا أَعْطَاكَ فَمَنَعَكَ، وَرُبَّمَا مَنَعَكَ فَأَعْطَاكَ.

Sometimes He gives while depriving you, and sometimes He deprives you in giving. [83]

It often happens that on account of the worldly adornments, luxuries and pleasures that Allāh Most High grants one, one becomes immoderately involved in these mundane activities—to the extent that one is deprived of the success and sweetness of obedience. When the ego is engaged in the pleasures of the world it cannot experience the pleasure of obedience.

It also often happens that one's deprivation of worldly pleasures is regarded as a misfortune; however, one is given the success and sweetness of worship in lieu. The servant should not, therefore, focus his gaze on the superficial (worldly) bestowals and deprivations. He should understand the reality (*ḥaqīqa*) of everything and discharge the right of every occasion.[26]

24 This is related on the authority of Muḥammad ibn Kaʿb al-Quraẓī (see ʿAynī, *Umdat al-Qārī*, "Chapter on the *ḥouris* and their description").

25 It is related that the Messenger of Allāh ﷺ said: "Allāh the Exalted has said: 'I have prepared for my righteous slaves what no eye has seen, no ear has heard, and the mind of no man has conceived.' If you wish, recite: *No person knows what is kept hidden for them of joy as a reward for what they used to do* (Qur'ān 32:17)" (*Bukhārī* no. 3072; *Muslim* no. 2825).

26 See Ibn Rajab, *Compendium*, 330–7, on the divine command to be content with destiny, whether of good fortune or hardship, and how such contentment is the state of the believers. Ibn

مَتَى فَتَحَ لَكَ بَابَ الْفَهْمِ فِي الْمَنْعِ .. عَادَ الْمَنْعُ عَيْنَ الْعَطَاءِ.

When He opens up your understanding of deprivation, the deprivation becomes the same as the gift. [84]

Perfect intelligence and true comprehension are only bestowed on the *ʿārifīn*. Others are deprived of this treasure. This treasure constitutes the fortune of this world and the next. The Shaykh ﵀ comments: O traveler! If Allāh Most High has withheld a worldly or religious favor from you, your heart should be devoid of regret; in such a state, you will have intelligently understood that your state of deprivation is the product of divine wisdom and mercy; therefore you must remain as pleased with Allāh as you would have been if a favor had been bestowed on you; then, your deprivation is in fact Allāh's gift [to you]. It would then be incorrect to think of it as a deprivation. This intelligence and state of contentment are far superior to the matter that was withheld from you.

اَلْعَطَاءُ مِنَ الْخَلْقِ حِرْمَانٌ، وَالْمَنْعُ مِنَ اللّٰهِ إِحْسَانٌ.

A gift from man is deprivation, and deprivation from God is beneficence. [88]

O traveler! Superficially, the bestowal of people appears to be beneficial for you because you have received something without effort. This gift is really a deprivation, because your attention will be on the people (who make gifts to you). Your distance from Allāh Most High is proportionate to your gaze (of desire and hope) on people. Your trust in Allāh will decrease.

On the other hand, if Allāh Most High keeps you in poverty and hardship, then although it may appear as deprivation, in reality it is His favor upon you. In this case, the true and original wealth (of gnosis) will increase. Your gaze will then not shift from your Master. Your humility and dependency on Him will increase. These are designed objectives.

Rajab includes the narration of *Aḥmad* in which the Prophet ﷺ was asked for "comprehensive and concise advice," and so he said: "Do not suspect Allāh with respect to His decree."

مَتى أَعْطَاكَ .. أَشْـهَدَكَ بِرَّهُ، وَمَتَى مَنَعَكَ .. أَشْهَدَكَ قَهْرَهُ، فَهُوَ فِي كُلِّ ذٰلِكَ مُتَعَرِّفٌ إِلَيْكَ وَمُقْبِلٌ بِوُجُودِ لُطْفِهِ عَلَيْكَ.

When He gives, He shows you His kindness; when He deprives, He shows you His power. And in all that, He is making Himself known to you and coming to you with His gentleness. [93]

The purpose of man's creation is that he acquires the gnosis of his Creator and His lofty attributes; hence He says that He did not create jinn and man except that they worship Him.

The ḥadīth literature clarifies that the acquisition of His gnosis is not possible without His bestowal. The way of gaining gnosis is to reflect on the predestined circumstances and conditions that might overtake one. In this way does the servant gain insight into the workings of his Master. Gnosis reaches the servant according to his circumstances. He who possesses proper intelligence will, therefore, gain gnosis from Allāh in every condition.

Expounding upon this concept, the Shaykh is saying: O traveler! When Allāh Most High bestows some bounty on you, He is in reality displaying His generosity and kindness to you; and when He withholds His gifts from you, involving you in difficulties and hardships, he displays to you His attribute of anger and power. The traveler who derives a lesson from every state is most fortunate. He derives the gnosis of his Master in every moment. His heart brims with delight on account of the treasure of gnosis.

The servant shorn of intelligence directs his attention to the gift bestowed upon him, while he is forgetful of Allāh. He regards himself deserving of the gift. He thus develops pride. During conditions of adversity, he suffers; hence he complains and proves his ingratitude. We seek refuge in Allāh!

إِنَّمَا يُؤْلِمُكَ الْمَنْعُ لِعَدَمِ فَهْمِكَ عَنِ اللّٰهِ فِيهِ.

Deprivation hurts you only because of the lack of your understanding of God in it. [94]

O traveler! The grief and annoyance of your heart when Allāh Most High afflicts you with difficulties and hardships are the products of your lack of intelligence. On account of your ignorance, you are unable to fathom the divine mercy, wisdom and grace underlying your adverse circumstances.

If you had not been ignorant, your state of adversity would have been just as pleasurable to you as your state of prosperity. In fact, your pleasure will be greater at the time of deprivation because poverty and hardship are the share (of gifts) reserved for the special servants of Allāh Most High.

رُبَّمَا فتَحَ لَكَ بَابَ الطَّاعَةِ وَمَا فتَحَ لَكَ بَابَ الْقَبُولِ،
وَرُبَّمَا قَضَى عَلَيْكَ بِالذَّنْبِ فَكَانَ سَبَبًا فِي الْوُصُولِ.

Sometimes He opens the door of obedience for you but not the door of acceptance; or sometimes He condemns you to sin, and it turns out to be a cause of arriving at Him. [95]

Very often Allāh Most High opens up the door of His obedience; hence one is able to engross oneself night and day in acts of obedience, supererogatory worship, contemplation, devotional exercises, recitation of the Qur'ān, etc. However, because of the lack of sincerity or vanity or because of despising other Muslims, the door of acceptance is not opened. Thus, your deeds remain unaccepted.

Sins frequently emerge from the worshipper. Although ostensibly the sin committed is a cause for divine rejection, on account of the exceptionally high degree of remorse, regret and repentance the sinner attains divine proximity. Thus, the sin becomes the medium of forgiveness.

Therefore, the servant should not look at the external form of everything. His gaze should be focused on the inner realities of things. If Allāh Most High has blessed one with worship and obedience, one should not despise those who are not involved in acts of piety, nor consider one's self to be superior. On the other hand, if a sin has been committed, one should not despair of Allāh's mercy by viewing the enormity of the external form of the sin.

مَتَىٰ كُنْتَ إِذَا أُعْطِيْتَ .. بَسَطَكَ الْعَطَاءُ، وإِذَا مُنِعْتَ .. قَبَضَكَ الْمَنْعُ، فَاسْتَدِلَّ بِذٰلِكَ عَلَىٰ ثُبُوتِ طُفُولِيَّتِكَ وَعَدَمِ صِدْقِكَ فِي عُبُودِيَّتِكَ.

If when given something, the giving expands you, and if when deprived of something, the deprivation contracts you, then take that as the proof of your immaturity and the insincerity of your servanthood. [147]

O traveler! If your condition is such that you worship and remember Allāh with concentration and relish when He showers favors on you, but when these favors are withheld you become disappointed and despondent in worship, then know that in the Divine Court you are not regarded as one of the people of Allāh (*ahl Allāh*). You are only claiming to be among the people of Allāh, but your claim is false. If you were truly among the people of Allāh, then this would not have been your condition. Your attitude indicates that you are not true in your servanthood and worship. Your state indicates that the quest for pleasures of the ego still lurks in you. You are still inclined to the acquisition of your ego's goals and hopes. This attitude is a negation of the state of servanthood and indicates slavery to the ego.

However, if the heart's constriction is on account of fear of a trial imposed by Allāh Most High—the trial being a manifestation of the wrath of Allāh Most High—and the uncertainty of maintaining patience and steadfastness during the trial, then it will not indicate falsity of one's servanthood. Such constriction of the heart and fear are natural human reactions. The attributes of humanity (*bashariyya*) remain in the *'ārif.*

نِعْمَتَانِ مَا خَرَجَ مَوْجُودٌ عَنْهُمَا، وَلَا بُدَّ لِكُلِّ مُكَوَّنٍ مِنْهُمَا: نِعْمَةُ الْإِيجَادِ، وَنِعْمَةُ الْإِمْدَادِ.

There are two graces from which no being can be separated and that are inevitable for every creature: the grace of existence, and the grace of sustenance. [97]

The graces of Allāh Most High limitlessly descend on every creature. However, there are two graces that are common to everything. The first is the act of creation: everything was non-existent prior to its existence. By the generosity of Allāh Most High, the gift of existence was bestowed. He thus created the object and eliminated non-existence.

Secondly, after coming into existence by way of creation, everything is wholly dependent on the aid of Allāh Most High for its endurance and sustenance. For this need it is dependent on Allāh Most High in every moment of its existence. Should Allāh Most High withhold His aid, everything will again return to the state of non-existence. He has created different ways and means for the existence of different objects; for example, for animals and humans He has created water, food, etc.

أَنْعَمَ عَلَيْكَ أَوَّلًا بِالْإِيجَادِ، وَثَانِيًا بِتَوَالِي الْإِمْدَادِ.

He bestowed His grace upon you, first, through giving you being, and, second, through uninterrupted sustenance. [98]

In the previous aphorism mention was made of the bounties of creation and assistance common to all created objects. The Shaykh ﵀ now addresses man in particular; in fact, the address is directed to the believer, whose attention is drawn to his earlier state of pure non-existence. From which Allāh Most High conferred on him the grace of being existent. The believer should thus understand that he is wholly dependent on Allāh Most High for his existence. Dependence is, therefore, man's natural and inherent attribute which he should never forget.

Secondly, with every breath and moment Allāh Most High ensures that man receives His favors, necessary for his physical and spiritual existence. Food, garments and a variety of preparations have been and are being continuously created for man's physical existence and survival. For man's spiritual existence, Allāh Most High constantly sends His aid in an uninterrupted flow. Without the spiritual aid of Allāh, the believer will go astray. Thus, it has been observed that when Allāh Most High terminates His aid from certain people, they fall headlong into deviation (*ḍalāl*).

Since it is not possible for one to be independent from the Lord for even a second, why do we feign independence? Why this self-esteem? Why this claim of excellence? How can these claims be correct? You should become a slave, keeping in mind one's origin and refrain from making boastful claims.

مَتَى أَوْحَشَكَ مِنْ خَلْقِهِ .. فَاعْلَمْ أَنَّهُ يُرِيدُ أَنْ يَفْتَحَ لَكَ بَابَ الْأُنْسِ بِهِ.

When He alienates you from His creatures, then know that He wants to open for you the door of intimacy with Him. [101]

O traveler! If your heart cannot find solace with anyone except in the invocation of Allāh and you are terrified of creatures, then understand this state to indicate Allāh's willing intimacy for you, and that He will keep you aloof from all things besides Him. On the other hand, if your heart derives comfort from creatures and you become bored and terrified of solitude and invocation, then understand that this condition is a great loss and misfortune for you.

إِذَا أَرَادَ أَنْ يُظْهِرَ فَضْلَهُ عَلَيْكَ .. خَلَقَ وَنَسَبَ إِلَيْكَ.

When He wants to show His grace to you, He creates states in you and attributes them to you. [123]

When Allāh Most High wishes to manifest His kindness and favor to a servant, He creates deeds and lofty states. On the occasions of praise, He relates these good deeds and attributes to the servant.

In reality, the servant's action and choice have no role in his righteous states, since Allāh Most High creates these states in him. Although Allāh Most High is the creator of these pious states, He relates the states to the servant who is then praised. Thus, if the servant is intelligent, he will not become vain and proud when he is blessed with the grace of Allāh Most High. On the contrary, he should be bashful and refrain from attributing any virtuous state to himself; and all beautiful attributes should be related to Allāh Most High.

Yet, evil and defects should be attributed to himself.

لَوْلَا جَمِيلُ سَتْرِهِ .. لَمْ يَكُنْ عَمَلٌ أَهْلًا لِلْقَبُولِ.

Were it not for the kindliness of His veiling, no deed would be worthy of acceptance. [131]

Only a deed entirely devoid of any egotistic contamination deserves to be accepted. Regardless of the degree of adornment and purification of the ego, there will remain to some extent ego in the self, even though this may not be discernible. The ego by nature is an embodiment of evil.

It is because of Allāh's grace and kindness that the evil and sins of the servant are overlooked and concealed by Him. He shows great forbearance by withholding His punishment from the sinful servant. Above all, He accepts the servant's defective deeds. In reality, no one's deeds deserve acceptance in His Lofty Court.

O traveler! Do not be overwhelmed by excessive grief on account of the deficiencies in your acts of virtue. In fact, when Allāh Most High accepts, He accepts our defective deeds and awards rewards for the very defective acts offered by His servants.

مَنْ أَكْرَمَكَ فَإِنَّمَا أَكْرَمَ فِيْكَ جَمِيلَ سَتْرِهِ، فَالْحَمْدُ لِمَنْ سَتَرَكَ، لَيْسَ الْحَمْدُ لِمَنْ أَكْرَمَكَ وَشَكَرَكَ.

Whoever honors you honors only the beauty of His veil in you. Therefore, praise is to Him who veiled you, not to the one who honored and thanked you. [134]

O traveler! When someone respects and honors you with praise or gifts, do not become proud. Do not gain the impression that you have in you some excellence. In reality, the person has not praised you. He has praised Allāh's attribute of veiling the sins and defects of people. If Allāh Most High had not concealed your egotistic evils, people would not even spit on you! All would have detested you because your ego is an embodiment of mischief and evil. Therefore, do not praise and flatter the one who praises you or one who treats you with respect, honor and kindness. The Being who has concealed your faults is truly deserving of praise.

The one who praises and honors you is not deserving of respect and praises [in essence]. However, there is nothing wrong in expressing gratitude to the one who is kind and shows respect to you, for it is Allāh Most High who bestowed the goodness to you via the agency of that person (who has honored you). But, the gaze should be on only Allāh Most High.

أَشْهَدَكَ مِنْ قَبْلِ أَنْ يَسْتَشْهِدَكَ .. فَنَطَقَتْ بِإِلٰهِيَّتِهِ الظَّوَاهِرُ، وَتَحَقَّقَتْ بِأَحَدِيَّتِهِ الْقُلُوبُ وَالسَّرَائِرُ.

He made you witness before He asked you to give witness. Thus, the outer faculties speak of His Divinity while the heart and the innermost consciousness have realized His Unity. [255]

O traveler! Do not think that there is no prior origin and cause for the testimony that you bear for His Unity here on earth and for the worship you are performing. Long ago, Allāh Most High demanded that you testify to His Unity. He had revealed His Unity in The Realm of the Souls.[27] After your appearance on earth, your spirit was fettered to the material form and made Him the object of worship on account of the spiritual perception it had experienced in The Realm of the Souls. Thus, the tongue proclaims His Unity and Lordship while the other physical limbs by their obedience imply that Allāh Most High is the True Being to be worshipped and obeyed. The limbs, therefore, go into prostration and bowing, while the heart and the other spiritual faculties have the certainty of His uniqueness. Were it not for that prior revelation in The Realm of the Souls, then in this physical world the physical body would not have testified to His Unity, and the heart would not have developed certitude.

The similitude for the aforementioned reality is like that of a city that you had seen and forgotten. On being reminded of this city, you recall it and your heart has certitude of its existence and description. However, if you had never seen the city, certitude would not develop, regardless of the efforts of a person to explain to you. Certitude is not possible when the form of a thing is not in one's subconscious mind (or already embedded in the imagination).

In the absence of the spiritual perception of the souls, certitude would not have been possible on the basis of only rational proofs of The Truth (*al-Ḥaqq*, a name of Allāh). Complete certitude is not based on rational proofs; it is like a lost item that is immediately recognized on sight. Similar to this is the

27 See Maghnīsāwī, *Al-Fiqh al-Akbar Explained,* 115–119, for a theological discussion of the "progeny of Ādam ﷺ" all being brought forth to testify to "His Lordship," so as not to claim that *We were unaware of this* (Qur'ān 7:172) on the Day of Resurrection.

perfect certitude in Allāh's Unity, the messages of His Messengers ﷺ and the matters of the Hereafter—the spirit was shown all of these higher realities.

When the spirit was imprisoned in this material body, it forgot the realities that were revealed to it, on account of the influences of the physical body. The Qur'ān, ḥadīth and Prophets of Allāh, therefore, remind man of this reality. If the grace of Allāh Most High is directed to the servant, the material veils of the physical body are lifted and the spirit then resumes its original perception. The physical body is subservient to the spirit; hence it becomes fully involved in obedience once its veils are lifted. *And that is the Bounty of Allāh. He grants it to whomever He wishes* (Qur'ān 57:21).

رُبَّمَا أَطْلَعَكَ عَلَى غَيْبِ مَلَكُوتِهِ، وَحَجَبَ عَنْكَ الْإِسْتِشْرَافَ عَلَى أَسْرَارِ الْعِبَادِ، مَنِ اطَّلَعَ عَلَى أَسْرَارِ الْعِبَادِ وَلَمْ يَتَخَلَّقْ بِالرَّحْمَةِ الْإِلٰهِيَّةِ .. كَانَ اطِّلَاعُهُ فِتْنَةً عَلَيْهِ وَسَبَبًا لِجَرِّ الْوَبَالِ إِلَيْهِ.

Whoever gets to know the secrets of servants without patterning himself on the divine mercifulness, finds his knowledge a tribulation and a cause for drawing evil upon himself. Sometimes He reveals to you the invisible domain of His Realm but veils you from knowing the secrets of servants. [158, 157]

O traveler! Sometimes Allāh Most High reveals to you, by way of illumination and inspiration, some of the hidden mysteries of the heaven and earth, such as future events or information of distant places; however, He does not make you aware of the secrets in the hearts of His servants. It is not appropriate for you to desire such information (of the hearts of people) because this awareness is withheld for your own benefit.

The knowledge of the secrets in the hearts of men is awarded to only such a person who has become a perfect human manifestation of mercy. Allāh's attribute of mercy embraces all. Despite His knowledge of the condition of men's hearts, He conceals their evil by virtue of His attribute of mercy and overlooks the errors and sins of ignoramuses. He does not hastily apprehend the perpetrators of evil. He conceals the faults of all people. A man who has imbued in himself an attribute of mercy is sometimes made aware of the secrets of men's hearts.

But one who lacks this attribute will be cast into trial by the revelation of such secrets of the heart because his concern with his ego will produce pride in him. Should such inner thoughts be revealed to one lacking in the attribute of perfect mercy, he will despise other Muslims while believing himself to be holy. Thus, this will be a trial constituting an avenue of misfortune for him.

Pride is a great misfortune for man. Greatness is an attribute that belongs exclusively to Allāh Most High. A man who lays claim to greatness will have his neck broken (by Allāh Most High).[28] Hence, it is best, and in the interests of the servant, that he is not informed of the secrets of men's hearts.

However, such revelation will not be a trial for a man who has inculcated mercy in his nature. Even if he is informed (by way of illumination or inspiration) of the secrets of the hearts, he will view the people with affection and mercy.

عَلِمَ أَنَّ الْعِبَادَ يَتَشَوَّفُونَ إِلَى ظُهُورِ سِرِّ الْعِنَايَةِ، فَقَالَ: ﴿يَخْتَصُّ بِرَحْمَتِهِ مَنْ يَشَاءُ﴾، وَعَلِمَ أَنَّهُ لَوْ خَلَّاهُمْ وَذٰلِكَ .. لَتَرَكُوا الْعَمَلَ اعْتِمَادًا عَلَى الْأَزَلِ، فَقَالَ: ﴿إِنَّ رَحْمَةَ اللّٰهِ قَرِيبٌ مِنَ الْمُحْسِنِينَ﴾.

He knew that servants would anticipate the emergence of the mystery of Providence in themselves, so He said, "He chooses whom He pleases for His Mercy." [Q. 2:105] And He knew that, had He left them at that, they would have abandoned all effort by relying on the Eternal, so He said. "Surely the Mercy of God is nigh to the doers of good." [Q. 7:56] [170]

The mercy of Allāh Most High is of two kinds: general (*āmma*) and special (*khāṣṣa*).

General mercy is for the entire creation. By virtue of this general mercy He bestowed existence on everyone and everything, as well as sustaining them until an appointed time. This mercy is not restricted to any particular being, but extends to all things. Thus, Allāh Most High tells us that His mercy embraces all things. This is the mercy of creation and sustenance.

28 The Messenger of Allāh ﷺ said, "Might is His lower garment and pride is His Outer garment, so, 'Whoever vies with Me, I will punish him.'" See Ibn Rajab, *Compendium*, 576.

Special mercy is His proximity and grace. Its basis is divine will. He bestows this special mercy on whomever He wills without any intermediate cause. By directing His special mercy to a person, He bestows His proximity to him. The Shaykh ﷺ refers to this special mercy.

In His eternal knowledge, Allāh Most High was aware that people would be desirous of His special mercy. They desire that the mysteries and secrets of the special mercy be revealed to them so that they attain His proximity. Motivated by this quest, they practice righteous deeds and supplicate for the realization of this aim. They feel that on account of their virtuous deeds they have become deserving of Allāh's special mercy. Dismissing this baseless idea, Allāh says (in the Qur'ān 2:105): *He chooses whom He pleases for His Mercy*. In other words, the quest and righteous deeds of people are not the basis for the acquisition of His special mercy. The basis for it is Allāh's will.

Although righteous deeds, supplication and effort are not the cause for the acquisition of Allāh's special mercy, they are undoubtedly signs of this special, eternal bounty. When, by that grace of Allāh Most High, the servant practices righteousness, it indicates that a servant might be one of the elect. The servant should understand that he must maintain this practice of righteous deeds in the hope that he will be delivered, ultimately, into Allāh's special mercy.

If, however, the servant was not exhorted to practice virtue, but was left with only the belief that Allāh Most High grants His special mercy to whomever He wills, he would have simply placed his reliance on destiny, thus refraining from righteous deeds. Hence, Allāh Most High says: *Surely the Mercy of Allāh is nigh to the doers of good* (7:56).

It is, therefore, improper to abandon righteousness. Along with righteousness, hope should be in Allāh Most High, not in one's deeds. Should one repose hope on one's deeds, it would be tantamount to reliance on one's self.

عِنَايَتُهُ فِيكَ لَا لِشَيْءٍ مِنْكَ، وَأَيْنَ كُنْتَ حِينَ وَاجَهَتْكَ عِنَايَتُهُ وَقَابَلَتْكَ رِعَايَتُهُ؟ لَمْ يَكُنْ فِي أَزَلِهِ إِخلَاصُ أَعْمَالٍ وَلَا وُجُودُ أَحْوَالٍ، بَلْ لَمْ يَكُنْ هُنَاكَ إِلَّا مَحْضُ الْإِفْضَالِ وَعَظِيمُ النَّوَالِ.

His providential care of you is not due to anything coming from you. Where were you when He confronted you

with His providence or met you face-to-face with His care? Neither sincerity of deeds nor the existence of states have any being in His Eternity. Instead, only pure bestowing and sublime giving are there. [169]

O traveler! Your understanding that your righteous deeds, spiritual states and effort bring about the special mercy and proximity of Allāh is due to deficiency in your thinking. What deed did you render in order to be brought to the focus of Allāh's mercy on you? The decree of His special mercy was applied to you when you and your deeds were non-existent. It was nothing but His grace; hence you should not consider your deeds as the cause for His grace. Remove your gaze from your efforts and focus it on the mercy of Allāh Most High.

لَا تَنْفَعُــهُ طَاعَتُكَ وَلَا تَضُرُّهُ مَعْصِيَتُكَ، وإِنَّمَا أَمَرَكَ بِهٰذِهِ وَنَهَاكَ عَنْ هٰذِهِ لِمَا يَعُودُ عَلَيْكَ.

Your obedience does not benefit Him, and your disobedience does not harm Him. It is only for your own good that He commanded the one and prohibited the other. [211]

O servant! Your obedience does not benefit Allāh Most High in any way whatsoever, because He is absolutely independent of all things. Your disobedience cannot harm Him in any way, either, because He is mighty and powerful.

You have been commanded to practice righteousness and abstain from transgression so that you acquire the benefit in this world and the Hereafter. He says in the Qur'ān that whoever practices righteousness, it is for himself; and whoever sins, it is on himself.

The demand therefore is that you perform righteousness, refrain from evil and never think that you have accomplished something wonderful. The idea of accomplishment would be proper if the actions rendered by you benefit another person. If you refrain from righteousness you are simply depriving yourself of benefits. You are not bestowing any favor on anyone.

قُرْبُكَ مِنْهُ أَنْ تَكُونَ مُشَاهِدًا لِقُرْبِهِ، وَإِلَّا فَمِنْ أَيْنَ أَنْتَ وَوُجُودُ قُرْبِهِ؟

Your nearness to Him is that you contemplate His nearness. Otherwise, what comparison is there between you and the existence of His nearness? [214]

It is a characteristic of the ego to liken others to itself. To a degree, this will be appropriate in regard to human beings, since all are of the same species. Man, however, on account of his ignorance and stupidity, sometimes thinks of Allāh Most High as he thinks of himself in some affairs. Some ignoramuses believe that, by their attention toward Allāh, they have elevated and adorned the religion; or some persons, who had previously aided the religion by acts of virtue, labor under the delusion that if they abstain from this service, or they die, the religion of Allāh will suffer a setback. Such delusions are clearly refuted by the Shaykh ﷺ.

إِنَّمَا أَجْرَى الْأَذَى عَلَى أَيْدِيهِمْ كَيْ لَا تَكُونَ سَاكِنًا إِلَيْهِمْ، أَرَادَ أَنْ يُزْعِجَكَ عَنْ كُلِّ شَيْءٍ حَتَّى لَا يَشْغَلَكَ عَنْهُ شَيْءٌ.

He only made affliction come at the hands of people so that you not repose in them. He wanted to drive you out of everything so that nothing would divert you from Him. [235]

O traveler! If you suffer any affliction at the hands of people—whether to your body, wealth or reputation—do not become despondent and disillusioned. There is much wisdom underlying their attitude. In reality, this discomfort has come to you from Allāh Most High. If, instead of the hurt, you are favored and comforted by people, you will then find repose with them and place your trust in them instead of in Allāh Most High.

Allāh Most High desires that your heart be completely disillusioned with people; hence He causes creation to hurt you. In consequence, you will free yourself from all others. When an intelligent person experiences ingratitude and fickleness in one or two of his associates, he realizes that others too are similar. He will, therefore, free his heart from all association. This in reality is a great mercy of Allāh Most High for one, in that nothing will make this servant neglectful of his True Master. He (the servant) now, in such a spiritual state, observes that everything is transitory; hence he will not derive pleasure in anything besides Allāh Most High.

إِذَا عَلِمْتَ أَنَّ الشَّيْطَانَ لَا يَغْفُلُ عَنْكَ .. فَلَا
تَغْفُلْ أَنْتَ عَمَّنْ نَاصِيَتُكَ بِيَدِهِ.

**If you know that the devil does not forget
you, then do not forget, for your part, Him
who has your forelock in His hand. [236]**

O believer and O traveler! You are aware that Allāh Most High has informed you that the devil is perpetually scheming to deviate and destroy you. Allāh Most High mentions the devil's vow in the Qur'ān: that he shall most certainly come to us from in front of us, from behind us, on our right sides and on our left sides.[29]

He vowed to attack the servants of Allāh from every side in an attempt to mislead them. Your plan to thwart the devil should be your alertness. You should not be neglectful of your Master in whose power is your life. Supplicate to Him. Only He can save you from your enemy.

جَعَلَهُ لَكَ عَدُوًّا لِيَحُوشَكَ بِهِ إِلَيْهِ، وَحَرَّكَ
عَلَيْكَ النَّفْسَ لِيَدُومَ إِقْبَالُكَ عَلَيْهِ.

**He made the devil your enemy so that, through
him, He could drive you toward Himself, and He
stirred up your soul against you so that your drawing near to Him would be permanent. [237]**

Allāh Most High informed mankind in the Qur'ān that the devil is their "open enemy" (Qur'ān 2:208).

---

29 This refers to the verses of the Qur'ān that start at 7:11 and detail the story of Ādam 🕊 and the devil (Ar. Iblīs or Shayṭān).

By virtue of Allāh's information and your own experience, you will realize without any doubt that the devil is your enemy in addition to your soul. While your soul is your enemy from within, the devil is an outside enemy. You will realize that he is the enemy of your welfare in both abodes. At the same time, you will know that on account of your weakness and the invisibility of your enemy, his plots to destroy you will be highly dangerous. Furthermore, you will not find any friend on earth to aid you against your enemy. When this knowledge becomes the condition of your heart, you will readily turn in supplication to Allāh Most High. You will be anxiously turning your attention to Him. This attitude is most desirable. This laudable attitude will, in fact, be the consequence of the devil's animosity for you.

Similarly, Allāh Most High has induced your soul to pursue desires. The soul is always demanding satiation of its pleasures. Sometimes the soul seeks expression of its desire to commit sin, and sometimes it desires the beauties and luxuries of the world. The traveler usually becomes perturbed by these demands because the domination of these desires prevents him from his actual goal (of divine proximity).

However, the wisdom and mercy of Allāh Most High for the servant in this trial is that he will struggle against his soul. Since the servant cannot overcome the soul by himself, he has no option but to supplicate to Allāh Most High for aid. His attention will, therefore, be fixed permanently toward Allāh Most High. Thus, he will ever be alert against this enemy.

It should be understood that the state of being permanently alert against the enemy is acquired when the knowledge of the soul's malice becomes one's attitude and disposition. Mere knowledge is not sufficient.

جَعَلَكَ فِي الْعَالَمِ الْمُتَوَسِّطِ بَيْنَ مُلْكِهِ وَمَلَكُوتِهِ لِيُعَلِّمَكَ جَلَالَةَ قَدْرِكَ بَيْنَ مَخْلُوقَاتِهِ، وَأَنَّكَ جَوْهَرَةٌ تَنْطَوِي عَلَيْكَ أَصْدَافُ مُكَوَّنَاتِهِ.

He put you in the intermediary world between His Kingdom and His Realm to teach you the majesty of your rank amongst His created beings and that you are a jewel wherein the pearls of His creations are hidden. [245]

O mankind! Allāh Most High has created you of two entities: physical and spiritual. You are not a totally physical being, nor a totally spiritual being, like the angels. You are a creation in a state between these two entities. Your intermediate status (between the physical and spiritual) is evident.

Allāh Most High created man between the heaven and earth. All things on earth have been created for man's use and benefit, and all things have been made subservient to him.

If man were only a physical creation, he would have been like all other physical and worldly creatures. He would then not have enjoyed superiority over them. Thus, it is clear that the essential substance of his constitution is something other than his physical matter. By virtue of his special spiritual essence, man enjoys superiority over all other creation. That special substance is his relationship with the spiritual realm.

Allāh Most High has created man a microcosm. He is an embodiment of all existing creation, consisting of lofty and lowly attributes and of physical and spiritual substances. He is thus physical and spiritual at the same time. He is earthly, as well as heavenly. On the one hand, he possesses the angelic qualities of intelligence, gnosis and worship; like the heavens, he is a substance for mysteries and celestial light; his heart is the abode of divine unveiling (*tajallī*). On the other hand, he has the capability of misleading others and being misled himself. He also has the attributes of rebellion and transgression. These are the animal and satanic attributes within him. In his state of anger, he is a lion. When lust dominates him, he is a pig. In the state of greed and adversity, he is a dog. When he deceives, he is a fox. His growth and development are like that of the trees. Like the ground, he is both hard and soft.

In short, man incorporates within him samples of every creation. It is for this reason that he is described as microcosm or "little world," and as the perfect substratum of the manifestation of the entire creation.

The aim underlying man's all-embracing constitution is for him to realize his significance and superiority over all creation. He will realize from his very constitution that he is a priceless pearl that embraces all aspects of the creation. When he has recognized this reality, he will not destroy himself by involvement in disobedience to his Master and Creator. He will maintain himself on the lofty and magnificent plane on which Allāh Most High has created him. The sole method for this is perpetual obedience to his Creator and abstention from transgression.

17

ON COMPANIONSHIP

لَا تَصْحَبْ مَنْ لَا يُنْهِضُكَ حَالُهُ وَلَا يَدُلُّكَ عَلَى اللهِ مَقَالُهُ.

Do not keep company with anyone whose state does not inspire you and whose speech does not lead you to God. [43]

THERE IS NOTHING more beneficial for the traveler than pious companionship; hence the Shaykh ﷺ states the principle in this regard, so that the traveler understands the company that will be beneficial and harmful for him.

Never choose the company of a man who does not inspire you toward Allāh. The state of the companion should be such that his entire attention is focused on Allāh. The gaze of his heart should be diverted from creation. In every affair his complete reliance should be on Allāh. In his lofty estimate, creation should have no significance and no rank. Obedience to the Sacred Law in all affairs should have become his natural disposition. His speech should guide toward the Path of Allāh. Such a person is qualified for companionship.

A man who lacks the aforementioned qualities is of no benefit. In fact, his company is harmful, even if overtly he has the appearance of a saint. Since his heart's relationship is with alien objects (i.e., things besides Allāh), his companionship is bound to exercise its influence. Those in his association will be similarly affected by his detrimental influence.

رُبَّمَا كُنْتَ مُسِيئًا فَأَرَاكَ الْإِحْسَانَ مِنْكَ
صُحْبَتُكَ مَنْ هُوَ أَسْوَأُ حَالًا مِنْكَ.

You might be in a bad state; then, your associating with one who is in a worse state makes you see virtue in yourself. [44]

It is incumbent on the believer to acquire the companionship of a person better than himself. In such company, you will see your own faults and you will become concerned with your moral and spiritual reformation. On the other hand, if you sit in the company of a man worse than yourself, its necessary consequence will be that, despite your evil, you will regard yourself to be pious. You will most certainly gain the impression that you are better than him. Thus your own deficiencies will not become discernible. You will be overtaken by vanity and be pleased with yourself.

مَا صَحِبَكَ إِلَّا مَنْ صَحِبَكَ وَهُوَ بِعَيْبِكَ عَلِيمٌ، وَلَيْسَ ذٰلِكَ إِلَّا مَوْلَاكَ
الْكَرِيمُ؛ خَيْرُ مَنْ تَصْحَبُ مَنْ يَطْلُبُكَ لَكَ لَا لِشَيْءٍ يَعُودُ مِنْكَ إِلَيْهِ.

No one is a companion of yours except the one who, while knowing your defects, is your companion, and that is only your generous Lord. The best one to take on as a companion is He who does not seek you out for the sake of something coming from you to Him. [135]

The friendship of worldly people is generally fickle. When they discover one's faults, they sever ties, and develop a dislike for the former friend. But the Creator maintains His relationship with His servants despite being aware of their innumerable deficiencies. Only He should be one's true Companion, for despite having full knowledge of the faults of His servants, He is always there for people to turn to.

Those servants of Allāh who have cultivated in themselves states of excellence also maintain their relationship with a person after discovering their defects. They will conceal even the greatest sin that they see in their associates. They do not sever their relationship. Thus, a man should establish his relationship with His Lord or with those who are linked to His Lord (i.e., saints).

Your best friend is a person who strives for your welfare without having any motive of self-gain for himself. Righteous Muslims also desire good for people, even their enemies. They do not cherish any hope for personal gain, because their hearts have been completely purified of egotistic motives. Their relationship with people is purely for the sake of Allāh. It is essential, then, to establish a bond with the righteous and to abandon all other friendships that are based on lowly motives.

18

ON AMBITIOUS DESIRE

مَا بَسَقَتْ أَغْصَانُ ذُلٍّ .. إِلَّا عَلَى بِذْرِ طَمَعٍ.

Were it not for the seeds of ambitious desire, the branches of disgrace would not be lofty. [60]

THE BRANCHES OF THE tree of disgrace grow and spread from the seed of ambitious desire that has taken root in the heart. Disgrace is always the consequence of greed and desire. When man's heart desires wealth and fame, then for its acquisition he will certainly establish a relationship with people and direct his appeals to them. This acquisition of wealth or fame is not possible without collusion with others. His desire constrains him to flatter and beg others. This is a great disgrace. *Ṭamaʿ* is thus part of the root of evil.

True respect lies in man's heart being devoid of any relationship with anyone besides Allāh. He remains independent from all. This treasure of true respect is acquired by the elimination of greed and the cultivation of contentment.

مَا قَادَكَ شَيْءٌ مِثْلُ الْوَهْمِ.

Nothing leads you like suspicion. [61]

This assertion is the proof for the previous aphorism. Nothing is as effective as suspicion for imprisoning man in greed and desire. As a result of suspicion, man becomes ensnared in the net of desire. One imagines or suspects that a certain person will be of benefit to one. One therefore turns the gaze of desire to him, expecting benefit from him. Or one imagines a particular trade, profession or occupation being beneficial for one. Greed then induces one to become involved in that pursuit.

All the chains of relationship that are fettering man's legs are the products of man's imagination or suspicion. It is only divine power, through the means of the righteous, which can free man from these chains.

The ego inclines greatly to imagination and suspicion and remains very far from higher spiritual realities. As long as the ego has not been purified, the elimination of this disease is difficult.

أَنْتَ حُرٌّ مِمَّا أَنْتَ عَنْهُ آيِسٌ، وَعَبْدٌ لِمَا أَنْتَ لَهُ طَامِعٌ.

In your despairing, you are a free man; but in your coveting, you are a slave. [62]

When desire and greed for an object arises in the heart, a strong relationship develops with it; and the heart becomes enslaved to it. This enslavement brings in its wake a variety of difficulties. In the bid for its acquisition, man bears the indignity of many a disgrace.

If the heart despairs of all things, it attains freedom from them and achieves perpetual peace and comfort. It does not behoove a Muslim, therefore, to disgrace himself in the pursuit of the lowly things of the world and to forget the Hereafter.

19

ON HUMILITY

مَنْ أَثْبَتَ لِنَفْسِهِ تَوَاضُعًا .. فَهُوَ الْمُتَكَبِّرُ حَقًّا، إِذْ لَيْسَ التَّوَاضُعُ إِلَّا عَنْ رِفْعَةٍ، فَمَتَىٰ أَثْبَتَّ لِنَفْسِكَ تَوَاضُعًا .. فَأَنْتَ الْمُتَكَبِّرُ حَقًّا.

He who attributes humility to himself is really proud, for humility arises only out of a sublime state. So when you attribute humility to yourself, then you are proud. [238]

HUMILITY IS THE BELIEF that one is the most contemptible and lowest being. The consideration of greatness in oneself is pride (*takabbur*).

The knowledge of a thing is gained from its opposite. In the absence of the opposite, the knowledge of a thing will not be possible. The knowledge of light is by virtue of darkness. If on earth there was only light, and no darkness whatsoever, the conception of light would not be possible. The knowledge of courage is on account of cowardice; if there was no cowardice, there would not have been the knowledge of courage. Thus the claim of humility made by a person is tantamount to pride. There is no doubt in defining such a person as proud. If his ego was fully imbued with true humility, he would not have been aware thereof because of the non-existence of its opposite of pride.

Since pride exists in the man who lays claim to humility, the Shaykh ﵀ says that the one who puts forth the claim that he is humble is in actual fact considering himself to be elevated. Thus, he is a man of pride.

The meaning of humility is that man views himself with all honesty to be so contemptible that the possibility of him having any rank does not even occur to his mind. He sees nothing but contemptibility in himself. When this degree of humility has been cultivated, one will make no claims—neither in regard to humility nor in regard to any other praiseworthy attribute.

لَيْسَ الْمُتَوَاضِعُ الَّذِي إِذَا تَوَاضَعَ .. رَأَى أَنَّهُ فَوْقَ مَا صَنَعَ،
وَلٰكِنَّ الْمُتَوَاضِعَ الَّذِي إِذَا تَوَاضَعَ .. رَأَى أَنَّهُ دُونَ مَا صَنَعَ.

The humble man is not the one who, when humble, sees that he is above what he does; instead, the humble man is the one who, when humble, sees that he is below what he does. [239]

Generally, people believe that a humble person is one who displays acts of humility; for example, a wealthy man rendering some service with his own hands to a poor person. People gain the impression from this display that the wealthy man is very humble when, in fact, he may be entirely devoid of any humility, because he thinks of himself as being superior to this act. While he overtly displays humility, he covertly believes that the act of humility in which he is involved is below his dignity. He feels conscious of having adopted humility and he believes that he has practiced virtue.

اَلتَّوَاضُعُ الْحَقِيقِيُّ هُوَ مَا كَانَ نَاشِئًا عَنْ شُهُودِ عَظَمَتِهِ وَتَجَلِّي صِفَتِهِ.

Real humility is the one which arises from the contemplation of His Sublimity and the illumination of His Attribute. [240]

Real humility is that condition of lowliness that is accepted by Allāh Most High. When the greatness of Allāh dawns on the heart of man and he vividly realizes the perfection of His attributes, then the rebellious ego melts away. The roots of rebellion and pride are then eradicated. The vain hopes of the ego are annihilated; humility then develops.

مَعْصِيَةٌ أَورَثَتْ ذُلًّا وَافْتِقَارًا خَيْرٌ مِنْ طَاعَةٍ أَوْرَثَتْ عِزًّا وَاسْتِكْبَارًا.

A disobedience that bequeaths humiliation and extreme need is better than an obedience that bequeaths self-infatuation and pride. [96]

The purpose of worship and invocation is to become humble and to be wholly dependent on Allāh Most High, eliminating the rebellion and arrogance of the ego. If a man commits a sin because of the frailty of human nature and is then torn by remorse, a humility might result that is better than the conceit that a man can develop as a consequence of his acts of worship and piety. Self-infatuation and pride can lead a person to despise other Muslims.

A dim-witted person should not now understand from this explanation that it is better to abandon worship and commit sins. The evil of sin and the virtue and beauty of obedience are self-evident facts. At this juncture, the Shaykh ﷺ is simply pointing out that the actual method of reaching the Divine Court is by way of acquiring true humility and dependence on Allāh—not through sin. We seek refuge in Allāh!

20

ON GRADUAL DELUSION

خَفْ مِنْ وُجُودِ إِحْسَانِهِ إِلَيْكَ وَدَوَامِ إِسَاءَتِكَ مَعَهُ أَنْ يَكُونَ ذٰلِكَ اسْتِدْرَاجًا لَكَ، ﴿سَنَسْتَدْرِجُهُمْ مِنْ حَيْثُ لَا يَعْلَمُونَ﴾.

Be fearful lest the existence of His generosity toward you and the permanence of your bad behavior toward Him not lead you step by step to ruin. "We shall lead them to ruin step by step from whence they know not."
[Q. 7:182] [65]

Allāh Most High does not always immediately take to task the transgressors. In spite of their rebellion and transgression, He gives them time and continues to shower His favors on them. When they completely lose themselves in sin and reach the point of no return, He suddenly apprehends them. The granting of such respite to the transgressors is called istidrāj, which is a matter of utmost gravity.

On the other hand, some servants of Allāh Most High are immediately forewarned when they commit any misdeed. As a result, they quickly engage in the invocation of Allāh Most High and abandon the transgression, so as to ward off the forgetfulness.

Here the Shaykh ﷺ discusses *istidrāj*. He says that Allāh's gentleness settles over you every moment, while you persist audaciously in bad behavior. You are not even being reprimanded. Instead your wishes are granted. This condition [of abundant blessings and not being punished despite one's persistence in sin] is fearful. You should fear this state, for perhaps it is respite allowed by Allāh Most High. Thereafter, He will suddenly apprehend you with His punishment. Proof for this is in the Qur'ān, which warns of Allāh's punishment arriving suddenly in the wake of the respite granted to the transgressors. When their transgression exceeds the limits, His punishment comes swiftly. The period of grace—the *istidrāj*—should, therefore, not be misunderstood. When Allāh Most High gives man respite, his forgetfulness increases in stages, but his [worldly] hopes and desires are fulfilled. When his forgetfulness has thoroughly set in, the divine chastisement suddenly overtakes him.

مِنْ جَهْلِ الْمُرِيدِ أَنْ يُسِيءَ الْأَدَبَ فَتُؤَخَّرَ الْعُقُوبَةُ عَنْهُ، فَيَقُولَ: لَوْ كَانَ
هٰذَا سُوءَ أَدَبٍ لَقَطَعَ الْإِمْدَادَ وَأَوْجَبَ الْإِبْعَادَ.. فَقَدْ يُقْطَعُ الْمَدَدُ عَنْهُ
مِنْ حَيْثُ لَا يَشْعُرُ، وَلَوْ لَمْ يَكُنْ إِلَّا مَنْعُ الْمَزِيدِ، وَقَدْ تُقَامُ مَقَامَ الْبُعْدِ
مِنْ حَيْثُ لَا تَدْرِي، وَلَوْ لَمْ يَكُنْ إِلَّا أَنْ يُخَلِّيَكَ وَمَا تُرِيدُ.

It is ignorance on the part of the novice to act improperly, and then, his punishment being delayed, to say, "If this had been improper conduct, He would have cut off help and imposed exile." Help could be cut off from him without his being aware of it, if only by blocking its increase. And it could be that you are made to abide at a distance without your knowing it, if only by His leaving you to do as you like. [66]

The closer one is to Allāh, the severer is the applicability of the laws. In many aspects, the general public is excused and not apprehended for misdeeds. However, the élite (*khawāṣ*) are immediately apprehended for any slips they make. On being apprehended, they readily understand the error for which they are being caught.

Sometimes the invoker or the traveler or the thankful-one utters a disrespectful word regarding The Truth Most High; for example, a word of complaint slips from his mouth because of some occurrence; or he complains to someone about the hardship on him; or he criticizes someone among the scholars; or he regards a disrespectful act of his as being insignificant because he was not immediately overtaken by punishment. He therefore thinks that if his act had been truly disrespectful, the physical and spiritual favors in which he is basking would have ceased.

The physical favors are wealth, children, health, strength and other material comforts. The spiritual favors are the rays of spiritual illumination that continuously cascade from the unseen realm into the heart of the traveler. The idea that this aid and favor would have terminated if Allāh had been displeased with one's disobedience is the result of extreme ignorance. It is not necessary for the traveler to be aware of the termination of inner illuminations, because such cessation can happen in several indiscernible ways.

Sometimes this happens by way of the cessation of further progress, and his spiritual station becomes stagnant. This stagnation leads to a gradual development of a barrier between the traveler and Allāh Most High, while the traveler labors under the impression of being on his former, elevated pedestal; but a great change has in fact taken place. We seek Allāh's protection from this.

This delusion can also occur as the traveler unknowingly drifts from closeness to Allāh. It can mean that a traveler is left to his whims and fancies, without Allāh aiding him in his spiritual efforts, as was previously the case. Here, the traveler is under the domination of his ego.

The seeker (*murīd*) should, therefore, live with the utmost respect and control of his speech and actions. It should be here understood that this type of disrespect is committed by a seeker who has not attained complete annihilation (*fanā'*).[30] After the attainment of *fanā'* the possibility of disrespect is entirely precluded.

---

30 On the subject of *fanā'* and *baqā'* (subsistence), Abū 'l-Qāsim al-Qushayrī writes: "By their use of the term annihilation (*fanā'*)—passing away—the sufis indicate the disappearance of blameworthy characteristics. By the term subsistence (*baqā'*)—abiding in Allāh—they indicate the establishment of praiseworthy characteristics. . . If the servant combats the character in his heart, refusing by his efforts its shallownesses and trivialities, Allāh will grant him the refinement of his character. Just so, if he continually takes pains to purify his actions to the best of his ability, Allāh in His grace will grant him the purification of his states—in fact, even the complete development of his states." See Qushayrī, *The Risālah*, 86–7. Qushayrī continues his explanation in the normative method of the sufis and their Orders, and it is clear that the "passing away," in his words, is due to a profound spiritual recognition of Allāh that impacts one's soul in a way that reforms the heart and one's actions; and this recognition, according to him, has various stages in the sufi path: "At first the annihilation [of the servant] is from himself and his attributes, through his subsistence in the attributes of the Real. Then his annihilation is from the attributes of the Real, through his witnessing of the Real. Then his annihilation is from his witnessing his annihilation, through his being absorbed in the existence of the Real" (op. cit. 88–9).

21

ON LITANY AND INSPIRATION

لَا يَسْتَحْقِرُ الْوِرْدَ إِلَّا جَهُولٌ، اَلْوَارِدُ يُوْجَدُ فِي الدَّارِ الْآخِرَةِ، وَالْوِرْدُ
يَنْطَوِي بِانْطِوَاءِ هٰذِهِ الدَّارِ، وأَوْلٰى مَا يُعْتَنٰى بِهِ مَا لَا يُخْلَفُ وُجُودُهُ،
اَلْوِرْدُ هُوَ طَالِبُهُ مِنْكَ، وَالْوَارِدُ أَنْتَ تَطْلُبُهُ مِنْهُ، وَأَيْنَ مَا هُوَ طَالِبُهُ مِنْكَ
مِمَّا هُوَ مَطْلَبُكَ مِنْهُ؟

Only the ignorant man scorns the recitation of litany. Inspiration is to be found in the Hereafter, while the litany vanishes with the vanishing of this world. But it is more fitting to be occupied with something for which there is no substitute. The litany is what He seeks from you, the inspiration is what you seek from Him. But what comparison is there between what He seeks from you and what you seek from Him? [112]

THE OUTWARD ACTS OF WORSHIP and inward or spiritual efforts are called the *wird* [translated as "litany"]. The inner "inspiration" (*al-wārid*, pl. *al-wāridāt*), by contrast, enters the heart of the servant involuntarily.

Sometimes the traveler commits the error of thinking that the formal worship and invocation that he practices with his own will are not as significant as the inspirations that he receives. The reason for this impression is that everyone practices such acts of worship by their own will and intention; on the other hand, inspirations are received without one's will or intention. Furthermore, due to the fact that inspiration is not the state of everyone, the ego attaches an exaggerated importance to inspirations—a view that is erroneous.

The Shaykh ﷺ dispels this error; hence he says that it is only the ignoramus who regards constancy in righteous actions and invocation as being less significant. There are two reasons for this misconception. Firstly, the incidence of inspiration will be more abundant in the Hereafter because here on earth contaminations, human nature and the physical body constitute impediments for such inspirations. But in the Hereafter these impediments will not exist. On the other hand, the litanies and works of invocation (*waẓā'if*, sing. *waẓīfa*) rendered with the physical body are only here on earth. There is no substitute for worship and litanies after death, whereas inspirations exist here and will exist in the Hereafter as well in even greater measure. It is of greater importance to guard the outer actions of worship that are called the *wird*.

Secondly, the one who demands the *wird* is Allāh Most High, while you (the traveler) desire inspirations. There is no comparison between your desire and Allāh's demand. It behooves you to attach much greater importance to His demand. It is, therefore, essential for the traveler to be constant in the observance of obedience and the *wird* that have been imposed on one. One should not regard the *wird* to be inferior to inspirations, because the normal cause of inspirations is also the *wird*. As a result of the traveler's *wird*, he is blessed with the incidence of inspirations.

إِذَا رَأَيْتَ عَبْدًا أَقَامَهُ اللّٰهُ تَعَالٰى بِوُجُودِ الْأَوْرَادِ، وَأَدَامَهُ عَلَيْهَا مَعَ
طُولِ الْإِمْدَادِ.. فَلَا تَسْتَحْقِرَنَّ مَا مَنَحَهُ مَوْلَاهُ لِأَنَّكَ لَمْ تَرَ عَلَيْهِ سِيمَا
الْعَارِفِينَ وَلَا بَهْجَةَ الْمُحِبِّينَ؛ فَلَوْلَا وَارِدٌ مَا كَانَ وِرْدٌ.

If you see a servant whom God has made to abide in the recitation of litanies and prolonged His help therein, do not disdain what his Lord has given him on the score that you do not detect the signs of gnostics on him nor the splendor of God's lovers. For had there not been an inspiration, there would have been no litany. [67]

The élite servants of Allāh Most High are of two kinds: *muqarrabīn* and *abrār*. The *muqarrabīn* are those whose choice and egotistical desires have been eliminated. Their spiritual state of subsistence (*baqā'*) is with the will and choosing of Allāh. They worship Allāh and discharge His rights by virtue of their enslavement to Him. Their motive is nothing else. The *abrār* are those in whom desires and personal will still exist. They worship Allāh for the attainment of Paradise and for salvation from Hell. Their gaze is set on the acquisition of lofty stations in Paradise.

The Glorious Qur'ān mentions both types of pious servants, either implicitly or explicitly. In his statement here, the Shaykh ﷺ mentions the *abrār*. He says that sometimes one sees a man steadfast on his worship and litanies, and at the same time observes divine aid with him, i.e., in fulfilling his devotional acts there are no obstacles in his path; Allāh Most High having freed him from the distraction of worldly activities and harnessed him into worship. But, at the same time, it is observed that the attributes normally to be found in the *ʿārifīn* are lacking in him—he indulges in certain pleasures, such as donning high quality garments and eating delicious foods and he also lacks in perpetual invocation and a state of divine perception; nor does there emanate from his face the radiance of the people of gnosis and divine love.

The Shaykh, then, warns observers of this type not to regard the treasure of their companion's constancy in outer worship as insignificant. Do not entertain the notion of his *wird* and *waẓā'if* being of no value simply on account of the qualities of the *ʿārifīn* not being discernible in him. Any such attitude is an act of extreme disrespect. It is not possible to display such steadfastness and determination without divine illuminations (*tajalliyāt*, sing. *tajallī*). It is this illumination in his heart that sustains and keeps him constant and steadfast in his worship, although it is conceded that he lacks the degree of divine illumination experienced by the *ʿārifīn*, whose desires, motives and choice have all been annihilated. But to despise him or to regard his state as inferior is the result of ignorance, and this attitude is an act of disrespect itself.

وُرُودُ الْإِمْدَادِ بِحَسَبِ الْاِسْتِعْدَادِ، وَشُرُوقُ
الْأَنْوَارِ عَلَى حَسَبِ صَفَاءِ الْأَسْرَارِ.

The arrival of sustainment is in accordance with receptivity, while the raying-out of lights is in accordance with the purity of the innermost being. [113]

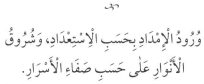

The incidence of spiritual illuminations and blessings on the heart of the servant is according to one's spiritual ability. Spiritual ability will be in the state of perfection on two conditions: firstly, if one is fully steadfast in his litanies, keeping his heart free from things besides Allāh; secondly, if the traveler is also constant and firm in maintaining physical purity.

The purpose of inspirations is certitude and gnosis of Allāh Most High. The radiance of the lights of certitude and gnosis is according to the degree of purity of the spiritual faculties, and the purity of the spiritual faculties is dependent on constancy in the acts of outer rituals of worship. It is, therefore, necessary for the servant to strive diligently, and to be constant in the observance of his acts of worship.

تَنَوَّعَتْ أَجْنَاسُ الْأَعْمَالِ لِتَنَوُّعِ وَارِدَاتِ الْأَحْوَالِ.

Actions differ because the inspirations of the states of being differ. [9]

Outer actions are subservient to the inspirations of the heart. It is observed that some travelers have a greater affinity with optional acts of ritual prayer, some with fasting, some with charity, some with supplication, some with the pilgrimage; while others have a greater preference for solitude (*khalwa*). These differences are due to differences in the inspirations that descend on the travelers from Allāh Most High.

In view of this reality, it is improper to criticize anyone [of these types]. Everyone is, in fact, constrained to act according to his inspirations. There is, however, no doubt in the superiority and excellence of the traveler in whose spiritual and physical states there is an attempt at imitating the way (*sunna*) of the Messenger of Allāh ﷺ, because the balanced way is only with following him. Although the most perfect, balanced way is exclusive to the Messenger of Allāh ﷺ, whoever acquires some share of it will be from among the outstanding luminaries of the age. But such persons are rare. Among millions there will be one who has been blessed with the vicegerency of the Messenger ﷺ. In such a vicegerent there are no extremes in him: his states and actions are balanced.

حُسْنُ الْأَعْمَالِ نَتَائِجُ حُسْنِ الْأَحْوَالِ، وَحُسْنُ
الْأَحْوَالِ مِنَ التَّحَقُّقِ فِي مَقَامَاتِ الْإِنْزَالِ.

Good works are the results of good states. Good states arise from the stations wherein those having spiritual realization abide. [46]

"Good works" here refers to the external or physical deeds of virtue. "Good states" refers to the states and attributes of the heart, such as abstinence (*zuhd*), contentment (*qanāʿa*), humility (*tawāḍuʿ*), sincerity (*ikhlāṣ*), etc. The abiding of the gnostic in the stations of realization is when he is drowned in the reflection of the divine attributes.

If the states are good and the heart is adorned with praiseworthy qualities, then the practical deeds of the servant will be good. This means that the calamities that are obstacles in the path of acceptance are non-existent, because the traveler is devoid of vanity (*ʿujb*). Such good works will be adorned with the state of divine perception and humility, and unassailed by satanic and stray thoughts.

If the traveler is steadfast in the state of realization, he will then be perfect in his works: if awe and reverence are predominant in him, the rebellion and pride of the ego will be defeated, and humility and abstinence will develop.

If the inspiration is not of a high degree, the traveler's states will suffer a proportionate deficiency, and his practical works will become correspondingly defective. Thus, showing-off and other spiritual aliments will influence the works of the traveler.

إِنَّمَا أَوْرَدَ عَلَيْكَ الْوَارِدَ لِتَكُونَ بِهِ عَلَيْهِ وَارِدًا، أَوْرَدَ عَلَيْكَ الْوَارِدَ لِيَتَسَلَّمَكَ مِنْ يَدِ الْأَغْيَارِ، وَلِيُحَرِّرَكَ مِنْ رِقِّ الْآثَارِ، أَوْرَدَ عَلَيْكَ الْوَارِدَ لِيُخْرِجَكَ مِنْ سِجْنِ وُجُودِكَ إِلَى فَضَاءِ شُهُودِكَ.

He only made an inspiration come upon you so that you would go to Him. He made an inspiration come upon you so as to get you out of the grip of alterities and free you from bondage to created things. He made an inspiration come upon you so as to take you out of the prison of your existence to the unlimited space of your contemplation. [52–54]

The meaning of "inspiration" here is gnosis, subtleties, mysteries and gifted knowledge that involuntarily enter into the heart of the traveler. The Shaykh mentions three factors that occasion the incidence of inspirations.

The first inspiration comes when the traveler initially engages in invocation and effort, and his heart is perplexed. He forcibly applies himself. This state remains for a short period of time. In this state, the heart begins to derive pleasure in invocation. This state progresses higher and the traveler desires to be perpetually engrossed in invocation. When invocation permeates the heart, the incidence of inspirations commences, i.e., he perceives with the eyes of the heart that all actions are the creation of The Creator (*al-Khāliq*). He then no longer attributes any act to any being besides Allāh.

The purpose of this inspiration is to increase enthusiasm in the traveler for obedience and invocation, so that he acquires admission to the lofty Divine Court. Even in this state, however, the desires of the ego remain intact and complete sincerity is not yet achieved in worship.

The second inspiration leads to the emancipation of the traveler from alterities and egotistic desires. The traveler will now be drawn to Allāh Most High in ecstasy. However, even after this second inspiration, the traveler's gaze is still on his ego and he reposes a measure of reliance on himself. He also regards himself to be in good stead. Thus, he still remains imprisoned in the narrow confines of existence.

Then follows a third inspiration that extricates the traveler from his existence (*wujūd*), i.e., the essential nothingness of his existence becomes an experiential fact for him. In this station the traveler breaks free from all the chains and fetters of the ego. He thus reaches the unlimited space of contemplation. In other words, with the inner eyes he vividly remembers his Master with a greater spiritual perception than the perception of the corporeal eyes in seeing physical objects. The realm into which the traveler now gains entry has been described as unlimited, because as long as there remains any vestige of the ego, the heart still dwells in a prison. When all vestiges of the ego have been eliminated, the traveler then emerges from his prison and steps into a complete freedom. Upon the traveler entering into this lofty realm, he becomes absorbed in contemplation—in all his conditions and circumstances. There now remains no trace of anxiety and uncertainty in him. In all circumstances he is content—be it sickness or health, adversity or prosperity.

Only those to whom these spiritual conditions occur understand and perceive the pleasure. Whoever has not tasted, does not know. May Allāh Most High make us of this lofty rank: *And that is not difficult for Him* (Qur'ān 14:20).

قَلَّمَا تَكُونُ الْوَارِدَاتُ الْإِلٰهِيَّةُ .. إِلَّا بَغْتَةً، صِيَانَةً لَهَا أَنْ يَدَّعِيَهَا الْعِبَادُ بِوُجُودِ الْاِسْتِعْدَادِ.

It is rare that divine inspirations come except suddenly, and this, in order that they be protected from servants' claiming them by virtue of the existence of receptivity on their part. [69]

It has earlier been mentioned, on several occasions, that the spiritual mysteries and subtleties inspired into the traveler's heart are not the product of his effort and choice. Sometimes the servant waits in expectation of divine inspirations, but they fail to transpire. In most cases, the occurrence of divine inspiration was at a time when it was least expected.

The reason underscoring this suddenness is to prevent the traveler from becoming a claimant of this occurrence. If inspirations could have been the effects of the traveler's volitional will, he would have suffered from the notion of his own capability and ability, and put forward claims. Such self-esteem would then lead to his corruption and destruction. Caught up in vanity, he would become completely forgetful of Allāh Most High.

Inspirations are like gifts. Whenever Allāh Most High wishes, He directs His grace to the servant and bestows this bounty of inspirations to his heart.

لَا يَنْبَغِي لِلسَّالِكِ أَنْ يُعَبِّرَ عَنْ وَارِدَاتِهِ .. فَإِنَّ ذٰلِكَ يُقِلُّ عَمَلَهَا فِي قَلْبِهِ، وَيَمْنَعُهُ وُجُودَ الصِّدْقِ مَعَ رَبِّهِ.

He who is progressing should not give expression to his inspirations, for that indeed diminishes their activity in his heart and strips him of sincerity with his Lord. [189]

It is highly inappropriate for the traveler to divulge the inspirations of his heart to anyone besides his shaykh. The ego derives pleasure when this information is divulged because the traveler's holiness, piety and greatness become confirmed in the estimation of others. This pleasure of the ego, which is really vanity, provides impetus for the lowly, bestial attributes. In consequence, the effect of the inspiration diminishes.

The actual purpose of such an inspiration was to destroy and suppress the rebellion of the ego. However, when the ego is strengthened, the effect of the inspiration will diminish and the traveler's bond of truth with his Lord will be adversely affected. The servant's relationship of truth with his Lord requires constant humility and submission in the Divine Court. The state of servanthood and fear of Allāh should never be absent.

اَلْحَقَائِقُ تَرِدُ فِي حَالِ التَّجَلِّي مُجْمَلَـةً، وَبَعْدَ الْوَعْيِ يَكُونُ الْبَيَانُ،
﴿فَإِذَا قَرَأْنَاهُ فَاتَّبِعْ قُرْآنَهُ ثُمَّ إِنَّ عَلَيْنَا بَيَانَهُ﴾.

The inner realities arrive synthetically in the state of illumination, while their explanation comes after retention. "So when We recite it, follow its recitation. Again on Us rests the explaining of it." [Q. 75:18–19] [215]

When the hearts of the *ʿārifīn* are freed from alterities and they emerge from the confines of their personal will, perpetually focusing their gaze on Allāh Most High, inner realities and spiritual knowledge are bestowed on them in the state of illuminations cascading into the heart. At the time of the manifestation of such knowledge, however, the inspiration overwhelms the heart and the senses. Thus, the inspirational knowledge acquired is concise. The clarity of the meanings of the inspiration is not attained at the precise time of the incidence of the inspiration because the comprehension of knowledge is the function of the senses. At the time of the inspiration of the spiritual knowledge all the senses become inoperative. Nevertheless, the concise meaning is impressed in the spiritual heart. Later, after the cessation of the inspiration, the traveler attains the meanings by virtue of his retention. He is then able to expound upon this inspirational knowledge.

During the incidence of the revelation [of the Majestic Qur'ān], the Messenger of Allāh ﷺ would recite simultaneously with Jibrīl ؑ in an attempt to memorize the revelation. Thereupon the following verse was revealed: *So when We recite it, follow its recitation. Again on Us rests the explaining of it* (7:18–19). The inspirational knowledge of the *ʿārifīn* resembles the incidence of divine revelation: the initial occurrence of the saint's inspiration is imprinted on the heart with a concise meaning, and its detailed elaboration follows later.

مَتٰى وَرَدَتِ الْوَارِدَاتُ الْإِلٰهِيَّةُ إِلَيْكَ .. هَدَمَتِ الْعَوَائِدَ عَلَيْكَ، ﴿إِنَّ الْمُلُوكَ إِذَا دَخَلُوا قَرْيَةً أَفْسَدُوهَا﴾، الْوَارِدُ يَأْتِي مِنْ حَضْرَةِ قَهَّارٍ، لِأَجْلِ ذٰلِكَ لَا يُصَادِمُهُ شَيْءٌ إِلَّا دَمَغَهُ، ﴿بَلْ نَقْذِفُ بِالْحَقِّ عَلَى الْبَاطِلِ فَيَدْمَغُهُ فَإِذَا هُوَ زَاهِقٌ﴾.

When divine inspirations come upon you, they demolish your habits. "Surely the kings, when they enter a town, ruin it." [Q. 27:34] The inspiration comes from the Presence of the Omnipotent. As a result, nothing opposes it without being smashed to bits. "Nay, but We hurl the Truth against falsehood, and it prevails against it, and lo! falsehood vanishes." [Q. 21:18][31] [216–217]

At this juncture, the Shaykh ﵁ explains the signs of inspirations: to distinguish these (inspirations) from imagination and personal thoughts. When inspirations settle in the heart, they completely annihilate and eradicate the evil and bestial attributes of the ego, and create in the traveler the lofty, angelic qualities of virtue and high states.

Inspirations are among the armies of Allāh Most High. When the royal army descends on a place, it destroys the enemy and overrides the place. Similarly, when inspirations descend on the ego, they overwhelm it and establish their domination. The true inspiration coming from Allāh Most High, The Dominator (*al-Qahhār*), is accompanied by the attributes of wrath and domination. Thus, human qualities and evil attributes in this situation are utterly destroyed and uprooted. Allāh Most High says in the Qur'ān: *Nay, but We hurl Truth against falsehood, and it prevails against it, and lo! falsehood vanishes* (21:18).

لَا تُزَكِّيَنَّ وَارِدًا لَا تَعْلَمُ ثَمَرَتَهُ .. فَلَيْسَ الْمُرَادُ مِنَ السَّحَابَةِ الْإِمْطَارَ، وَإِنَّمَا الْمُرَادُ مِنْهَا وُجُودُ الْإِثْمَارِ.

Do not attest to the validity of an inspiration whose

31 This aphorism has been moved up from the end of the chapter due to greater relevance here.

fruits you know not. The purpose of rainclouds is not to give rain; their only purpose is to bring forth fruit. [220]

The actual aim of the inspirations descending on the traveler is the suppression of the ego's rebellion, the elimination of evil attributes, progress in obedience and attention on Allāh Most High. When an inspiration occurs that does not produce such an effect, leaving the ego in its former state, the traveler should not be happy, because the actual aim has not been achieved. There is no benefit in an inspiration that leaves the ego stagnant in its present state, without producing any elevation in the traveler's humility, fear and servanthood.

Many travelers hanker after inspirations and spiritual states while being deficient in external deeds of virtue. This is a grave deception.

لَا تَطْلُبَنَّ بَقَاءَ الْوَارِدَاتِ بَعْدَ أَنْ بَسَطَتْ أَنْوَارَهَا وَأَوْدَعَتْ أَسْرَارَهَا ..
فَلَكَ فِي اللّٰهِ غِنًى عَنْ كُلِّ شَيْءٍ، وَلَيْسَ يُغْنِيكَ عَنْهُ شَيْءٌ.

After the lights of inspirations have rayed out and their mysteries have been deposited, do not seek their continuance, for you have in God one who enables you to dispense with everything; but nothing enables you to dispense with God. [221]

Frequently, the traveler deriving pleasure from an inspiration turns his concentration toward it. He sometimes gains the erroneous impression that this state (of receiving inspirations) has become his permanent condition, and he derives great pleasure therein. But when the effect of this state dissipates, he is overtaken by grief. He therefore hankers after the acquisition of this condition, little realizing that he has already achieved the purpose of the inspiration and that he still possesses the achievement—in spite of the inspiration's effect having disappeared. He no longer perceives the existence of the inspiration's benefit, however, because his disposition has already become accustomed to it, whereas initially he had derived pleasure since the experience of the inspiration was new to him. Yet, the permeation of his outer and inner being with the illuminations of the inspiration imposes the condition of servanthood on the entire existence of the traveler. He does not, therefore, perceive it since it is no longer a new experience.

It is for this reason that the Shaykh ﷺ instructs us: when the illuminations of the inspiration permeate you, and your outer and inner being become elevated (on account of the state of servanthood produced by the inspiration, resulting in the spiritual realization of the divine attributes), do not then desire the perpetuation of the inspirations. You should not expect the initial state of dominance to endure endlessly, nor become despondent on account of the dissipation of this initial state.

Rather, engross yourself in the solid state of spiritual presence that you have developed with Allāh Most High. The desire for a temporary state of a spiritual experience in which the traveler derives much ecstatic pleasure is in reality a desire for matters besides Allāh. You should become absorbed in divine perception—which will induce in you independence from all things besides Allāh Most High. Never permit other things to divert you from Allāh Most High, whereby they induce in you an attitude of independence from Him.

There is no benefit for you in the domination of the inspiration. You have already achieved its purpose. Concern yourself with your true occupation: your relationship with Allāh Most High.

22

ON THE STATES OF THE PATH

قَوْمٌ أَقَامَهُمُ الْحَقُّ لِخِدْمَتِهِ وَقَوْمٌ اخْتَصَّهُمْ بِمَحَبَّتِهِ، ﴿كُلًّا نُمِدُّ هٰؤُلَاءِ وَهٰؤُلَاءِ مِنْ عَطَاءِ رَبِّكَ وَمَا كَانَ عَطَاءُ رَبِّكَ مَحْظُورًا﴾.

God makes some people abide in the service of Him, and He singles out others to love Him. "All do we aid—these as well as those—out of the bounty of thy Lord, and the bounty of thy Lord is not limited." [Q. 17:20] [68]

This topic has already been discussed earlier when classifying the élite servants of Allah into the *muqarrabīn* and the *abrār*.

The *abrār* are fully engaged, day and night, in the worship of Allāh, and serving mankind for His sake; and they are abstinent with regards to the finery of life—and they are called *zuhhād* and *ʿubbād*. Their purpose in worship is entry into Paradise and protection from Hell.

The *muqarrabīn* have been selected by Allāh Most High for His love and proximity. Their external acts of worship are less than those performed by the *abrār*. Yet their actual deeds are with their hearts. At all times they are concerned with Allāh Most High. His invocation permeates their hearts. For them, there is nothing besides Allāh Most High in their hearts. They are not concerned with Heaven and Hell.[32]

---

32 This statement is, indeed, controversial, because it implies that an advanced stage in the spiritual path of the sufis leads to an indifference to one's ultimate fate: whether to the delights of Paradise or the torments of Hell—all because one is only occupied with the love of Allāh, and nothing besides.

This discussion relates to Aḥmad Sirhindī's contrasting of the way of "sainthood" (*wilāyat*) and the way of "Prophethood" (*nubuwwa*). He explains: "Son! In the way of *wilāyat* one has to wash one's hands of this world as well as the next, one has to believe that the love of the other

At the end of this aphorism, the Qur'ānic verse is applied to these two groups: Allāh aids both according to their goal: the *abrār* are permitted to occupy themselves in pursuit of the next world; and the *muqarrabīn* are facilitated in expunging everything except Allāh from their hearts, by the means of being given a pure intention, which is to only desire Allāh Himself.

Likewise, the people who only desire this world are given blessings of comfort and luxury. Thus they engross themselves in worldly pleasure, and forget their Lord and lapse into transgression.

لَيْسَ كُلُّ مَنْ ثَبَتَ تَخْصِيصُهُ كَمُلَ تَخْلِيصُهُ، رُبَّمَا
رُزِقَ الْكَرَامَةَ مَنْ لَمْ تَكْمُلْ لَهُ الِاسْتِقَامَةُ.

Not all who are most certainly amongst the chosen go on to perfect their liberation. Sometimes a charisma is bestowed upon someone whose righteousness is not perfect. [111, 179]

The masses are in awe of the display of charismas—customarily known as "miracles'—and they place great faith in those who demonstrate such abilities. In fact, they consider such a condition to be the criterion of sainthood (*wilāya*). However, the true and actual charisma, or miracle, is firmness upon the Sacred Law and purification of the soul from evil qualities.

Here the Shaykh ﷺ dispels the error of judgment. It does not follow from the demonstration of miraculous acts that the person has attained complete freedom from the evil attributes of the ego; sometimes even the imperfect man is endowed with such ability. In fact, similar acts—known as

world is nothing better than the love of this world, and that the craving for the Hereafter is just as undesirable as the craving for this life. . . In the way of *nubuwwa*, on the other hand, the love of the next world is commendable, and the concern for the life Hereafter is good and desirable. . . In the course of his journey when a sufi experiences *fanā'*, he forgets, to be sure, this world and the next, and brackets the love of the latter with the love of the former. But when he attains *baqā'* and completes his work, and participates to some extent in the perceptions of *nubuwwa*, he has only one concern: the Hereafter. He is all fear for Hell and all love for Paradise. The trees, rivers, maidens, and servants of Paradise are not to be compared with the objects of this world. . . To sum up: the Hereafter is loved either by the common man or by the elect of the elect (*akhaṣṣ al-khawāṣṣ*). The average elect (*khāṣṣ*) does not love the Hereafter. . ." Sirhindī, of course, endorses the superiority of the way of *nubuwwa*. See Ansari, *Sufism and Shari'ah*, 211-221, for a fuller explanation by Sirhindī of the two methods.

istidrāj—are displayed by even non-Muslims. Thus the display of miraculous acts is not the criterion for sainthood.[33]

اَلسَّتْرُ عَلٰى قِسْمَيْنِ: سَتْرٌ عَنِ الْمَعْصِيَةِ وَسَتْرٌ فِيهَا، فَالْعَامَّةُ يَطْلُبُونَ مِنَ اللّٰهِ السَّتْرَ فِيهَا خَشْيَةَ سُقُوطِ مَرْتَبَتِهِمْ عِنْدَ الْخَلْقِ، وَالْخَاصَّةُ يَطْلُبُونَ السَّتْرَ عَنْهَا خَشْيَةَ سُقُوطِهِمْ مِنْ نَظَرِ الْمَلِكِ الْحَقِّ.

Veiling is of two kinds: veiling of disobedience, and veiling in it. Common people seek God's veiling in disobedience out of the fear of falling in rank amongst mankind. The elect seek the veiling of disobedience out of the fear of falling from the sight of the Real King. [133]

The servants of Allāh Most High who seek the veiling of disobedience are of two types. The first kind seek the veiling *of* disobedience, and the second group seeks veiling *in* disobedience. The former group consists of those who possess a natural propensity to disobey and transgress, but Allāh Most High saves them "before" the commission of disobedience. The latter group seeks veiling "after" they have committed the sins.

The people of the second group are motivated to supplicate for forgiveness and veiling (of their disobedience) in order to avoid being publicly disgraced. This motive is underlined by their deficiency in faith and their ignorance of the reality of faith. Also, the perception of people is dominant in them and they have the hope of gaining some benefit from people. They have a great fear of people; hence they supplicate to Allāh Most High to conceal their misdeeds.

While the concern of ordinary people is the estimation of others, the elite—who are the first group mentioned in this aphorism—are only concerned with Allāh Most High. They desire their egos to be concealed and saved from disobedience solely for the sake of Allāh Most High. They fear being distanced from His mercy. Their gaze is not on others. They do not concern themselves with the criticism and praise of people. They neither have hope in people, nor do they fear them. Their aim is only to secure the pleasure of their Master; hence they seek to be protected from even committing an act of disobedience.

---

33 For a fuller discussion of miracles and *istidrāj* see Maghnīsāwī, *Al-Fiqh al-Akbar Explained,* 161–166.

رُبَّمَا عَبَّرَ عَنِ الْمَقَامِ مَنِ اسْتَشْرَفَ عَلَيْهِ، وَرُبَّمَا عَبَّرَ عَنْهُ مَنْ وَصَلَ إِلَيْهِ، وَذٰلِكَ مُلْتَبِسٌ إِلَّا عَلَى صَاحِبِ الْبَصِيرَةِ.

Sometimes he who draws near to a station expresses himself about it, and sometimes he who is united with it expresses himself about it. That is confusing save to him who has insight. [188]

A "station" refers to one of the branches of faith, such as abstinence (*zuhd*), scrupulousness (*wara*ʿ), trusting in Allāh (*tawakkul*), contentment (*qanāʿa*), etc. For it to be called a "station" it must become an entrenched attribute, inseparable from the heart. When any of these attributes fluctuate in the traveler it is referred to as a "state" (*ḥāl*).

Sometimes a man who is approaching a station discusses and explains the station that he has not yet reached; and people who have achieved a certain rank do sometimes talk about their "state," which has not yet become a "station."

There is usually little difference in the exposition and style of both the one who is approaching the station under discussion and the one who has achieved it. Consequently, people are—generally speaking—unable to distinguish between the two. Such discernment is often the vocation of the people of insight (*baṣīra*), who perceive the degrees between the speakers.

The one who is drawing near to a station can become pleased with his exposition, and this satisfaction can lead to a delusion which prevents him from actually attaining the station that he was so close to: he contents himself with the rhetoric and elaborate explanation of the station, as opposed to achieving the state of heart that is the reality of the station. On the other hand, one sometimes finds that the discourse of the one who has attained the station will resemble normal talk, devoid of the frills and trappings of rehearsed speeches.

The efficacy of the discourses of these two persons often differs. The speech of the one deficient in his spiritual rank will initially attract people, making an impression on them. However, the effect of his speech will soon dissipate, and those who were initially so enamored will find themselves quite near to the spiritual state they were in when they first encountered such an eloquent speaker. On the other hand, the speech (as well as the company) of the fully qualified may not be so impressive in the beginning, but the effect of his talk will be enduring.

Sometimes a man who has no qualification in either states or stations undertakes the discourse on the topic. He studies books and delivers speeches to ensure a following. Such a person simply advertises piety. The sign of such a person is his inability to explain matters of *taṣawwuf* that he has not yet read in the books of the discipline. In contrast, the accomplished man, who has reached the stations, will tender convincing answers in such cases.

قَوْمٌ تَسْبِقُ أَنْوَارُهُمْ أَذْكَارَهُمْ، وَقَوْمٌ تَسْبِقُ أَذْكَارُهُمْ أَنْوَارَهُمْ، [وَقَوْمٌ تَتَسَاوَى أَذْكَارُهُمْ وَأَنْوَارُهُمْ، وَقَوْمٌ لَا أَذْكَارَ وَلَا أَنْوَارَ.. نَعُوذُ بِاللّٰهِ مِنْ ذٰلِكَ،] ذَاكِرٌ ذَكَرَ لِيَسْتَنِيرَ قَلْبُهُ، وَذَاكِرٌ اسْتَنَارَ قَلْبُهُ فَكَانَ ذَاكِرًا، [وَالَّذِي اسْتَوَتْ أَذْكَارُهُ وَأَنْوَارُهُ فَبِذِكْرِهِ يُهْتَدٰى وَبِنُورِهِ يُقْتَدٰى].

The lights of some people precede their invocations, while the invocations of some people precede their lights. [There are some whose invocations and lights come together, while some people have no invocations or lights. We seek refuge in Allāh from this.] There is the invoker who invokes so that his heart be illumined; and there is the invoker whose heart has been illumined and he invokes. [The one whose invocations and lights come together, is guided by his invocation and follows his light.][34] [253]

This aphorism is differentiating between the *majdhūb* (the ecstatic) and the *sālik* (the traveler).[35]

There are also people whose spiritual effulgence and engagement in invocation are simultaneous. The lights illumine their hearts the very moment they engage in invocation. These lights draw them to Allāh Most High.

34 The bracketed portion in this aphorism is not present in Danner's translation and is our translation. Some of the Arabic editions contain those sentences while others do not (see *Al-Ḥikam al-ʿAṭā'iyya* (Damascus: Al-Maktaba al-ʿArabiyya), p. 68.

35 The discussion of the definition and differences between the traveler and the ecstatic has been covered in the commentary of the last aphorism of chapter eight. Therefore this section has been abbreviated by the editor.

The spiritual journey requiring effort and the magnetic attraction towards Allāh Most High of these people are simultaneous.

There is another group of people who are bereft of invocation and spiritual lights. This group does not obey Allāh Most High, nor do their hearts incline towards obedience and worship. We seek Allāh's protection!

دَلَّ بِوُجُودِ آثَارِهِ عَلٰى وُجُودِ أَسْمَائِهِ، وَبِوُجُودِ أَسْمَائِهِ عَلٰى ثُبُوتِ
أَوْصَافِهِ، وَبِوُجُودِ أَوْصَافِهِ عَلٰى وُجُودِ ذَاتِهِ، إِذْ مُحَالٌ أَنْ يَقُومَ
الْوَصْفُ بِنَفْسِهِ، فَأَرْبَابُ الْجَذْبِ يَكْشِفُ لَهُمْ عَنْ كَمَالِ ذَاتِهِ، ثُمَّ
يَرُدُّهُمْ إِلٰى شُهُودِ صِفَاتِهِ، ثُمَّ يُرْجِعُهُمْ إِلَى التَّعَلُّقِ بِأَسْمَائِهِ، ثُمَّ يَرُدُّهُمْ
إِلٰى شُهُودِ آثَارِهِ، وَالسَّالِكُونَ عَلٰى عَكْسِ هٰذَا: فَنِهَايَةُ السَّالِكِينَ بِدَايَةُ
الْمَجْذُوبِينَ، وَبِدَايَةُ السَّالِكِينَ نِهَايَةُ الْمَجْذُوبِينَ؛ لٰكِنْ لَا بِمَعْنًى
وَاحِدٍ، فَرُبَّمَا الْتَقَيَا فِي الطَّرِيقِ، هٰذَا فِي تَرَقِّيهِ، وَهٰذَا فِي تَدَلِّيهِ.

By the existence of His created things, He points to the existence of His Names, and by the existence of His Names, He points to the immutability of His Qualities, and by the existence of His Qualities, He points to the reality of His Essence, since it is impossible for a quality to be self-subsistent. He reveals the perfection of His Essence to the possessors of attraction; then He turns them back to the contemplation of His Qualities; then He turns them back to dependence on His Names; and then He turns them back to the contemplation of His created things. The contrary is the case for those who are progressing: the end for those progressing is the beginning for the ecstatics, and the beginning for those progressing is the end for the ecstatics. But this is not to be taken literally, since both might meet in the Path, one in his descending, the other in his ascending. [249]

The sun, the earth, the moon, the stars and the entire magnificent creation indicate that the Creator of these objects is mighty, knowledgeable, majestic, wise and All-Powerful. By contemplating upon these acts of Allāh's creation we are guided to understanding the divine names, such as *Qādir* (All-Powerful), *ʿĀlim* (Omniscient), *Ḥakīm* (Wise), etc. The recognition of these attributes leads to our concluding His perfect Being (*dhāt*). This is the state of the *sālik* who goes from creation to the Creator.

In contrast, the majdhūb attains the experience of the Being of Allāh, then he proceeds to recognize the attributes and their relationship to The Being, and then his spiritual gaze turns to the relationship of the attributes to the creation.

Thus the *sālik* and *majdhūb* are travelling in opposite directions, so to speak. The end of the *sālik's* path is the beginning of the *majdhūb's*, and vice versa, roughly speaking.

Yet the difference is that the *sālik* takes a considered course in which he is put to considerable toil and struggle to attain the goal, as he has to proceed through all the valleys of the ego. Thus when he eventually attains the goal of arrival he is alert, and accompanied by firm obedience and firmness. In contrast, the *majdhūb*, on his descent, is aware of the goal, but he is unaware of the tricks of the ego. Therefore he lacks the firmness of the *sālik* upon the Sacred Law. Such people can even be so afflicted so as to leave off obligatory (*farḍ*) aspects of the religion. However, such people have literally lost their minds, so they are not liable for punishment because they are excused from having to abide by the Sacred Law. These are a people whose intellects have been overwhelmed by the lights [of their illumination], and hence they have lost the faculty of rational discernment.[36]

Another difference is that the beginning of the *sālik* is different to the end of the *majdhūb* because the *sālik* does not perceive the attributes and Being of Allāh in the beginning; yet the end of the *majdhūb* [who attains the goal] is one of perfection in which he is not heedless of the attributes and the Being—but now, in that end state, he actually sees the relationship between the attributes and creation.

The *sālik* progresses through invocation, effort, worship and righteous action, and gradually his ego is annihilated in the state of *fanā'*, and he then attain *baqā'* with the attributes and the Being. The ego of the *majdhūb* is annihilated at the beginning. His way is one of *baqā'*; and the more he travels, the more alert he becomes.

36 For a discussion of the conditions for the responsibility for one's actions see *Reliance*, 40–46, which includes an explanation of "sound mind."

It is possible for the two to meet, so to speak, as one "ascends" and the other "descends."

The *sālik* is superior to the *majdhūb*. People derive benefit from the sālik. On the contrary, the *majdhūb* cannot benefit people as long as he is in the state of absorption (*jadhb*). Therefore he cannot be a Shaykh [of an Order] to guide others. Nevertheless, on the termination of his descent, he is capable of being a Shaykh on the condition that he is not dominated by jadhb. Likewise, as long as the *sālik* does not attain the stage of witnessing (*mushāhada*) and illumination (*tajallī*), he does not possess the qualities of being a Shaykh.

شَــتَّانَ بَيْنَ مَنْ يَسْتَدِلُّ بِهِ أَوْ يَسْــتَدِلُّ عَلَيْهِ: الْمُسْتَدِلُّ بِهِ عَرَفَ الْحَقَّ لِأَهْلِــهِ، فَأَثْبَتَ الْأَمْرَ مِنْ وُجُودِ أَصْلِهِ، وَالِاسْــتِدْلَالُ عَلَيْهِ مِنْ عَدَمِ الْوُصُولِ إِلَيْهِ .. وَإِلَّا فَمَتَى غَابَ حَتَّى يُسْتَدَلَّ عَلَيْهِ؟ وَمَتَى بَعُدَ حَتَّى تَكُونَ الْآثَارُ هِيَ الَّتِي تُوْصِلُ إِلَيْهِ؟

What a difference between one who proceeds from God in his argumentation and one who proceeds inferentially to Him! He who has Him as his starting-point knows the Real as It is, and proves any matter by reference to the being of its Origin. But inferential argumentation comes from the absence of union with Him. Otherwise, when was it that He became absent that one has to proceed inferentially to Him? Or when was it that He became distant that created things themselves will unite us to Him? [29]

This aphorism emphasizes the great difference between the methods of the *sālik* and the *majdhūb,* as discussed previously, with regards to their spiritual paths.

The *majdhūb* substantiates the existence of creation on the basis of the Divine Existence, thus confirming that true existence is only true of Him. In reality, all other things have figurative existence [in a sense, because only He is willing their existence].

[The amazing thing about] the inferential argumentative nature of the *sālik* is that they seek to establish the existence of the Necessary Being on the basis of temporal things, due to their distance and deprivation from the Divine Court. Such a person thus substantiates the conspicuous on the basis of the inconspicuous. To not declare such a person as distant or deprived would be to conclude that Allāh Most High is absent, but the reality is that He is never absent; hence such a deduction is redundant. He is not "far away" so that external impressions must prove His existence for us. Indeed, He is actually closer to us than our own selves. Moreover, He is more conspicuous than the external facades of creation. Such inferential reasoning is a conclusive proof of such a person's loss and impoverishment.

The inferential reasoning (*istidlāl*) in this context does not refer to purely rational reasoning, or the method of logic employed in an academic sense. Rather, it refers to inspirational (*wijdānī*) and experiential (*dhawqī*) "logic," which is the result of contemplation and meditation on the creation in order to arrive at transcendental truths.

﴿لِيُنْفِقْ ذُو سَعَةٍ مِّنْ سَعَتِهِ﴾: الْوَاصِلُونَ إِلَيْهِ، ﴿وَمَنْ قُدِرَ عَلَيْهِ رِزْقُهُ
[فَلْيُنْفِقْ مِمَّا آتَاهُ اللَّهُ]﴾: السَّائِرُونَ إِلَيْهِ.

Those who are united[37] with Him: "Let him who has abundance spend out of his abundance." [Q. 65:7] Those who are voyaging toward Him: "And whoever has his means of subsistence straitened to him [let him spend of that which Allāh has given him]." [Q. 65:7] [30]

The first part of the Qur'ānic verse mentioned in this aphorism pertains to divorced women who breast-feed their babies, and who after divorce have to be paid maintenance for the infant from the father. If the father is a man of wealth he should pay generously, and if he lacks substantial means he should give whatever he can afford.

Although the circumstances that had occasioned the revelation of this verse were specific, the text is general. The Shaykh ﷺ generalizes the meaning of this Qur'ānic verse, and applies it analogically to the case of the accomplished sufi who has arrived (*wuṣūl*) at the goal of the Path: namely, to the experiential knowledge and spiritual perception of Allāh. Their

37 For an explanation of being "united" with Allāh, refer to the editor's preface.

hearts have been emancipated from the vision [metaphorically-speaking] of all things besides Allāh Most High. They have arrived in the spacious field of Allāh's Oneness and their gaze is limitless. Divine knowledge and mysteries have unraveled for them. They have thus acquired a substantial treasure that they should now start sharing by imparting it to others. They should spend as much as they desire. This treasure that they possess will not decrease, because the door of limitless knowledge has opened up for them.

The second part of this blessed verse applies to those who are currently engaged in the journey of the Path and have not yet reached the station of perception (*maqām al-mushāhada*). Their hearts have not yet been freed from beings other-than-Allāh Most High; hence they are still confined in the narrow limits of suspicion and baseless ideas. They should share with others whatever knowledge they have acquired from Allāh Most High, according to their ability, and aid them. However, they are not free to spend as they please because their capital is very little. They are in a very restrictive circle.

اِهْتَدَى الرَّاحِلُونَ إِلَيْهِ بِأَنْوَارِ التَّوَجُّهِ، وَالْوَاصِلُونَ لَهُمْ أَنْوَارُ الْمُوَاجَهَةِ، فَالْأَوَّلُونَ لِلْأَنْوَارِ، وَهٰؤُلَاءِ الْأَنْوَارُ لَهُمْ .. لِأَنَّهُمْ لِلّٰهِ لَا لِشَيْءٍ دُونَه، ﴿قُلِ اللّٰهُ ثُمَّ ذَرْهُمْ فِي خَوْضِهِمْ يَلْعَبُونَ﴾.

Those who are voyaging to Him are guided by the lights of their orientation, whereas those who are united to Him[38] have the lights of face-to-face confrontation. The former belong to their lights, whereas the lights belong to the latter, for they belong to God and not to anything apart from Him. "Say: Allāh! Then leave them prattling in their vain talk." [Q. 6:91] [31]

This statement illustrates the difference in the states of the travelers and those who have arrived.

Those servants of Allāh who are traversing the Path, and who have not yet reached the station of perception and illumination, are guided along to Allāh Most High by the inner lights of their struggle against the ego. Their concentration is on these inner lights because the attainment of their goal is by virtue of these.

38 For an explanation of being "united" with Allāh, refer to the editor's preface.

Those who have already reached the lofty Divine Court possess inner lights of vision and presence. Thus their lights are a divine emanation that is on account of the relationship of nearness and love of Allāh that they enjoy.

While the first group's efforts are for the achievement of lights, the lights of the second group cascade upon them without their effort. Lights are not the goal of the second group, as they are for the first. Allāh Most High has rendered them independent [or uncaring] of such lights. Their state is reflected in the Qur'ānic verse: *Say: Allāh! Then leave them prattling in their vain talk* (6:91). For the accomplished sufis there is only Allāh Most High.

قَطَعَ السَّائِرِينَ لَهُ وَالْوَاصِلِينَ إِلَيْهِ عَنْ رُؤْيَةِ أَعْمَالِهِمْ وَشُهُودِ أَحْوَالِهِمْ:
أَمَّا السَّائِرُونَ .. فَلِأَنَّهُمْ لَمْ يَتَحَقَّقُوا الصِّدْقَ مَعَ اللّٰهِ فِيهَا، وَأَمَّا
الْوَاصِلُونَ .. فَلِأَنَّهُ غَيَّبَهُمْ بِشُهُودِهِ عَنْهَا.

He prevents those who are voyaging to Him from witnessing their deeds and those who are united with Him from contemplating their states. He does that for the voyagers because they have not realized sincerity toward God in those works; and He does that for those united with Him because he makes them absent from contemplating those states by contemplating Him. [59]

The difference between the travelers and those who have arrived is here discussed from another angle. Allāh Most High has diverted the gaze of the first group from their outward acts of worship and the gaze of the second group from contemplating their spiritual states. The reason for these diversions differs for the two groups.

Whenever the traveler's attention is drawn to any of his acts or states he does not see sincerity therein. He discerns some sort of spiritual calamity in his actions, such as showing-off, vanity, etc. This results in a disturbance in his concentration on Allāh. After repeated scrutiny of his actions, the traveler finally refrains from looking at his own deeds and states. He then concludes that his deeds are futile, hence being concerned with them will only increase his trial and agitation. In this way has Allāh Most High prevented them from the perception of their own deeds.

On the other hand, the accomplished sufis are completely absorbed in divine perception. This absorption makes them oblivious to their own deeds and stages. They attribute their deeds and states to Allāh Most High, and do not regard their deeds as being their own volitional commission. In fact, they have abandoned their own will and intention.[39]

رُبَّ عُمُرٍ اتَّسَعَتْ آمَادُهُ وَقَلَّتْ أَمْدَادُهُ، وَرُبَّ
عُمُرٍ قَلِيلَةٌ آمَادُهُ كَثِيرَةٌ أَمْدَادُهُ.

Many a life is long in years but meager in fruits, and many a life is short in years but rich in fruits. [257]

The apparent fate of living a long time is that one achieves greater benefit for others, as well as gaining more capital for one's self in the Hereafter. Alas, one can observe the opposite in those whose long lives are spent in deriving little benefit, as they do not receive divine aid, while squandering their lives in forgetfulness and preoccupation in the fulfillment of base desires. Such a waste of time can lead to either total or partial deprivation.

In contrast, some people live very short lives, but the divine aid for them is considerable; hence their time is filled with worship, invocation and the performance of righteous deeds.

This latter condition is also applicable to the community (*umma*) of Muḥammad ﷺ and its rank over other communities: its life span is short, but its virtues are more. *And that is the Bounty of Allāh. He grants it to whomever He wishes* (Qur'ān 57:21).

Yet there are other people who spend the greater part of their life in negligence, but then toward the end of their life they are engulfed by the grace of Allāh. Therefore within a short while they compensate for their previous misbehavior. In fact, such gains can be so fruitful that they surpass the efforts of those who seemingly spent their entire lives in abundant worship. This surpassing by those who have started to worship later in life is due to the excellence of sincerity, and not the abundance of action with

39 This statement should not lead to a complete sense of abandonment; rather, the pious Muslim intends and wills, while knowing that their success in achieving what they intend and will is wholly dependent on Allāh's willing such occurrences for them. The Prophetic method is one that stresses striving to one's utmost ability in the worship of Allāh, while simply relying on Allāh for success—and Gangōhī has emphasized these same sentiments elsewhere in this work.

less sincerity. Precisely for this reason, one *rakʿa* (cycle) of the ritual prayer by an *ʿārif* is superior to a thousand cycles by others.

مَنْ بُورِكَ لَهُ فِي عُمُرِهِ.. أَدْرَكَ فِي يَسِيرٍ مِنَ الزَّمَنِ مِنْ مِنَنِ اللّٰهِ تَعَالَى
مَا لَا يَدْخُلُ تَحْتَ دَوَائِرِ الْعِبَارَةِ وَلَا تَلْحَقُهُ الْإِشَارَةُ.

He who has been blessed in life attains, in a short time, to such gifts from God that no expression or symbolic allusion could describe. [258]

The meaning of having been blessed in one's life is the divine gift of such alertness and diligence that the traveler begins to value every moment of his life. Thus he treasures every breath, without permitting wastage. Furthermore, he expends his full effort in physical and spiritual acts of worship.

Due to the purity and subtlety of a person's actions, they can acquire wonderful bounties from Allāh Most High in a short time, which are beyond description or even detection. For example, the Night of Power [in the month of Ramadan] is better than a thousand nights, despite it being only one night.

The grace of Allāh Most High is not based on anyone's logic, and nor is it confined to any person or specific time.

23

ON CONTRACTION AND EXPANSION

بَسَطَكَ كَيْ لَا يُبْقِيَكَ مَعَ الْقَبْضِ، وَقَبَضَكَ كَيْ لَا يَتْرُكَكَ
مَعَ الْبَسْطِ، وَأَخرَجَكَ عَنْهُمَا كَيْ لَا تَكُونَ لِشَيْءٍ دُونَهُ.

He expanded you so as not to keep you in contraction, and contracted you so as not to keep you in expansion, and He took you out of both so that you not belong to anything apart from Him. [80]

Qabḍ AND *basṭ* ARE two alternating states for the *sālik*.

In the state of *qabḍ* the heart is concentrated on the divine attributes of splendor (*jalāl*) and wrath (*qahr*). In this state the heart is under the shadow of despondency, and there is unrest in invocation and worship.

Basṭ is the state in which the heart is concentrated on the divine attributes of beauty and mercy. In this state the heart is elated with an exhilaration beyond the traveler's control, and his happiness is overflowing.

The traveler who has advanced beyond the initial stages of the Path will experience *qabḍ* and *basṭ*. In the beginning of the Path these stages are called "fear" and "hope." The difference between *qabḍ/basṭ* and fear/hope is that the latter is the product of reflecting on a future event, whereas the former is the consequence of the incidence of inspiration at the present time.

Here the Shaykh is elaborating on the wisdom of the two spiritual states of *qabḍ* and *basṭ* that alternate over the seeker during the Path. Addressing the *sālik* he says that each one replaces the other at an opportune moment so that one doesn't remain in either state. Addressing the traveler he says that the purpose of *basṭ* is to take the traveler out of the state of *qabḍ*. If it were not for *basṭ*, the traveler would perpetually remain in the state of *qabḍ*. A few days in the state of *qabḍ* is unbearable for the traveler. It will not be surprising, then, if he is destroyed. In fact, such episodes of self-destruction have happened. It is for this reason that the state of *basṭ* is bestowed upon him.

The state of *qabḍ* is imposed on the traveler so that he does not always remain in the state of *basṭ,* because in this latter condition the ego derives pleasure. Thus the state of continuous expansion will bring about a reduction in the attribute of servanthood. The longer this state remains, the graver the danger.

These two states do not exist in the accomplished sufi. He experiences a condition in-between *qabḍ* and *basṭ.* Neither state is predominant. Hence the traveler is ultimately taken out of these two states so that his attention is focused only on Allāh Most High. In the states of *qabḍ* and *basṭ* the traveler's attention is diverted to his states, because these two states, when present in one, dominate over the traveler: in the state of *qabḍ*, the traveler will endeavor to eliminate the impressions of despondency and grief; while the heart derives pleasure in the state of *basṭ.* Thus in both states the attention is not toward Allāh Most High. The state of the accomplished sufi is equilibrium (*iʿtidāl*): his state can neither be called *qabḍ* nor *basṭ.*

Steadfastness (*istiqāma*) and equilibrium are achieved by way of qabḍ and *basṭ.* After the ups and downs of these two states, a state of equilibrium settles on the heart.

اَلْعَارِفُونَ إِذَا بُسِطُوا أَخْوَفُ مِنْهُمْ إِذَا قُبِضُوا، وَلَا
يَقِفُ عَلَى حُدُودِ الْأَدَبِ فِي الْبَسْطِ إِلَّا قَلِيلٌ.

It is more dreadful for gnostics to be expanded than to be contracted, for only a few can stay within the limits of proper conduct in expansion. [81]

Since the state of *basṭ* conforms to the desires of the ego, the gnostics (*ʿārifīn*) are more fearful in this state than they are when in the state of *qabḍ.* In *basṭ* the ego may lose itself in pleasure and proclaim its spiritual conditions and miracles. There is the danger of the traveler making claims of loftiness. Sometimes when the state of *basṭ* becomes intense, the traveler utters such statements that are in conflict with the lofty rank of those of Allāh Most High. It is for this reason that the Shaykh says that only a few among the travelers succeed in observing the limits of proper conduct.

On the contrary, since *qabḍ* is a state in conflict with the ego, the attributes of humility, weakness and servitude prevail in one, because the traveler perceives himself overwhelmed by the divine attributes of majesty and power.

اَلْبَسْطُ تَأْخُذُ النَّفْسُ مِنْهُ حَظَّهَا بِوُجُودِ الْفَرَحِ،
وَالْقَبْضُ لَا حَظَّ لِلنَّفْسِ فِيهِ.

Through the existence of joy the soul gets its share in expansion, but there is no share for the soul in contraction. [82]

The basis for the previous aphorism is given here.

In the state of *basṭ* the limits of proper conduct are generally not observed because the ego receives its share of pleasure in the condition. Forgetfulness is the necessary corollary of the ego's derivation of pleasure. Moreover, the ego asserts itself in this state. The acquired inspirational knowledge, mysteries, subtleties and stations of elevation are here in front of the traveler. Thus in the state of *basṭ* he considers himself to be among the élite. These attitudes are in opposition to the states of servanthood. On the other hand, the ego obtains no pleasure in the state of *qabḍ*. It therefore remains within the limits of rectitude. Hence the gnostics prefer the state of *qabḍ* to the state of *basṭ*.

رُبَّمَا أَفَادَكَ فِي لَيْلِ الْقَبْضِ مَا لَمْ تَسْتَفِدْهُ فِي إِشْرَاقِ
نَهَارِ الْبَسْطِ، ﴿لا تَدْرُونَ أَيُّهُمْ أَقْرَبُ لَكُمْ نَفْعًا﴾.

Sometimes He makes you learn in the night of contraction what you have not learned in the radiance of the day of expansion. "You do not know which of them is nearer to you in benefit." [Q. 4:11] [150]

Qabḍ is displeasing to the ego, while *basṭ* is pleasurable. The traveler fears the state of *qabḍ* and thinks of it as a means of distancing him from divine proximity, while he loves *basṭ* and regards it to be a medium for attaining divine proximity. The Shaykh ﵁ therefore now explains the wisdom of *qabḍ*.

Qabḍ is compared to night because in this state the traveler is motionless.

The ego is broken and forlorn, hence it does not move toward its excellences. Nor does it advance claims of loftiness. In this forlorn and motionless condition it turns in supplication to Allāh Most High.

The state of *basṭ* is described as "radiance of the day of expansion" because the ego is in motion, just as people are in motion during daytime. In this latter state, the ego is desirous of displaying its knowledge of spiritual realities.

The traveler is advised not to fear the state of *qabḍ*, because sometimes in the state of *qabḍ* the traveler is granted transcendental knowledge and mysteries that he does not attain in the state of *basṭ*. This is occasioned by the humility and forlornness of the ego produced by the state of *qabḍ*. Humility is the means for Allāh's grace and kindness. The treasure of knowledge and gnosis is granted to the traveler in this state of extreme humility.

The Shaykh 🕮 then cites the following from a Qur'ānic verse: *You do not know which of them is nearer to you in benefit* (4:11). This verse discusses the issue of inheritance, and the instruction contained therein is to execute the laws of inheritance as commanded. Therefore people are commanded to not use their own opinion [in opposition to Allāh's law] in matters pertaining to this issue.

On the basis of this verse, the Shaykh 🕮 instructs the traveler that Allāh Most High knows what is best for him, and that he should trust in His Lord's willing for him, whether that means that he is consigned to *qabḍ* or *basṭ*. Indeed, the traveler's inability to discern which condition is better for him is even more obscure than the inheritance laws regarding heirs, because of the complex nature of spiritual issues over other everyday matters.

24

ON SPIRITUAL LIGHTS AND THEIR CATEGORIES

اَلْأَنْوَارُ مَطَايَا الْقُلُوبِ وَالْأَسْرَارِ.

Lights are the riding-mounts of hearts and of their innermost centers. [55]

According to the sufis, "heart" in this context refers to the physical heart, and "innermost centers" means the spiritual heart. The people of spiritual insight perceive these faculties.

The heart is divided into several departments. The lights that the traveler acquires from worship and spiritual struggle are the riding-mounts that deliver the travelers to their destination: the divine presence. Thus it behooves the traveler to impose worship and discipline upon himself. The traveler should not regard the lights and the pleasure he experiences to be the goal; rather, they are the means for the attainment of the goal. Just as the riding-mounts are not the goal of the travelers, the lights are not the goal.

اَلنُّورُ جُنْدُ الْقَلْبِ كَمَا أَنَّ الظُّلْمَةَ جُنْدُ النَّفْسِ، فَإِذَا أَرَادَ اللّٰهُ أَنْ يَنْصُرَ عَبْدَهُ .. أَمَدَّهُ بِجُنُودِ الْأَنْوَارِ، وَقَطَعَ عَنْهُ مَدَدَ الظُّلَمِ وَالْأَغْيَارِ.

Light is the army of the heart, just as darkness is the army of the soul. So when God wishes to come to the help of His servant, He furnishes him with armies of Lights and cuts off from him the reinforcements of darkness and alterities. [56]

In the terminology of the sufis, the propensity or capacity in man to incline toward evil is termed the "soul" (*nafs*). It stirs man to adopt disgraceful qualities. The heart (*qalb*) is the substratum of the praiseworthy attributes of man.

The soul of man is so self-absorbed in self-esteem, vanity, ignorance and [base] emotions that it remains oblivious to these evils in itself. Its engrossment in these evils precludes it from perceiving them. Its natural inclination is evil and corruption.

Yet, in the heart of the believer there is also the light of Allāh's Oneness that has been bestowed by Allāh, which draws him onwards toward the attributes of worship and obedience.

The meaning of "darkness" is the attributes of the soul; and the "light" refers to the illumination of the heart. Darkness is the army of the soul, while the light is the army of the heart. The conflict between these opposites is perpetual. The soul with its army attacks the heart, preventing it from acting according to the demands of virtue. Meanwhile, the heart endeavors to conquer the soul by means of its army. Sometimes the soul gains the upper hand, leading to the servant committing sin and abstention from obedience. On other occasions, the light of the heart asserts its dominance, overwhelming the soul.

If Allāh Most High has decreed success for the servant, He aids him with an army of light in his struggle against the soul. Here Allāh Most High reveals to him the contemptibility of this world and its transitory nature. The evils of the soul are exposed for him and darkness and all alien objects are dispelled from the heart. These foreign bodies that had taken up an abode in the heart and were being supported by the soul are then deprived of their aid when the light becomes dominant. Gradually, the goal is attained.

If misfortune is decreed for the servant—may Allāh protect us—the darkness gains in intensity. This intensity is an incremental process resulting in the complete disappearance of the heart's light. The world then dominates the person.

When a struggle ensues between the soul and the heart, the traveler should turn his attention to Allāh Most High, supplicating for His aid. He should increase his invocation and repose his trust in Allāh. The demands of the soul will be subjugated and the heart's light will prevail, Allāh-willing.

اَلنُّورُ لَهُ الْكَشْفُ، وَالْبَصِيرَةُ لَهَا الْحُكْمُ، وَالْقَلْبُ لَهُ الْإِقْبَالُ وَالْإِدْبَارُ.

Insight belongs to the Light, discernment to the intellect, and both progression and retrogression belong to the heart. [57]

The corporeal eye visualizes objects with the aid of external light, such as the sun's light or candlelight. In the absence of such light, the eye is unable to see. The operation of the heart's vision is similar. As long as it lacks the aid of light it is unable to exercise spiritual vision. Light here means the light of certitude and faith that Allāh Most High bestows on his special servants. By virtue of the light of certitude, insight becomes conspicuous to the heart.

This revelation is the result of the light that has been acquired. This is like a person who has knowledge of the contents in a room, yet is unable to see them in the darkness—on account of the absence of light. When a light is produced his eyes perceive the objects with great clarity. Thus, the function of light is to render visible the transcendental realities of knowledge. The heart's vision then perceives them. If the heart possesses vision, it will perceive, otherwise not.

Once insight is attained, then it is the heart's function to move in the direction of virtue and to diverge from evil: away from the transitoriness of the world toward the perpetuity of the Hereafter. The physical limbs of the body are subservient to the heart, so they will move swiftly toward the true goal once the heart has been corrected.

أَنَارَ الظَّوَاهِرَ بِأَنْوَارِ آثَارِهِ، وَأَنَارَ السَّرَائِرَ بِأَنْوَارِ أَوْصَافِهِ .. لِأَجْلِ ذٰلِكَ
أَفَلَتْ أَنْوَارُ الظَّوَاهِرِ، وَلَمْ تَأْفُلْ أَنْوَارُ الْقُلُوبِ وَالسَّرَائِرِ، وَلِذٰلِكَ قِيلَ:
إِنَّ شَمْسَ النَّهَارِ تَغْرُبُ بِاللَّيْلِ وَشَمْسُ الْقُلُوبِ لَيْسَتْ تَغِيبُ.

He illumined exterior phenomena with the lights of His created things; and He illumined the innermost hearts with the uncreated lights of His attributes. For that reason, the lights of exterior phenomena[40] set, whereas the lights of hearts and of the innermost hearts do not set. That is why it is said, "Verily, the sun of the day sets at night, but the Sun of hearts never sets!" [104]

---

40 This word appears to have been mistyped in the second sentence as "phenonema" in the Brill 1984 edition. It has been corrected here as it is in the first sentence.

The sun, the moon, the stars and all of creation are the effects of Allāh's power and wisdom. Allāh Most High has illumined exterior phenomena with the light of created things. Therefore we are able to derive benefit from the good things and abstain from the harmful ones.

Moreover, He has illumined the innermost dimension of the heart with the light of His attributes of beauty (*jamāl*) and majesty (*jalāl*). Thus inspirational knowledge and transcendental realities are revealed to the innermost recesses of the hearts of the gnostics. The latter perceive the inner spiritual attributes, and therefore adopt praiseworthy ones (*awṣāf ḥamīda*) while abstaining from the evil ones (*awṣāf radhīla*).

Since the light of the heavens and earth is temporal, being acquired from the sun and moon, it becomes overshadowed and recedes into concealment, because temporal things undergo changes. On the other hand, since the light of the spiritual heart emanates from the attributes of Allāh Most High, and since Allāh's attributes are eternal, this divine light is never overshadowed; hence it cannot be hidden. However, the perception of this light diminishes when human qualities assert their domination.

The intelligent man chooses the eternal and abandons the temporal entities that undergo change.

مَطَالِعُ الْأَنْوَارِ الْقُلُوبُ وَالْأَسْرَارُ.

The hearts and the innermost centers of being are the places where lights arise. [151]

The emanation of gnosis and subtle knowledge is from the innermost centers of the gnostics. Their hearts resemble the heaven in which lie the horizons for the rising of the sun and moon. The light emanating from their hearts is infinitely superior to the radiance of the sun and moon. It is mentioned in the ḥadīth that if the light of the faith of the lowest ranking Muslim is manifested, then the east and west would be illuminated and the light of the sun and moon would be eclipsed. When this is the brilliance of the light of the lowest ranking Muslim, then the light of the gnostics is beyond description.

نُورٌ مُسْتَوْدَعٌ فِي الْقُلُوبِ، مَدَدُهُ مِنَ النُّورِ الْوَارِدِ مِنْ خَزَائِنِ الْغُيُوبِ،
نُورٌ يَكْشِفُ لَكَ بِهِ عَنْ آثَارِهِ، وَنُورٌ يَكْشِفُ لَكَ بِهِ عَنْ أَوْصَافِهِ.

There is a light deposited in hearts which is nourished by the Light coming from the treasuries of the invisible realms. There is a light wherewith He unveils for you His created things, and there is a Light wherewith He unveils for you His Attributes. [152–153]

The light of certitude embedded in the hearts of the gnostics progresses with the aid of the light that descends from the treasuries of the invisible realms. The stages of the gnostics' certitude rise continuously because such stages are infinite. This increase in the light of the gnostic's certitude is from the light emanating from the eternal divine attributes.

The light entrusted to the hearts of the gnostics is of two kinds. The first kind is the medium for unveiling the created things of Allāh, the True Cause, that is to say, the conditions and circumstances of creation are revealed to one. This type of revelation is called "the disclosure of forms" (*kashf ṣūrī*). The other kind is the light by means of which the attributes of Allāh's majesty and beauty are unveiled. This light is the emanation of the manifestation of the divine attributes, and it is called "the disclosure of meaning" (*kashf maʿnawī*).

أَنْوَارٌ أُذِنَ لَهَا فِي الْوُصُولِ، وَأَنْوَارٌ أُذِنَ لَهَا فِي الدُّخُولِ.

There are lights that are allowed to arrive and lights that are allowed to enter. [204]

The light of divine knowledge and mysteries that settles in the hearts of the gnostics from the treasuries of the invisible realm illuminates their hearts. There are two types of these lights. The first type only "arrive" on the outer façade of the heart, while the second type "enters" into the innermost recesses of the heart.

The effect of the light settling on the outer façade of the heart is the perception by the heart of its ego as well as of Allāh. Both this world and the Hereafter are kept in view. The presence of foreign things still remains in the heart. Thus the traveler sometimes inclines to his ego and sometimes to Allāh. Sometimes he desires the Hereafter and sometimes the world.

The effect of the lights that enter the innermost recesses of the heart is the entrenchment of Allāh's invocation in the heart. Only [the remembrance of] Allāh Most High is in the heart. All other things are expelled from the heart of the traveler by these lights. He is not enslaved to anyone besides Allāh.

According to some gnostics, as long as faith is confined to the outer façade of the heart, the servant is the lover of both Allāh and the world. Such a servant is sometimes in communion with Allāh Most High and sometimes in collusion with his ego. When faith enters the interior of the heart, the servant renounces the world.

رُبَّمَا وَرَدَتْ عَلَيْكَ الْأَنْوَارُ، فَوَجَدَتِ الْقَلْبَ مَحْشُوًّا
بِصُوَرِ الْآثَارِ، فَارْتَحَلَتْ مِنْ حَيْثُ نَزَلَتْ، فَرِّغْ قَلْبَكَ
مِنَ الْأَغْيَارِ .. تَمْلَأْهُ بِالْمَعَارِفِ وَالْأَسْرَارِ.

Sometimes lights come upon you and find the heart stuffed with forms of created things; so they go back from whence they descended. Empty your heart of alterities and you will fill it up with gnostic intuitions and mysteries. [205–206]

The heart of man is a celestial faculty that has the ability of reflecting divine knowledge, mysteries and gnostic intuitions. However, on account of man's preoccupation with mundane matters and emotional issues, the "forms" of created things becomes impressed on his mind. These impressions are then mirrored in the heart, resulting in the diminishing of the heart's inherent ability of inner spiritual perception. It then resembles a mirror on whose surface dust and grime have settled, blurring the images or impeding visionary perception.

When the traveler engages in invocation and spiritual struggle, adopts solitude, decreases speech, reduces association with people and concentrates on the purification of his soul, then the grace of Allāh Most High focuses on him. He becomes polished and illumined. He gains the ability to absorb the lights from the Divine.

Sometimes the outer heart receives lights and gains the ability to reflect them. However, when the lights reach a heart and they find it engrossed in worldly preoccupations, they return to their celestial abode whence they had emanated. Consequently, it is essential for the traveler to cleanse his heart from all created things. He should keep the mirror of the heart thoroughly polished and Allāh Most High will fill it with divine knowledge, mysteries and intuitions.

لَا يُعْلَمُ قَدْرُ أَنْوَارِ الْقُلُوبِ وَالْأَسْرَارِ إِلَّا فِي غَيْبِ الْمَلَكُوتِ، كَمَا لَا تَظْهَرُ أَنْوَارُ السَّمَاءِ إِلَّا فِي شَهَادَةِ الْمُلْكِ.

It is only in the invisible world of the Realm that the value of the lights of the hearts and of the innermost centers of being is known, just as the lights of the sky do not manifest themselves except in the visible world of the Kingdom. [250]

Inasmuch as this universe is the substratum for the manifestation of the light of the sun, the moon and the stars, the Hereafter is the abode of the manifestation of the light of man's spiritual faculties. Since these lights are concealed from the vision of people, their value is neither appreciated nor understood in this world.

The intelligent traveler should not grieve on account of this attitude of people; nor should he care, because the world is not the substratum for the manifestation of these lights. The light of the unknown men of Allāh living in renunciation and seclusion will glitter in the Hereafter. It is in that abode where their worth and value will be appreciated.

رُبَّمَا وَقَفَتِ الْقُلُوبُ مَعَ الْأَنْوَارِ، كَمَا حُجِبَتِ النُّفُوسُ بِكَثَائِفِ الْأَغْيَارِ.

Sometimes hearts stop at lights the same way souls are veiled by the opacities of alterities. [154]

Some hearts stop at the lights of the stations (*maqāmāt*) without reaching their goals. They are veiled from reaching the same way that souls are veiled by the opacities of perceptibles from attaining the subtle implications (*maʿānī*) and comprehended meanings (*mafhūmāt*). This is either due to the absence of a spiritual shaykh or due to weak aspiration.[41]

41 Both the aphorism and commentary are missing from Gangōhī's work and the commentary added here is from Ibn ʿAjība (*Īqāẓ al-Himam fī Sharḥ al-Ḥikam* 265).

25

ON THE SERVANT'S PROXIMITY TO ALLĀH AND NATURAL DISPOSITION

وُصُولُـكَ إِلَى اللهِ وُصُولُكَ إِلَى الْعِلْمِ بِهِ، وَإِلَّا فَجَلَّ رَبُّنَا أَنْ يَتَّصِلَ بِهِ شَيْءٌ أَوْ يَتَّصِلَ هُوَ بِشَيْءٍ.

Your union with God is union through knowledge of Him. Otherwise, God is beyond being united[42] with anything or anything being united with Him! [213]

THE MEANING OF *wuṣūl* to Allāh is not a physical union as is the fusion of two physical objects. Allāh Most High is devoid of physical or material dimensions. The sufi concept of *wuṣūl* is a spiritual state in which the servant experientially sees [the existence] of Allāh Most High, with a clarity that negates the need for any rational proof.[43] This certitude is realized at such a high degree that it even surpasses the confidence of an observer participating in the physical visualization of objects. It is possible for the eye to err sometimes in its vision, but such an error does not occur in the state of certitude, which—when achieved—is a constant attribute of the heart, as vision is an attribute of the eye. This perception is called *wuṣūl*, *tajallī* and *fayḍ al-Raḥmān* (the Grace of the Infinitely Good).

42 For an explanation of being "united" with Allāh, refer to the editor's preface.

43 See the footnote from Sirhindī at the beginning of chapter three on the vision of Allāh being reserved only to the next world for the believers, and it is not for this world.

قُرْبُكَ مِنْهُ أَنْ تَكُوْنَ مُشَاهِدًا لِقُرْبِهِ، وَإِلَّا فَمِنْ أَيْنَ أَنْتَ وَوُجُوْدُ قُرْبِهِ.

Your nearness to Him is that you contemplate His nearness. Otherwise, what comparison is there between you and the existence of His nearness? [214]

All attributes of excellence and perfection in reality belong exclusively to Allāh. Such attributes apply figuratively to the servant. It is Allāh Most High who in reality has "nearness" with the servant. The Qur'ān says: *When my servant asks you about Me, then [know that], verily, I am near [to him]* (2:186).

The meaning of the servant's nearness to Allāh Most High is that he perceives Allāh's nearness with his spiritual eyes. The effect of such a witnessing is that the servant will observe, at all times, the etiquette of the Divine Court: he will be firm on the Sacred Law.

Divine nearness does not mean physical nearness, which is a characteristic of material objects.

لَوْ أَنَّكَ لَا تَصِلُ إِلَيْهِ إِلَّا بَعْدَ فَنَاءِ مَسَاوِيكَ وَمَحْوِ دَعَاوِيكَ .. لَمْ تَصِلْ إِلَيْـهِ أَبَدًا، وَلٰكِنْ إِذَا أَرَادَ أَنْ يُوصِلَكَ إِلَيْهِ .. سَـتَرَ وَصْفَكَ بِوَصْفِهِ، وَغَطَّى نَعْتَكَ بِنَعْتِهِ، فَوَصَلَكَ إِلَيْهِ بِمَا مِنْهُ إِلَيْكَ لَا بِمَا مِنْكَ إِلَيْهِ.

If you were to be united with Him only after the extinction of your vices and the effacement of your pretensions, you would never be united with Him. Instead, when He wants to unite you to Himself, He covers your attribute with His Attribute and hides your quality with His Quality. And thus He unites you to Himself by virtue of what comes from Him to you, not by virtue of what goes from you to Him. [130]

The *wuṣūl* or *mushāhada* (witnessing) described earlier is attained when the ego becomes lifeless, when every evil quality and demand has been expelled from it and it no longer has any motives or desires. It becomes like a lifeless person in the custody of a living person. The attainment of such a stage is beyond the ability of the servant [on the basis of his own efforts].

If Allāh Most High had decreed that a servant can never reach Him unless he kills his ego by means of his own efforts, then no one would have attained His proximity, because evil is the natural propensity of the ego. When Allāh wishes to favor a servant with His proximity, He illuminates the servant with the rays of His lofty attributes. The servant's attributes are then overshadowed and concealed. Thus the servant reaches Allāh Most High by virtue of divine grace and mercy. The servant does not attain *wuṣūl* on the strength of his own actions and struggle. In fact, that is not possible.

The elimination of the natural, despicable qualities of the ego does not occur; rather, these lowly attributes are overshadowed by the manifestation of the radiance of the divine attributes. Despite this, there is no escape from righteous actions, struggle and purification for the servant since it is the divine custom (*ʿādat Allāh*) that when the servant strives he receives the grace of Allāh Most High. The cause of attaining Allāh's proximity is therefore not the traveler's effort, but the grace of Allāh. While the traveler should not relax in his performance of righteous actions and struggle, his trust should be only on the grace of Allāh Most High. If the traveler places his reliance on his deeds, then it will become an obstacle in his reaching the court of Allāh, as the object is to rely on none other than Him.

كُنْ بِأَوْصَافِ رُبُوبِيَّتِهِ مُتَعَلِّقًا، وَبِأَوْصَافِ عُبُودِيَّتِكَ مُتَحَقِّقًا.

Cling to the attributes of His Lordship and realize the attributes of your servanthood! [125]

The attributes of Lordship are the perfect and excellent attributes of Allāh, such as power, majesty, knowledge, wisdom, etc. Examples of the attributes of servanthood are poverty, weakness, disgrace, ignorance, dependence, etc.

The entire creation, along with its being and attributes, is the impression of Allāh's attributes. True Existence is the attribute of only Allāh Most High. The existence of all other objects is secondary and is the result of divine bestowal. The brightness on the wall produced by the sun will figuratively belong to the wall. Thus, truly speaking, no object has any inherent quality. There is only a connection with the true attributes of Allāh in that all objects are the impressions of the divine attributes.[44]

---

44 ʿAlī al-Qārī has written: "The essence of things is indeed real. . . This is a direct rebuttal to the Sophists (*sufista'iyya*) and others who deny the real essences of things (*ḥaqā'iq al-ashyā'*) and

But man is oblivious of this reality, thinking that the attributes belong to him. He thinks, therefore: "I have existence. I am knowledgeable. I am wealthy. I am honorable." Little does he understand that only Allāh truly exists. Only He, really, has knowledge. Only He has treasure. Only He has honor.

The Shaykh 🙏, admonishing the believer, tells him to keep in mind the connection that he should have with the divine attributes. He should banish ignorance, which means abandonment of the personal attributes to which he lays claim. His existence and attributes are merely the impressions of the divine attributes. All of man's attributes are subservient to the divine attributes and have no independent existence. The believer should engender in himself the attributes of servanthood. He should view his contemptibility in relation to the true honor of Allāh Most High, and compare the wealth of Allāh with his own poverty. He should perceive and recognize his own weakness in relation to Allāh's power, and understand his own ignorance by contemplating true knowledge, i.e., the divine attribute of knowledge.

مَنَعَـكَ أَنْ تَدَّعِيَ مَا لَيْسَ لَكَ مِمَّا لِلْمَخْلُوقِينَ، أَفَيُبِيحُ لَكَ أَنْ تَدَّعِيَ
وَصْفَهُ، وَهُوَ رَبُّ الْعَالَمِينَ؟

He has prohibited you from claiming for yourself what does not belong to you amongst the qualities of created beings; so would He permit you to lay claim to His Attribute, He who is the Lord of the Universe? [126]

This statement is presented as proof for the earlier assertion. It is prohibited to claim something that belongs to another person, even though in reality that claimant is not even the true owner of that object—since only Allāh Most High owns anything in reality. When it is improper for man to claim ownership of the property of a person who, in fact, is not even the actual owner, then how can it be permissible for him to lay claim to the attributes of Lordship, such as honor, dignity, power, knowledge, etc.?

Allāh is the Lord of the entire universe and the attributes of Lordship belong exclusively to Him. It is, therefore, the duty of the believer to confine himself to these limits by understanding that all attributes of excellence

---

believe that the world is all imaginary and fantasy like dreams. Close to this opinion is that of the heretic pantheists (*wujūdiyya ilḥādiyya*), the incarnationists (*ḥulūliyya*), and those like them among the ignorant *sufis*" (see Maghnīsāwī, *Al-Fiqh al-Akbar Explained*, 106).

belong to Allāh alone. He should never attempt to even substantiate his own existence[45]—so that he remains free from all vestiges of associationism. Thus will his faith remain pure.

تَحَقَّقْ بِأَوْصَافِكَ .. يُمِدَّكَ بِأَوصَافِهِ، تَحَقَّقْ بِذُلِّكَ
.. يُمِدَّكَ بِعِزَّتِهِ، تَحَقَّقْ بِعَجْزِكَ .. يُمِدَّكَ بِقُدْرَتِهِ،
تَحَقَّقْ بِضَعْفِكَ .. يُمِدَّكَ بِحَوْلِهِ وَقُوَّتِهِ.

Realize your attributes and He will help you with His Attributes; realize your lowliness and He will help you with His Sublimity; realize your impotence and He will help you with His Power; realize your weakness and He will help you with His Might and Force! [178]

In the previous aphorism we have the exhortation to free ourselves from claiming any of the attributes that belong to Allāh and His Lordship. The ego has a very strong relationship with its imagined attributes of excellence: it is proud of its honor, strength, power, etc. It remains entrapped in these fanciful ideas, deriving pleasure from such vain and false hopes. In fact, it dreads the very thought of abandoning these baseless desires.

The believer is, therefore, here reminded of the divine aid that he will gain when he renounces such vain and false desires. When the servant is firm in his condition of servanthood, Allāh Most High will not abandon him. Prior to the abandonment of desires, the servant would seek aid from his imagined attributes. In most cases, he was unsuccessful. However, after freeing himself from his imagined excellences, Allāh Most High aids him with His attributes of reality.

لَا يُخْرِجُكَ عَنِ الْوَصْفِ .. إِلَّا شُهُودُ الْوَصْفِ.

Only the contemplation of His Attribute can dislodge you from your attribute. [241]

45 This instruction should be understood as a command to never substantiate one's own existence as though it is independent and free of Allāh's control. Gangōhī strikes this very point two aphorisms later, when he says: "In fact, the ego will even regard itself to have independent existence."

The attribute of the ego in this context refers to qualities of excellence that the ego imagines in itself, such as greatness, independence, power, knowledge, etc. In fact, the ego will even regard itself to have independent existence. These are all imaginary ideas of the ego. As long as man dwells in such fantasy, he will not reach Allāh Most High.

The expulsion of these egotistic attributes cannot be achieved by means of struggle alone. It is only when Allāh Most High directs the illumination of His attributes to the servant that the ego, then, contemplates the True Divine Being; a process that leads to the imagined attributes of the ego being displaced.

Man has the awareness of the greatness of Allāh Most High; however, this knowledge is not sufficient to displace his pride. Only when the reflection of Allāh's attribute of greatness falls on him, and he vividly perceives it, will his imagined greatness be eliminated. This is the case with all his other imagined attributes.

Thus, only after witnessing Allāh's attribute of Being does the servant achieve nearness and communion with Allāh Most High.

إِنَّمَا وَسِعَكَ الْكَوْنُ مِنْ حَيْثُ جُثْمَانِيَّتِكَ، وَلَمْ
يَسَعْكَ مِنْ حَيْثُ ثُبُوتِ رُوحَانِيَّتِكَ.

The Cosmos envelops you in respect to your corporeal nature, but it does not do so in respect to the immutability of your spiritual nature. [246]

Man consists of body and spirit. While the physical body belongs to this material world, the spirit is a spiritual substance belonging to the invisible, celestial realm. Yet, the spirit has a relationship with its physical body.

The physical body depends on physical provisions, such as food and water, for its subsistence. On the other hand, the spirit, being a spiritual substance, does not subsist on material nourishment. Its nourishment is invocation and obedience to Allāh Most High.

Thus, the material world can sustain man's physical body, but not his spiritual being. There is no affinity between the spirit and the physical world, which is a prison for the spirit. Therefore, if man fully engrosses himself in this perishable abode, the spirit will initially become terrified and its strength will gradually dissipate. If one's effort is only on developing the physical body and the spirit is neglected, the spirit will be rendered impotent.

It is therefore necessary that man only take from this material world that which is merely required to sustain his body. He should not involve himself in elaborate schemes for the sake of the physical body. Allāh Most High Himself has assumed the responsibility of providing for man. Man should, consequently, apply his undivided attention to the nourishment and development of his spirit and eliminate the pollution that has settled on the spirit as a result of its relationship with the material body. He is to cleanse his spirit from this pollution by means of invocation, obedience and struggle. In this way will he gain complete freedom from the physical body and be vouchsafed the everlasting life.

لَا يَلْزَمُ مِنْ ثُبُوتِ الْخُصُوصِيَّةِ عَدَمُ وَصْفِ الْبَشَرِيَّةِ،
إِنَّمَا مَثَلُ الْخُصُوصِيَّةِ كَإِشْرَاقِ شَمْسِ النَّهَارِ ظَهَرَتْ فِي
الْأُفُقِ وَلَيْسَتْ مِنْهُ، تَارَةً تُشْرِقُ شُمُوسُ أَوْصَافِهِ عَلَى لَيْلِ
وُجُودِكَ، وَتَارَةً يَقْبِضُ ذٰلِكَ عَنْكَ فَيَرُدُّكَ إِلَى حُدُودِكَ،
فَالنَّهَارُ لَيْسَ مِنْكَ إِلَيْكَ، وَلٰكِنَّهُ وَارِدٌ عَلَيْكَ.

The permanence of sanctity does not necessitate that the attribute of human nature be non-existent. Sanctity is analogous to the illumination of the sun in daytime: it appears on the horizon but it is not part of it. Sometimes the suns of His Attributes shine in the night of your existence, and sometimes He takes that away from you and returns you to your existence. So daytime is not from you to you, but instead, it comes upon you. [248]

The attributes of the saints (*awliyā'*) are of several kinds. Some attributes are necessary for them, like being devoid of disgraceful characteristics such as pride, malice, vanity, etc. and being adorned with lofty qualities such as dependence on Allāh, humility, sincerity, constancy in invocation, etc. These attributes are with them every moment. Some attributes are the natural human qualities, for example, physical weakness and the propensity to be affected by an episode of grief.

When the divine attributes [of Allāh Most High] illuminate the saints, all other human attributes are overwhelmed. The saints then demonstrate such wonderful feats that are beyond the ability of others: when the divine attribute of knowledge radiates on them, they proclaim such wonderful knowledge that other people of similar knowledge are dumbstruck.

When there is no illumination through the divine attributes, the human qualities are conspicuous. The episodes of the saints bear testimony to this fact. Sometimes they elaborate on issues of great intricacy, while sometimes they are unaware of even common, everyday matters.

The term "sanctity" here refers to the wonderful impressions [of the divine attributes] that are occasionally manifested. The existence of sanctity does not mean that the human attributes of the saints have become non-existent—human attributes are common to all people, even the illustrious saints. This "sanctity" resembles the sunlight that spreads in the entire horizon. All creation become visible and the impression is conveyed that the light is the inherent quality of all objects that have become visible, but in reality this is not so. The rays of sanctity similarly illuminate the darkness of the material existence of the saints, but at that time special impressions become manifest.

When the rays of divine illumination are withheld, the human attributes of the saints become more manifest. All human weaknesses are again clearly discernible in them. Thus the radiance of this light is not inherent in them nor does it form an integral part of their being. They have no control over it and cannot acquire it by choice.

Some people labor under the misconception that divine proximity is achieved only when all human attributes are eradicated. This idea is utterly baseless and deceptive. Many people are involved in associationism (*shirk*) on account of this misconception. As a result of this fallacy, they believe the saints to be partners with Allāh Most High in His exclusive attributes. Even the Prophets do not share the attributes of Allāh, such as knowledge of everything. We seek refuge in Allāh! The Messenger of Allāh ﷺ too was not aware of certain things, such as the episode when Lady 'Ā'isha ﵂ was maliciously slandered. Moreover, as a result of extreme hunger he would tie stones on his blessed stomach. At other times, he would feed thousands, inform people of far-away happenings and reveal the knowledge of former and later times.

26

ON THE DIVINE'S PROXIMITY TO CREATION AND HIS MANIFESTATION OF THINGS BY DIRECTION AND GUIDANCE

اَلْكَوْنُ كُلُّهُ ظُلْمَةٌ وَإِنَّمَا أَنَارَهُ ظُهُورُ الْحَقِّ فِيهِ، فَمَنْ رَأَى الْكَوْنَ وَلَمْ يَشْــهَدْهُ فِيهِ أَوْ عِنْدَهُ أَوْ قَبْلَهُ أَوْ بَعْدَهُ.. فَقَــدْ أَعْوَزَهُ وُجُودُ الْأَنْوَارِ، وَحُجِبَتْ عَنْهُ شُمُوسُ الْمَعَارِفِ بِسُحُبِ الْآثَارِ.

The Cosmos is all darkness. It is illumined only by the manifestation of God in it. He who sees the Cosmos and does not contemplate Him in it or by it or before it or after it is in need of light, and is veiled from the sun of gnosis by the clouds of created things. [14]

EXISTENCE IS LIGHT; non-existence is darkness. The entire creation in the Cosmos with regard to its being is pure non-existence [in essence]. The manifestation of Allāh's attributes bestowed existence and brightness on the Cosmos. Creation is for this reason illuminated with the radiance of existence, and made visible. Thus, in reality, there is only one [true] existence: the existence of Allāh Most High.

There are various kinds of perception of the people of spiritual insight, whose gaze is fixed on reality. Some of these saintly people, when their gaze falls on creation, perceive the Creator first. As a result of inner illumination, creation recedes into oblivion [for them]. After having attained the perception of the Creator, they perceive the creation. For others, creation is presented as a mirror for the beauty and grandeur of the Creator's works. Thus they perceive Allāh in or with creation [so to speak—not literally]. Those who gaze only on creation, not perceiving the Creator in any way, are completely deprived of the light of gnosis. The mysteries of gnosis, which are like the sun's light, are concealed in the clouds of physical creation. They are, therefore, deprived of this treasure.

The true reality of perception and its elucidation are not rational concepts, but are comprehended by intuition (*dhawq*) and inspiration (*wijdān*).

مِمَّا يَدُلُّكَ عَلَىٰ وُجُودِ قَهْرِهِ سُبْحَانَهُ أَنْ
حَجَبَكَ عَنْهُ بِمَا لَيْسَ بِمَوْجُودٍ مَعَهُ.

That which shows you the existence of His Omnipotence is that He veiled you from Himself by what has no existence alongside of Him. [15]

Earlier it was mentioned that true existence belongs only to Allāh Most High, who has no partner. A concept that posits true existence for any being other than Allāh Most High is to be condemned as associationism (*shirk*) in the divine attribute of existence (*wujūd*).

Here the Shaykh ﷺ mentions the wonderful power of Allāh Most High. A conspicuous proof of His wrath is that he prevents people from seeing Him by "veiling" Himself with objects that are devoid of true existence. These objects are the material items of creation. People fix their gaze on these material objects and cannot look beyond. While they see things that lack true existence, their gaze fails to discern the One who truly exists. When there is no intervening obstacle, according to reason, one should be able to perceive the Truly Existent, since the material obstacle is devoid of true existence. By virtue of His power, however, Allāh has prevented people from perceiving Him even though there is, in reality, no intervening object.

In the following aphorism, the Shaykh ﷺ presents several arguments for the contention that creation cannot be—rationally speaking—a screen for the Divine Being.

كَيْفَ يُتَصَوَّرُ أَنْ يَحْجُبَهُ شَيْءٌ وَهُوَ الَّذِي أَظْهَرَ كُلَّ شَيْءٍ! كَيْفَ يُتَصَوَّرُ
أَنْ يَحْجُبَهُ شَـيْءٌ وَهُوَ الَّذِي ظَهَرَ بِكُلِّ شَيْءٍ! كَيْفَ يُتَصَوَّرُ أَنْ يَحْجُبَهُ

شَيْءٌ وَهُوَ الَّذِي ظَهَرَ فِي كُلِّ شَيْءٍ! كَيْفَ يُتَصَوَّرُ أَنْ يَحْجُبَهُ شَيْءٌ وَهُوَ الَّذِي ظَهَرَ لِكُلِّ شَيْءٍ! كَيْفَ يُتَصَوَّرُ أَنْ يَحْجُبَهُ شَيْءٌ وَهُوَ الظَّاهِرُ قَبْلَ وُجُودِ كُلِّ شَيْءٍ! كَيْفَ يُتَصَوَّرُ أَنْ يَحْجُبَهُ شَيْءٌ وَهُوَ أَظْهَرُ مِنْ كُلِّ شَيْءٍ! كَيْفَ يُتَصَوَّرُ أَنْ يَحْجُبَهُ شَيْءٌ وَهُوَ الْوَاحِدُ الَّذِي لَيْسَ مَعَهُ شَيْءٌ! كَيْفَ يُتَصَوَّرُ أَنْ يَحْجُبَهُ شَـــيْءٌ وَهُوَ أَقْرَبُ إِلَيْكَ مِنْ كُلِّ شَيْءٍ! كَيْفَ يُتَصَوَّرُ أَنْ يَحْجُبَهُ شَيْءٌ وَلَوْلَاهُ لَمَا كَانَ وُجُودُ كُلِّ شَيْءٍ! يَا عَجَبًا كَيْفَ يَظْهَرُ الْوُجُودُ فِي الْعَدَمِ! أَمْ كَيْفَ يَثْبُتُ الْحَادِثُ مَعَ مَنْ لَهُ وَصْفُ الْقِدَمِ!

How can it be conceived that something veils Him, since He is the one who manifests everything? How can it be conceived that something veils Him, since He is the one who is manifest through everything? How can it be conceived that something veils Him, since He is the one who is manifest in everything? How can it be conceived that something veils Him, since He is the Manifest to everything? How can it be conceived that something veils Him, since He was the Manifest before the existence of anything? How can it be conceived that something veils Him, since He is more manifest than anything? How can it be conceived that something veils Him, since He is the One alongside of whom there is nothing? How can it be conceived that something veils Him, since He is nearer to you than anything else? How can it be conceived that something veils Him, since, were it not for Him, the existence of everything would not have been manifest? It is a marvel how Being has been manifested in non-being and how the contingent has been established alongside of Him who possesses the attribute of Eternity! [16]

When Allāh Most High has bestowed the light of existence on everything, after extracting it from the darkness of non-existence, how could it be conceivable for such objects to prevent the conception of Him?

When all objects of creation point to His existence, how can they constitute veils concealing Him? They reveal Him. They do not conceal Him.

All objects of creation are the impressions of the lofty attributes and names of Allāh Most High. His attributes shine out in every object of creation. Living objects manifest His attribute of giving life: He is The Life-Giver (al-Muḥyī). Dead objects manifest His attribute of causing death: He is The Slayer (al-Mumīt). If everything represents an attribute of Allāh, it then follows that nothing can conceal Him.

The illumination of Allāh Most High is on every object. All things have knowledge of Him in proportion to the degree of divine illumination on them. Hence all things glorify Him and submit to Him, although we are not able to understand. Therefore, if every object is a substratum for divine illumination, how is it possible for them to conceal Him?

Manifestation—to be conspicuous—is His eternal attribute that existed before the existence of creation. The manifestation of creation is, in fact, the shadow of His attribute of manifestation. Nothing in creation can, therefore, conceal Him.

Allāh says in the Glorious Qur'ān that He is closer to man than his jugular vein (50:16). When Allāh is closer to man than even his own life, nothing can conceal Him from man. It is only our own existence that has become a "veil."

Earlier it was mentioned that creation, in reality, is non-existent and only Allāh Most has true existence. The conspicuous nature of existence—in contrast to non-existence—is self-evident. Thus the manifestation of Allāh Most High is greater than the manifestation of creation . On account of the intensity of divine conspicuousness, the intelligence (*ʿaql*) [of many] fails to comprehend Him, just as the eye cannot stare at the sun. The mole that cannot see the sun's light because of visual incapacity cannot say that the sun is inconspicuous. Nothing can, therefore, conceal Him.

Finally, when only Allāh has true existence and all else is false and non-existent, it is truly amazing how Being was made manifest in non-being, despite their being opposites. It is also truly amazing that the contingent exist with the Eternal,. However, the Eternal is true and the temporal is false, since how can the false endure with the existence of the True. Thus Allāh says in the Qur'ān: *And say: The truth has come, and falsehood has vanished; surely falsehood is ever certain to vanish* (17:81) and *Everything will be destroyed except His face* (28:88). Furthermore, the poet Labīd said, "Everything except Allāh is vain." The commentator of the Ḥikam states that if there had not been any subject matter in this work besides this one it would have been sufficient.[46]

46 "The commentator of the *Hikam*" seems to undoubtedly be Ibn ʿAbbād al-Rundī, because

اَلْحَقُّ لَيْسَ بِمَحْجُوبٍ عَنْكَ، وَإِنَّمَا الْمَحْجُوبُ أَنْتَ عَنِ النَّظَرِ إِلَيْهِ، إِذْ لَوْ حَجَبَهُ شَيْءٌ .. لَسَتَرَهُ مَا حَجَبَهُ، وَلَوْ كَانَ لَهُ سَاتِرٌ .. لَكَانَ لِوُجُودِهِ حَاصِرٌ، وَكُلُّ حَاصِرٍ لِشَيْءٍ فَهُوَ لَهُ قَاهِرٌ، ﴿وَهُوَ الْقَاهِرُ فَوْقَ عِبَادِهِ﴾.

The Real is not veiled from you. Rather, it is you who are veiled from seeing It, for, were anything to veil It, then that which veils It would cover It. But if there were a covering to It, then that would be a limitation of Its Being: every limitation of anything has power over it. "And He is the Omnipotent, above His servants." [Q. 6:18] [33]

Allāh Most High is conspicuous. His Being, attributes, beauty and grandeur shine out in everything and in every place. He is not under any kind of veil. The veil is from the side of people whose spiritual insight is impeded by the veil of egotistic attributes.

If one desires to perceive His beauty and grandeur, then one should lift this veil of egotistic cravings by means of struggle [against the ego], righteous actions, invocation and obedience to a genuine shaykh (*shaykh kāmil*). When this has been achieved one will see nothing other-than-Allāh.

How is it possible for anything to conceal Him when He encompasses all things?

شُعَاعُ الْبَصِيرَةِ يُشْهِدُكَ قُرْبَهُ مِنْكَ، وَعَيْنُ الْبَصِيرَةِ تُشْهِدُكَ عَدَمَكَ لِوُجُودِهِ، وَحَقُّ الْبَصِيرَةِ يُشْهِدُكَ وُجُودَهُ، لَا عَدَمَكَ وَلَا وُجُودَكَ.

The ray of light of the intellect makes you witness His nearness to you. The eye of the intellect makes you witness your non-being as due to His Being. The Truth of the intellect makes you witness His Being, not your non-being nor your being. [36]

When the traveler engrosses himself in the quest for Allāh Most High,

this exact statement is found in his work. See Ibn 'Abbād al-Nafazī al-Rundī, *Al-Hikam al-'Aṭā'iyya li Ibn 'Aṭā'illāh al-Iskandarī: Sharḥ Ibn 'Abbād* (Cairo: Mu'assasat al-Ahrām, 1408/1988), 128.

executing all acts of obedience, together with loud and silent invocation according to the instruction of a genuine shaykh, then Allāh Most High—by His special grace—expands his heart, imbuing it with a light. This light is called "light of the intellect" or "the knowledge of certainty" (*'ilm al-yaqīn*). By virtue of this attribute, the traveler attains the perception of divine proximity, through which the traveler perceives that he is close to Allāh Most High at every moment of his life. The effect of this perception is the disappearance of rebellion from the ego: the domination of evil qualities and contamination are broken. Shame will then become dominant. The traveler will abstain from prohibitions and be ever prepared to submit to the commands of Allāh Most High.

When this condition becomes entrenched, Allāh Most High bestows another light on the heart, which is called the "eye of intellect" or "the eye of certainty" (*'ayn al-yaqīn*). By virtue of this light, the traveler sees everything besides Allāh to be non-existent [in essence]. He regards himself and all things to be absolute nothingness [in essence]. After having achieved the first light, the traveler has perceived himself to be in the presence of Allāh Most High, which means that the traveler recognizes his own existence. After acquisition of the second light, the existence of all creation passes into oblivion: only the [absolute] existence of Allāh Most High is in view.

The effects of this witnessing will be total reliance on only Allāh Most High. The traveler will have absolutely no trust in and reliance on anything in creation, and his gaze will remain diverted from all things besides Allāh Most High. On reaching this station (*maqām*), the traveler acquires the attributes of consigning everything to Allāh (*tafwīḍ*), trust in the Divine (*tawakkul*), satisfaction with the divine decree (*riḍā bi 'l-qaḍā'*) and submission (*taslīm*).

Thereafter a third light comes upon the heart. It is called the "Truth of the intellect" or "the Truth of certainty" (*ḥaqq al-yaqīn*). In this state the traveler only witnesses the Being (*dhāt*) of Allāh: neither the existence nor the non-existence of creation remains in view. The traveler perceived the non-existence of all things in the stage of the second light. This leads to the condition in which the traveler still considers his ego, even though it pertains to his non-existence. At this stage he has not yet attained complete annihilation (*fanā'*). The awareness of one's existence and non-existence also constitutes a veil.

The meaning of complete annihilation (*fanā' kāmil*) is to be so absorbed in annihilation that one is not even aware of it. This state is achieved after the traveler has been endowed with the third light. Yet higher than this stage is the rank of subsistence (*baqā'*), where the traveler is returned to creation. A brief explanation of this stage was given earlier.

كَانَ اللّٰهُ وَلَا شَيْءَ مَعَهُ، وَهُوَ الْآنَ عَلٰى مَا عَلَيْهِ كَانَ.

God was, and there was nothing with Him, and He is now as He was. [37]

Since Allāh Most High is eternal, He has always existed. Just as He was unique in His existence prior to the appearance of creation, so too is He after the appearance of creation. No one is associated in His attribute of [necessary] existence.

The traveler who has attained a perfect *fanā'* sees nothing with him besides Allāh Most High. Now he perceives the unique existence of Allāh Most High, because previously he was behind a veil; hence he would perceive other entities along with Allāh's existence. After the lifting of the veil, his spiritual comprehension has been rectified, enabling him to observe the one and unique existence of Allāh Most High.

اَلْعَجَبُ كُلُّ الْعَجَبِ مِمَّنْ يَهْرُبُ مِمَّا لَا انْفِكَاكَ لَهُ عَنْهُ،
وَيَطْلُبُ مَا لَا بَقَاءَ لَهُ مَعَهُ، ﴿فَإِنَّهَا لَا تَعْمَى الْأَبْصَارُ
وَلٰكِنْ تَعْمَى الْقُلُوبُ الَّتِي فِي الصُّدُورِ﴾.

How astonishing is he who flees from what is inescapable and searches for what is evanescent! "For surely it is not the eyes that are blind, but blind are the hearts which are in the breasts." [Q. 22:46] [41]

Man is inseparable from his True Master, Allāh Most High. In spite of this, he seeks to flee. This is most astonishing. His submission to his ego is in fact his attempt to flee from Allāh Most High. Man thus abandons the righteousness that brings him closer to Allāh Most High.

On the other hand, man desires and pursues the world that will perish. This attitude of man is gross stupidity that is the result of spiritual blindness. While they see with their physical eyes, the spiritual vision of their hearts is blinded.

إِنَّمَا يَسْتَوْحِشُ الْعُبَّادُ وَالزُّهَّادُ مِنْ كُلِّ شَيْءٍ لِغَيْبَتِهِمْ عَنِ اللّٰهِ فِي كُلِّ شَيْءٍ، فَلَوْ شَهِدُوهُ فِي كُلِّ شَيْءٍ .. لَمْ يَسْتَوْحِشُوا مِنْ شَيْءٍ.

The devotees and the ascetics are alienated from everything only because of their absence from God in everything. For had they contemplated Him in everything, they would not have been alienated from anything. [115]

The devotees are those who are always engaged in righteous deeds. They consider this to be the medium of divine proximity as they are unaware of the way of divine love and gnosis (*maʿrifa*). The ascetics are those persons who have renounced the world and all its pleasures. They regard their renunciation to be the medium of divine proximity.

The people of divine love and gnosis have no reliance on their righteous deeds, nor do they consider abandonment of a lawful desire to be the medium for the acquisition of the goal. The devotees and ascetics detest association with people and shun even lawful pleasures because they believe these to be impediments in attaining the goal of divine proximity. However, the gaze of the gnostic is only on Allāh Most High. He is not concerned with anything's existence or non-existence. Besides the Lord Himself, the gnostic perceives nothing else. He sees the manifestation of Allāh's attributes in everything. From this angle, then, the gnostic neither detests nor fears anything. At the same time, he has no love for anything.[47]

This attitude of the gnostic should not be misconstrued. It does not mean that he is absolutely devoid of the attributes of love, affection, fear and detestation. It is not possible to entirely eradicate man's natural attributes. However, all the attributes of the gnostic are for the sake of Allāh and from Allāh. The ego has absolutely no influence in the attributes of the gnostic. On the other hand, the devotees and the ascetics will have love and affection for a good act or a saintly man because they see in it or in him benefit for their ego and consider it a medium for divine proximity. Similarly, they

47 The original South African translation presents a lengthy note here clarifying that Gangōhī is not saying that the "way and attitude" of the devotees and ascetics is "erroneous," but merely that the way of the gnostics is "superior"; but both, nevertheless, are saints. It then emphasizes that the "Sunna" calls for the "abandonment of desires, solitude" and firmness in worship, and that most people only attain to gnosis after having "traversed the difficult valleys" of worship and abstinence. See *Ikmālush Shiyam*, 225.

will detest and fear something or someone because they discern harm for themselves therein and believe it to be a cause for distancing themselves from Allāh Most High.

The gnostic has no consideration for his ego. All motives and relationships are negated. Nothing besides Allāh Most High truly exists for him. The ego has no share in anything the gnostic does. The condition of the gnostics is described in the following ḥadīth: "Whoever loves for the sake of Allāh, detests for the sake of Allāh, gives for the sake of Allāh and withholds for the sake of Allāh—verily, he has perfected his faith."[48]

Thus the devotee or ascetic lacking in gnosis is still trapped by the ego. Everything, therefore, is a veil for them; hence they detest and fear objects [of creation].

تَطَلُّعُكَ إِلَى بَقَاءِ غَيْرِهِ دَلِيلٌ عَلَى عَدَمِ وِجْدَانِكَ لَهُ،
وَاسْتِيحَاشُكَ لِفُقْدَانِ مَا سِوَاهُ دَلِيلٌ عَلَى عَدَمِ وُصْلَتِكَ بِهِ.

The proof that you have not found Him is that you strive for the permanency of what is other than He, and the proof that you are not united[49] to Him is that you feel estranged at the loss of what is other than He. [222]

When man desires that a thing remains with him forever—whether it be worldly wealth, property, or spiritual states, unveiling (*kashf*) and miracles (*karāmāt*)—it indicates that he lacks the gift of *wuṣūl* to Allāh. If he had attained *wuṣūl*, his heart would not have hankered after these things. Similarly, when man fears the loss or reduction of these objects, it is indicative of him lacking *wuṣūl*.

If man acquires the true treasure of Divine Proximity, he will never be concerned by the loss of any other object. For example, take a man who possesses a copper coin of insignificant value and a gold coin of considerable value. If he loses the copper coin, but has possession of the gold coin, he will not be perturbed. Yet if such a man became despondent at the loss of a copper coin of insignificant worth, it will be concluded that he does not have gold, hence his concern for the copper. Thus the seeker who lays

48 Narrated by Abū Dāwūd in his *Sunan* (no. 4681) from Abū Umāma ﷺ.
49 For an explanation of being "united" with Allāh, refer to the editor's preface.

claim to Divine Proximity should examine himself on this standard. If he does not hanker after the perpetuation of things nor does the loss of things affect him, then this state of his heart indicates attainment of proximity to Allāh Most High.

مَا تَجِدُهُ الْقُلُوبُ مِنَ الْهُمُومِ وَالْأَحْزَانِ
فَلِأَجْلِ مَا مُنِعَتْهُ مِنْ وُجُودِ الْعِيَانِ.

That which hearts find in the way of worries and sadnesses is due to that which prevents their having inner vision. [224]

All grief, pain and worry experienced by people are due to their deprivation of inner vision. If they possessed this wealth, they would never experience grief and worry. Grief and worry are the consequence of the ego being denied its aims. Therefore a man who is perpetually in the presence of his Master, having become oblivious of the desires and aims of his ego, will always be happy. The heart of the gnostic is illumined with the light of gnosis (*nūr al-maʿrifa*). The world and its pleasures have no worth in his heart; hence he is always in happiness, whether he has material possessions or not. His heart is never grief-stricken.

This condition of spiritual happiness is not negatory of natural emotional feelings. It does not mean that the gnostic will be without emotion even if near and close ones die, or he himself is overtaken by illness and physical pain. Rather, the happiness of the gnostic is everlasting while that of the novice is temporary. In reality, the superficial happiness of the novice is grief and pain.

مَتَى آلَمَكَ عَدَمُ إِقْبَالِ النَّاسِ عَلَيْكَ أَوْ تَوَجُّهُهُمْ بِالذَّمِّ إِلَيْكَ .. فَارْجِعْ
إِلَى عِلْمِ اللهِ فِيكَ، فَإِنْ كَانَ لَا يُقْنِعُكَ عِلْمُهُ .. فَمُصِيبَتُكَ بِعَدَمِ
قَنَاعَتِكَ بِعِلْمِهِ أَشَدُّ مِنْ مُصِيبَتِكَ بِوُجُودِ الْأَذَى مِنْهُمْ.

When it pains you that people do not come to you, or that they do so with rebukes, then return to the knowledge

of God in you. But if the knowledge of Him in you does not satisfy you, then your affliction at not being content with that knowledge is greater than your affliction at the pain coming from people. [234]

The criticism and praise of people are neither harmful nor beneficial. Therefore, when the traveler is pained by the criticism of people, or when they shun him, he should be satisfied with Allāh's awareness of his condition. He should know that since Allāh Most High is aware of his sincerity, and since He accepts his deeds, the criticism and opposition of people cannot harm him in any way whatsoever.

On the other hand, if he is rejected by Allāh Most High, then the praises and support of people will not avail him in any way. The traveler should ingrain this conception in his heart. He will then suffer no grief.

O traveler! If you are not content with Allāh's awareness of your state—but you are grieved on account |of your regard for people's attention, criticism and ignoring—then know that this pain is, in reality, not a hardship. The great calamity, in fact, is the abominable state of your heart: your discontentment and lack of confidence in the knowledge of Allāh Most High. You should reflect and endeavor to discover the cause of this deplorable state of your heart. Why are you concerned with the praise and criticism of people? It does not behoove the traveler to be concerned with and affected by the praise or criticism of people. By Allāh Most High, it will be of no benefit!

مَا حَجَبَكَ عَنِ اللهِ وُجُودُ مَوْجُودٍ مَعَهُ، إِذْ لَا شَيْءَ مَعَهُ، وَلٰكِنْ حَجَبَكَ عَنْهُ تَوَهُّمُ مَوْجُودٍ مَعَهُ.

It is not the existence of any being alongside of Him that veils you from God, for nothing is alongside of Him. Rather, the illusion of a being alongside of Him is what veils you from Him. [137]

An existent being does not veil a person from Allāh nor does it deprive him of divine perception. People that are deprived of divine proximity, dwelling behind the veil of forgetfulness and failing to see beyond material creation, have been cast into deprivation by things that they imagine exist [of their own independence]. Believing non-existents to exist [independently], they lapse into forgetfulness and are deprived of the state of witnessing.

Since the gnostic's gaze is only on Allāh Most High Himself and on the impressions of the divine attributes, he regards the whole universe as the shadow of Allāh's attributes [in the sense that they are evidence of the attributes, and not that the attributes literally cast shadows]. Thus this universe does not constitute a veil for his spiritual vision, just as the reflection or shadow of trees in the water does not impede the motion of the boat. However, if the pilot is overwhelmed by his imagination and believes the shadows to be trees, he will bring the boat to a halt. He will not advance. In his imagination the trees have become obstacles impeding the boat's movement.

The person whose imagination constitutes a veil can also be likened to a man who hears the roaring of the wind outside his home. He imagines it to be the roaring of a lion and remains indoors fearing the lion that he has imagined. This person is prevented from emerging, not by any real existent, but by his baseless imagination.

لَوْلَا ظُهُورُهُ فِي الْمُكَوَّنَاتِ .. مَا وَقَعَ عَلَيْهَا وُجُودُ إِبْصَارٍ، وَلَوْ ظَهَرَتْ
صِفَاتُهُ .. اضْمَحَلَّتْ مُكَوَّنَاتُهُ.

Had it not been for His manifestation in created beings, eyesight would not have perceived them. Had His Qualities been manifested, His created beings would have disappeared. [138]

This subject has already been discussed several times. The entire universe by itself is, in fact, non-existent [in origin]. The only necessary existent is the One, True Existent: Allāh Most High. This very same subject is here presented in another style.

The universe that you behold is, in fact, the reflection of the [command of the] True Existent. If not for the divine illumination and reflection this universe would not have existed.

If the divine attributes had to radiate on the universe without intervening veils, the entire creation would perish. It can never bear the direct radiation of the divine attributes. When the divine illumination appeared on Mount Ṭūr it was reduced to bits and Moses ﷺ fell unconscious.

أَظْهَرَ كُلَّ شَيْءٍ لِأَنَّهُ الْبَاطِنُ، وَطَوٰى وُجُودَ كُلِّ شَيْءٍ لِأَنَّهُ الظَّاهِرُ.

He manifests everything because He is the Interior, and He conceals the existence of everything because He is the Exterior. [139]

The Exterior and The Interior are among the beautiful names of Allāh. Just as Allāh has no partner in His Existence, so too has He no partners in His attributes. The attribute of being "interior" [or "hidden'] dictates that none is associated with His quality of being concealed; He has, therefore, made everything conspicuous. Similarly, His attribute of "exteriority" [or being "manifest'] demands that there be no partner with Him in His quality of being conspicuous; thus He has placed [the reality of] everything in concealment. Only He is truly manifest and truly hidden. The manifestation and concealment of all creation are secondary, allegorical and shadow-like.

إِنَّمَا حَجَبَ الْحَقَّ عَنْكَ شِدَّةُ قُرْبِهِ مِنْكَ. إِنَّمَا احْتَجَبَ لِشِدَّةِ ظُهُورِهِ، وَخَفِيَ عَنِ الْأَبْصَارِ لِعِظَمِ نُورِهِ.

Only His extreme nearness to you is what veils God from you. Only because of the intensity of His manifestation is He veiled, and only because of the sublimity of His light is He hidden from view. [164–165]

Here the Shaykh ﷺ states three reasons why Allāh's true reality is incomprehensible to man's intellect. The first reason is the intensity of His proximity. As explained earlier, only Allāh Most High has true proximity to creation. The reality of this proximity is such that Allāh Most High is closer to us than our own selves. The full comprehension of an object is possible when proximity to and distance from an observer are at the correct degree. If an object is at a great distance, visibility is reduced and it becomes invisible when the distance is excessive. Similarly, an object placed against the eyes cannot be properly seen. The same rule applies to spiritual vision and comprehension.

Now, since Allāh Most High is closer to the servant than his own being, neither his physical faculty of vision nor his spiritual faculty of vision can comprehend Him. No one, therefore, can comprehend Him. Even the comprehension of Allāh Most High by His saints is infinitesimal because of His closeness. Thus, extreme proximity constitutes a veil. This is one reason for man's inability to comprehend Allāh Most High.

Another reason is that Allāh is more conspicuous than everything else. As a result of intense manifestation, He is beyond the comprehension of the physical and spiritual eyes. The gaze of man is unable to stare even at the sun by virtue of the intensity of its illumination although the sun is a lowly creature of Allāh Most High. What then can be imagined of the light of the Creator? Indeed, it is a limitless manifestation. The witnessing, proximity and arrival that the sufis experience are simply the [experiencing of the] certainty of His Being and of their perception of closeness to Him. Total comprehension of the Divine Being is an impossible.

كَيْفَ يَحْتَجِبُ الْحَقُّ بِشَيْءٍ، وَالَّذِي يَحْتَجِبُ
بِهِ هُوَ فِيهِ ظَاهِرٌ، وَمَوْجُودٌ حَاضِرٌ؟

How can God be veiled by something, for He is apparent and has actual being in that wherewith He is veiled? [218]

An object cannot be comprehended or perceived on account of two reasons: one, intensity of proximity and manifestation; two, being distant. The first is confirmed for the Essence of Allāh, but the second does not apply to Him.

Here the Shaykh رحمه الله states that it is inconceivable that Allāh Most High be veiled by anything or at a distance from anything. Allāh's illumination is conspicuous, even in an object that is regarded to be a veil. He exists, is present and is conspicuous, and therefore nothing can veil Him. Every object is a reflection of His beauty and splendor.

The stray thoughts (*wasāwis*) are to be regarded by the traveler as a veil caused by the impoverished state of his spiritual insight. If this insight is correct, then stray thoughts will not perturb him nor appear as a veil.

أَبَاحَ لَكَ أَنْ تَنْظُرَ مَا فِي الْمُكَوَّنَاتِ، وَمَا أَذِنَ لَكَ أَنْ تَقِفَ مَعَ ذَوَاتِ
الْمُكَوَّنَاتِ، ﴿قُلِ انْظُرُوا مَاذَا فِي السَّمٰوَاتِ﴾، فَبِقَوْلِهِ: ﴿قُلِ انْظُرُوا

مَاذَا فِي السَّمٰوَاتِ﴾ فَتَحَ لَكَ بَابَ الْأَفْهَامِ، وَلَمْ يَقُلْ: انْظُرُوا السَّمٰوَاتِ لِئَلَّا يَدُلَّكَ عَلٰى وُجُودِ الْأَجْرَامِ.

He has permitted you to reflect on what is in created beings, but He has not allowed you to stop at the selfsame creatures. "Say: Behold what is in the heavens and the earth!" [Q. 10:101] Thus, with His words, "Behold what is in the heavens," He opened up the door of instruction for you. But He did not say, "Behold the heavens," so as not to lead you to the mere existence of bodies. [140]

Allāh Most High has instructed man to recognize the beauties and splendor of Allāh's attributes by meditating on His creation. However, man has not been instructed to confine his gaze to the outer manifestations of the physical objects only, because viewing creation in this manner constitutes a veil for the inner recognition of Allāh Most High; and such a gaze upon only the scenery [of creation] is to dwell in forgetfulness.

The verse of the Qur'ān [here quoted] is the proof for the need to look beyond the mere presence of objects. The command is to here meditate on the attributes of Allāh Most High that are displayed *in* the created objects present in the heavenly realm. The order is not, however, to simply view the heavens. The contemplative study of these created objects is to open up a wonderful vista of understanding, in which one progresses past witnessing the creation to actually witnessing the Creator.

The material objects are in reality non-existent, because they have no independent existence. They are the veils of Allāh Most High. The purpose of looking at them is to find a way toward the Creator.

اَلْأَكْوَانُ ثَابِتَةٌ بِإِثْبَاتِهِ وَمَمْحُوَّةٌ بِأَحَدِيَّةِ ذَاتِهِ.

The Universe is permanent through His making it permanent, and it is annihilated by the Unity of His Essence. [141]

By itself, creation has no existence. Its existence is like a shadow and reflection, and only gained through the divine command.

If the gaze is directed to His absolute Unity, then creation is absolutely annihilated. This concept should not be misunderstood. It should not be inferred that the creation is Allāh or that Allāh incarnates creation—we seek refuge in Allāh! Indeed, the Creator forever remains the Creator and the creation forever remains the creation, and the two can never fuse.

When a person is not endowed with spiritual insight, he is neither able to comprehend transcendental and spiritual realities nor to employ intelligence. When Allāh Most High graces man with spiritual vision, these mysteries become clear.[50]

أَمَرَكَ فِي هٰذِهِ الدَّارِ بِالنَّظَرِ فِي مُكَوَّنَاتِهِ، وَسَيَكْشِفُ
لَكَ فِي تِلْكَ الدَّارِ عَنْ كَمَالِ ذَاتِهِ.

He commanded you in this world to reflect upon His creations; but in the Hereafter He will reveal to you the Perfection of His Essence. [116]

Allāh Most High has ordered His servants to reflect and ponder on His creation so that they acknowledge Him and understand His attributes of knowledge, power and wisdom. After meditation, when belief has become grounded, the servant will gain the ability to perceive the manifestation of the [signs of the] divine attributes in Allāh's creation. After contemplating and meditating on the attributes, he will witness Allāh with his spiritual vision.

In this earthly abode, the servant is only able to perceive the divine illumination with the eyes of the heart; however, soon [in the Hereafter] the Lord Himself will become manifest. However, the vision of Allāh with the physical eyes in the Hereafter will be in proportion to the spiritual vision of man here on earth. The greater the perception with the inner eyes here on earth, the greater will be man's physical vision of Allāh in the Hereafter.[51]

---

50 For a relevant discussion of reality and the meaning of the divine name *al-Ḥaqq* (The Truth) see Ghazālī, *The Ninety-Nine Beautiful Names*, 124–126.

51 Imām Ṭaḥāwī discusses the beatific vision in the next world: "The 'Seeing of Allāh by the People of the Garden' is true, without their vision being all-encompassing and without the manner of their vision being known. . . A man's belief in the 'seeing of Allāh by the people of the Garden' is incorrect if he tries to imagine what it is like or interprets it according to his own understanding. For the interpretation of this 'seeing,' indeed the meaning of any of the subtle phenomena which are in the realm of Lordship, can only be achieved by strict submission. Interpretation must be avoided. Those who do not avoid negating Allāh's attributes and of likening Allāh to something

عَلِمَ مِنْكَ أَنَّكَ لَا تَصْبِرُ عَنْهُ، فَأَشْهَدَكَ مَا بَرَزَ مِنْهُ.

When He knew that you would not renounce Him,[52] He made you contemplate that which issues from Him. [117]

The true believers have an intense love for Allāh Most High, as Allāh Most High has described them in the Qur'ān [at 2:165]. Allāh Most High is the true love, and every one [of the believers] loves Him. The lover can have no rest without seeing his Beloved. However, the vision of Allāh Most High in this world is not permitted due to the limitations of this lowly physical existence.

Allāh Most High was ever aware that His lovers would be restless because of their inability to see Him. He, therefore, displayed the illumination of [the knowledge of] Himself and His attributes from behind the veils of His creation to enable the believer to perceive Him according to the degree of his spiritual vision. Every believer enjoys a degree of this witnessing. Thus belief in the Divine Being is common to all believers. This belief is also a kind of witnessing.

The grace of Allāh focuses more on some believers, hence they have greater spiritual witnessing. The degree of their spiritual certitude is similar to physical vision for which there is no need to adduce any proof. The lovers of Allāh derive contentment from this witnessing. If this spiritual witnessing was not vouchsafed to them, they would have become destroyed and annihilated.

In the Hereafter, however, they will be blessed with the great fortune of beholding Allāh Most High.

---

else, have gone astray and have failed to understand Allāh's Glory. For our Lord, the Glorified and the Exalted, can only be described in terms of Oneness and Absolute Singularity. No creation is in any way like Him." See points 35 and 37 in Ṭaḥāwī, *Islamic Belief.*

52 According to Islamic theology, Allāh and His Attributes are eternal. Consequently, it should be noted that His knowledge is, likewise, an eternal attribute which entails that Allāh has *always* known *everything* that is necessary, impossible and possible, without ever being ignorant of anything—and this shall always be the case. So the use of language in this aphorism should not be misunderstood as implying that Allāh or His attributes (in this case His knowledge) are subject to imperfection at any moment: it is merely a figure of speech. See the commentary of point 28 of *Jawharat al-Tawḥīd* of Laqānī.

أَنْتَ مَعَ الْأَكْوَانِ مَا لَمْ تَشْهَدِ الْمُكَوِّنَ، فَإِذَا

شَهِدْتَهُ .. كَانَتِ الْأَكْوَانُ مَعَكَ.

So long as you have not contemplated the Creator, you
belong to created beings; but when you have contemplated Him, created beings belong to you. [247]

As long as man is unable to recognize Allāh Himself and His attributes
in creation, and the gaze of his heart remains confined to creation, he will
remain subservient to creation. Those engrossed in wealth, children and land
will remain entrapped in these worldly pursuits. They will be the worshippers
of materialism. Those pursuing fame will be subservient to this pursuit. In
short, if the pursuit is not Allāh Most High, man will remain the slave of
whatever he is pursuing.

When man recognizes that creation is the substratum for the manifestation of Allāh's illumination and all things besides Allāh are banished from
his mind, then the entire creation becomes subservient to this servant, who,
from that moment, gains independence from creation.

When creation becomes subservient to man, his love permeates the
hearts of others. They all love him while there is no room in his heart for
anyone's love. He remains aloof from everyone and everything besides Allāh
Most High.[53]

مَنْ عَرَفَ الْحَقَّ .. شَهِدَهُ فِي كُلِّ شَيْءٍ، وَمَنْ فَنِيَ بِهِ .. غَابَ عَنْ كُلِّ

شَيْءٍ، وَمَنْ أَحَبَّهُ .. لَمْ يُؤْثِرْ عَلَيْهِ شَيْئًا.

He who knows God contemplates Him in everything. He
who is extinguished by Him is absent from everything.
He who loves Him prefers nothing to Him. [163]

Here, the Shaykh 🙏 discusses gnosis (ma'rifa), fanā' and love (maḥabba).

---

53 The seemingly absolutist terms of the commentary here should neither be taken literally
nor out of context. As highlighted by Gangōhī earlier in the work, human sentiments are natural,
and they are acceptable as long as the love of matters other than Allāh do not exceed or compete
with one's love for the Divine.

The signs of the person who has acquired these three stages are explained. The three stages are mentioned in order of priority.

When, by virtue of Allāh's grace, a man is made a perfect gnostic, then there is nothing in creation that can prevent him from being spiritually aware of his Lord, in a manner that is not characteristic of normal human beings. He does not regard everything non-existent, as does one who is in the stage of *fanā'* and has not yet reached the stage of *baqā'*. Since the gnostic is annihilated from all things and perpetually aware of Allāh Most High and His attributes, he sees everything. However, his gaze upon created objects does not deflect his invocation of Allāh, as is the case with people in general; rather, he is able to perceive Allāh's attributes in all of creation.

The one in the stage of *fanā'* does not see anything, since he has disappeared from all and everything, so much so that he becomes oblivious of his own existence. On earth, if a person is in love with someone, the beloved is constantly in his mind and heart. In spite of others being in his presence, he remains detached from them and sometimes is not even aware of their presence.

When a man who has not yet attained the stage of *fanā'* loves Allāh, then he will not give preference to creation over Allāh, despite still witnessing the existence of creation. He will accord priority to the pleasure of Allāh Most High and crush his own desires.

اَلنَّعِيـــمُ وإِنْ تَنَوَّعَتْ مَظَاهِرُهُ إِنَّمَا هُوَ بِشُـــهُودِهِ وَاقْتِرَابِهِ، وَالْعَذَابُ وَإِنْ تَنَوَّعَتْ مَظَاهِرُهُ إِنَّمَا هُوَ لِوُجُودِ حِجَابِهِ، فَسَبَبُ الْعَذَابِ وُجُودُ الْحِجَابِ، وإِتْمَامُ النَّعِيمِ بِالنَّظَرِ إِلَى وَجْهِ اللّٰهِ الْكَرِيمِ.

While varied in its manifestations, felicity is only for the sake of contemplating and drawing near to Him; and, while varied in its manifestations, suffering is due only to the existence of His veil. Therefore, the existence of the veil is the cause of the suffering, and the perfection of felicity is through the vision of the Countenance of God, the Generous. [223]

Things are the medium for the heart to derive comfort and pleasure, as well as hurt and grief by way of punishment.

There are numerous worldly objects of comfort and happiness, such as a spouse, children, wealth, prestige, etc. However, true happiness only occurs if inner witnessing of the Divine accompanies the use of these objects of pleasure.

If this inner state of witnessing Allāh Most High does not accompany the use of these things, then these things are a punishment, even if one derives happiness at the time and does understand their reality. But soon will one comprehend the reality. Sometimes this punishment becomes manifest here on earth, when these material possessions are lost or when one is no longer capable of utilizing them. Grief then overwhelms a person.

Assuming that he is not overtaken by this punishment during his lifetime, then at the time of death he will be forced to leave everything. At that critical juncture, he will experience absolute regret and suffering.

On the contrary, if inner witnessing accompanies these pleasures and comforts, then even when man is separated from them he is still in possession of inner tranquility, because he has arrived at the knowledge of Allah. Such a state of comfort and happiness is perpetual for the one who has arrived at this spiritual station.

There are numerous hardships and pain in this world, such as sickness, poverty, starvation, etc. Furthermore, the Hereafter possesses a variety of chastisements. Yet, true punishment is when man undergoes these trials while deprived of witnessing the Divine. When such a person is veiled and far from Allāh, then these difficulties will be an absolute punishment.

However, these similar trials will not be a hardship for the person with the wealth of witnessing and arrival, even though they have the external form of it. This is due to the fact that happiness and grief is in the heart, and his heart is full of joy with the Divine. The man in whose heart there exists the treasure of inner witnessing and arrival will never be prepared to exchange his hardships for a world full of comforts and pleasures if the price he has to pay is the loss of the spiritual treasure he possesses. Thus, true suffering and punishment for such a person is being deprived of proximity to Allāh, and true felicity for him is the wealth of inner perception.

اَلْكَائِنُ فِي الْكَوْنِ، وَلَمْ تُفْتَحْ لَهُ مَيَادِينُ الْغُيُوبِ،
مَسْجُونٌ بِمُحِيطَاتِهِ، وَمَحْصُورٌ فِي هَيْكَلِ ذَاتِهِ.

So long as the domains of the Invisible Worlds have not been revealed to him, the being in the Cosmos is imprisoned by his surroundings and confined in the temple of his nature. [246]

A man born on earth and entrapped in forgetfulness is diverted from Allāh Most High. In consequence, he is deprived of spiritual knowledge and insight. Such a person dwells within the confines of his lowly desires. He remains unaware of the spacious field of Divine Unity (*tawḥīd*). He wanders aimlessly in his own existence, in circles, never progressing beyond his starting point. All his efforts are for the sake of his ego.

In contrast to this slave of the ego is the traveler who has emerged from these lowly confines and is progressing in the vast planes of Divine Unity. He has attained freedom from the narrow limits of the desires of his ego and imaginary ideas. He has acquired a pure, holy and free life. He does not suffer grief as a result of worldly hardships and events. Changing conditions do not overwhelm him. In fact, he dominates. He is sustained by the attributes of Allāh Most High. His existence is not coupled to worldly objects. Although he may appear to be affected superficially by worldly circumstances, his heart is as firm as a mountain.

27

ON THE SPECIAL TRAITS OF THE GNOSTICS

مَا الْعَارِفُ مَنْ إِذَا أَشَـارَ .. وَجَدَ الْحَقَّ أَقْرَبَ إِلَيْهِ مِنْ إِشَـارَتِهِ، بَلِ الْعَارِفُ مَنْ لَا إِشَارَةَ لَهُ، لِفَنَائِهِ فِي وُجُودِهِ وَانْطِوَائِهِ فِي شُهُودِهِ.

The gnostic is not one who, when he makes a symbolic allusion, finds God nearer to himself than his allusion. Rather, the gnostic is he who has no symbolic allusion due to his self-extinction in His Being and self-absorption in contemplating Him. [77]

Before expounding on this topic, it is necessary to present a few points.

Firstly, the servant in the state of *fanā'* is like a dead body in the hands of a living person. The dead body has neither movement nor rest of its own; rather, it is moved by the will of the living. Thus the person of *fanā'* is completely subservient to the will of Allāh, since he does not discern any attribute in himself. He is even oblivious of his own existence. He dwells only in the witnessing of the One Being as the true enactor of all actions and attributes. The adequate description of this state of the traveler comes in the ḥadīth that says: "With Me he hears and with Me he sees."[54]

---

54 This is a reference to a longer famous ḥadīth which is a wonderful summation of the spiritual path of Islam: Abū Hurayra ﵁ narrates that the Messenger of Allāh ﷺ said, "Allāh, exalted is He, said, 'Whoever shows enmity to a close friend of Mine, then I declare war on him. My slave does not draw closer to Me with anything more beloved to Me than that which I made obligatory upon him. My slave continues to draw closer with optional extra acts until I love him. When I love him, *I am his hearing with which he hears, his sight with which he sees,* his hand with which he grasps and his foot with which he walks. If he asks Me I will definitely give him, and if he seeks refuge with Me I will definitely give him refuge'" (*Bukhārī*). Ibn Rajab writes in explanation of this ḥadīth: "whoever exerts himself to draw closer to Allāh by [performance of] the obligatory acts and moreover with optional extra acts, then He will draw him closer to Him, and make him

Secondly, when a man speaks about an object there are three things present in his mind: the speaker, the discussion and the object of discussion.

Thirdly, [one must consider] the extreme proximity of Allāh to His servant. Indeed, as explained earlier, He is closer to man than himself. [Usually,] when remembering something, the implication is that there is some distance between the one remembering and the one being remembered. Also, in such cases, there is the presupposition between the two. Thus when a man remembers the Divine Unity, it implies that his ego has not yet been annihilated.

Fourthly, in the terminology of the sufis, "allusion" (*ishāra*) means to remember or discuss the of Divine Unity that are inspired in the heart. If in the course of such discourse the gnostic finds Allāh Most High closer to himself than his allusion, then it is clear that he has not yet attained any rank in *fanā'*. The gnostic in the course of such discourses should not be like a lecturer who has in mind the three matters usual to normal discourse.

The condition of the gnostic should be one of absolute closeness to Allāh Most High. True annihilation is only when there remains absolutely no duality in the gnostic's mind. There should be no difference and distance in his mind regarding his discourse of Allāh's Oneness. His state of *fanā'* should be absolute absorption and annihilation in the witnessing of Allāh Most High. In spite of his discourse on Oneness he should remain unaware thereof. While he is ostensibly a speaker, he in reality speaks by another power. He is like a lifeless man in the power of a living being.

مَطْلَبُ الْعَارِفِينَ مِنَ اللّٰهِ تَعَالَى الصِّدْقُ فِي
الْعُبُودِيَّةِ وَالْقِيَامُ بِحُقُوقِ الرُّبُوبِيَّةِ.

That which the gnostics seek from God is sincerity in servanthood and performance of the claims of Lordship. [79]

The gnostics only supplicate to Allāh for these two things mentioned in this aphorism. They are not motivated by the bounties of this world or the Garden.

---

ascend from the degree of *īmān* to the degree of *iḥsān* so that he will come to worship Allāh in presence and in vigilant watchfulness as if he sees Him, and so that his heart will fill with gnosis of Allāh, exalted is He, His love, His greatness, fear of Him, awe of Him, magnification of Him, intimacy with Him, and longing for Him until this gnosis which is in his heart becomes the act of witnessing Him with inner sight. . ." See Ibn Rajab, *Compendium*, 617 and 629.

The attributes of servanthood include: gratitude for bounties; patience in adversity; love and hatred for the sake of Allāh only; annihilation of [total reliance upon] one's schemes and plans; contentment with the divine will; maintaining the heart's gaze and attention constantly on Allāh Most High; the acquisition of humility; dependency on only Him; and fearing Him.

The claims of Lordship mean that the gnostics expend themselves in the performance of acts of worship, while maintaining the spiritual body (*rūḥ*) in the perpetual invocation of Allāh.

These two desires alone are the primary motives of the gnostics, while others follow their emotional desires: seeking the things of this world or the next world [like the damsels and mansions of Paradise], or spiritual states [like inspirations and miracles], or pursue customary knowledge while turning away from the knowledge of reality.

اَلْعَارِفُ لَا يَزُولُ اضْطِرَارُهُ، وَلَا يَكُونُ مَعَ غَيْرِ اللّٰهِ قَرَارُهُ.

The imperative need of the gnostic never vanishes, nor is his repose in anyone but God. [103]

The gnostic is fully aware of his ego and its attributes. The greater his insight and recognition of his ego the greater will be his gnosis of Allāh Most High. In this regard a ḥadīth says: "Whoever has recognized his self has recognized his Lord.'[55] The gnostic thus views his ego as an embodiment of defect and evil since its aim, at every moment, is to gain the pleasures of the world. The gnostic, being fully aware of this corrupt state of the ego, diverts his attention at all times to Allāh Most High. He remains restless and supplicates to Allāh Most High to aid and save him from the evil of the ego. This attitude becomes an inseparable quality of the gnostic.

Since the aim of the gnostic is to worship Allāh, he cannot find rest in anything besides Allāh. His heart finds support with only Allāh Most High.

---

55 Sakhāwī relates from Abū 'l-Muẓaffar ibn al-Samʿānī that this ḥadīth is not known through any chain that reaches the Prophet ﷺ; rather, it has been related from Yaḥyā ibn Muʿādh al-Rāzī. Nawawī has similarly said that it is not established (Sakhāwī, *Al-Maqāṣid al-Ḥasana*) and Ṣaghānī (and a number of others) have considered it to be a fabrication (*Mawḍūʿāt al-Ṣaghānī*). ʿAjlūnī discusses this ḥadīth in detail and mentions that Suyūṭī has written a treatise on it entitled *Al-Qawl al-Ashbah fi Ḥadīth Man ʿArafa Nafsahū ʿArafa Rabbah* (which forms part of his *Al-Ḥawī li 'l-Fatāwā*). He then quotes that in Māwardī's *Adab al-Dīn wa 'l-Dunya* a similar meaning has been related from the Prophet ﷺ by ʿĀ'isha (see ʿAjlūnī, *Kashf al-Khafā'*). Ghazālī uses the ḥadīth as an aphorism without attributing it to the Prophet ﷺ (see Ghazālī, "Condemnation of Self-Delusion," *Iḥyā' ʿUlūm al-Dīn*).

اَلزُّهَّادُ إِذَا مُدِحُوا .. انْقَبَضُوا لِشُهُودِهِمُ الثَّنَاءَ مِنَ الْخَلْقِ، وَالْعَارِفُونَ إِذَا مُدِحُوا .. انْبَسَطُوا لِشُهُودِهِمْ ذٰلِكَ مِنَ الْمَلِكِ الْحَقِّ.

When ascetics are praised, they are contracted, for they witness the praise as coming from mankind; but when gnostics are praised, they are expanded, for they witness the praise as coming from the Real King. [146]

The veil of other-than-Allāh is in the view of the spiritual insight of the ascetic. He therefore flees from every worldly object because he regards them to be a veil screening him from Allāh. When someone praises him, then his heart is grieved, because he deems the praise to be the act of the one praising, and so he fears being entrapped in corruption. It should be understood that this idea of the ascetic is actually correct, because praise does corrupt many people.

Nevertheless, since the gaze of the gnostic is perpetually on only Allāh, he sees everything with the gaze of reality and truth. He understands all actions as being the emanation of Allāh's power and His display of marvels. When someone praises the gnostic, he then understands the praise as an emanation of Allāh. He therefore feels elated. In this state of elation he experiences further spiritual progress. Such praise does not affect him adversely because his ego has already been annihilated. The pleasures of the world no longer pose attractions for him. The danger of vanity and self-esteem does not exist in relation to the gnostic. His pleasure when being praised is purely for the sake of Allāh. It is, therefore, not detrimental to him.

When a man praised someone in his presence, the Messenger of Allāh ﷺ said: "Woe upon you! You have cut the throat of your brother."[56] In view of the fact that such high-ranking gnostics, devoid of all vestiges of the ego, are extremely rare, this ḥadīth has in general declared praise to be a trial [which corrupts the ego].

---

56 Nawawī includes in its entirety the ḥadīth referred to above: "Mention of a man was made to Allāh's Messenger ﷺ and someone praised him whereupon he ﷺ said, 'Woe be to you! You have broken the neck of your friend!' He repeated this several times and added, 'If one of you has to praise his friend at all, he should say: "I reckon him to be such and such and Allāh knows him well," if you think him to be so-and-so, you will be accountable to Allāh because no one can testify the purity of others against Allāh'" (*Bukhārī* and *Muslim* on the authority of Abū Bakra). See *Riyāḍ us-Ṣāliḥīn*, trans. Muhammad Amin and Abu Usamah Al-Arabi bin Razduq (Riyadh: Darussalam, 1998), 1331-2.

28

ON INTUITIVE KNOWLEDGE AND REASONING

مَنْ رَأَيْتَهُ مُجِيبًا عَنْ كُلِّ مَا سُئِلَ، وَمُعَبِّرًا عَنْ كُلِّ مَا شَهِدَ،

وَذَاكِرًا كُلَّ مَا عَلِمَ .. فَاسْتَدِلَّ بِذٰلِكَ عَلَى وُجُودِ جَهْلِهِ.

Infer the existence of ignorance in anyone whom you see answering all that he is asked or giving expression to all that he witnesses or mentioning all that he knows. [70]

A SUFI OR TRAVELER who answers every question posed to him, never proclaiming his lack of knowledge on any matter, and who reveals his spiritual experiences is in fact an ignoramus. Only a being whose knowledge encompasses everything has the ability to answer every question, and this attribute belongs exclusively to Allāh Most High, the Knower of the Visible and the Unseen. Man's knowledge is meager in comparison.

It is also necessary for the scholar (*ʿālim*) to take into account the intellectual capacity of the one who poses a question to him, and answer in an appropriate manner. Thus, if he discerns a lack of comprehension in the questioner, then he should refrain from answering.

When the traveler reveals the mysteries and subtleties that he has acquired along the path, he betrays his ignorance, because spiritual secrets and knowledge are a trust (*amāna*) from Allāh Most High; as such, the disclosure of them is an abuse of that trust. In addition, people will not be equipped to handle such mysteries because their inner perception has not been developed, so the words will be incomprehensible to them. Words cannot convey the meanings of this affair [of *taṣawwuf*]. Moreover, the disclosure of such secrets to the unprepared and ignorant can be detrimental, and may lead to strife due to the audience misconstruing the actual meaning of the words uttered. Consequently, silence is a much more suitable course of action for the traveler; it is, in fact, imperative.

مِنْ عَلَامَاتِ النُّجْحِ فِي النِّهَايَاتِ الرُّجُوعُ إِلَى اللهِ فِي الْبِدَايَاتِ.

Amongst the signs of success at the end is the turning to God at the beginning. [26]

Just as there is a beginning to any matter, there is also an end; and the Path is the same: it has the initiation and the goal. The goal of the Path is known as *wuṣūl* (arrival) and *mushāhada* (witnessing).

When the traveler turns to Allāh in the beginning of his journey and relies on Him alone in every affair, without reliance upon himself or his spiritual efforts and struggles, it indicates that he will achieve success in reaching the end of the Path.

If in the beginning the traveler is deceived by his own efforts, believing that he will attain perfection thereby, or he hankers after lofty spiritual stations only, he will fail to reach the true goal—even though he acquires knowledge of the ultimate goal by virtue of his association with a shaykh. It is, therefore, imperative that the traveler seeks Allāh's aid in everything. He should at no time consider his efforts of spiritual struggle (*mujāhada*) to be significant. Moreover, his quest should only be Allāh Most High. This is the basic principle of the Path.

مَنْ أَشْرَقَتْ بِدَايَتُهُ .. أَشْرَقَتْ نِهَايَتُهُ.

He who is illumined at the beginning is illumined at the end. [27]

In the beginning, the traveler's spiritual affairs are connected with deeds and forms of invocation (*awrād*). These acts are related to the physical body. In the final stage these affairs are transferred from the physical body to the spiritual body—the spirit. In other words, the heart becomes radiant with lights and gnosis, and spiritual activity is performed in the heart.

The traveler who spends his time constructively in the beginning, adorning his state with obedience and worship and refraining from futility, will be successful in the end. The sun of spiritual illuminations and gnosis will rise in him.

On the other hand, the one who is indolent and lethargic in the beginning, refraining from steadfastness and regularity in observing obedience and worship, will have a weak end. The perfection of the final stage is dependent on the perfection of the initial stage.

مَنْ وَجَدَ ثَمَرَةَ عَمَلِهِ عَاجِلًا .. فَهُوَ دَلِيلٌ عَلَى وُجُودِ الْقَبُولِ آجِلًا.

Whoever finds the fruit of his deeds coming quickly has proof of the existence of acceptance. [72]

Although the true reward for worship is obtainable in the Hereafter, many servants of Allāh acquire a reward while on earth. Such reward [here called "the fruit of his deeds'] is the heart's experience of pleasure and sweetness while engaging in the acts of righteousness. This is a proof of the acceptance of his deeds in the Hereafter, and their ensuing reward.

However, the pleasure of worship should not be understood as a goal, for such a pursuit is a negation of sincerity. Worship should be rendered for the pleasure of Allāh Most High, irrespective of any pleasure or displeasure to the ego. Thus the traveler should worship in all states and circumstances.

Should the traveler perform an act of worship while not experiencing a sweetness and pleasure, he should not conclude that the act is to be worthless in the Hereafter. The fruit of his deeds is merely a sign of acceptance, but it is not a condition (*sharṭ*) or cause of acceptance. Often an act devoid of pleasure [to one] is more acceptable to Allāh Most High than an act in which one derives sweetness and pleasure.

وِجْدَانُ ثَمَرَاتِ الطَّاعَاتِ عَاجِلًا بَشَائِرُ
الْعَامِلِينَ بِوُجُودِ الْجَزَاءِ عَلَيْهَا آجِلًا.

For those who do good, finding the fruits of acts of obedience in this world is glad tidings of their recompense in the Hereafter. [251]

Those who at the outset experience the sweetness of their efforts should rejoice at attaining His vision (*mushāhada*). Whoever does not experience this should not despair of Allāh's mercy, for Allāh sends a breeze that blows over the hearts and they find themselves in the morning by the Knower of the Hidden (*'Allām al-Ghuyūb*).

Or you can say, whoever finds the fruits of his acts in this world he should [also] rejoice at finding the rewards of his acts later in the Hereafter... However, this reward at which he rejoices should not be intended or sought, so that it does not damage his sincerity.[57]

إِذَا أَرَدْتَ أَنْ تَعْرِفَ قَدْرَكَ عِنْدَهُ .. فَانْظُرْ فِي مَاذَا يُقِيمُكَ.

If you want to know your standing with Him, look at where He has made you abide now. [73]

The servant that desires to know if Allāh has accepted or rejected him, and whether he is fortunate or unfortunate, should ponder on his own condition. He should look at the activity in which Allāh Most High has placed him. If he is involved in noble acts that he executes for the sake of Allāh's pleasure, he should understand that he might be of the accepted-ones—and in such a situation he is a man of fortune. If he is involved in disobedience and transgression, then he should fear that he stands rejected by Allāh Most High—as such, he is most unfortunate.

اَلْحُزْنُ عَلَى فُقْدَانِ الطَّاعَةِ مَعَ عَدَمِ النُّهُوضِ
إِلَيْهَا مِنْ عَلَامَاتِ الْإِغْتِرَارِ.

One of the signs of delusion is sadness over the loss of obedience coupled with the absence of resolve to bring it back to life. [76]

Some people grieve much because they lack in obedience and virtues. They even shed tears in profusion. Despite their grief, they do not initiate the process of worship nor do they abstain from sins. Such sorrow is false and the deception of the ego. True regret leads one to practice virtue and shun evil.

57 Both the aphorism and commentary are missing from Gangōhī's work and the commentary added here is from Ibn 'Ajība (*Īqāẓ al-Himam fī Sharḥ al-Ḥikam* 399).

مِنْ عَلَامَاتِ إِقَامَةِ الْحَقِّ لَكَ فِي الشَّيْءِ
إِدَامَتُهُ إِيَّاكَ فِيهِ مَعَ حُصُولِ النَّتَائِجِ.

A sign that it is God who has put you in a certain state is that He keeps you in it while its fruits mature. [180]

When Allāh Most High establishes a servant in a certain situation—be it a worldly occupation [such as trade, farming or employment] or a religious state [such as learning or renunciation of the worldly agencies]—and the fruits of this state are also experienced, then it is the sign of Allāh's pleasure for the state of the servant: that Allāh loves him to remain in this state, provided that his occupation does not interfere with any religious duties. Since Allāh Most High sees goodness for the servant in this condition, He keeps him involved therein. The servant should, therefore, neither wish to be extricated from his occupation nor should he attempt to withdraw from it. He should be grateful to Allāh Most High and remain in his occupation.

مِنْ عَلَامَاتِ اتِّبَاعِ الْهَوَى الْمُسَارَعَةُ إِلَى نَوَافِلِ
الْخَيْرَاتِ، وَالتَّكَاسُلُ عَنِ الْقِيَامِ بِالْوَاجِبَاتِ.

A sign of compliance with passion is haste in supererogatory good deeds and sluggishness in fulfilling obligatory deeds. [193]

Some people who exhibit considerable enthusiasm for supererogatory worship—such as litanies, fasting and ritual prayer—are lax in the performance of obligatory duties. They are, for example, lax in paying their debts and fulfilling the rights of others. They do not attach importance to the obligation of pilgrimage to Mecca (*ḥajj*), or they fail to pay the poor-due tax (*zakāt*) that they owe for previous years, or they do not seek pardon from people whom they have wronged. This attitude is a deception of the ego. In such circumstances, the enthusiasm for optional acts is subservience to base desires of the ego. The ego loves fame that is acquired by indulgence in supererogatory worship.

Of what benefit will optional acts be when one is loaded with the liability of compulsory duties? Supererogatory worship is like the profit in trade, while the obligations are like the [essential] capital. Thus, the compulsory acts have priority over the optional acts.

مَا اسْتُوْدِعَ فِي غَيْبِ السَّرَائِرِ .. ظَهَرَ فِي شَهَادَةِ الظَّوَاهِرِ.

Whatever is deposited in the invisible world of innermost hearts is manifested in the visible world of phenomena. [28]

A sign of a man of spiritual accomplishment is that the blessings and impressions of the lights and gnosis hidden in his heart become conspicuous on his face, hands and feet.

29

ON EXHORTATION AND ITS EFFECT ON THE HEART

مَنْ أُذِنَ لَهُ فِي التَّعْبِيرِ .. فُهِمَتْ فِي مَسَامِعِ
الْخَلْقِ عِبَارَتُهُ، وَجُلِّيَتْ إِلَيْهِمْ إِشَارَتُهُ.

Whoever has been given permission to speak out will have his expression understood by his listeners, and his symbolic allusion will be clear to them. [184]

THE SPIRITUAL MYSTERIES that are inspired by Allāh Most High in the hearts of his close servants are secret trusts, the revelation of which is not permissible without divine consent; hence the gnostics do not reveal the divine mysteries entrusted to them without this special consent.

Those who are granted this permission are such men whose speech is for the sake of Allāh only. There is no vestige of their ego associated with their speech. They do not speak of their own accord. They are instruments in the divine will. While it superficially appears as if they are speaking, the speech in fact is a divine inspiration.

The speech of such august personalities consists of two kinds: clear speech with no ambiguity (*taṣrīḥ*); and speech that is ambiguous in outward meaning, which is essentially communicated by symbolic allusion (*ishāra*).

The nature of *taṣrīḥ* is that it is easily understood by people upon hearing it. The nature of *ishāra* is that it is clear and evident to the audience, even when the meaning is not fully comprehended.

Since the speech of the gnostics is by Allāh's command, and the underlying purpose is to benefit others, the audience readily understands what is being conveyed of the divine mysteries, even when the use of symbolic allusion is the method of conveying. Such expounders are mere instruments for the divine will, from which the speech emanates and settles into the hearts of the listeners like torrents of rain.

On the contrary, the talk of a man who is not divinely authorized to divulge divine mysteries will not strike a responsive chord in the hearts of the audience. People will not understand his discourse on higher spiritual realities and gnosis. Furthermore, he will not be able to present a simple exposition. He will speak laboriously and in circles. The minds of people will not incline to accept his speech nor will they be impressed.

It is incumbent for the traveler to refrain from speech as long as permission has not been granted to him. The sign of divine permission is the entry of transcendental subjects into his heart and their simultaneous manifestation on his tongue. He thus becomes a pure instrument of divine knowledge. Such speech is beneficial and impressive.

رُبَّمَا بَرَزَتِ الْحَقَائِقُ مَكْسُوفَةَ الْأَنْوَارِ إِذَا لَمْ يُؤْذَنْ لَكَ فِيهَا بِالْإِظْهَارِ.

Sometimes the lights of inner realities will appear eclipsed when you have not been given permission to give expression to them. [185]

When the traveler seeks to elaborate on spiritual mysteries and realities without divine permission, his own choice and intention play a role. He then ceases to be purely an instrument of the divine will. His elaboration lacks an illuminative quality, owing to the darkness of the non-Divine that has contaminated it. Even if he makes some impression, it will be short-lived.

تَسْبِقُ أَنْوَارُ الْحُكَمَاءِ أَقْوَالَهُمْ، فَحَيْثُ صَارَ التَّنْوِيرُ وَصَلَ التَّعْبِيرُ.

The lights of sages precede their words, so that, wherever illumination occurs, the expression arrives there. [182]

When the gnostics intend to counsel or admonish the servants of Allāh, their hearts turn toward Allāh Most High in supplication before speaking. They supplicate for the hearts of people to be endowed with the ability to absorb the advice. At that juncture a light arises from the light in their hearts.

This light, then, enters the hearts of the audience and produces the required ability. Thus, even prior to the discourse of the gnostic, his light reaches their hearts. His speech then follows. The hearts that have already been rendered fertile by the luminosity of the lights readily absorb the statements of the gnostic. The advice is, therefore, impressive and beneficial.

كُلُّ كَلَامٍ يَبْرُزُ وَعَلَيْهِ كِسْوَةُ الْقَلْبِ الَّذِي مِنْهُ بَرَزَ.

Every utterance that comes forth does so with the vestment of the heart from which it emerged. [183]

The tongue is the translator of the heart and it reveals the state of the heart. Therefore, if the speech originates from an illumined heart, then the speech, too, will be luminous; it will make an impression on the listeners.

On the contrary, if the heart is polluted with darkness the speech will also be cloaked in darkness. It will not enter the hearts of men; it will exercise no benefit.

عِبَارَتُهُم إِمَّا لِفَيَضَانِ وَجْدٍ، أَوْ لِقَصْدِ هِدَايَةِ مُرِيدٍ .. فَالْأَوَّلُ: حَالُ السَّالِكِينَ، وَالثَّانِي: حَالُ أَرْبَابِ الْمَكِنَةِ وَالْمُحَقِّقِينَ.

Their expression is either because of the overflow of ecstasy or for the purpose of guiding a disciple. The former case is that of those who progress; the latter case is that of those who possess a function and have realization. [186]

When torrents of spiritual knowledge and inspiration cascade into the heart of the traveler in the initial stage of his spiritual sojourn, he is unable to contain them, and they spill over on to his tongue.

In contrast, the heart of the complete gnostic (*ʿārif kāmil*) is extremely spacious. His heart is able to contain all the spiritual mysteries inspired into it. He remains in control of the knowledge in his heart. He does not, therefore, reveal it. However, when the need arises to instruct and guide a disciple, he speaks as the occasion necessitates.

اَلْعِبَارَةُ قُوتٌ لِعَائِلَةِ الْمُسْتَمِعِينَ، وَلَيْسَ لَكَ إِلَّا مَا أَنْتَ لَهُ آكِلٌ.

An expression is nourishment to needy listeners, and your share in it is only what you can eat thereof. [187]

Just as food and water are the nourishment of the physical body, so too are knowledge and gnosis the nourishment of the spirit. The various discourses of knowledge and gnosis are the nourishment for listeners who are in need of such sustenance.

In the same way that not every person is able to digest all kinds of food, not everyone is able to comprehend and absorb every item of spiritual nourishment. Thus, it is wrong to believe that every aspect of spiritual knowledge is appropriate for every man. Different people absorb such spiritual nourishment in accordance with their inherent abilities.

30

ON THANKFULNESS

مَنْ لَمْ يُقْبِلْ عَلَى اللهِ بِمُلَاطَفَاتِ الإِحْسَانِ

.. قِيْدَ إِلَيْهِ بِسَلَاسِلِ الإِمْتِحَانِ.

Whoever does not draw near to God as a result of the caresses of love is shackled to Him with the chains of misfortune. [63]

THOSE SERVANTS IN whom nobility and lofty intelligence are inherent do not become proud and arrogant as a result of the bounties of Allāh that they are awarded. They do not lose themselves in indolence, forgetfulness and worldly love. The bounties serve to increase their love for their True Benefactor. In consequence, they become engrossed in obedience and worship.

Those who consider these bounties to be the goal to pursue do not direct their attention to Allāh Most High. As a result, they are caught up in many trials and hardships. These misfortunes act like chains by means of which these recalcitrant servants are forcibly drawn to Allāh Most High. As such, the trials and hardships are in reality a blessing for them.

مَنْ لَمْ يَشْكُرِ النِّعَمَ .. فَقَدْ تَعَرَّضَ لِزَوَالِهَا،

وَمَنْ شَكَرَهَا .. فَقَدْ قَيَّدَهَا بِعِقَالِهَا.

Whoever is not thankful for graces runs the risk of losing them, and whoever is thankful fetters them with their own cords. [64]

The one who is ungrateful for the graces of Allāh Most High is in reality pursuing the elimination of them. Thankfulness entails abandonment of transgression and the adoption of obedience. Only the One Being should be acknowledged as the giver of all graces.[58] Ingratitude leads to the disappearance of graces.

The one who is grateful for the bounties and recognizes the True Giver has ensured the perpetuation of the graces of Allāh. In fact, the favors will be increased. In this regard, Allāh Most High states in the Qur'ān: *If you are grateful, most certainly I shall increase the bounties for you. And, if you are ungrateful, then [know] that My punishment is severe* (14:7).

رُبَّمَا وَرَدَتِ الظُّلْمُ عَلَيْكَ، لِيُعَرِّفَكَ قَدْرَ مَا مَنَّ بِهِ عَلَيْكَ.

Sometimes darknesses come over you in order that He make you aware of the value of His blessings upon you. [198]

The condition of the servant here on earth is not always the same. Sometimes the light of obedience settles on him, and at other times the darkness of the contamination of desires and forgetfulness settles in his heart.

If he only experienced illumination, he would not have known its value. Furthermore, the reality of light is understood from its opposite: darkness. When there is no appreciation, the servant will not express gratitude to his Master. For this reason, sometimes the darkness of forgetfulness and the dominance of lowly desires dominate the traveler so that he values the light of obedience and all other blessings.

مَنْ لَمْ يَعْرِفْ قَدْرَ النِّعَمِ بِوِجْدَانِهَا .. عَرَفَهَا بِوُجُودِ فُقْدَانِهَا.

He who does not know the value of graces when they are present knows their value when they are absent. [199]

58 One should refer to the treatises' section of this work, where one will read Ibn ʿAṭā'illāh saying in the second treatise: "If the eye of the heart (*ʿayn al-qalb*) sees that Allāh is One (*wāḥid*) in His blessings (*minna*) the Law (Sharīʿa) requires nevertheless that thanks be given to His creatures."

There are innumerable graces of Allāh Most High on man at every moment. Man is, in reality, engulfed by graces. Most people, however, fail to appreciate the graces and remain ungrateful. Some people even complain about Allāh Most High and always remain dissatisfied. Such people will only appreciate the value of graces after they have been snatched away.

لَا تُدْهِشْكَ وَارِدَاتُ النِّعَمِ عَنِ الْقِيَامِ بِحُقُوقِ شُكْرِكَ
.. فَإِنَّ ذٰلِكَ مِمَّا يَحُطُّ مِنْ وُجُودِ قَدْرِكَ.

The inspirations of grace should not so dazzle you as to keep you from fulfilling the obligations of thankfulness, for that would indeed bring you down in rank. [200]

Two things constrain a man to become unmindful of fulfilling the rights of gratitude: either the graces of Allāh are regarded as insignificant and few, or they are viewed to be so abundant that one feels unable to offer adequate thanks and appreciation. Laboring under this latter misconception can lead to one abstaining from expressing gratitude altogether.

Any neglect with regard to the fulfillment of the rights of gratitude will diminish the rank of the traveler. Allāh Most High has elevated your rank solely by His kindness and favor. Every act rendered by you is rewarded tenfold and more. He magnifies your little and insignificant deeds. This demands that you always pursue thankfulness and righteousness.

Your refraining from thankfulness points to your stark ignorance. It appears that you believe in your own ability and effort. You labor under the notion that you practice virtue by your own strength and effort. This is total ignorance. Allāh Most High is the Owner of all your [good] actions. He activates your body and limbs. Despite Allāh Most High being the True Actor of your righteousness, He honors and ennobles you by permitting people to award you with titles of nobility, such as pious-one, thankful-one and invoker of Allāh.

Ponder and endeavor to fathom your origin. In reality you lack the strength to move a particle. It is by virtue of His pure kindness that you are considered to be a possessor of elevated rank. Therefore, never abandon thankfulness nor be found wanting in the discharge of its obligations.

مَتٰى رَزَقَكَ الطَّاعَةَ وَالْغِنٰى بِهِ عَنْهَا .. فَاعْلَمْ أَنَّهُ قَدْ أَسْبَغَ عَلَيْكَ نِعَمَهُ ظَاهِرَةً وَبَاطِنَةً.

When He gives you obedience, making you unaware of it because of Him, then know that He has showered you liberally with His graces both inwardly and outwardly. [74]

When Allāh Most High involves a servant in obedience He bestows on him the attribute of independence from all others besides Him. It should be understood, then, that He has awarded the servant with inward and outward graces in full measure.

Outward graces are the application of the physical body to acts of obedience. Inward graces are the heart's attainment of freedom from the slavery of all others besides Allāh Most High. These are the bounties for which the servant should perpetually express gratitude.

مِنْ تَمَامِ النِّعْمَةِ عَلَيْكَ أَنْ يَرْزُقَكَ مَا يَكْفِيكَ وَيَمْنَعَكَ مَا يُطْغِيكَ.

Part of the completeness of grace accorded you lies in His providing you with what suffices and holding you back from what makes you exceed bounds. [225]

Abundant sustenance often leads to a man's transgression and rebellion. He becomes unmindful of Allāh while he basks in the luxury of the graces. On the other hand, if the graces are insufficient for his needs he is disturbed and his heart finds no rest. He consequently drifts from the path of his Master. However, the bestowal of graces that suffice his needs—neither too many nor too few—is Allāh's completeness of grace on the servant. The servant who has sufficient means for his needs should, therefore, wholeheartedly apply himself to the invocation of Allāh Most High.

مَتٰى جَعَلَكَ فِي الظَّاهِرِ مُمْتَثِلًا لِأَمْرِهِ، وَرَزَقَكَ فِي الْبَاطِنِ الْإِسْتِسْلَامَ لِقَهْرِهِ .. فَقَدْ أَعْظَمَ الْمِنَّةَ عَلَيْكَ.

When He makes you submissive to His command outwardly and provides you with resignation to His power inwardly, then He has enhanced the greatness of the favor accorded you. [110]

There is no greater grace than these two bounties [mentioned above in this aphorism] that Allāh Most High confers on a servant. Firstly, [the author mentions] the man who outwardly obeys the commands of Allāh Most High with his body. Secondly, [this person is] he who is contented with, or resigned to, all circumstances divinely ordained for him, from the power of Allāh; regardless of whether these are pleasing or displeasing to his disposition he wholeheartedly submits to the decrees of his Master.

All goodness is within the confines of these two graces. Thereafter, there is no need for a servant to look for anything, because the excellence of a person is in servanthood. The servant to whom these two blessings have been bestowed is in possession of both outward and inward servanthood.

لَا يَزِيدُ فِي عِزِّهِ إِقْبَالُ مَنْ أَقْبَلَ عَلَيْهِ، وَلَا
يَنْقُصُ مِنْ عِزِّهِ إِدْبَارُ مَنْ أَدْبَرَ عَنْهُ.

His Sublimity is not increased when someone draws near to Him, and His Sublimity is not decreased when someone draws away from Him. [212]

"His Sublimity is not increased when someone draws near to Him" because His Sublimity is beginninglessly eternal, and "His Sublimity is not decreased when someone draws away from Him" because He is self-subsistent and independent of creation. Therefore, it states in a ḥadīth *qudsī* that Allāh says, "If the first of you and the last of you, the human of you and the jinn of you came together as the heart of the most pious man among you, then it would not increase My dominion in the least. If the first of you and the last of you, the human of you and the jinn of you came together as the heart of the most sinful man among you, then it would not diminish My dominion in the least."[59]

59 *Muslim*, no. 2577. Both this aphorism and commentary appear to be missing from Gangōhī's work and the commentary added here is summarized from Ibn ʿAjība (*Īqāẓ al-Himam fī Sharḥ al-Ḥikam* 339).

PART 2

المراسلات

The Treatises

THE FIRST TREATISE

وَقَالَ رَضِيَ اللّٰهُ عَنْهُ مِمَّا كَتَبَ بِهِ لِبَعْضِ إِخْوَانِهِ:[60]

أَمَّا بَعْدُ، فَإِنَّ الْبِدَايَاتِ مَجَلَّاةُ النِّهَايَاتِ، وَإِنَّ مَنْ كَانَتْ بِاللّٰهِ بِدَايَتُهُ كَانَتْ إِلَيْهِ نِهَايَتُهُ، وَالْمُشْتَغَلُ بِهِ هُوَ الَّذِي أَحْبَبْتَهُ وَسَارَعْتَ إِلَيْهِ، وَالْمُشْتَغَلُ عَنْهُ هُوَ الْمُؤْثَرُ عَلَيْهِ، وَإِنَّ مَنْ أَيْقَنَ أَنَّ اللّٰهَ يَطْلُبُهُ .. صَدَقَ الطَّلَبَ إِلَيْهِ، وَمَنْ عَلِمَ أَنَّ الْأُمُوْرَ بِيَدِ اللّٰهِ .. انْجَمَعَ بِالتَّوَكُّلِ عَلَيْهِ، وأَنَّهُ لَا بُدَّ لِبِنَاءِ هٰذَا الْوُجُودِ أَنْ تَنْهَدِمَ دَعَائِمُهُ وأَنْ تُسْلَبَ كَرَائِمُهُ، فَالْعَاقِلُ مَنْ كَانَ بِمَا هُوَ أَبْقٰى أَفْرَحَ مِنْهُ بِمَا هُوَ يَفْنٰى، قَدْ أَشْرَقَ نُورُهُ وَظَهَرَتْ تَبَاشِيرُهُ، فَصَدَفَ عَنْ هٰذِهِ الدَّارِ مُغْضِيًا، وَأَعْرَضَ عَنْهَا مُوَلِّيًا، فَلَمْ يَتَّخِذْهَا وَطَنًا وَلَا جَعَلَهَا سَكَنًا، بَلْ أَنْهَضَ الْهِمَّةَ فِيهَا إِلَى اللّٰهِ تَعَالٰى، وَسَارَ فِيهَا مُسْتَعِينًا بِهِ فِي الْقُدُومِ عَلَيْهِ، فَمَا زَالَتْ مَطِيَّةُ عَزْمِهِ لَا يَقِرُّ قَرَارُهَا، دَائِمًا تَسْيَارُهَا، إِلٰى أَنْ أَنَاخَتْ بِحَضْرَةِ الْقُدْسِ وَبِسَاطِ الْأُنْسِ، مَحَلِّ الْمُفَاتَحَةِ وَالْمُوَاجَهَةِ وَالْمُجَالَسَةِ وَالْمُحَادَثَةِ وَالْمُشَاهَدَةِ وَالْمُطَالَعَةِ.

60 ʿAlī Muttaqī incorporates this treatise at the end of the twenty-second chapter of his arrangement.

فَصَارَتِ الْحَضْرَةُ مُعَشَّشَ قُلُوبِهِمْ؛ إِلَيْهَا يَأْوُونَ، وَفِيهَا يَسْكُنُونَ، فَإِذَا نَزَلُوا إِلٰى سَمَاءِ الْحُقُوقِ أَوْ أَرْضِ الْحُظُوظِ .. فَبِالْإِذْنِ وَالتَّمْكِينِ وَالرُّسُوخِ فِي الْيَقِينِ، فَلَمْ يَنْزِلُوا إِلَى الْحُقُوقِ بِسُوءِ الْأَدَبِ وَالْغَفْلَةِ، وَلَا إِلَى الْحُظُوظِ بِالشَّهْوَةِ وَالْمُتْعَةِ، بَلْ دَخَلُوا فِي ذٰلِكَ كُلِّهِ بِاللّٰهِ وَلِلّٰهِ وَمِنَ اللّٰهِ وَإِلَى اللّٰهِ.

﴿وَقُلْ رَبِّ أَدْخِلْنِي مُدْخَلَ صِدْقٍ وَأَخْرِجْنِي مُخْرَجَ صِدْقٍ﴾، لِيَكُونَ نَظَرِي إِلٰى حَوْلِكَ وَقُوَّتِكَ إِذَا أَدْخَلْتَنِي، وَاسْتِسْلَامِي وَانْقِيَادِي إِلَيْكَ إِذَا أَخْرَجْتَنِي، ﴿وَاجْعَلْ لِي مِنْ لَدُنْكَ سُلْطَانًا نَصِيرًا﴾ يَنْصُرُنِي وَيَنْصُرُ بِي وَلَا يَنْصُرُ عَلَيَّ؛ يَنْصُرُنِي عَلٰى شُهُودِ نَفْسِي وَيُفْنِينِي عَنْ دَائِرَةِ حِسِّي.

Among the things that he wrote to some of his friends, he said (may God be pleased with him!):

Now then, beginnings are the places where endings are revealed, so that whoever begins with God ends up with Him. He is the one you love and rush to in whatever occupies you, and He is the one you prefer in whatever you turn away from. Whoever is certain that God seeks him is sincere in seeking Him. He who knows that all matters are in God's hands is recollected through trust in Him. Indeed, it is inevitable that the pillars of this world's house of existence be destroyed and that its precious things be stripped away. For the intelligent man is more joyous over the permanent than he is over the evanescent. His light rays out, glad tidings have come to him. Thus, he turns away from this world, takes no notice of it, shuns it altogether. He does not therefore take it as a homeland, nor does he turn it into a home, but rather, while in it, he arouses his fervor toward God [Most High] and seeks His help in going to Him. His determination, a riding-mount, is restless and ever on the move till it comes to kneel down in the Presence of the Holy on the carpet of intimacy, the place of reciprocal disclosure, confrontation, companionship, discussion, contemplation, and viewing.

The Presence is the nesting-place of the hearts of initiates: they take refuge in it and dwell in it. Then, when they descend to the heaven of obligations and the earth of varied fortune, they do so with authority, stability, and profundity of certitude. For they have not so

> descended to obligations through improper conduct or forgetfulness, nor to fortune through passion and pleasure; but instead, they have entered therein by God and for God and from God and to God.
>
> "And say: My Lord, make me enter a truthful entering, and make me go forth a truthful going forth," [Q. 17:80] so that I will see Your strength and power when You make me enter, and will submit and conform myself to You when You make me go out. Give me an authority from You, an ally that helps me or that helps others through me, but not one that goes against me: one that helps me against self-regard and extinguishes me from the realm of my senses.

The initial spiritual state of the traveler is for him like a mirror and a source of illumination of his final state. This means that the state of spiritual elevation which the traveler will reach at the end of his journey will correspond to his initial spiritual condition. The final state can be assessed from the initial condition. If in the beginning the traveler expends all his endeavors in worship, invocation and exertion, then it indicates that a wonderful portion of Allāh's grace will be opened up for him. Furthermore, this traveler will quickly reach his goal. Yet, if his initial state is weak, such as his worship being defective, then it indicates that his final condition too will be weak and defective.

When the initial state of the traveler starts off with consciousness of Allāh—with the traveler seeking aid from Allāh Most High in all his affairs, both worldly and religious—then his end will be the meeting with Allāh Most High. He will be completely detached from all creation and the means and agencies [of normal life]. On the contrary, if in the beginning there is deficiency in his attribute of total dependence on Allāh, his reliance being on material agencies and on his own intelligence, then its effect will manifest in the traveler's end condition: his reliance upon Allāh will be defective even in the end.

When the traveler abandons worldly occupations and engrosses himself in the remembrance of Allāh, then sometimes the ego motivated by ignorance and worldly love yearns for the occupations which were abandoned. Thus it is said that it is worthwhile to involve oneself in only such deeds of virtue which were loved and quickly adopted for Allāh's sake. However, the lower desires which were abandoned earlier for the sake of Allāh Most High should never again be adopted. It is imperative to steer away from them.

When man fully understands and believes that Allāh Most High expects him to worship Him and to discharge the rights of servanthood, he will expend all his endeavors in a genuine quest for reaching Allāh Most High, and abandon his egotistic desires. The deficiency in man's quest for Allāh corresponds to the degree of the deficiency in his trust in Allāh Most High. The greater the deficiency in trust, the more defective will be the quest of the traveler. The deficiency is the result of lack of sincerity in the quest. When the motivation is only Allāh's pleasure, it indicates that there is sincerity in the traveler's quest. The aim of worship should be only divine pleasure.

When man is convinced that every occurrence is in the control and power of Allāh Most High, his trust will be fully in Allāh Most High. In view of this attitude, he will relieve himself of all worries by assigning them to Allāh's will. The result of this attitude is the abandonment of all worries. Worries, in fact, are the consequence of placing reliance on one's own intelligence and efforts.

The traveler should be true in his quest and rely on Allāh Most High for the attainment of his goal. He should not place trust in his efforts and schemes, neither should he bring worries upon himself. Everything should be done calmly. When a person's reliance is on his own plans and intelligence, Allāh Most High assigns him to the machinations of his ego.

Fearing the loss of worldly pleasures, many people do not involve themselves with the Path. Novices of a weak disposition are sometimes accosted by this fear. Allaying their fears, the Shaykh ﵀ says that at some time or the other the world has to be either given up or the world itself will abandon man. At that time all the delightful things of man will be snatched away. The man of intelligence will, therefore, choose the everlasting abode of the Hereafter: he will be more pleased with the Hereafter. This does not necessarily mean that he does not derive any pleasure from worldly things—such a condition is beyond human nature. It only means that in relation to this world, his pleasure and yearning for the Hereafter are greater.

Initially, when the intelligent traveler musters up courage to abandon the world, its delights and pleasures, he experiences some strain and difficulty. However, after a short period, a light begins to kindle in his heart on account of his attempted abandonment of the world. The glitter of this light becomes manifest on his face and body. This is the sign of the acceptance of his endeavors. Therefore this intelligent traveler closes his eyes on this ephemeral existence. Thus he does not regard this world as his abode or home. His heart does not derive peace on earth. Instead, he concentrates on his advance towards divine proximity. In this endeavor he seeks only

Allāh's aid. With divine aid he continues his advance and he does not rely on his own efforts for achieving the goal.

No one can achieve salvation on the strength of his efforts and deeds alone. Every gain is because of Allāh's grace. The traveler whose gaze is not on his efforts, but is focused on Allāh's mercy and kindness, will reach his destination. This is the initial state of the traveler.

A variety of spiritual states draw the traveler. Among those states are pleasure (*ladhdhāt*), happiness (*faraḥ*), delight (*surūr*), spiritual rays of illumination (*anwār*), miracles (*karāmāt*), revelations (*mukāshafāt*), higher-spiritual realities (*ḥaqā'iq*) and divine mysteries (*asrār*).

If the traveler becomes overly attracted to any of these states he becomes stagnant. His progress comes to a halt. However, if Allāh's grace is upon him and his success is decreed, the traveler will leave all these states and continue his journey of progress towards Allāh. In such a state of restlessness, he presses onwards until he reaches Allāh's Lofty Court and the stations of:

- Reciprocal disclosure (*mufātaḥa*): where the heart attains true love and pleasure. In this station divine blessings and benefit commence their decent on his heart.
- Confrontation (*muwājaha*): where the traveler is a focus of Allāh's mercy.
- Companionship (*mujalasa*): the state of the traveler's ecstasy while experiencing the divine proximity.
- Discussion (*muḥādasa*): with the showering of mysteries, secrets and subtle divine knowledge upon the traveler's heart.
- Contemplation (*mushāhada*): where the traveler perceives Allāh Most High with his inner eyes, while he is oblivious of his physical senses.
- Viewing (*muṭalaʿā*): the state of absolute entrenchment: the reality of arrival to the goal.

After attaining the divine presence, the travelers take it as their home, or nesting-place; and here they find the peace that is the culmination of their journey. Ostensibly, the now-accomplished sufi associates with people, but his heart remains in a tranquility that remains focused on Allāh. This stage is the station of annihilation (*fanā'*) and station is also called the station of ascension (*ʿurūj*) and of union (*jamaʿ*): the end of the journeying.

When the traveler is firmly entrenched in the state of *fanā'*, i.e. all things besides Allāh are completely erased from his heart, he becomes completely absorbed in the perception of divine beauty and majesty. His attention is diverted from all things [that impede the fulfillment of the servant's obligations to Allāh]. After having attained this elevated station, if Allāh Most High wishes to appoint the traveler as a spiritual guide for others, He bestows on him the station of "subsistence" (*baqā'*) and "separation" (*farq*).

When this state of *fanā'* becomes entrenched and leads to *baqā'*, the traveler is granted a state of pressing concern for the creation. However, there is a big difference between this current concern for people and the earlier concern prior to the completion of the Path. While the former concern was in the state of being oblivious of Allāh Most High, with other motives being the cause of the concern, the present concern is in reality directed to Allāh Most High. In this stage, the gaze toward creation is like looking in a mirror at the reflection of the Divine Being since the entire creation is the manifestation of His beauty and splendor.[61]

At this juncture, these accomplished sufis are the medium of spiritual benefit and guidance for others. They then associate with people. This station is here described as "the heaven[62] of obligations" and "earth of varied fortune." In this portrayal, the idea of the difficulty of the task of these people is presented. The rights that devolve upon them as a result of their association with people are comparable to the heaven. Just as it is difficult and almost impossible to ascend into the heaven, so too is the fulfillment of these obligations. It is not within the reach of everyone to do justice to the obligations arising from association with people.

When these illustrious people descend from their lofty station to these rights and desires, it is only by the commend of Allāh Most High. If they had a choice in the matter they would never prefer to emerge from the state of *fanā'* and descend to creation.

This descent occurs after the state of annihilation has been entrenched, which is achieved after entrenchment in certainty and gnosis. Hence their

61 Abū 'l-Qāsim al-Qushayrī says: "By their use of the term annihilation (*fanā'*)—passing away—the sufis indicate the disappearance of blameworthy characteristics. By the term subsistence (*baqā'*)—abiding in God—they indicate the establishment of praiseworthy characteristics" (*The Risalah*, 86). Shaykh Aḥmad Sirhindi, seeking to dispel the mistaken notions of some with regards to these states, says: "*Fanā,* passing away from the self, and *baqā'*, abiding in God, are experiential (*shuhūdī*) not existential (*wujūdī*). Man does not become God and is not united with Him. The servant is servant for ever, and the Lord is Lord eternally. They are wicked heretics who think that *fanā'* and *baqā'* are existential" (*Sufism and Shari'ah*, 181).

62 The translation of *samā'* as "heaven" in this context must be understood as something like "the vault of sky overhanging the earth" (see *The Chambers Dictionary*, 1997 reprint, under "heaven"), as a way of trying to convey the meaning of a huge expanse, which is what the commentary makes clear; hence the word "heaven" should not be confused with the Heaven that is Paradise.

descent toward such rights is not accompanied by negligence and disrespect. The earlier state before annihilation was one of being unmindful of the rights of others, but now this no longer exists: heedlessness is completely abandoned, and they are perpetually alert. If anyone persecutes them they do not seek revenge because the heart is attached to Allāh at all times. They recognize that it is Allāh Most High who has imposed on them the persecutor. If someone praises them, they do not forget their ego. In short, in the fulfillment of their duties and discharge of the rights there is no carelessness. They execute their obligations with maximum diligence and concern. They are never unmindful of Allāh Most High, not even for a moment.

Their descent into the realm of emotion is not for the acquisition of carnal desire and pleasure. It is not for personal benefit. Prior to the state of *fanā'*, eating, food, garments and sex were for self-gratification and pleasure. Now after the attainment of the lofty state of *fanā'*, their indulgence in these mundane acts is with the aid and consent of Allāh Most High and solely for Him Most High. The ego has absolutely no share in these seemingly worldly activities.

When the traveler enters this stage, he gains greater perfection. This is the second journey of the traveler. The first journey is called *taraqqī* or *'urūj* (elevation) and the second journey is termed *nuzūl* (descent). The Shaykh ﴾ substantiates both these journeys on the basis of the Qur'ānic verse: *And Say: My Lord, make me enter a truthful entering, and make me go forth a truthful going forth* (17:80).

The "truthful entering" is a reference to the journey of elevation, because this journey leads the traveler into the Divine Court in a state of *fanā'*, where his heart dissociates completely from creation.

The meaning of "a truthful going forth" is the journey of descent. This journey takes the traveler towards creation and he passes on his spiritual treasure to people.

In his upward journey of truth, the traveler perceived only the might and power of Allāh Most High. In the state of descent, the traveler is in absolute submission to his Creator. He is pleased with whatever station to which Allāh Most High dispatches him. His ego displays no desire for remaining in the station of elevation because he has wholeheartedly submitted himself to the duty imposed on him by Allāh Most High.

At the end of this subject, the Shaykh offers a supplication for steadfastness. The accomplished sufi constantly supplicates for divine aid, and Allāh's help is often near at hand for such a blessed one.

THE SECOND TREATISE

وَمِمَّا كَتَبَ بِهِ لِبَعْضِ إِخْوَانِهِ:[63]

إِنْ كَانَتْ عَيْنُ الْقَلْبِ تَنْظُرُ إِلٰى أَنَّ اللّٰهَ وَاحِدٌ فِي مِنَّتِهِ .. فَالشَّرِيعَةُ تَقْتَضِي أَنَّهُ لَا بُدَّ مِنْ شُكْرِ خَلِيقَتِهِ. وإِنَّ النَّاسَ فِي ذٰلِكَ عَلٰى ثَلَاثَةِ أَقْسَامٍ:

- غَافِلٌ مُنْهَمِكٌ فِي غَفْلَتِهِ، قَوِيَتْ دائِرَةُ حِسِّهِ، وَانْطَمَسَتْ حَضْرَةُ قُدْسِهِ، فَنَظَرَ الْإِحْسَانَ مِنَ الْمَخْلُوقِينَ وَلَمْ يَشْهَدْهُ مِنْ رَبِّ الْعَالَمِينَ: إِمَّا اعْتِقَادًا .. فَشِرْكُهُ جَلِيٌّ، وَإِمَّا اسْتِنَادًا .. فَشِرْكُهُ خَفِيٌّ.

- وَصَاحِبُ حَقِيقَةٍ غَابَ عَنِ الْخَلْقِ بِشُهُودِ الْمَلِكِ الْحَقِّ، وَفَنِيَ عَنِ الْأَسْبَابِ بِشُهُودِ مُسَبِّبِ الْأَسْبَابِ .. فَهٰذَا عَبْدٌ مُوَاجَهٌ بِالْحَقِيقَةِ، ظَاهِرٌ عَلَيْهِ سَنَاهَا، سَالِكٌ لِلطَّرِيقَةِ، قَدِ اسْتَوْلٰى عَلٰى مَدَاهَا، غَيْرَ أَنَّهُ غَرِيقُ الْأَنْوَارِ مَطْمُوسُ الْآثَارِ، قَدْ غَلَبَ سُكْرُهُ عَلٰى صَحْوِهِ، وَجَمْعُهُ عَلٰى فَرْقِهِ، وَفَنَاؤُهُ عَلٰى بَقَائِهِ، وَغَيْبَتُهُ عَلٰى حُضُورِهِ.

- وَأَكْمَلُ مِنْهُ عَبْدٌ شَرِبَ فَازْدَادَ صَحْوًا، وَغَابَ فَازْدَادَ حُضُورًا، فَلَا جَمْعُهُ يَحْجُبُهُ عَنْ فَرْقِهِ، وَلَا فَرْقُهُ يَحْجُبُهُ عَنْ جَمْعِهِ، وَلَا فَنَاؤُهُ يَصْرِفُهُ عَنْ بَقَائِهِ، وَلَا بَقَاؤُهُ يَصُدُّهُ عَنْ فَنَائِهِ، يُعْطِي كُلَّ ذِي قِسْطٍ قِسْطَهُ، وَيُوفِي كُلَّ ذِي حَقٍّ حَقَّهُ.

وَقَدْ قَالَ أَبُو بَكْرٍ الصِّدِّيقُ رَضِيَ اللّٰهُ عَنْهُ لِعَائِشَةَ رَضِيَ اللّٰهُ عَنْهَا لَمَّا نَزَلَتْ بَرَاءَتُهَا مِنَ الْإِفْكِ عَلٰى لِسَانِ رَسُولِ اللّٰهِ صَلَّى اللّٰهُ عَلَيهِ وَسَلَّمَ: «يَا عَائِشَةُ، اشْكُرِي رَسُولَ اللّٰهِ صَلَّى اللّٰهُ عَلَيْهِ وَسَلَّمَ.» فَقَالَتْ: «وَاللّٰهِ، لَا أَشْكُرُ إِلَّا اللّٰهَ»، دَلَّهَا أَبُو بَكْرٍ عَلَى الْمَقَامِ الْأَكْمَلِ؛ مَقَامِ الْبَقَاءِ الْمُقْتَضِي لِإِثْبَاتِ الْآثَارِ، وَقَدْ قَالَ اللّٰهُ تَعَالٰى: ﴿أَنِ اشْكُرْ لِي وَلِوَالِدَيْكَ إِلَيَّ الْمَصِيرُ﴾ وَقَالَ صَلَوَاتُ اللّٰهِ وَسَلَامُهُ عَلَيْهِ: «لَا يَشْكُرُ اللّٰهَ مَنْ لَا يَشْكُرُ النَّاسَ»، وَكَانَتْ فِي ذٰلِكَ الْوَقْتِ مُصْطَلَمَةً عَنْ شَاهِدِهَا، غَائِبَةً عَنِ الْآثَارِ، فَلَمْ تَشْهَدْ إِلَّا الْوَاحِدَ الْقَهَّارَ.

63 ʿAlī Muttaqī included this treatise at the end of the thirtieth chapter of his arrangement.

Among the things that he wrote to some of his friends, he said (may God be pleased with him!):

If the eye of the heart sees that God is One in His blessings, the Law requires nevertheless that thanks be given to His creatures.

Indeed, in the matter of blessings, people fall into three classes. The first is that of the forgetful person, immersed in his forgetfulness, strong in the domain of his senses, blurred in inner vision. He sees generosity as coming from mankind and does not contemplate it as coming from the Lord of the Universe, either out of conviction, in which case his associationism is evident, or else out of dependence, in which case his associationism is hidden.

The second is that of the possessor of a spiritual reality who, by contemplating the Real King, is absent from mankind, and who, by contemplating the Cause of effects, is extinguished from the effects. He is a servant brought face to face with Reality, the splendor of which is apparent in him. A traveler in the Path, he has mastered its extent, except that he is drowned in lights and does not perceive created things. His inebriety prevails over his sobriety, his union over his separation, his extinction over his permanence, and his absence over his presence.

The third is that of a servant who is more perfect than the second: he drinks, and increases in sobriety; he is absent, and increases in presence; his union does not veil him from his separation, nor does his separation veil him from his union; his extinction does not divert him from his permanence, nor does his permanence divert him from his extinction. He acts justly toward everyone and gives everyone his proper due.

Abū Bakr al-Ṣiddīq said to ʿĀ'isha, when her innocence was revealed through the tongue of the Prophet, "O ʿĀ'isha, be grateful to the Messenger of God!" Then she said, "By God, I will be grateful only to God!"[64] Abū Bakr had pointed out to her the more perfect station, the station of permanence which requires the recognition of created things. God says, "Give thanks to Me and to thy parents." [Q. 31:14] And the Prophet said, "He who does not thank mankind

64 As pointed out by Ibn ʿAjība the correct version is that it was her mother who told her to stand up (see *Īqāẓ al-Himam fī Sharḥ al-Ḥikam* 426). This is also the version related by Bukhārī (no. 2518).

does not thank God."[65] At that time she was extinguished from her external senses, absent from created things, so that she contemplated the One, the Omnipotent.

The Stages of Thankfulness

The eyes of the heart perceive the transcendental reality of things. Man with a developed spiritual vision sees with clarity that Allāh Most High is unique in His attribute of kindness and in the bestowal of favors. He clearly perceives that the only benefactor is Allāh Most High. Despite man's spiritual realization of the True Benefactor's munificence and kindness, the Sacred Law orders man, in this material world of cause and effect, to fulfill the duty of thankfulness. He is instructed to even express gratitude to the overt agencies through whose medium the divine bounties reach him. In this regard the noble ḥadīth says: "He who does not thank mankind does not thank Allāh." In this regard there are three types of people.

The first consists of people who are unmindful of Allāh. They remain uncaring while they are concerned with only the physical creation. They do not step beyond the confines of the material creation in the slightest degree. They are spiritually blind and unable to understand the glory of Allāh Most High. His attributes are incomprehensible to them. They perceive the good things as gifts and favors of people without realizing that everything is an emanation from the Creator. For example, an employer is believed by such a person to be the bestower of one's wages. If this idea has become a belief in a person, then he has renounced his faith and entered into disbelief (*kufr*) because his associationism is clear. He has associated creation with the Creator in His attribute of providence. Only Allāh Most High is The Bestower (*al-Muʿṭī*). However, if the belief is that Allāh is the actual bestower, but on account of men being the medium for the acquisition of the bounties these bestowals are attributed to them, then such a belief is hidden associationism. According to this belief, man is considered to be a bestower of bounties to a certain degree.

The second type is a servant whose gaze of perception has shifted from this external material world. His gaze has gained the ability to see realities. Being engrossed in the witnessing of the true Sovereign of the universe, he has become oblivious of creation. He has emerged from all vestiges of duality and has entered the realm of Unity. Having gained the perception of the

65 Bukhārī, *Al-Adab al-Mufrad* (no. 218).

Cause of all causes, he becomes unaware of the intermediate agencies. The material or worldly agents, the means and ways, have disappeared from in front of his gaze.

The servant in this lofty state is complete in relation to the people of heedlessness. However, he has not reached the best and most perfect stage, nor has he yet mounted the stage of consciousness because he is absorbed in the ocean of divine illumination. His gaze of perception, therefore, is unable to see creation. Besides Unity, there is nothing in his presence. His state of obliviousness is greater than his state of consciousness. The contemplation of Allāh is dominant in him. His stage of separation is overwhelming. The vision of Allāh along with the perception of creation is termed *farq*. The state of *fanā'* permeates him. He lacks the stage of *baqā'*, which succeeds *fanā'*. Absence dominates this person's being, and creation does not feature in his presence.

This servant is perfect in the thankfulness that he discharges for the bounties of Allāh. He expresses gratitude to only Allāh Most High and to no one else. This servant is exempted from discharging the thankfulness of people, which has devolved as an incumbent duty on him. In view of his state of annihilation, he is excused from the obligation of expressing thankfulness to people. He lacks the ability to express thankfulness to beings besides Allāh Most High because his gaze has completely shifted from the intermediate agencies.

The third kind of person occupies the highest rank. He is superior to the second type. He has drunk from elixir of Oneness, and after having traversed *fanā'* and all states higher he has arrived at the station of *baqā'*. For him creation has become the mirror for viewing the splendor and beauty of Allāh Most High.

The servant in this elevated and most perfect state discharges everyone's right correctly. While expressing gratitude to people, he discharges Allāh's rights of thankfulness in proper measure. He is neither like the heedless one, nor like the annihilated one. He is on the highest and most perfect stage of thankfulness.

The Shaykh ﵀ illustrates the latter two stages of thankfulness by citing the episode of 'Ā'isha the Truthful ﵂.

The hypocrites had leveled a slanderous accusation against Lady 'Ā'isha ﵂. As a result, the Messenger of Allāh ﷺ grieved for many days. In the beginning, Lady 'Ā'isha ﵂ was unaware of the slanderous rumor about her. When she was informed thereof, she was smitten with grief. She lost much weight as a consequence of the great worry and heartache which overwhelmed her. Furthermore, she was deprived of the earlier attention which the Messenger of Allāh ﷺ used to give her. This was the severest blow for her. Meanwhile, the Messenger of Allāh ﷺ investigated the allegations. Unable to bear the sorrow and grief, Lady ʿĀ'isha, with the permission of the Messenger of Allāh ﷺ, left for the home of her parents. One day the Messenger of Allāh ﷺ went to meet her. He said: "O ʿĀ'isha! If you have sinned, repent." Lady ʿĀ'isha requested her parents to reply on her behalf. They declined, commenting: "What can we say in the Messenger of Allāh's presence?" On hearing this comment, Lady ʿĀ'isha stood up and after reciting the praise of Allāh said:

> Our condition is like that of Yusuf's father. When Yusuf's brothers reported to their father that a wolf had eaten Yusuf, they even brought along Yusuf's bloodstained shirt; and Yaʿqūb said that patience is beautiful, and Allāh is the one from whom aid is sought regarding that which they had narrated.

She then sat down. As she sat, the revelation began. After termination of the revelation, the blessed face of Messenger of Allāh ﷺ was glowing radiantly with happiness. He exclaimed: "O ʿĀ'isha! Be happy, for Allāh Most High has proclaimed your innocence." He then recited those verses of Sūrat al-Nūr which were just revealed to proclaim her innocence and to announce severe punishment for those who slander chaste women. It was on this occasion that His Honor Abu Bakr the Truthful ordered ʿĀ'isha to express thankfulness to the Messenger of Allāh ﷺ because he was the medium for the announcement of her innocence. In response, ʿĀ'isha took an oath and declared that, besides Allāh Most High, she will not express thankfulness to anyone.

This episode is the basis for both the stages of *fanā'* and *baqā'*. His Honor Abu Bakr directed Lady ʿĀ'isha towards the station of *baqā'* while, in her prevalent state, she was in the state of *fanā'*, hence oblivious of all others. It was for this reason that she was unable to direct thankfulness to anyone besides Allāh Most High. Although this was the state of Lady ʿĀ'isha at that specific occasion, her usual condition at all times was *akmal* (most perfect) having attained both stages of *fanā'* and *baqā'*.

THE THIRD TREATISE

وَقالَ رَضِيَ اللّٰهُ عَنْهُ:[66]

لَمَّا سُئِلَ عَنْ قَوْلِهِ صَلَوَاتُ اللّٰهِ عَلَيْهِ وَسَلَامُهُ «وَجُعِلَتْ قُرَّةُ عَيْنِي فِي الصَّلَاةِ»: هَلْ ذٰلِكَ خَاصٌّ بِالنَّبِيِّ صَلَّى اللّٰهُ عَلَيْهِ وَسَلَّمَ أَمْ لِغَيْرِهِ مِنْهُ شِرْبٌ وَنَصِيبٌ؟ فَأَجَابَ:

إِنَّ قُرَّةَ الْعَيْنِ بِالشُّهُودِ عَلَى قَدْرِ الْمَعْرِفَةِ بِالْمَشْهُودِ، فَالرَّسُولُ صَلَّى اللّٰهُ عَلَيْهِ وَسَلَّمَ لَيْسَ مَعْرِفَةٌ كَمَعْرِفَتِهِ، فَلَيْسَ قُرَّةُ عَيْنٍ كَقُرَّتِهِ، وَإِنَّمَا قُلْنَا أَنَّ قُرَّةَ عَيْنِهِ فِي صَلَاتِهِ بِشُهُودِهِ جَلَالَ مَشْهُودِهِ لِأَنَّهُ قَدْ أَشَارَ إِلَى ذٰلِكَ بِقَوْلِهِ: «فِي الصَّلَاةِ»، وَلَمْ يَقُلْ: «بِالصَّلَاةِ»، إِذْ هُوَ صَلَاةُ اللّٰهِ عَلَيْهِ وَسَلَامُهُ لَا تَقَرُّ عَيْنُهُ بِغَيْرِ رَبِّهِ، وَكَيْفَ وَهُوَ يَدُلُّ عَلَى هٰذَا الْمَقَامِ وَيَأْمُرُ بِهِ مَنْ سِوَاهُ بِقَوْلِهِ صَلَوَاتُ اللّٰهِ عَلَيْهِ وَسَلَامُهُ: «اُعْبُدِ اللّٰهَ كَأَنَّكَ تَرَاهُ»، وَمُحَالٌ أَنْ يَرَاهُ وَيَشْهَدَ مَعَهُ سِوَاهُ.

فَإِنْ قَالَ لَهُ قَائِلٌ: قَدْ تَكُونُ قُرَّةُ الْعَيْنِ بِالصَّلَاةِ لِأَنَّهَا فَضْلٌ مِنَ اللّٰهِ، وَبَارِزَةٌ مِنْ عَيْنِ مِنَّةِ اللّٰهِ، فَكَيْفَ لَا يَفْرَحُ بِهَا؟ وَكَيْفَ لَا تَكُونُ قُرَّةُ الْعَيْنِ بِهَا، وَقَدْ قَالَ سُبْحَانَهُ: ﴿قُلْ بِفَضْلِ اللّٰهِ وَبِرَحْمَتِهِ فَبِذٰلِكَ فَلْيَفْرَحُوا﴾؟ .. فَاعْلَمْ أَنَّ الْآيَةَ قَدْ أَوْمَأَتْ إِلَى الْجَوَابِ لِمَنْ تَدَبَّرَ سِرَّ الْخِطَابِ، إِذْ قَالَ: ﴿فَبِذٰلِكَ فَلْيَفْرَحُوا﴾، وَمَا قَالَ: «فَبِذٰلِكَ فَافْرَحْ يَا مُحَمَّدُ،» قُلْ لَهُمْ: فَلْيَفْرَحُوا بِالْإِحْسَانِ وَالتَّفَضُّلِ، وَلْيَكُنْ فَرَحُكَ أَنْتَ بِالْمُتَفَضِّلِ، كَمَا قَالَ فِي الْآيَةِ الْأُخْرَى: ﴿قُلِ اللّٰهُ ثُمَّ ذَرْهُمْ فِي خَوْضِهِمْ يَلْعَبُونَ﴾.

He said (may God be pleased with him!):

When he was asked with regard to the Prophet's words [God's blessings and peace be upon him], "And my eye's refreshment has been made to be in ritual prayer,"[67] whether that was particular with the Prophet or whether anyone else had a share or part in it, he answered:

66 This treatise was placed by ʿAlī Muttaqī at the end of the fourth chapter of his arrangement.

67 This is part of a ḥadīth from Thābit ibn Anas ﷺ which reads: "I have been enamored of three things in this world of yours: perfume, women, and my solace in ritual prayer" (*Nasāʾī* 3950; *Ḥākim* 2676; *Aḥmad* 12315).

In truth, the eye's refreshment through contemplation is commensurate with the gnosis of the Object of contemplation. The gnosis of the Messenger is not like the gnosis of someone else; accordingly, someone else's refreshment of eye is not like his.

We have said that the refreshment of his eye in his ritual prayer was through his contemplating the Majesty of the Object of contemplation only because he himself indicated as much by his words, "in ritual prayer." For he did not say, "by means of ritual prayer," since his eye was not refreshed by means of something other than his Lord. How could it be otherwise? For he points to this station, and commands others to realize it, with his words, "Adore God as if you were seeing Him," since it would have been impossible for him to see Him and at the same time to witness someone other than He alongside Him.

Suppose someone were to say, "The refreshment of the eye can be by means of ritual prayer because it is a grace of God and emerges from God's blessing itself. So, how is it one cannot ascend by means of it, or how is it the eye's refreshment cannot be had by means of it? For God says, 'Say: In the grace of God and in His mercy, in that they should rejoice.'" [Q. 10:58]

If that were said, then you must know that the significance of the verse, for those who meditate on the secret of the statement, is to be found in the main clause, for He says, "In that they should rejoice," and not, "in that you should rejoice, O Muḥammad." In other words, "Say to them: Let them rejoice by means of generous acts and kindness, but let your rejoicing be with Him who is kind," just as, in another verse, He says, "Say: Allāh! Then leave them prattling in their vain talk." [Q. 6:91]

The ḥadīth indicates that the Messenger ﷺ experienced great pleasure and happiness in the ritual prayer.

Someone had asked the author whether this rank was exclusive with the Messenger of Allāh ﷺ or do others too have a share in this experience? In reply, the author said that coolness of the eyes, happiness and pleasure of the heart in the ritual prayer are experienced as a result of perceiving the Divine's beauty and splendor. This is experienced by the gnostics.

The pleasure experienced in the ritual prayer will be in proportion to the gnosis which one possesses of Allāh Most High. It is apparent that Messenger's gnosis surpasses the levels of all; hence he experienced greater pleasure and coolness of the eyes than everyone else.

This answer means that pleasure and coolness of the eyes in the ritual prayer are not exclusive with the Messenger of Allāh ﷺ, but others too enjoy this experience in lesser degree according to their ranks.

This pleasure and coolness of the eyes are experienced in the ritual prayer by a man who is not afflicted with egotistic and devilish thoughts. A man who is afflicted with such thoughts will not experience coolness of the eyes in the ritual prayer.

It was contended that the cause of the Messenger of Allāh ﷺ experiencing pleasure and coolness of the eyes in the ritual prayer was his perception of Allāh and not because of the ritual prayer itself. The reason for this contention is that the ḥadīth indicates this in its wording.

In other words, while *in* the state of the ritual prayer the Messenger of Allāh ﷺ derived pleasure on account of perceiving the Divine. He did not say: "The coolness of my eyes is *with* the ritual prayer," because such coolness was not attainable from objects besides Allāh. It is evident that the ritual prayer itself is also other than Allāh. How is it possible for The Messenger of Allāh's eyes ﷺ to find coolness in other than Allāh when he has instructed us to worship Allāh Most High in such a manner as if we are seeing Him?

When the servant attains this exalted stage, there remains then nothing for him other than Allāh. His attention is completely diverted from all others. Even his actions and existence pale into annihilation. Since the ritual prayer is an act of the servant, it too is an object besides Allāh. As such it becomes oblivious to him. At that time, in the ritual prayer, the coolness of the eyes and spiritual pleasure are experienced only because of the divine presence.

It is argued that coolness of the eyes and spiritual pleasure are attainable from the ritual prayer itself because the ritual prayer is the consequence of Allāh's grace and mercy; hence the servant who is in love with Allāh will necessary derive spiritual pleasure from the performance of the ritual prayer. Furthermore, pleasure with Allāh's grace has been commanded by Allāh Most High. He thus says in the Qur'ān: *Say: In the grace of Allāh and in His mercy, in that they should rejoice* (10:58). In view of the ritual prayer also being Allāh's grace and mercy, there will be happiness and pleasure in it.

The answer to this argument is that the verse itself indicates the answer. The instruction is that the people should be pleased with only grace and mercy. The verse does not command: "O Muḥammad! Become happy with it."

Thus the meaning of this answer is that while people become happy with the grace, mercy and favor of Allāh, the Messenger ﷺ should be happy with Allāh Himself. This view is substantiated elsewhere in the Qur'ān where the instruction is: *Say: Allāh! Then leave them prattling in their vain talk* (6:91). In other words: "Say that I am pleased with Allāh, and then leave them to play in their vain talk."

THE FOURTH TREATISE

وَقَالَ رَضِيَ اللّٰهُ عَنْهُ مِمَّا كَتَبَ بِهِ لِبَعْضِ إِخْوَانِهِ:[68]

اَلنَّاسُ فِي وُرُودِ الْمِنَنِ عَلٰى ثَلَاثَةِ أَقْسَامٍ:

– فَرِحٌ بِالْمِنَنِ، لَا مِنْ حَيْثُ مُهْدِيهَا وَمُنْشِئِهَا، وَلٰكِنْ بِوُجُودِ مُتْعَتِهِ فِيهَا .. فَهٰذَا مِنَ الْغَافِلِينَ، يَصْدُقُ عَلَيْهِ قَوْلُهُ تَعَالٰى: ﴿حَتّٰى إِذَا فَرِحُوا بِمَا أُوتُوا أَخَذْنَاهُمْ بَغْتَةً﴾.

– وَفَرِحٌ بِالْمِنَنِ مِنْ حَيْثُ أَنَّهُ شَهِدَهَا مِنَّةً مِمَّنْ أَرْسَلَهَا، وَنِعْمَةً مِمَّنْ أَوْصَلَهَا، يَصْدُقُ عَلَيْهِ قَوْلُهُ تَعَالٰى: ﴿قُلْ بِفَضْلِ اللّٰهِ وَبِرَحْمَتِهِ فَبِذٰلِكَ فَلْيَفْرَحُوا هُوَ خَيْرٌ مِمَّا يَجْمَعُونَ﴾.

– وَفَرِحٌ بِاللّٰهِ، ما شَغَلَهُ مِنَ الْمِنَنِ ظَاهِرُ مُتْعَتِهَا وَلَا بَاطِنُ مِنَّتِهَا، بَلْ شَغَلَهُ النَّظَرُ إِلَى اللّٰهِ عَمَّا سِوَاهُ، وَانْجَمَعَ عَلَيْهِ فَلَا يَشْهَدُ إِلَّا إِيَّاهُ، يَصْدُقُ عَلَيْهِ قَوْلُهُ تَعَالٰى: ﴿قُلِ اللّٰهُ، ثُمَّ ذَرْهُمْ فِي خَوْضِهِمْ يَلْعَبُونَ﴾، وَقَدْ أَوْحَى اللّٰهُ إِلٰى دَاوُدَ عَلَيْهِ السَّلَامُ: «يَا دَاوُدُ، قُلْ لِلصِّدِّيقِينَ: بِي فَلْيَفْرَحُوا، وَبِذِكْرِي فَلْيَتَنَعَّمُوا».

وَاللّٰهُ تَعَالٰى يَجْعَلُ فَرَحَنَا وَإِيَّاكَ بِهِ وَبِالرِّضَا مِنْهُ، وَأَنْ يَجْعَلَنَا مِنْ أَهْلِ الْفَهْمِ عَنْهُ، وَأَنْ لَا يَجْعَلَنَا مِنَ الْغَافِلِينَ، وَأَنْ يَسْلُكَ بِنَا مَسْلَكَ الْمُتَّقِينَ .. بِمَنِّهِ وَكَرَمِهِ.

Among the things that he wrote to some of his friends, he said (may God be pleased with him!):

With regard to the advent of blessings, people are of three categories. To the first belongs the one who rejoices at blessings, not in respect to their Bestower or Originator, but in respect to his pleasure in

68 This treatise was placed by ʿAlī Muttaqī at the end of the thirtieth chapter of his arrangement after the second treatise above.

> them. This man belongs to the forgetful, and God's words hold true for him: "Until, when they rejoiced in that which they were given, We seized them suddenly." [Q. 6:44]
>
> To the second category belongs the one who rejoices at blessings inasmuch as he sees them as blessings from Him who sent them or as grace from Him who brought it to him. God refers to him with His words: "Say: In the grace of God and in His mercy, in that they should rejoice. It is better than that which they hoard." [Q. 10:58]
>
> To the third category belongs the one who rejoices in God. Neither the exterior pleasure of blessings nor their interior graces divert him. Instead, his vision of God, his concentration on Him, divert him from what is other than He, so that he contemplates only Him. God refers to him with His words: "Say: Allāh! Then leave them prattling in their vain talk." God revealed to David: "O David, say to the truthful: Let them rejoice in Me, let them find joy in My invocation!" [Q. 6:92].
>
> May God make your joy and ours in Him and in the contentment that comes from Him; may He put us amongst those who understand Him; may He not put us amongst the forgetful; and may He voyage with us in the path of the God-fearing with His grace and generosity!

Of the three classes of people with regard to the advent of blessings, the first kind consists of such people who are driven to pride by the possession of bounties. Their happiness and pleasure are not expressions of gratitude to Allāh Most High for His favors, but are solely because of the advantage and enjoyment they derive from the bounties. Lost in their pleasures, they completely forget their Benefactor, Allāh Most High. Allāh's punishment suddenly overtakes them. For such people the Qur'ān says: *Until, when they rejoiced in that which they were given, We seized them suddenly* (6:54).

The second class consists of those people whose happiness is an expression of gratitude to the Benefactor and is the result of truly contemplating Him. The following statement of Allāh Most High applies to them: *Say: In the grace of Allāh and in His mercy, in that they should rejoice. It is better than that which they hoard* (10:58). They do not become happy because of the bounty. Their happiness is on account of the kindness of Allāh Most High. They are concerned with the Being who has awarded the bounty. They express their gratitude to their Benefactor. This class of people is not unmindful of their Master and Benefactor even though they have not yet attained the state of perfection in relation to those who are accomplished and superior (*afḍal*).

People in this second class do not in entirely direct their attention to Allāh Most High. Their ego does turn towards the bounties as well. Thus they do entertain a desire for bounties to a certain degree.

The third class do not become unmindful of Allāh Most High by indulgence in the external benefits of the bounties and favors, nor do they concern themselves with the spiritual dimension of the bounties by considering these blessings as being the signs of Allāh's kindness. In any such attitude there is also the element of diversion of turning the attention to objects besides Allāh. They are in contemplation of the Beatific Vision of the True Beloved. Their absorption in this contemplation has expelled from their hearts whatever is a blessing or not.

The third class, unlike the former two classes, are totally immersed in the perception of divine beauty. The variety of intentions and desires of their hearts have all gathered in the Being of The True Benefactor. Their attention is not on the bounty from any angle whatsoever. The following Qur'ānic verse pertains to the people in this class: *Say: Allāh! Then leave them prattling in their vain talk* (6:91). Allāh is their Beloved. They are concerned with Him alone. Everyone else and everything else are expelled from their hearts.

The instruction to David ﷺ commands that man seeks for happiness and peace of mind in the pleasure and invocation of Allāh.

PART 3

المناجات الإلهية

The Intimate Discourses

وقال رضي اللّٰه عنه:

And he said (may God be pleased with him!):

إِلٰهِي، أَنَا الْفَقِيرُ فِي غِنَايَ، فَكَيْفَ لَا أَكُونُ فَقِيرًا فِي فَقْرِي؟

My God, I am poor in my richness, so why should I not be poor in my poverty? [1]

Man's original and natural attribute is poverty (*faqr*). He is, therefore, dependent on Allāh Most High. This dependence is inseparable from him. A state of wealth (*ghinā'*) is a temporary acquisition. Even in the state of wealth he is entirely dependent on Allāh. Thus man's dependence is greater in the state of poverty.

إِلٰهِي، أَنَا الْجَاهِلُ فِي عِلْمِي، فَكَيْفَ لَا أَكُونُ جَهُولًا فِي جَهْلِي؟

My God, I am ignorant in my knowledge, so why should I not be most ignorant in my ignorance? [2]

إِلٰهِي، إِنَّ اخْتِلَافَ تَدْبِيرِكَ وَسُرْعَةَ حُلُولِ مَقَادِيرِكَ مَنَعَا عِبَادَكَ
الْعَارِفِينَ بِكَ عَنِ السُّكُونِ إِلٰى عَطَاءٍ وَالْيَأْسِ مِنْكَ فِي بَلَاءٍ.

My God, the diversity of Your planning and the speed of Your predestined decrees prevent Your servants, the gnostics, from relying on gifts or despairing of You during trials. [3]

The divine decrees are ever-changing. A man is sometimes in poverty and then Allāh Most High bestows wealth to him; and sometimes the rich are reduced to penury. Health is transformed into sickness and vice versa. Strength into weakness and weakness into strength. Honor is snatched away and disgrace sets in. The lowly is elevated and granted respect and rank.

These ever-changing conditions are part of predestination (*taqdīr*) which unravel with swiftness. These two factors prevent the gnostics from smugness in the comforts and bounties they are endowed with; hence they do not focus their attention on the material and spiritual bounties awarded to them. They have understood the temporary nature of these awards. These are things which come and go. It is, therefore, not worthwhile to attach the heart to things which will disappear.

They also do not lose hope in Allāh's mercy when calamities descend on them. They are fully aware that these calamities too are not enduring. These too will disappear.

إِلٰهِي، مِنِّي مَا يَلِيقُ بِلُؤْمِي، وَمِنْكَ مَا يَلِيقُ بِكَرَمِكَ.

My God, from me comes what is in keeping with my miserliness, and from You comes what is in keeping with Your generosity. [4]

Transgression, sin and unmindfulness originate from man's evil and contemptibility. It is man's inherent quality to fail in the execution of the rights (*ḥuqūq*) of Allāh Most High. Allāh's relationship with man is one of grace, kindness and forgiveness.

إِلٰهِي، وَصَفْتَ نَفْسَكَ بِاللُّطْفِ وَالرَّأْفَةِ بِي قَبْلَ وُجُودِ ضَعْفِي، أَفَتَمْنَعُنِي مِنْهُمَا بَعْدَ وُجُودِ ضَعْفِي؟

My God, You have attributed to Yourself gentleness and kindness toward me before the existence of my weakness; so, would You then hold them back from me after the existence of my weakness? [5]

Allāh Most High is The Merciful (*al-Raḥīm*) and The All-Pitying (*al-Ra'ūf*). His mercy and kindness are limitless. His attributes are eternal, hence His kindness and grace are perpetually with man.

إِلٰهِي، إِنْ ظَهَرَتِ الْمَحَاسِنُ مِنِّي .. فَبِفَضْلِكَ، وَلَكَ الْمِنَّةُ عَلَيَّ، وَإِنْ ظَهَرَتِ الْمَسَاوِئُ مِنِّي .. فَبِعَدْلِكَ، وَلَكَ الْحُجَّةُ عَلَيَّ.

My God, if virtues arise from me, that is because of Your grace: it is Your right to bless me. And if vices arise from me, that is because of Your justice: it is Your right to have proof against me. [6]

Man's obedience and acts of virtue are not by virtue of his effort and strength, but are the result of Allāh's grace and kindness which He confers to man. On the contrary, the perpetration of evil is not injustice by Allāh Most High. It is His justice. He, being the true King, is entitled to act in His kingdom as He pleases. Thus when He refrains from preventing man from the commission of evil, He is not being unjust to him. His action is just.

In man's commission of evil is also the confirmation of Allāh's indictment against man who will not be able to deny his evil in the Divine Court.

إِلٰهِي، كَيْفَ تَكِلُنِي إِلٰى نَفْسِي وَقَدْ تَوَكَّلْتَ لِي؟ وَكَيْفَ أُضَامُ وَأَنْتَ النَّاصِرُ لِي؟ أَمْ كَيْفَ أَخِيبُ وَأَنْتَ الْحَفِيُّ بِي؟ هَا أَنَا أَتَوَسَّلُ إِلَيْكَ بِفَقْرِي إِلَيْكَ، وَكَيْفَ أَتَوَسَّلُ إِلَيْكَ بِمَا هُوَ مُحَالٌ أَنْ يَصِلَ إِلَيْكَ؟ أَمْ

كَيْفَ أَشْـكُو إِلَيْكَ حَالِي وَهُوَ لَا يَخْفَى عَلَيْكَ؟ أَمْ كَيْفَ أُتَرْجِمُ لك بِمَقَالِي وَهُوَ مِنْكَ بَرَزَ إِلَيْكَ؟ أَمْ كَيْفَ تَخِيبُ آمَالِي وَهِيَ قَدْ وَفَدَتْ إِلَيْكَ؟ أَمْ كَيْفَ لَا تَحْسُنُ أَحْوَالِي وَبِكَ قَامَتْ وَإِلَيْكَ؟

My God, how can You leave me to myself, for You are responsible for me? And how could I be harmed while You are my Ally? Or how could I be disappointed in You, my Welcomer? Here am I seeking to gain access to You by means of my need of You. How could I seek to gain access to You by means of what cannot possibly reach you? Or how can I complain to You of my state, for it is not hidden from You? Or how can I express myself to You in my speech, since it comes from You and goes forth to You? Or how can my hopes be dashed, for they have already reached You? Or how can my states not be good, for they are based on You and go to You? [7]

Allāh is man's Ally (*al-Nāṣir*). The supplication is, therefore, to be saved from becoming trapped by the ego which destroys man.

Allāh is man's helper. His aid is, therefore, with man. With Allāh's aid, the servant will never be disgraced. The servant will not suffer failure when Allāh's kindness manifests itself. When the servant is truly dependent on Allāh, His aid will most certainly be forthcoming.

Since man's deeds are insignificant, he cannot present them as a medium for attaining divine proximity. Rather, the servant presents his poverty as a medium for attaining closeness to Allāh Most High.

Something which has a relationship with the object of intercession is offered as a medium (*wasīla*). If there is no relationship, the appointment of the medium as the intercessor will be futile. The medium should have the ability to enter into the presence of the one to whom the intercession is to be presented. But poverty and dependence lack this ability and relationship. There is no relationship between Allāh Most High and poverty. Hence the Shaykh retracts this supplication saying, "How could I seek to gain access to You by means of what cannot possibly reach you."

Furthermore, when the servant considers his state of poverty to be of the quality which renders it significant enough to act as his medium, then it indicates dependence on his poverty and implies a claim of poverty made by the servant. He thus reposes reliance on one of his personal attributes.

The poverty is, therefore, defective. Perfect poverty is to focus the attention solely on Allāh Most High.

Why should man complain when all his conditions are conspicuous to Allāh Most High? A complaint is lodged to a being who is unaware. Yet, everything is His command. Everything is therefore beautiful and beloved. There is no need for the servant to despair.

إِلٰهِي، مَا أَلْطَفَكَ بِي مَعَ عَظِيمِ جَهْلِي، وَمَا أَرْحَمَكَ بِي مَعَ قَبِيحِ فِعْلِي!

My God, how gentle You are with me in spite of my great ignorance, and how merciful You are with me in spite of my ugly deeds! [8]

When hardships settle on man, he becomes resentful although there is benefit for him in these calamities. In view of his childishness and shortsightedness he cannot fathom the wisdom underlying the hardships imposed on him by divine decree. But Allāh's mercy is with him.

Although man deserves to be eliminated on account of his transgression, Allāh's wide mercy always encompasses him.

إِلٰهِي، مَا أَقْرَبَكَ مِنِّي وَمَا أَبْعَدَنِي عَنْكَ!

My God, how near You are to me, and how far I am to You! [9]

إِلٰهِي، مَا أَرْأَفَكَ بِي، فَمَا الَّذِي يَحْجُبُنِي عَنْكَ؟

My God, how kind You are to me! So what is it that veils me from You? [10]

Allāh is closer to man than his own life, but man, on account of his egotistic attributes, is far from Allāh. Not a moment passes without Allāh's mercy and grace being on the servant. When Allāh is so magnanimous and gracious to his servant, nothing can impede him from the perception of Allāh.

إِلٰهِي، قد عَلِمْتُ بِاخْتِلَافِ الْآثَارِ وَتَنَقُّلَاتِ الْأَطْوَارِ أَنَّ مُرَادَكَ مِنِّي
أَنْ تَتَعَرَّفَ إِلَيَّ فِي كُلِّ شَيْءٍ حَتّٰى لَا أَجْهَلَكَ فِي شَيْءٍ.

My God, from the diversity of created things and the changes of states, I know that it is Your desire to make Yourself known to me in everything so that I will not ignore You in anything. [11]

The changing circumstances and conditions occurring to man are numerous. Richness, poverty, health, sickness, respect, happiness, despondency, etc. are among man's changing conditions. When the servant reflects on the different conditions occurring to him, he will realize that Allāh Most High is encouraging him to recognize Him. The servant should not be ignorant of recognizing Allāh in all things.

If the servant's condition was static, undergoing no change, his cognizance of Allāh would remain defective. If, for example, the servant's state of health and wealth remained constant, his recognition of Allāh would remain imperfect because Allāh is also the eliminator of sickness and poverty, but the servant would be denied the appreciation of this latter reality. Similarly, if he remained perpetually in the state of sickness, the servant would have been deprived of the cognizance of Allāh being the bestower of health.

إِلٰهِي، كُلَّمَا أَخْرَسَنِي لُؤْمِي أَنْطَقَنِي كَرَمُكَ،
وَكُلَّمَا آيَسَتْنِي أَوْصَافِي أَطْمَعَتْنِي مِنَّتُكَ

My God, whenever my miserliness makes me dumb, Your generosity makes me articulate, and whenever my attributes make me despair, Your grace gives me hope. [12]

Sins silence the servant's tongue which supplicates for Allāh's proximity. This pursuit is the result of closeness and love which are the products of obedience to Allāh Most High. Since the servant is devoid of obedience and possesses only defect and incompetence, the tongue of pursuit is silenced. But the kindness of Allāh activates the tongue with speech. When the servant realizes that Allāh is gracious, he musters up courage.

Evil attributes have created despair in the servant who feels that he is unable to adopt steadfastness and firmness in the Path of Allāh Most High. However, each time the despair is displaced by hope as a result of Allāh's kindness and favor.

إِلٰهِي، مَنْ كَانَتْ مَحَاسِنُهُ مَسَاوِيَ .. فَكَيْفَ لَا تَكُونُ مَسَاوِيهِ مَسَاوِيَ؟
وَمَنْ كَانَتْ حَقَائِقُهُ دَعَاوِيَ .. فَكَيْفَ لَا تَكُونُ دَعَاوِيهِ دَعَاوِيَ؟

My God, if someone's virtues are vices, then why cannot his vices be vices? And if someone's inner realities are pretensions, then why cannot his pretensions be pretensions? [13]

On account of ostentation and vanity, the virtuous deeds of the servant are also evils. What then is the condition of his evil deeds?

The inner reality of the servant is mere claim making. The Shaykh, because of humility and modesty, feels that his knowledge of transcendental realities is only an empty claim. When the glory and splendor of Allāh Most High are realized by the servant, he sees the emptiness of whatever knowledge he possesses.

إِلٰهِي، حُكْمُكَ النَّافِذُ وَمَشِيئَتُكَ الْقَاهِرَةُ لَمْ يَتْرُكَا
لِذِي مَقَالٍ مَقَالًا، وَلَا لِذِي حَالٍ حَالًا.

My God, Your penetrating decision and Your conquering will have left no speech to the articulate nor any state to him who has a state. [14]

Allāh's command operates in everything and His will dominates all things. Thus a man who gives discourses on higher spiritual realities should not labor under any deception of him being a great researcher and a man of subtle knowledge. He should not be vain on account of his eloquence in elaborating on such matters. Allāh's command and will can snatch away whatever the man of knowledge thinks he knows. Such episodes have already transpired.

Also, a man of spiritual rank should not be vain because of his rank of elevation. Ranks of spiritual elevation are divine bounties which Allāh Most High is fully capable of snatching away. There were many men of such ranks who were demoted and had their loftiness snatched away. Thus no one should repose confidence in his excellences.

إِلٰهِي، كَمْ مِنْ طَاعَةٍ بَنَيْتُهَا وَحَالَةٍ شَيَّدْتُهَا هَدَمَ
اعْتِمَادِي عَلَيْهَا عَدْلُكَ، بَلْ أَقَالَنِي مِنْهَا فَضْلُكَ!

My God, how often has Your justice destroyed the dependence I built up on obedience or the state I erected! Yet, it was Your grace that freed me of them. [15]

The servant offers many deeds of obedience outwardly. He also purifies his spiritual states from contaminations through sincerity. The servant, therefore, gains the impression of having gained entry into a powerful fortress. He feels that he is protected against the subtleties of ostentation and vanity. But when the servant reflects on the justice of Allāh, his reliance on his assumed fortress dissipates.

The demand of divine justice is that Allāh does as He pleases. It is, therefore, within the purview of His justice to ignore the obedience and worship of His servants and even punish man for their worship.

The Shaykh progresses further and says that, in fact, it is Allāh's kindness which has constrained the servant to abandon dependence on his obedience and worship. Thus the servant's reliance is on Allāh's grace, not on his deeds of virtue.

إِلٰهِي، إِنَّكَ تَعْلَمُ وَإِنْ لَمْ تَدُمِ الطَّاعَةُ مِنِّي فِعْلًا
جَزْمًا .. فَقَدْ دَامَتْ مَحَبَّةً وَعَزْمًا.

My God, You know that, even though obedience has not remained a resolute action on my part, it has remained as a love and a firm aspiration. [16]

The servant is deficient in being constant in worship. His constancy is erratic. Nevertheless, he is constant in his love for worship and in his aspiration for obedience. This constancy too is the consequence of Allāh's grace. Many people are deprived of this constancy.

إِلٰهِي، كَيْفَ أَعْزِمُ وَأَنْتَ الْقَاهِرُ، وَكَيْفَ لَا أَعْزِمُ وَأَنْتَ الْآمِرُ؟

My God, how can I resolve while You are the Omnipotent, or how can I not resolve while You are the Commander? [17]

Allāh's power and control extends over all things. How could it then be possible for the servant to resolve to be obedient and refrain from transgression? It is quite possible that Allāh may neutralize the servant's resolution. Furthermore, how is it possible for the servant to refrain from forming a resolution when Allāh Most High commands righteousness and prohibits evil? The servant is, therefore, in bewilderment between these two opposites. What should he do? He is helpless and unable to plan. He lacks the ability for firm resolution, but he is under pressure not to abandon resolution. Thus the servant has no option other than resigning (*taslīm*) himself to Allāh Most High and reposing his fill reliance on Him.

In view of this bewilderment, the gnostics abstain from making resolutions. They assign all their affairs to Allāh Most High. This state of resignation is called *tafwīḍ*. It is because of this attitude that it is said: "The gnostic has no heart."

إِلٰهِي، تَرَدُّدِي فِي الْآثَارِ يُوجِبُ بُعْدَ الْمَزَارِ،
فَاجْمَعْنِي عَلَيْكَ بِخِدْمَةٍ تُوصِلُنِي إِلَيْكَ.

My God, my wavering amongst created things inevitably makes the Sanctuary distant, so unite me to You by means of a service that leads me to You. [18]

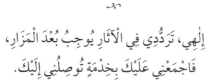

The servant's heart flutters about indecisively in the different conditions attendant to creation. Sometimes the servant strikes up a relationship with one person and then again with another person. Sometimes he pursues spiritual conditions and experiences. The servant's vacillation in these aspects of creation impedes him from reaching Allāh's proximity. His aimless wanderings increase his distance from the Divine Court. The servant should, therefore, supplicate to be applied entirety to such a service which ensures that his bond with creation be severed so that he reaches Allāh Most High.

إِلٰهِي، كَيْفَ يُسْتَدَلُّ عَلَيْكَ بِمَا هُوَ فِي وُجُودِهِ مُفْتَقِرٌ إِلَيْكَ؟ أَيَكُونُ لِغَيْرِكَ مِنَ الظُّهُورِ مَا لَيْسَ لَكَ حَتّٰى يَكُونَ هُوَ الْمُظْهِرَ لَكَ؟ مَتٰى غِبْتَ حَتّٰى تَحْتَاجَ إِلٰى دَلِيلٍ يَدُلُّ عَلَيْكَ؟ وَمَتٰى بَعُدْتَ حَتّٰى تَكُونَ الْآثَارُ هِيَ الَّتِي تُوصِلُ إِلَيْكَ؟

My God, how can one argue inferentially of You by that which depends on You for its existence? Does anything other than You manifest what You do not have, so that it becomes the manifester for You? When did You become so absent that You are in need of a proof giving evidence of You? And when did You become so distant that it is created things themselves that lead us to You? [19]

Here the Shaykh ﵀ expresses surprise at the attempt to prove the existence of Allāh Most High by the utilization of created objects in the process of logical deduction (*istidlāl*). If Allāh Most High had not created these objects, they would not have existed. Their very existence is dependent on Allāh Most High. How can such dependents constitute proof for His existence? The proof (*dalīl*) is always more conspicuous than the object it sets out to prove (*madlūl*). Is it then possible for created objects to be more conspicuous than the Creator? Obviously not! Creation, therefore, cannot be an adequate basis to prove His existence. In fact, His intense conspicuousness makes His existence self-evident, requiring no proof. Proof is required to confirm what is absent; but He is never absent. He is not far away; hence there is no need to deliver creation to Him. He is omnipresent and more conspicuous than every object in creation. Thus the exercise in logical deduction to prove His existence is redundant and superfluous.

إِلٰهِي، عَمِيَتْ عَيْنٌ لَا تَرَاكَ عَلَيْهَا رَقِيبًا، وَخَسِرَتْ
صَفْقَةُ عَبْدٍ لَمْ تَجْعَلْ لَهُ مِنْ حُبِّكَ نَصِيبًا.

My God, blind is the eye that does not see You watching over it, and vain is the handclasp of a servant who has not been given a share of Your love. [20]

The servant who fails to discern that Allāh Most High watches and guards him is blind. The servant who does not act to achieve the love of Allāh will always flounder in loss even though he does not understand this.

إِلٰهِي، أَمَرْتَ بِالرُّجُوعِ إِلَى الْآثَارِ فَارْجِعْنِي إِلَيْهَا بِكِسْوَةِ
الْأَنْوَارِ وَهِدَايَةِ الْاِسْتِبْصَارِ .. حَتَّى أَرْجِعَ إِلَيْكَ مِنْهَا كَمَا
دَخَلْتُ إِلَيْكَ مِنْهَا؛ مَصُونَ السِّرِّ عَنِ النَّظَرِ إِلَيْهَا، وَمَرْفُوعَ
الْهِمَّةِ عَنِ الْاِعْتِمَادِ عَلَيْهَا، إِنَّكَ عَلَى كُلِّ شَيْءٍ قَدِيرٌ.

My God, You have commanded me to return to created things, so return me to them with the raiment of lights and the guidance of inner vision, so that I may return from them to You just as I entered You from them, with my innermost being protected from looking at them and my fervor raised above dependence on them. For, truly, You have power over everything. [21]

Once the servant attains arrival and contemplation. Allāh Most High orders him to return to his earthly relationships, such as family and wealth. He is ordered to pay attention to the rights and obligations connected with creation. The servant is. therefore, fearful of being deprived of Allāh's contemplation by his worldly associations. He thus supplicates for divine aid and guidance. He petitions Allāh to enshroud him with His illumination and to strengthen his heart so that even while he is physically with creation, he should see only Allāh Most High.

The servant supplicates for inner vision so that he is always guided and prevented from engrossment in creation, so that the contemplation of Allāh appears to him in everything. Since Allāh has power over everything, He can fulfill all supplications.

إِلٰهِي، هٰذَا ذُلِّي ظَاهِرٌ بَيْنَ يَدَيْكَ، وَهٰذَا حَالِي لَا يَخْفَى عَلَيْكَ، مِنْكَ أَطْلُبُ الْوُصُولَ إِلَيْكَ، وَبِكَ أَسْتَدِلُّ عَلَيْكَ.. فَاهْدِنِي بِنُورِكَ إِلَيْكَ، وَأَقِمْنِي بِصِدْقِ الْعُبُودِيَّةِ بَيْنَ يَدَيْكَ.

My God, here is my lowliness manifest before You, and here is my state unhidden from You. From You, I seek union with You. I proceed from You in my argumentation about You. So guide me to You with Your light and set me up before You through sincerity of servanthood! [22]

Man's original state of neediness is open to Allāh Most High. The condition of the servant is not concealed from Allāh Most High. In reality, the revelation to man of his own state of neediness is respect. The servant who is unaware of his neediness and thinks of himself as being honorable is truly contemptible.

The servant supplicates to reach Allāh with His aid. His gaze is never on his own efforts and deeds. He seeks to be guided to Allāh's recognition by Allāh Himself. Unlike others, he does not resort to the process of logical deduction to recognize and attain Him. Someone asked an *ʿārif*: "How did you recognize Allāh?" He replied: "I recognized my Lord by my Lord."

The supplication of the servant is, therefore, to be guided to Allāh Most High by His light, which means the heart being inspired with gnosis.

The servant further petitions to be permitted to stand in the Divine Presence as a true slave by submission to the attributes of Lordship and the manifestation of the qualities of servanthood. These are the attributes of humility, lowliness, weakness and neediness.

إِلٰهِي، عَلِّمْنِي مِنْ عِلْمِكَ الْمَخْزُونِ، وَصُنِّي بِسِرِّ اسْمِكَ الْمَصُونِ.

My God, make me know by means of Your treasured-up Knowledge, and protect me by means of the mystery of Your well-guarded Name. [23]

إِلٰهِي، حَقِّقْنِي بِحَقَائِقِ أَهْلِ الْقُرْبِ، وَاسْلُكْ بِي مَسَالِكَ أَهْلِ الْجَذْبِ.

My God, make me realize the inner realities of those drawn nigh, and make me voyage in the path of those possessed by attraction. [24]

Hidden knowledge refers to divine mysteries and secrets which are bestowed to the saints (*awliyā'*). The guarded Names are the Beautiful Names of Allāh Most High, which are protected against defilement and disgrace. The secrets of these Names refer to the illumination emanating from them. The servant seeks protection against all evils with the aid of the divine illumination of His Names.

إِلٰهِي، أَغْنِنِي بِتَدْبِيرِكَ عَنْ تَدْبِيرِي، وَبِاخْتِيَارِكَ لِي عَنِ اخْتِيَارِي، وَأَوْقِفْنِي عَلٰى مَرَاكِزِ اضْطِرَارِي.

My God, through Your direction make me dispense with self-direction, and through Your choosing for me make me dispense with my choosing; and make me stand in the very center of my extreme need. [25]

The servant supplicates for only divine dispensation. The gaze should be only on the plan and decree of Allāh Most High, not on the plans and efforts of man. When man is concerned with his own schemes, he becomes trapped in his ego. He then drifts away from Allāh's presence.

All affairs of the servant should be directed only by the divine will. The individual's will should not feature in any affair. When the servant operates his own will, he clashes with the divine will.

The center of extreme need refers to the lowly attributes of man, such as humility, weakness and neediness. In these conditions the servant always supplicates to Allāh Most High. It behooves the servant to keep in view his weakness and neediness.

إِلٰهِي، أَخْرِجْنِي مِنْ ذُلِّ نَفْسِي وَطَهِّرْنِي مِنْ شَكِّي وَشِرْكِي قَبْلَ حُلُولِ رَمْسِي، بِكَ أَسْتَنْصِرُ .. فَانْصُرْنِي، وَعَلَيْكَ أَتَوَكَّلُ .. فَلَا تَكِلْنِي، وَإِيَّاكَ أَسْأَلُ .. فَلَا تُخَيِّبْنِي، وَفِي فَضْلِكَ أَرْغَبُ .. فَلَا تَحْرِمْنِي، وَلِجَنَابِكَ أَنْتَسِبُ .. فَلَا تُبْعِدْنِي، وَبِبَابِكَ أَقِفُ .. فَلَا تَطْرُدْنِي.

My God, pull me out of my self-abasement and purify me of doubting and associationism before I descend into my grave. I seek Your help, so help me; in You I trust, so entrust me to no one else; You do I ask, so do not disappoint me; Your kindness do I desire, do not refuse me; it is to You that I belong, so do not banish me; and it is at Your door that I stand, so do not cast me away. [26]

The greed of the ego means man's desires and hopes are placed in others besides Allāh Most High. Doubt here means the constriction of the heart when something displeasing happens. This constriction produces darkness in the heart. Cleansing the heart for the attainment of purity means the development of certainty which expands the heart. True peace and pleasure from Allāh Most High settles in the heart which has been purified.

Associationism here refers to the heart's indifference of the true Cause and its relationship with the external agencies.

When the darkness of doubt becomes dominant, the light of certainty diminishes. The heart then inclines towards associationism because Divine Unity (*tawḥīd*) cannot be visualized without the light of certainty. Man then turns towards the external agencies and superficial causes of things. The servant, therefore, is to supplicate for purification of doubt and associationism.

إِلٰهِي، تَقَدَّسَ رِضَاكَ عَنْ أَنْ تَكُونَ لَهُ عِلَّةٌ مِنْكَ، فَكَيْفَ تَكُونُ لَهُ عِلَّةٌ مِنِّي؟ أَنْتَ الْغَنِيُّ بِذَاتِكَ عَنْ أَنْ يَصِلَ إِلَيْكَ النَّفْعُ مِنْكَ، فَكَيْفَ لَا تَكُونُ غَنِيًّا عَنِّي؟

My God, Your contentment is too holy for there to be a cause for it in You, so how can there be a cause for it

in me? Through Your Essence, You are independent of any benefit coming to You, so why should You not be independent of me? [27]

Contentment is a divine attribute. All attributes of Allāh Most High are eternal. The eternal has no cause. Since Allāh's attribute of contentment is eternal with no cause, it is inconceivable that any act of the servant can ever be the cause for the contentment of Allāh. Nothing can act upon Allāh Most High. Change does not come to Him. Allāh's contentment is not dependent on the servant's actions. The servant's good deeds and conditions are the effects of Allāh's contentment.

إِلٰهِي، إِنَّ الْقَضَاءَ وَالْقَدَرَ غَلَبَنِي، وَإِنَّ الْهَوٰى بِوَثَائِقِ الشَّهْوَةِ أَسَرَنِي، فَكُنْ أَنْتَ النَّصِيرَ لِي حَتّٰى تَنْصُرَنِي وَتَنْصُرَ بِي، وَأَغْنِنِي بِفَضْلِكَ حَتّٰى أَسْتَغْنِيَ بِكَ عَنْ طَلَبِي. أَنْتَ الَّذِي أَشْرَقْتَ الْأَنْوَارَ فِي قُلُوبِ أَوْلِيَائِكَ حَتّٰى عَرَفُوكَ وَوَحَّدُوكَ، وَأَنْتَ الَّذِي أَزَلْتَ الْأَغْيَارَ مِنْ قُلُوبِ أَحِبَّائِكَ حَتّٰى لَمْ يُحِبُّوا سِوَاكَ، وَلَمْ يَلْجَأُوا إِلٰى غَيْرِكَ، أَنْتَ الْمُؤْنِسُ لَهُمْ حَيْثُ أَوْحَشَتْهُمُ الْعَوَالِمُ، وَأَنْتَ الَّذِي هَدَيْتَهُمْ حَتّٰى اسْتَبَانَتْ لَهُمُ الْمَعَالِمُ، مَاذَا وَجَدَ مَنْ فَقَدَكَ وَمَاذَا فَقَدَ مَنْ وَجَدَكَ؟ لَقَدْ خَابَ مَنْ رَضِيَ دُونَكَ بَدَلًا، وَلَقَدْ خَسِرَ مَنْ بَغٰى عَنْكَ مُتَحَوِّلًا.

My God, destiny and the decree of fate have overcome me, and desire with its passional attachments has taken me prisoner. Be my Ally so that You may help me and others through me. Enrich me with Your kindness, so that, content with You, I can do without asking. You are the one who makes the lights shine in the hearts of Your saints so that they know You and affirm Your Oneness. You are the one who makes alterities disappear from the hearts of Your lovers so that they love none but You and take refuge in none but You. You are the one who befriends them when the world makes them forlorn. You are the one who guides them till the landmarks

become clear for them. He who has lost You—what has he found? He who has found You—what has he lost? Whoever takes someone other than You as a substitute is disappointed, and whoever wants to stray away from You is lost. [28]

When the servant contemplates resolving to practice obedience or abstain from transgression, his resolution is negated by fate. The servant is also fettered by the strong chains of the ego. He, therefore, has no alternative other than divine aid. The servant in his supplication should also include his relatives and associates. Independence from all things besides Allāh is an attribute for which the servant supplicates so that he remains independent from even his own motives. When the servant is endowed with perpetual contemplation, he will be annihilated and oblivious of even his own motives and desires.

The servant is able to recognize Allāh Most High by the illumination of gnosis with which He brightens the heart. As a result, the servants of Allāh affirm His unity and perceive His reality. It is Allāh who purifies the hearts of His friends from all alterities. All things besides Allāh are expelled from their hearts which become the repositories of divine love. They discern the path of truth by means of divine light which guides them along.

The one who observes creation with his eyes and heart without perceiving the Most High with his heart has, in reality, seen nothing, because creation is pure non-existence. He has, therefore, gained nothing by his observation. On the other hand, whoever has gained the contemplation of Allāh has found everything despite him being deprived of the good things of the world.

إِلٰهِي، كَيْفَ يُرْجَى سِوَاكَ وَأَنْتَ مَا قَطَعْتَ الْإِحْسَانَ؟ وَكَيْفَ يُطْلَبُ
مِنْ غَيْرِكَ وَأَنْتَ مَا بَدَّلْتَ عَادَةَ الْإِمْتِنَانِ؟ يَا مَنْ أَذَاقَ أَحِبَّاءَهُ حَلَاوَةَ
مُؤَانَسَتِهِ فَقَامُوا بَيْنَ يَدَيْهِ مُتَمَلِّقِينَ، وَيَا مَنْ أَلْبَسَ أَوْلِيَاءَهُ مَلَابِسَ
هَيْبَتِهِ فَقَامُوا بِعِزَّتِهِ مُسْتَعِزِّينَ، أَنْتَ الذَّاكِرُ مِنْ قَبْلِ الذَّاكِرِينَ، وَأَنْتَ
الْبَادِيُ بِالْإِحْسَانِ مِنْ قَبْلِ تَوَجُّهِ الْعَابِدِينَ، وَأَنْتَ الْجَوَّادُ بِالْعَطَاءِ
مِنْ قَبْلِ طَلَبِ الطَّالِبِينَ، وَأَنْتَ الْوَهَّابُ لَنَا، ثُمَّ أَنْتَ لِمَا وَهَبْتَهُ لَنَا
مِنَ الْمُسْتَقْرِضِينَ.

My God, how could hope be put in what is other than You, for You have not cut off Your benevolence? And how could someone other than You be asked, for You have not changed the norms for conferring blessings? O He who makes His beloved friends taste the sweetness of intimacy with Himself so that they stand before Him with praise, and O He who clothes His saints with the vestments of reverential fear toward Himself so that they stand glorifying His glory—You are the Invoker prior to invokers, You are the Origin of benevolence prior to servants turning to You, You are the Munificent in giving prior to the asking of seekers, and You are the Giver who, in respect to what You have given us, asks us for a loan! [29]

The limitless ocean of Allāh's kindness is eternal; it never diminishes. The servant should, therefore, not have any hope except in the Most High. Allāh Most High is always the bestower of bounties to His servants. The servant should not, therefore, ask from others besides Allāh Most High.

The happiness felt from the contemplation of the beauty of the Beloved is termed *uns*. When the servant experiences the pleasure of divine love, all other relationships are expelled from his heart and he stands with love and humility in the presence of Allāh Most High.

The "vestments of reverential fear" refers to the dignity and awe which surround the personalities of Allāh's saints. People are awed simply by looking at the saints. The saints derive their respect and honor from divine grandeur, not from any worldly agency.

Long before the invoking servant came into existence, Allāh Most High remembered him by virtue of His kindness. In consequence of His remembrance, he bestowed the gift of existence. Even prior to the servant becoming a worshiper and a suppliant, Allāh Most High turned His gaze of mercy to the servant by granting him the wonderful existence.

Whatever Allāh Most High bestows to the servant, He asks it as a loan. The Qur'ān says: *Who will give Allāh a beautiful loan?* (57:11).[69] The reward

69 Regarding this "loan," Mawlānā 'Āshiq Ilāhī says: "A 'beautiful' loan refers to charity that is given with sincerity and with a happy heart. Everyone and everything belongs to Allaah, even the wealth that one possesses. It is Allaah's grace that he rewards people for spending the wealth that belongs to Him. Spending in good causes is termed as a loan only because it resembles a

for advancing this loan to Allāh Most High will be granted in the afterlife. Allāh Most High does not acquire any benefit from the loan that the servant advances to Him. The term loan is used figuratively and indicates Allāh's love for His servants. It is like giving a child a gift, then asking it on loan and returning a superior item.

إِلٰهِي، اُطْلُبْنِي بِرَحْمَتِكَ حَتّٰى أَصِلَ إِلَيْكَ،
وَاجْذُبْنِي بِمِنَّتِكَ حَتّٰى أُقْبِلَ عَلَيْكَ.

My God, seek me with Your grace so that I may reach You, and attract me with Your blessings so that I may draw near to You. [30]

إِلٰهِي، إِنَّ رَجَائِي لَا يَنْقَطِعُ عَنْكَ وَإِنْ عَصَيْتُكَ،
كَمَا أَنَّ خَوْفِي لَا يُزَايِلُنِي وَإِنْ أَطَعْتُكَ.

My God, my hope is not cut off from You even though I disobey You, just as my fear does not leave me even though I obey You. [31]

إِلٰهِي، قَدْ دَفَعَتْنِي الْعَوَالِمُ إِلَيْكَ، وَقَدْ أَوْقَفَنِي عِلْمِي بِكَرَمِكَ عَلَيْكَ.

My God, the world has pushed me toward You, and my knowledge of Your generosity has made me stand before You. [32]

The servant cannot reach Allāh Most High on the strength of his defective deeds and efforts. The servant, therefore, supplicates for divine assistance to be drawn to Him by His grace and kindness.

The servant should never despair of the mercy of Allāh despite his acts of disobedience. The kindness and forgiveness of Allāh are not dependent on any cause.

---

loan. In reality, Allaah needs nothing and the person spending has everything to gain." See Ilāhī, *Illuminating Discourses on the Noble Quran* 9:353.

The servant should not become audacious on account of his acts of obedience and worship. Allāh does as He pleases. Even if He punishes the servant for worshipping, it will be proper and just. He is the true King.

When the servant is conscious of reality, he realizes that everything in creation pushes him towards Allāh Most High. Everything sends out the message: "I am perishable. Do not strike up a relationship with me." The servant's knowledge of the fact that Allāh Most High is merciful and kind constrains him to turn towards Allāh. He, therefore, never relents in his endeavors to reach his Creator.

إِلٰهِي، كَيْفَ أَخِيبُ وَأَنْتَ أَمَلِي، أَمْ كَيْفَ أُهَانُ وَعَلَيْكَ مُتَّكَلِي؟

My God, how could I be disappointed while You are my hope, or how could I be betrayed while my trust is in You? [33]

إِلٰهِي، كَيْفَ أَسْتَعِزُّ وَ فِي الذِّلَّةِ أَرْكَزْتَنِي، أَمْ كَيْفَ لَا أَسْتَعِزُّ وَإِلَيْكَ نَسَبْتَنِي؟ أَمْ كَيْفَ لَا أَفْتَقِرُ وَأَنْتَ الَّذِي فِي الْفَقْرِ أَقَمْتَنِي؟ أَمْ كَيْفَ أَفْتَقِرُ وَأَنْتَ الَّذِي بِجُودِكَ أَغْنَيْتَنِي؟ أَنْتَ الَّذِي لَا إِلٰهَ غَيْرُكَ، تَعَرَّفْتَ لِكُلِّ شَيْءٍ فَمَا جَهِلَكَ شَيْءٌ، وَأَنْتَ الَّذِي تَعَرَّفْتَ إِلَيَّ فِي كُلِّ شَيْءٍ فَرَأَيْتُكَ ظَاهِرًا فِي كُلِّ شَيْءٍ، فَأَنْتَ الظَّاهِرُ لِكُلِّ شَيْءٍ. يَا مَنِ اسْتَوٰى بِرَحْمَانِيَّتِهِ عَلٰى عَرْشِهِ، فَصَارَ الْعَرْشُ غَيْبًا فِي رَحْمَانِيَّتِهِ، كَمَا صَارَتِ الْعَوَالِمُ غَيْبًا فِي عَرْشِهِ، مَحَقْتَ الْآثَارَ بِالْآثَارِ، وَمَحَوْتَ الْأَغْيَارَ بِمُحِيطَاتِ أَفْلَاكِ الْأَنْوَارِ. يَا مَنِ احْتَجَبَ فِي سُرَادِقَاتِ عِزِّهِ عَنْ أَنْ تُدْرِكَهُ الْأَبْصَارُ، يَا مَنْ تَجَلّٰى بِكَمَالِ بَهَائِهِ فَتَحَقَّقَتْ عَظَمَتَهُ الْأَسْرَارُ، كَيْفَ تَخْفٰى وَأَنْتَ الظَّاهِرُ؟ أَمْ كَيْفَ تَغِيبُ وَأَنْتَ الرَّقِيبُ الْحَاضِرُ؟

My God, how can I deem myself exalted while You have planted me in lowliness, or why should I not deem myself exalted, for You have related me to Yourself? Why should I not be in need of You, for You have set

me up in poverty, or why should I be needy, for You have enriched me with Your goodness? Apart from You there is no God. You have made Yourself known to everything, so nothing is ignorant of You. And it is You who have made Yourself known to me in everything; thus, I have seen You manifest in everything, and You are the Manifest to everything. O He who betakes Himself to His throne with His clemency, so that the throne is hidden in His clemency, just as the Universe is hidden in His throne—You have annihilated created things, and obliterated alterities with the englobing spheres of light! O He who, in His pavilions of glory, is veiled from the reach of sight, O He who illumines with the perfection of His beauty and whose Infinity is realized by the gnostics' innermost being—how can You be hidden, for You are the Exterior? Or how can You be absent, for You are the Ever-Present Watcher? [34]

When the servant's hope is in Allāh, he will not despair. When he derives support from Allāh, he can never be disgraced. Man's origin is non-existence (*ʿadam*). He, therefore, cannot have honor as his original attribute. Eternal honor is the attribute of Allāh Most High alone. Since the servant is connected to Allāh Most High by virtue of his love and obedience, he derives honor and respect from Allāh's honor. Thus, in relation to his origin, man is contemptible, but in relation to his bond with Allāh he is honorable.

With regard to his origin, the servant is a pauper and dependent. With the existence of Allāh, the servant is rendered free from dependence on others. When the servant has acquired the treasure of Allāh's nearness, he can never then be in need of others.

Allāh is the only Being who deserves worship. Besides Him there is no object of worship. Every object in creation recognizes Allāh according to the degree of gnosis bestowed to it. Every object is like a mirror reflecting Allāh's beauty for the servant who perceives Allāh's manifestation in all things. Thus Allāh is conspicuous and revealed to everyone and everything.

Allāh's limitless mercy has ensconced the Throne, just as the entire universe is an infinitesimal atom having seemingly disappeared under the vast canopy of the Divine Throne.

The *athar* mentioned first refers to the heavens, the planets, the Tablet, the Pen and all other aspects of creation besides the Divine Throne. The second *athar* refers to the glorious Throne of Allāh Most High. All creation recedes In comparison to the Throne. This is the meaning of annihilation in this context.

Alterities in this context also means the glorious Throne. In relation to divine spheres of light it is described as an alterity, i.e. something besides Allāh Most High. The infinite mercy of Allāh Most High encompasses the Throne and renders it an insignificant, infinitesimal spectacle which has receded into oblivion. Entire creation, including the Throne, is entirely encompassed by the infinite mercy of Allāh.

Eyes are unable to perceive Allāh Most High. Seeing Allāh Most High with the corporeal eyes in this world is an absolute impossibility. In the Hereafter, while the physical eyes will be empowered to see Allāh Most High, the sight will not be encompassing. Created objects cannot see or comprehend the eternal Being in entirety and totality. Total vision of Allāh Most High is an impossibility, even in the Hereafter.

Allāh Most High is never concealed from the gnostics, whose hearts have been permeated by the radiant illumination of Allāh's Beautiful Attributes, such as grandeur and beauty. Their hearts are imbued with great respects for the grandeur of Allāh Most High.

Allāh is more conspicuous than all things. He is, therefore, invisible. He stands guarding and protecting entire creation.

وَاللّٰهُ الْمُوَفِّقُ، وَبِهِ أَسْتَعِينُ.

God is the Granter of success, and in Him I take refuge!

وَصَلَّى اللّٰهُ عَلٰى سَيِّدِنَا مُحَمَّدٍ وَآلِهِ وَصَحْبِهِ أَجْمَعِينَ.

May Allāh send peace upon our master Muḥammad, and upon all of his folk and Companions.

All praise belongs to Allāh. The commentary on *Itmām al-Niʿam* has been accomplished on 11th Rabīʿ al-Thānī 1237 on Tuesday. May Allāh Most High make it beneficial by His grace.

Index

garments 95, 145, 146, 182, 199, 204, 225, 317
gaze 107, 117, 118, 135, 149, 175, 187, 191–192, 194–196, 201, 211, 224–225, 228, 230, 243–245, 269–270, 274, 283, 341
  of desire 213
  of Allāh 345
  of man 283
  of perception 321
  of the gnostic 276, 280, 294
  of the seeker 237, 241, 320
  of the servant 340
  on creation 287
  on one's own efforts 206
generosity 102–103, 196, 319, 324, 330, 334
generosity of Allāh 198–199, 212, 219, 327, 346
gentleness of Allāh 191, 196, 219, 331, 333
genuine shaykh (*shaykh kāmil*) 273–274
al-Ghafūr 166
al-Ghazālī, Abū Ḥāmid 176, 193, 284, 293
gifts from Allāh 175, 177, 179–180, 194–198, 229, 247, 330, 345
gifts from people 149, 195, 201
giving 277, 346
giving up 96
glad tidings 297, 312
glorifying Allāh 119, 272, 345
glory (*ʿizza*) of Allāh 134, 285, 320, 335
gnosis (*maʿrifa*) 146, 185, 189–190, 195–196, 210, 226–228, 252, 256, 269, 276–277, 286, 293, 296–297, 300, 304, 316, 324, 340, 344
  degrees of 348
gnostic (*ʿārif*) 161, 163, 172–173, 175, 176, 177, 187, 195, 198, 224, 225, 227, 230–231, 246–247, 250, 251, 256–259, 278, 291–295, 301–303, 324, 330, 337
  aim of 293
  attributes of 276
  condition of 277, 292
  has no heart 337
  hearts of 349
  illumination of 349
  innermost being of 347–348
  intuitions of 258–259
  motives of 293
  needs of 293
  perfect 287
  qualities of 293
  speech of 301
goal 244–245, 253, 254, 255, 260, 276, 296, 297, 305
goal of the seeker 100–102, 104, 105, 151, 158, 174–175, 209, 236, 241
good deeds 105, 107, 137–138, 162, 163, 200, 201, 227, 232, 276, 299, 343. *See also* righteous deeds (*aʿmāl ṣāliḥa*)
goodness 131, 139, 199, 309, 347, 348
good opinion of Allāh 97, 164
grace (*faḍl*) of Allāh 96, 98, 102, 106, 113, 120–121, 123, 126–127, 131, 137, 159, 162, 167, 173, 178, 190, 197–201, 203, 205, 206, 229, 246–247, 252, 258, 263, 273–274, 284, 287, 305–309, 313, 315, 324, 325, 327, 330–331, 333–336, 345, 346
graces
  bestowal of 308
  completeness of 308
  inward 308
  outward 308
grandeur 269, 273, 349
gratitude (*shukr*) 100, 102, 123, 126, 159, 190, 201, 293, 299, 306, 320
  expressing 307, 321
  perpetual 308
  rights of 307
gratitude (*shukr*) to Allāh 319, 327
grave 342
greatness of Allāh 204, 216, 266, 292
greed 112, 137, 210, 213–214, 342
grief 106, 138, 163, 191, 196, 201, 232, 250, 259, 267, 278, 287–288, 289, 294, 298, 322

human 203–204
mercy of Allāh 98, 102, 106, 108, 131, 140, 147, 161, 163, 164, 166, 169–170, 177, 191, 192, 196–197, 203–204, 207–208, 237, 249, 263, 297, 315, 324, 325, 327, 330, 333, 345, 346, 348
infinite 349
kinds of 204–205
never despair of 346
meritorious (*mustaḥabb*) acts 158
Messenger of Allāh 321, 324–325
mind 194, 287, 292, 302
mindful of Allāh 317, 327–328
mingling with people 117
minor sin (*ṣaghīra*) 96
miracles 268, 293
miracles (*karāmāt*) 141, 154, 170, 250, 315
miracles (*muʿjizāt*) 170
mirror 269
mirror of the heart 258–259
miserliness 330, 334
misfortune 128, 190–191, 194, 204, 254, 305
misleading others 210
miʿrāj 113
moderation 163
modesty 118, 171, 335
moon 119, 120, 194, 240, 256–257, 259
moral reformation 125, 169, 212
Moses 280
mosquito, wing of 143
motives 262, 277, 344
Mount Ṭūr 280
Munificent, the 345
al-Muntaqim 166
muqarrabīn 224, 235–236
Muslims 193, 197, 212, 246, 256
mutajarrid. See isolation (*tajrīd*)
mutasabbib 181
Muttaqī, ʿAlī 311, 318, 323, 326
mysteries 284, 295, 302, 303, 315, 340
mysteries of gnosis 269–270
mystical secrets (*asrār*) 146

N

nafs 125
names of Allāh 110, 134–135, 190, 240, 271–272, 281, 284, 340, 341
al-Nāṣir 332
natural disposition 211, 329
Nawawī, Imām 176, 293
nearness (*qurb*) to Allāh 207, 262, 266, 271, 273, 281–282, 287, 291, 305, 333, 348. *See also* proximity (*qurb*) to Allāh
need 146–147, 170–169, 173, 175, 177, 216, 308, 332, 340, 341, 347
extreme 341
of others 348
neglect 124, 307
negligence 130, 152, 208, 246
night 247, 251
night journey (*miʿrāj*) 113
Night of Power 247
nobility 305, 307
noble acts 298
non-being 271, 272, 273
non-Divine 302
non-existence (*ʿadam*) 198–199, 269, 271, 272, 274, 276, 279–280, 283, 287, 348
of the universe 280
non-Muslims 118, 236–237
nothingness 142, 228, 274
nourishment 266, 304
nourishment, spiritual 267
novice 278

O

obedience (*ṭāʿa*) 94, 97, 102–103, 106, 112, 114–115, 117, 123, 126, 128, 131–134, 152, 155, 157–160, 178, 182, 189, 202, 206, 211, 216, 224, 228, 240, 241, 254, 273, 296–297, 306, 308, 309, 334, 336, 344
acts of 273–274, 297, 308, 347
aspiration for 337
beauty of 217
deficiency in 185